# Nietzsche and Politicized Identities

# Nietzsche and Politicized Identities

Edited by
REBECCA BAMFORD
and ALLISON MERRICK

Cover art owned by Allison Merrick, Nietzsche Haus, Sils Maria, 2022.

Published by State University of New York Press, Albany

© 2024 State University of New York

All rights reserved

Printed in the United States of America

No part of this book may be used or reproduced in any manner whatsoever without written permission. No part of this book may be stored in a retrieval system or transmitted in any form or by any means including electronic, electrostatic, magnetic tape, mechanical, photocopying, recording, or otherwise without the prior permission in writing of the publisher.

For information, contact State University of New York Press, Albany, NY
www.sunypress.edu

### Library of Congress Cataloging-in-Publication Data

Names: Bamford, Rebecca, editor. | Merrick, Allison, editor.
Title: Nietzsche and Politicized Identities / edited by Rebecca Bamford and Allison Merrick.
Description: Albany : State University of New York Press, [2024] | Includes bibliographical references and index.
Identifiers: ISBN 9781438497174 (hardcover : alk. paper) | ISBN 9781438497198 (ebook) | ISBN 9781438497181 (pbk. : alk. paper)
Further information is available at the Library of Congress.

10 9 8 7 6 5 4 3 2 1

# Contents

Acknowledgments — ix

Note on Abbreviations — xi

Introduction — 1
    *Rebecca Bamford and Allison Merrick*

## Part I
## On the Origins of Identities and Modes of Subjection

Chapter 1
Contending Selfhood: Nietzschean Contributions to the
Question of Political Identity — 17
    *Lawrence J. Hatab*

Chapter 2
Nietzsche and Tragic Identity — 37
    *Paul Kirkland*

Chapter 3
Passionate Actors and Wounded Apes: Nietzsche on
Identity Formation — 61
    *Robert Guay*

Chapter 4
How We Became Who We Are: Retracing Nietzsche's
Genealogy of Politicized Identity — 79
    *Allison Merrick*

Chapter 5
Perspectivism, World-Traveling, and the Multiplicitous Self:
Rereading Nietzsche through Latinx Decolonial Feminist Philosophy   99
   *Rebecca A. Longtin*

## Part II
## Elitism and Political Hierarchies

Chapter 6
Shame, Humiliation, and *Whiplash*: The Case of the Ascetic Priest   123
   *Daniel Conway*

Chapter 7
Freedom against Equality: Nietzsche's Aristocratic Politics   153
   *Rebecca Aili Ploof*

Chapter 8
Masters, Slaves, "Terrorists": On Elitism and Existential Threats   171
   *C. Heike Schotten*

## Part III
## Emancipatory Possibilities

Chapter 9
Nietzsche and Feminine Subjectivity   207
   *Elif Yavnık*

Chapter 10
Sexism Is Exhausting: Nietzsche and the Emotional Dynamics
of Sexist Oppression   229
   *Kaitlyn Creasy*

Chapter 11
"The Great Seriousness Begins": Nietzsche's Tragic Philosophy
and Philosophy's Role in Creating Healthier Racialized Identities   265
   *Jacqueline Scott*

Chapter 12
"To Affirm while Resisting": Ralph Ellison and Friedrich Nietzsche
on Overcoming History                                              289
   *Jeremy Fortier*

Chapter 13
Disability, Power, and Life                                        323
   *Rebecca Bamford*

Contributors                                                       347

Index                                                              351

# Acknowledgments

The editors thank the authors for their contributions to this volume and for their patience and understanding. The editors also thank the staff at SUNY Press, including former editor Andrew Kenyon and especially Michael Rinella, for their support. Finally, the editors thank Richard Ansell-Pearson for his excellent indexing assistance.

The editors are grateful to Cambridge University Press for granting permission to reprint Jacqueline Scott's 2019 essay " 'The Great Seriousness Begins': Nietzsche's Tragic Philosophy and Philosophy's Role in Creating Healthier Racialized Identities," in *Nietzsche's Metaphilosophy: The Nature, Method, and Aims of Philosophy*, eds. Paul S. Loeb and Matthew Meyer, 247–64 (Cambridge: Cambridge University Press).

Rebecca Bamford thanks the School of History, Anthropology, Philosophy and Politics and the Faculty of Arts, Humanities and Social Sciences at Queen's University Belfast for providing essential research support that has facilitated the completion of this project, and in particular the Centre for Gender and Politics, Keith Breen, Catherine Hamilton-Cooper, Kathrina Rafferty, and Carole Maslowski. She also thanks the College of Arts and Sciences at Quinnipiac University for its initial support for this research project. Finally, she thanks Allie Merrick and Simon Stratford.

# Note on Abbreviations

Abbreviations of the titles of Nietzsche's works have been standardized throughout the essays in this volume. We follow the style of abbreviations used by the *Journal of Nietzsche Studies*. In texts where a section number is not sufficient to identify sections of texts clearly, Roman numerals are used to indicate text volume number. A component text title abbreviation, or an abbreviation of a chapter title, is used where necessary to further clarify the source of quotations from Nietzsche's texts.

| | |
|---|---|
| KSA | *Kritische Studienausgabe* |
| KGB | *Briefwechsel: Kritische Studienausgabe* |
| eKGWB and BVN | *Digital Critical Edition of Nietzsche's Works and Letters* |
| PTAG | *Philosophy in the Tragic Age of the Greeks* |
| TL | "On Truth and Lying in an Extra-Moral Sense" |
| BT | *The Birth of Tragedy* |
| UM | *Untimely Meditations* |
| HH | *Human, All Too Human* |
| AOM | *Assorted Opinions and Maxims* |

| | |
|---|---|
| *WS* | *The Wanderer and His Shadow* |
| *D* | *Dawn* |
| *GS* | *The Gay Science* |
| *Z* | *Thus Spoke Zarathustra* |
| *BGE* | *Beyond Good and Evil* |
| *GM* | *On the Genealogy of Morality/Morals* |
| *CW* | *The Case of Wagner* |
| *TI* | *Twilight of the Idols* |
| *EH* | *Ecce Homo* |
| *AC* | *The Antichrist* |
| *NCW* | *Nietzsche Contra Wagner* |
| *NF* | *Notebook Material and Fragments* |
| *WP* | *The Will to Power* |

# Introduction

REBECCA BAMFORD AND ALLISON MERRICK

It may be something of a truism these days to note that contemporary political struggles often find their origins in conflicts that are based on social group identities, including race, ethnicity, religion, geographic region, gender, sexuality, disability, and nationality, as well as class. However obvious a point this may be, questions about how inequities, injustices, and social problems are connected with politicized identities remain pressing.[1] Research in a range of disciplines has shown that our social group identities directly affect the material conditions of our lives.[2] Conflicts and inequities that are grounded in the particularities of social group identities have been shown to affect democracy itself, as well as participation in democracy.[3] These material issues are not confined to one nation, or to any single world region, and neither are they are purely twenty-first-century problems, since they are grounded in our histories and deeply embedded in our understanding of and critical engagement with those histories. We propose that we would do well to continue to ask questions about why politicized identities bear so much political weight in determining who counts as a member of a social group, and in whether and how it is possible to respond to the specific political challenges that affect social groups cogently, collectively, and justly.

This volume aims to make better sense of the extent to which the work of Friedrich Nietzsche incorporates conceptual resources that are necessary to address current and pressing political and social issues grounded in engagements amongst, and about, politicized identities. We take our inspiration for the volume from Nietzsche's remarks in aphorism 6 of *Beyond Good and Evil*, where Nietzsche describes every great philosophy as the confession of its originator and as a form of autobiography, "a type of involuntary and unself-conscious memoir; in short, that the moral (or immoral) intentions in every philosophy constitute the true living seed from which the whole plant has always grown" (*BGE* 6). Nietzsche's concern in this aphorism is of course to point out the lack of awareness and involuntariness involved in current philosophers' incorporating of the personal into their—our—practice of philosophy. As part of Nietzsche's continuing engagement with free spiritedness in this text, this aphorism prompts us to interrogate the prejudices and assumptions that we all bring to the practice of philosophy, including and especially our moral prejudices and assumptions. And, at the same time, Nietzsche's aphorism also opens up space in which we may consider how to respond to the personal as already forming a constituent part of our philosophical engagements, not least since, as Carol Hanisch has pointed out, the personal is political.[4]

In this volume, we encouraged authors to incorporate autobiographical components into their chapters, including insights from their lived experiences in academic philosophy as well as in their personal lives. However, we determined that it was important for authors to be supported in choosing how much, and in what ways, to speak from, or about, lived standpoints.[5] We think it is important to note that philosophers and political theorists, including volume authors, live with the issues of politicized identities addressed by the chapters collected here every day: lived experiences are a valuable component of scholarly engagement with politicized identities. In addition, it bears mention that since we asked authors to ground their work in engagements with lived standpoints, not all politicized identities are or could be represented directly in this volume. Even so, we think the scholarly analysis here is relevant and timely to the question of how to engage critically and constructively with politicized identities, which continues to be taken up in a variety of contexts internationally.

Also underlying our approach to this volume is a return to genealogy, by which we mean two things: first, a return to engagement with Nietzsche's text *On the Genealogy of Morality* as a political philosophical text; second, a return to emphasis on critical engagement with Nietzsche's concept of genealogy as a tool for engagement with social and political issues affecting diverse social groups in particular ways. These two, of course, often come bundled together. That is, by attending to Nietzsche's *On the Genealogy of Morality* and to the origins, the histories, and the psychological needs that shape forms of life and their moral worth, one also opens up the methodological issue of whether this distinctive mode of investigating is up to the task of clarifying how our vexed concepts function or of addressing, and perhaps redressing, any number of urgent social issues.[6]

One particularly notable place in which the two have shown up together is Wendy Brown's essay "Wounded Attachments," which is notable for its sustained critical engagement with identity politics and examines the *ressentiment* of identities that she treats as grounded in their formative, historical, socio-political injuries.[7] Therein Brown develops a genealogical account of politicized identity as a product of what Nietzsche calls "willing which has taken its direction from the ascetic ideal" (*GM* III:28).[8] On this basis, she contends that all liberal subjects, not just markedly disenfranchised ones, are vulnerable to *ressentiment* by virtue of their situatedness within, and production by, power, as well as by liberal discourse's denial of this situatedness and production: as she suggests, in attempting to displace their suffering, identities structured by *ressentiment* become problematically invested in their own subjection.[9] In her assessment of Patricia Williams's defense of rights, which forms part of her account, Brown points out that rights may ultimately abet the damages of privatization, which include the fragmentation of a political culture of responsibility and the disguise of the workings of class—workings that mean the promise of rights may ultimately be kept only for the few and not for the many.[10] Yet as C. Heike Schotten has pointed out, while Brown's account constitutes a definitive statement of left Nietzscheanism, it contrasts a Nietzschean freedom that is not clearly liberatory with what ultimately amounts to a straw version of identity politics.[11] Hence, it is Schotten's claim that a more robust account of politicized identity is available, one that incorporates insights from Nietzsche but calls upon us to grapple with questions of liberation anew.

Brown and Schotten, however, are not alone. Indeed, a significant body of scholarship has deployed Nietzsche's thought in response to ongoing social and political concerns that are bound up with politicized identities, of which a number also focus on, or point to the critical importance and continuing relevance of, Nietzsche's genealogy as an analytic tool. For example, Ofelia Schutte has used Nietzschean resources to develop an account of political identity in which she points out the significance of genealogical accounts of liberation struggles, which provide unifying collective memory for oppressed social groups.[12] Further still, as Robert Bernasconi has shown, in Foucault's critical engagement with his own genealogical perspective,

Foucault connects his methodology to that of Nietzsche, which according to Bernasconi, raises questions about Nietzsche's role in the history of race and racism as well as about Foucault's own role. Otherwise put, a clear-eyed engagement with the methods of genealogy ought to, or so Bernasconi argues, raise a fundamental critical issue: the question, that is, "of how easy it is to pass from tracing a history to praising it."[13] The worry, as Bernasconi has it, is that Nietzsche's thinking on heredity and breeding is tied up with concerns of race. Hence, even while evidence of Nietzsche's agreement with biopolitical anti-Semitism of some of his peers is clear, the evidence of Nietzsche's anti-Black racism cannot be, as Bernasconi maintains, explained away.[14] Accordingly, in assiduously attending to the history, the origins, and the very tracings of complex histories one may inadvertently usher in a host of normative commitments that, in Bernasconi's view, one would do well to be alert to and bear in mind.

Further still many scholars have drawn on Nietzsche's philosophy to strengthen interconnections between diverse and intersectional accounts of and engagements with politicized identities. For instance, in the first of her three books that interrogate the concept of the feminine in post-Hegelian philosophy, Luce Irigaray critically examines Nietzsche's relationship to the feminine.[15] A wide range of scholars have followed Irigaray in critical assessment of Nietzsche, women, and feminist theory.[16] More recently, Maudemarie Clark has written on questions of Nietzsche's receptivity to feminism, to the project of gay liberation, and to democracy.[17] Further still, Nietzschean conceptual tools for addressing and critically engaging with racialized identities have been explicitly developed in a collection of essays on the critical affinities between Nietzsche and African American thought edited by Jacqueline Scott and Todd Franklin.[18] Work by Robert Gooding-Williams has critically examined interconnections between Nietzsche and Black studies.[19] Lewis Gordon has deployed Nietzsche's thought in his critical engagements with racialized and colonized identities, noting where Nietzschean tools are useful to the advancement of justice, including in cases where Nietzsche himself may have been unsympathetic to an observation that may be appropriately grounded in his philosophy.[20]

The chapters in this volume pick up on some of the threads developed in earlier scholarship and seek to connect these with contemporary concerns. As such, the volume is divided into three main thematic areas, with chapters grouped according to these themes. The first section examines questions pertaining to the origins of identities and modes of subjection of identities. In section two, a more specific focus on elitism and political hierarchies is maintained. In the third and final section, a range of emancipatory possibilities of Nietzsche's political and philosophical thinking are considered and assessed.

## Part I: On the Origins of Identities and Modes of Subjection

One of the grounding questions of this volume is that of identity formation and development. How, for Nietzsche, do varying modes of identity form and acquire legitimacy? These questions are tied to conceptual and textual interpretation questions concerning Nietzsche's thinking on subjectivity and drive psychology. If it is the case that Nietzsche contests a unitary subject, offering an account of the sense of self as a composite of competing, often conflicting, drives, then what sense can we make of identity and of its role as the locus of agency or action? Any cogent answer to these questions requires provision of an account for the disjunction between Nietzsche's attempts to dissolve the self into a fluid, fluctuating set of drives and the stability of a unified and autonomous sense of ourselves as agents. To elaborate further on this point, we might also consider in what ways our philosophical accounts of ourselves serve to constrain us or to limit our conceptions of what is possible. We might even imagine how our understanding of ourselves might be reshaped.

Lawrence Hatab takes up these thematic issues in his contribution in chapter 1, arguing that Nietzsche's ostensibly inconsistent views on agency can be reconciled if one brings together Nietzsche's account of agonistic psychology with a mode of narrative identity structure. The narrative form, claims Hatab, offers a sense of self over time, yet that very *sense* of identity is itself constituted by an agonistic psychology: our drives and affects, both conscious and unconscious, often conflict and compete to gain a place of prominence in that story. Once we recognize this—that "selfhood" is a matter of conscious and unconscious agonistically contended perspectives—we can also appreciate how identity claims to nationality or ethnicity, for instance, follow a similar structure. By way of conclusion, Hatab draws on his own biography and evolving identities to further demonstrate the feasibility of the Nietzschean account he proposes.

In chapter 2, Paul Kirkland points out that what Nietzsche offers us is a new way of thinking about identity as a site of politicized contest. As Kirkland shows, Nietzsche develops a conception of identity that focuses on multiplicity and on agonal contestation, which roots identity in the thoroughly tragic. By emphasizing these dynamic elements—the sense of self as the product of a mix of competing drives, for instance—Kirkland shows how Nietzsche offers us a more nuanced conception of identity that seeks to hold unease as a component of identity itself, rather than seeking to reconcile or otherwise do away with internal conflict. According to Kirkland, the tragic view of identity is precisely the one Nietzsche offers us through his self-portrait in *Ecce Homo*.

Robert Guay's chapter 3 explores the themes of identity formation and of their legitimacy. Nietzsche, Guay holds, sees all identity formation as aspirational, as inevitably striving to meet an ideal. As Guay puts it: "Identity itself is idealizing." The problem, however, is that these ideals after which we strive are often unreflectively or unconsciously internalized, making our identities self-estranging. Expanding on Nietzsche's concerns that identity formation, so understood, leads to homogenous normalizing, Guay demonstrates that social institutions can also produce conformity through abnormal and marginalized identities. If our identity is formed and shaped by both individual and social norms, which are at once available to conscious reflection and to the unconscious, how might we respond, how might identities be reshaped? One answer, Guay suggests, is to be found in a recognition of the idealizing structure of identity formation, which may show us a meaningful way of being who we are.

Allison Merrick agrees that identity formation, for Nietzsche, is thoroughly politicized. In exploring why a psychologist would undertake the genealogical study of morality, Merrick's chapter 4 demonstrates that historical, socio-political conflicts and contexts organize self-experience (*EH* "Genealogy"). If Nietzsche's account of those conflicts and contexts are persuasive then we can notice that genealogical investigations extend much further than excavating our taken-for-granted notions, reclaiming subjugated histories, and examining how forms of life have been contingently constructed. What Merrick's analysis shows is that Nietzsche's genealogical accounts also help us to understand how our affective, which is to say psychic, lives have come to be ordered and shaped. Attending to the genealogist as psychologist then carries some renewed significance for projects of political action: it reminds us that even as we must attend to subjugated histories we must also keep in view the psychic structures they produce.

In her contribution in chapter 5, Rebecca Longtin examines the enduring significance of Nietzsche's perspectivism to contemporary engagement with politicized identities. As Longtin points out, perspectivism situates knowledge within concrete embodied standpoints and their socio-political-cultural contexts, shifts between different perspectives to challenge universal frameworks and dogmatic hegemonies and resists essentialist identity categories. Longtin compares Nietzsche's perspectivism with the work of Latin American decolonial feminist philosophers María Lugones, Gloria Anzaldúa, and Mariana Ortega in order to illuminate the contemporary political significance of perspectivism, which as she argues is of enduring significance if we want to theorize in intersectional ways that do real justice to multiple standpoints and worldviews.

## Part II: Elitism and Political Hierarchies

In chapter 6, Daniel Conway also takes his cue from *On the Genealogy of Morality*. In focusing on the psychological profile of ascetic priest, Conway demonstrates the ways that the character type marshals shame to shape identity. As a means of illuminating and assessing Nietzsche's attempts to politicize the figure and role of the ascetic priest, Conway draws on the 2014 Damian Chazelle film *Whiplash*, which tells the story of a sadistic music teacher, Terence Fletcher (played by J. K. Simmons) and his talented protégé, Andrew Neiman (played by Miles Teller). What emerges from their interactions is a view of shame as a tool of subjection. Open, then, is the question of whether Andrew's overcoming of Fletcher is possible for the "new philosophers" Nietzsche envisages. Can we use Chazelle's film, the very template he lays down, to complete the Nietzsche's genealogical account? Might the priests too take pride in and feel himself awakened and invigorated by the whiplashing he has received from his erstwhile ward and protégé, the philosopher?

Conway's chapter, of course, opens up a number of pointed but often neglected questions: Why does Nietzsche need the character of the priest to be so terribly inflexible in their allegiance to the ascetic ideal? Is that a flaw in Nietzsche's account, an internal weakness? Or is there a more promising explanation? Might the priests come to recognize a problem in the way that they have maintained their power and forgo their ways? This raises, in a rather acute way, the questions of what values, and of whose values, should be prioritized and why. This is, of course, to grapple and contend with Nietzsche's aristocratic politics.

Rebecca Aili Ploof takes up this task in chapter 7. In focusing on a mode of ontological freedom as historically discovered and deployed by an aristocratic class, Ploof contends that, according to Nietzsche, so too with us: the rewards of such freedoms, far from being democratically distributed, will be the purview of the elite. Ploof's explanation for Nietzsche's aristocratic elitism focuses on the value of freedom. According to her, Nietzsche identifies how the political drive toward ever greater equality jeopardizes the freedom for humans to become otherwise. As Ploof shows, projects focused on equality entrench a form of human being that is unhealthy and harmful to itself through the universalization of ascetic ideals, scientism, and democracy. Ploof therefore suggests that Nietzsche proposes we should seek to reinvigorate freedom as the most valuable value, because freedom is the value that enables the transformation of human being itself, even while this transformation is limited to the few.

In a similar vein, C. Heike Schotten suggests in chapter 8 that we must recognize that Nietzsche's critique of slave morality is written from the vantage point of those in power. Instead of reprimanding Nietzsche for situating his critique "from above," as a mode of elitism, Schotten uses that perspective to draw out the misplaced *ressentiment* of the Right. In so doing, Schotten demonstrates through her analysis of the US "terrorism" discourse that Nietzsche's critique can be usefully directed toward the "reactionary rightwing powerholders ascendant in our current moment"—and as she also points out, this is also, in some sense, "every moment hitherto in the existence of these United States."

## Part III: Emancipatory Possibilities

The final group of chapters in this volume examine the question of whether Nietzsche's engagement with questions of politicized identities and his wider political thought are best viewed as descriptive or whether his philosophy offers us a therapeutic or even normative political agenda. That is, these contributions explore whether Nietzsche simply helps us to better diagnose the ills of modernity or whether he also offers us a means of redress for the conditions in which we find ourselves. Can we deploy Nietzsche usefully in support of political action, and if so, in what way and to what extent is such action limited by Nietzsche's own prejudices and presumptions? Moreover, these contributors consider what it is that we get from Nietzsche that we cannot get from other political philosophers and theorists concerned with issues of politicized identity, especially with regard to contemporary political projects that drive at egalitarian or democratic ends.

In chapter 9, Elif Yavnik takes up these questions in relation to the issue of feminine subjectivity in Nietzsche. Yavnik argues that the Nietzschean performative *summoning* of the feminine can be viewed as a call to the possibility of being and living differently. As Yavnik explains, this is to open oneself up to living in a world shaped by diverse experiences, bodies, and sensibilities as well as to encountering hitherto less apparent facets of oneself and of understanding oneself differently. In line with the diagnostic dimension of Nietzsche's relevance to contemporary issues of politicized identities, Yavnik proposes that what Nietzsche offers to us today is a signpost to the possibility of overcoming the understanding of identity through male perspectives and masculine discourses and orders.

Kaitlyn Creasy also assesses Nietzsche's agenda as being descriptive rather than normative. In chapter 10, offering an account of the transpersonal nature of the affects, Creasy shows that Nietzsche illuminates the affective dynamics of oppression and internalizing of harmful social norms resulting in harms that range from extreme to subtle and insidious. According to Creasy, a Nietzschean analysis of the affective dynamics of oppression, especially gender-based oppression, can help to explain the affective productions of patriarchal culture that subject women to particular cultural or social norms that potentially result in exhaustion, self-estrangement, or even self-loathing. In so doing, Creasy shows how her Nietzschean account fleshes out a critical affective mechanism of what Sandra Bartky has termed psychological oppression.

Jacqueline Scott proposes a therapeutic account in chapter 11, focusing on issues of race in her assessment of Nietzsche's relevance to politicized identities. Scott makes plainer how one of Nietzsche's goals in his later works was to experiment with the aims and methods of philosophy, in order that—in the face of a tragic view of life—the healthiest psychological types may affirm their lives. With this specific form of philosophical experimentation in mind, Scott argues that we need to adopt a tragic view of our racialized lives in the contemporary world in order to affirm our lives as racialized subjects in a racialized society. According to Scott, doing so will enable us to accept the endemic and chronic nature of racism in society, acceptance that is necessary to enable action to revalue racialized identities in ways that make real differences to the material conditions of people's lives and to their capacity to affirm their racialized lives. For example, she applies Nietzschean tragic affirmation to explain the transformative potential in a case examined by Lani Guinier and Gerald Torres, in which prisoners might experiment with their racialized identities in order to create the solidarity across racial identities necessary to improve their incarcerated working conditions and their lives after prison. As Scott also points out, the problem of racialized division and the need for tragic affirmation to combat it is not solely an American problem: it is also a problem for philosophy as a discipline.

Jeremy Fortier also adopts a therapeutic approach to the issue of emancipatory possibility from a different angle: How might we affirm the past, Fortier wonders in chapter 12, particularly a past that we may like to resist, in whole or in part? Can one affirm the past while also at the same time resisting it, or at least certain of its political implications? Fortier shows how both Nietzsche and Ralph Ellison wrestled productively and insightfully with these questions. As Fortier demonstrates, both Nietzsche and Ellison concluded that finding something to *affirm* in one's history is a precondition for effectively resisting, and transcending, that history. As Fortier makes clear, what both Nietzsche and Ellison demonstrate is the interconnection of self-knowledge and historical knowledge, which enables our critical questioning of contemporary values while also supporting a space in which to create values. As such, Fortier's comparison of Ellison and Nietzsche shows us how each man's work can illuminate the other's, as well as illustrating the continuing relevance of their thinking to political thought.

Rebecca Bamford's account in chapter 13 shows how Nietzsche's philosophy has been used to provide support for disability justice projects in the past. Similar to Scott and Fortier, Bamford takes a therapeutic-normative approach. She argues that Nietzsche's critique of *Mitleid* (pity or compassion) and the free spirit works in which this critique is grounded, still count as a helpful resource for disability justice projects. As Bamford suggests, Nietzsche's critique of *Mitleid* can help to unpick the structural conditions that perpetuate ableism, promote disabled people's agency and independence, and provide a useful tool to help us understand how moral, social, and political philosophical assumptions and prejudices—particularly when these are predicated on the assumed universal moral and social correctness of *Mitleid*—hinder the elimination of ableism from philosophy as well as from wider society.

~

As is clear, not all topics and issues pertinent to politicized identities and the social and political issues tied to them could be covered in any single volume.[21] We therefore make no claim for the completeness of this volume's coverage of the plethora of complex issues concerning experiences of intersectional injustice to which politicized identities remain vulnerable. Rather, the chapters gathered in this volume constitute a current appraisal of Nietzsche's contemporary relevance to understanding, and responding effectively to, some of the important range of social and political issues that are inextricable from politicized identities in their diversity and intersectionality. As Kimberlé Crenshaw has pointed out in a key contribution on intersectionality, identity, and the political, the social power in delineating difference may be "the source of social empowerment and reconstruction" rather than a source of domination.[22] Nietzsche's philosophy is neither an unproblematic tool nor always the best tool for seeking social empowerment or for pursuing projects of social justice. Our contention here is the modest one that Nietzsche may be a useful tool toward such ends and that it is worthwhile to continue to ask when and why political philosophy and theory grounded in Nietzsche can do useful liberatory work that may make a meaningful difference in people's lives and experiences. Our hope, of course, is that this volume achieves just that.

## Notes

1. We have opted for the term of art "politicized identity." The reason is that the papers collected in this volume argue that Nietzsche places identity itself on the scene of agonal socio-political and historical struggles.

2. Major, Dovidio, and Link 2018; Valentine 2022.

3. Brown-Dean 2019.

4. Hanisch 1970 (2006). As Hanisch notes in her 2006 introduction to the text, the title of her essay was suggested by Shulamith Firestone and Anne Koedt.

5. Indeed, some of our contributors comment on their approaches in their biosketches for the volume.

6. Bernard Williams, as is well known, draws upon Nietzsche's *On the Genealogy of Morality* to clarify how the concept of truthfulness may be said to function (2002). Others have marshaled the text and its methods to clarify and combat a number of urgent social issues, including racism, sexism, and ableism (e.g., McWhorter 2009; Scott 2006; Tremain 2017). Others still have made use of the mode of genealogical inquiry to illuminate our current historical contexts and the ways it shapes modes of life (e.g., Erlenbusch-Anderson 2018).

7. Brown 1993. See also Elisabeth Anker 2022. Indeed, it is worth pointing out that Brown's approach can be neatly contrasted with the complaints about

identity politics that focus on vague appeals to a focus on identity being somehow problematically "woke."

    8. Brown 1993, 401–2.
    9. Brown 1993, 401–2.
    10. Brown 1993.
    11. Schotten 2019.
    12. Schutte 1993, 16.
    13. Bernasconi 2017a, 174.
    14. Bernasconi 2017b.
    15. Irigaray 1991.
    16. Oppel 2005; Patton 1993; Diethe 2013.
    17. Clark 2015.
    18. Scott and Franklin 2006.
    19. Gooding-Williams 2006.
    20. See for example Gordon 2022, 207; Gordon 1997.
    21. Though to offer one example, Longtin's piece (chapter 5 of this volume) does indeed touch upon issues of colonialism, though we acknowledge that more work could have been included that would have also clarified the extent to which Nietzsche's work may be a resource for anti-colonial movements. Further still, and on another front, Allie Merrick has recently shown that Nietzsche's *Antichrist* draws upon and makes use of the genealogical mode of inquiry to make plain that, in Nietzsche's view at least, the origins of Christianity rest on a reinterpretation of the type of the redeemer. Hence, open here is another avenue of scholarship, one that illuminates Nietzsche's account of the origins, motivations, and histories of religious identities as well as a critical evaluation of those claims, but one that for reasons of shape could not be taken up by this volume (Merrick 2023).
    22. Crenshaw 1991.

## References

Anker, Elisabeth. 2022. "States of Freedom." *Polity* 54.3: 583–90.
Bernasconi, Robert. 2017a. "Making Nietzsche's Thought Groan: The History of Racisms and Foucault's Genealogy of Nietzschean Genealogy in *Society Must Be Defended*." *Research in Phenomenology* 47.2: 153–74.
———. 2017b. "Nietzsche as a Philosopher of Racialized Breeding." In *The Oxford Handbook of Philosophy and Race*, edited by Naomi Zack, 54–64. Oxford: Oxford University Press.
Brown-Dean, Khalilah L. 2019. *Identity Politics in the United States*. Cambridge: Polity Press.
Brown, Wendy. 1993. "Wounded Attachments." *Political Theory* 21.3: 390–410.

Clark, Maudemarie. 2015. *Nietzsche on Ethics and Politics*. Oxford: Oxford University Press.
Crenshaw, Kimberlé. 1991. "Mapping the Margins: Intersectionality, Identity Politics, and Violence against Women of Color." *Stanford Law Review* 43.6: 1241–1299.
Diethe, Carol. 2013. *Nietzsche's Women: Beyond the Whip*. Berlin: De Gruyter.
Erlenbusch-Anderson, Verena. 2018. *Genealogies of Terrorism: Revolution, State Violence, Empire*. New York: Columbia University Press.
Gooding-Williams, Robert. 2006. *Look, a Negro!: Philosophical Essays on Race, Culture and Politics*. New York: Routledge.
Gordon, Lewis R. 2022. *Fear of Black Consciousness*. London: Penguin (Allen Lane).
———, ed. 1997. *Existence in Black: An Anthology of Black Existential Philosophy*. London: Routledge.
Hanisch, Carol. 1970 (2006). "The Personal Is Political." *Women of the World, Unite! Writings by Carol Hanisch* (website). https://www.carolhanisch.org/CHwritings/PIP.html.
Irigaray, Luce. 1991. *Marine Lover of Friedrich Nietzsche*. Translated by Gillian C. Gill. New York: Columbia University Press.
Koopman, Colin. 2019. *How We Became Our Data: A Genealogy of the Informational Person*. Chicago: University of Chicago Press.
Major, Brenda, John F. Dovidio, and Bruce G. Link, eds. 2018. *The Oxford Handbook of Stigma, Discrimination, and Health*. Oxford: Oxford University Press.
McWhorter, Ladelle. 2009. *Racism and Sexual Oppression in Anglo-America: A Genealogy*. Bloomington: Indiana University Press.
Merrick, Allison. 2023. "Concerning the Psychological Type of the Redeemer: Nietzsche on the Methods of Philosophy." *European Journal of Philosophy* 31.1: 151–62. https://doi.org/10.1111/ejop.12774.
Nietzsche, Friedrich. 2007. *On the Genealogy of Morality*. Translated by Carol Diethe. Cambridge, MA: Cambridge University Press.
Oppel, Frances Nesbitt. 2005. *Nietzsche on Gender: Beyond Man and Woman*. Charlottesville: University of Virginia Press.
Patton, Paul. 1993. *Nietzsche, Feminist, and Political Theory*. London: Routledge.
Schotten, C. Heike. 2019. "Wounded Attachments?: Slave Morality, the Left, and the Future of Revolutionary Desire." In *Nietzsche and Critical Social Theory: Affirmation, Animosity, and Ambiguity*, edited by Christine A. Payne and Michael J. Roberts, 31–59. Leiden, NL: Brill.
Schutte, Ofelia. 1993. *Cultural Identity and Social Liberation in Latin American Thought*. Albany: State University of New York Press.
Scott, Jacqueline. 2006. The Price of the Ticket: A Genealogy and Revaluation of Race. In *Critical Affinities: Nietzsche and African American Thought*. Edited by Jacqueline Scott and A. Todd Franklin, 149–71. Albany: State University of New York Press.

Scott, Jacqueline, and Todd Franklin. 2006. *Critical Affinities: Nietzsche and African American Thought*. Albany: State University of New York Press.

Tremain, Shelley. 2017. *Foucault and Feminist Philosophy of Disability*. Ann Arbor: University of Michigan Press.

Valentine, Desiree. 2022. "Racialized Disablement and the Need for Conceptual Analysis of 'Racial Health Disparities.'" *Bioethics* 36.3: 336–45.

Williams, Bernard. 2002. *Truth and Truthfulness: An Essay in Genealogy*. Princeton, NJ: Princeton University Press.

# Part I

# On the Origins of Identities and Modes of Subjection

1

# Contending Selfhood

## Nietzschean Contributions to the Question of Political Identity

LAWRENCE J. HATAB

In our time there are growing impulses toward ethnic nationalism and against multicultural identity politics. Immigration policies have been fractious in Europe and America. In this chapter I offer an interpretation of Nietzsche's thinking on selfhood and his concept of the good European in order to suggest a viable response to vexing contemporary questions concerning political identity. Identity in my discussion has nothing to do with philosophical conceptions of a substantive self that is "identical" throughout temporal movement, within changing circumstances, or despite human variations. I work with the familiar sense of *personal* identity, not what one is but who one is, namely those narratives driven by existential meanings and values, which figure in how political life is exercised from multiple personal, social, and cultural perspectives. Nietzsche surely stresses this sense of identity, because for him even philosophy is driven by personal drives: "I have gradually come to realize what every great philosophy so far has been . . . a type of involuntary and unnoticed memoir. . . . There is absolutely nothing impersonal about the philosopher; and in particular his morals bear decided and decisive witness to *who he is*" (*BGE* 6).

## Nietzsche on Human Selfhood[1]

Nietzsche's approach to selfhood is complicated and elusive. With his philosophy of becoming, any talk of a "self" cannot connote something substantive or enduring. Selfhood, for Nietzsche, is ever emergent within a dynamic of life forces, which rules out "identity" in the sense of sameness, either within or between selves. A self is not a unified subject that grounds attributes or launches actions as a causal source (*BGE* 19–21). There is no substantial self behind or even distinct from performance: "There is no 'being' behind doing, effecting, becoming; 'the doer' is merely a fiction added to the deed—the deed is everything" (*GM* I:13). Human experience and thinking are decentered processes, but the grammar of subjects and predicates, nouns and verbs, tricks us into assigning an "I" as the source of behavior and thought (*BGE* 17). Words like "will" and "self" can supply a nominal unity but experience and action are too fluid and complicated to be reduced to the supposed reference of a linguistic unit (*BGE* 19).

The fluidity of selfhood is not simply a function of changes because it is energized agonistically: as an arena for the conflict of different drives, each seeking mastery (*BGE* 6, 36). Whatever comes to thought and awareness stems from an interactive struggle of multiple pockets of force (*BGE* 12; *KSA* 11:40 [42]). Nietzsche's agonistic psychology does not mean that the self is an utter chaos; he does allow for shaping the self, but this is a difficult and demanding process of counter-cropping the drives so that a certain mastery can be achieved. The self embodies differing perspectives, and their conflicts can be orchestrated by a capacity to manage one's "for" and "against" as alternating displays in different interpretive contexts (*GM* III:12). The arena of drives fits Nietzsche's long-standing emphasis on the body, which is better construed as the lived body of carnal experience rather than a physiological object. Indeed, one of Nietzsche's specific renditions of a "self" is tied to the body and its impulses, rather than an "ego" (*Z* I: "Despisers of the Body").

Agonistic relations obtain not only within selves but between selves as well. Here we can approach Nietzsche's notorious concept of will to power and its often misunderstood meaning. The conflict of drives is explained by Nietzsche as a function of will to power (*BGE* 36), which cannot be centered in any particular drive or its achievements because it is a field-concept radiating throughout the whole of existence (*KSA* 13:14 [79]). It is a medial structure between drives that does not come to rest in any single site of force. Will to power manifests itself *only* against resistances, which is why it seeks out and needs resistance (*KSA* 12:9 [151]), namely a conflicting power to be *overcome*. Something important needs to be stressed here: since power needs resistance, it is essentially related to counter-powers; if resistance were eliminated, destroyed, or neutralized by sheer domination, one's power would evaporate, it would no longer *be* power. Will to power within selves can therefore never be resolved into some harmony or teleological completion. And will to power between selves is really a social phenomenon because different selves and their power interests continually shape each other in reciprocal competition. This is one way to understand Nietzsche's objection to atomic individualism (*TI* "Skirmishes" 33; *BGE* 12). Finally, power is not confined to physical force, so there are socio-cultural manifestations of power in any human worldview. That is why the ascendancy of slave morality over master morality (in Nietzsche's genealogical account) is a matter of will to power, as would be something like pacifism, an aim to overcome human violence (*KSA* 13:11 [111]). Indeed, when it comes to cultural production, counter-powers are always in play, and so at least in this sphere "there is no annihilation" (*KSA* 12:7 [53]).

Nietzsche's objection to individualism stems from his rejection of *any* grounding conception in a discrete self. Yet individuality in some sense can be construed in his promotion of creative types juxtaposed against herd conformity. There is also a kind of default individuation when considering the particular nexus of drives operating in each person. Yet this nexus is ever in flux as intersections of competing drives, which cannot be completely controlled or even grasped cognitively by the conscious mind (see *D* 109, 119). Indeed, for Nietzsche consciousness is a late development in the human animal and not preeminently strong or effective (*GS* 11). Surprisingly, in Nietzsche's account what we mean by consciousness is only a function of social communication because we only attend to ourselves reflectively when we turn to words for the sake of commerce in common linguistic meanings that render us comprehensible to others (*GS* 354). Accordingly, self-knowledge (a crucial ingredient in traditional philosophical methods) is only an internalization of socio-linguistic signs that are mutually communicable. When we engage in conscious self-awareness, we are only translating ourselves into common constructions. What is truly "individual" then is not indicated in consciousness because the instruments of self-analysis omit whatever might be unique in experience (*GS* 354). We are each unique, but only in an unconscious configuration of drives that eludes both social communication and self-comprehension.

Accordingly, our sense of identity, of who we are, is mostly drawn from narrative meanings that cannot be fully expressive of our individual nature, which at best might be called a singularity, construed as a negative trace that exceeds description and conscious self-awareness. There is always more to a person than what can be brought to overt comprehension. This does not mean that expressive identity is utterly false, but it cannot pretend to be the full truth. Moreover, narrative identity follows the unstable contest of differing drives, because when we consider who we are, we attend to multiple perspectives of meaning and value: personal interests, social relations, family ties, occupation, ethnicity, nationality, gender, sexual orientation, language, religion, geography, and so on. Such perspectives are rarely stable or in harmony, either within or between their orientations.

Political institutions represent formats that bear on these human perspectives and (at least in democratic societies) that stand as sites for perspectival contestation. The ongoing effects and conflicts in institutions constitute the life of politics. Americans for decades have been engaged in fights over identity politics, generally with respect to matters of ethnicity, gender, sexual orientation, and religion—particularly regarding marginalized identities and targets of prejudice or discrimination. Even those who complain about identity politics (a factor in the 2016 US presidential election) often do so from an unacknowledged vantage point of ethnic, gender, or religious identities, and from fears for their own status, whether real or imagined. I believe that my sketch of Nietzsche's carnal agonistic perspectivism can well address issues of personal selfhood and identity politics in American democracy. A pluralized will to power helps gather these issues into focus and alerts us to the central flaw driving most political energies: an inability to bear the finitude of identity, by which I mean (1) we are mortal and vulnerable to suffering, lack, and loss; (2) we each embody a plurality of tensional identities that are not resolvable into a stable unity; (3) our identities follow unconscious drives that cannot be fully controlled or explained; and (4) neither ourselves nor others can be reduced to, and confined by, any particular identity or summary description. Human selfhood is agonistically unsettled and ever open. The finitude of identity is not easy to bear and therefore susceptible to projects of resolution or closure. All of us are able to commit what Nietzsche called the "original sin of philosophers" (*AOM* 5), namely substantivizing cultural phenomena that are simply "approximate indications" (*ungefährer Fingerzeig*), a mistake amounting to a false reification (*Verdinglichung*) stemming from a rage for generalization (*Verallgemeinerung*). Yet such errors are more affective/conative than cognitive, more an impulse to corral other persons for exclusion or conversion, usually to protect one's own identity out of fear spawned by otherness. Even justified defenses of identity against discrimination and bias can turn solidarity into tribalism.

With coming discussions, I concede a hermeneutical appropriation of Nietzsche's thinking that may not always fit his intentions. My work in bringing a Nietzschean perspective to democratic politics has not been limited to exegesis of his texts alone or to his own commitments. Rather, I have found Nietzsche's philosophy to be an effective engine for rethinking democracy in important ways. In what follows I take that hermeneutical path with respect to citizenship, nationalism, and immigration, all through the prism of identity politics. Here I leave aside the question of Nietzsche's elitist objections to democratic equality, which I have engaged elsewhere.[2]

## Citizenship

Being a citizen is part of my identity as an American, but that intersects with other parts of identity and cannot have any privileged status. Citizenship is a certain perspective, namely being a participant in a political community, whether local, state, or national. Politics can have significant bearing on much of my personal identity and that of other Americans, so citizenship has significant valence. Democratic citizenship, in a constitutive sense apart from specific political interests, abstracts from other elements of identity because it entails an allegiance to the law and not persons or personal needs alone. It is noteworthy that Nietzsche's discussion of law and justice (*GM* II:10–11) can be pertinent here. Legal justice, he says, is not a slavish reactive phenomenon but an active power that converts human abuses into "crimes," which bypasses personal offense and vengefulness on behalf of the *impersonal* force of law. Vengeful dispositions in people can be "distracted" from the personal damage done to them. Moreover, Nietzsche offers an agonistic conception of justice, which transforms brute force into political power, which creates new avenues of power because legal provisions do not eliminate conflict but rather reroute it into an ongoing "conflict of power-complexes." I have read this account as fitting democratic political contests and the American provision for separation of powers.[3]

## Will to Power and Politics

In my work I have drawn from Nietzsche the notion of agonistic perspectivism and applied it to democratic politics. The agonistic structure of will to power shows that one's achievements are structurally related to resistance. Accordingly, one *needs* a contending Other for meaningful achievement. Nietzsche talks about the "spiritualization of hostility," wherein one must affirm the presence and power of opponents as implicated in one's own posture (*TI* "Morality" 3), both internally and externally. This agonistic concept is explicitly associated with politics in the passage at hand. If we add perspectivism, which rules out a decisive baseline truth, we notice the contours of democracy: democratic politics assumes veridical openness, because otherwise, inviting citizen participation would be an irresponsible courting of error; the only way to achieve a political result, then, is a competition of ideas, the award of temporary victory by a tally of votes, and periodic repetitions of the political contest. Agonistic openness means that citizen identities can be participants in the process, but no political result can be defined according to any victorious perspective because it must open itself to possible defeat in coming elections. In other words, democratic citizenship cannot be constituted by any particular identity.

A radical agonistic politics, I have argued, rules out violence, which stems from an impulse to eliminate conflict and competition by annihilating or incapacitating an opponent—thus bringing the contest to an end. In a notebook passage (*KSA* 12:10 [117]), Nietzsche claims that he fights Christianity "not with the aim of destroying it but only of putting an end to its *tyranny* and clearing the way for new ideals," which themselves must desire the continuance of Christianity because they must have "*strong* opponents, if they are to become *strong*." Democratic citizenship in this respect would therefore require *agonistic respect*, which means (1) allowing, even affirming political opposition; (2) acknowledging defeat in a fair political contest; and (3) yielding to the (temporary) political power of a perspective that one opposes. Such agonistic respect is an unwritten civic disposition that is neither instinctive nor easy to cultivate, which is the main reason why democracy can fail and has not been the rule in political history. Political "antagonism," being against the agon, stems from an incapacity for or refusal of agonistic respect, a compression within a particular identity, or an impulse toward eliminativism.

## Identity Politics

A driving force in identity politics has been attention to, and rectification of, injustices visited upon citizens and their identities along cultural lines listed earlier. What causes such injustice and what should rectification mean? Nietzsche is provocative on this score and I think his offerings have merit. Will to power, as we have seen, presupposes and cannot be eliminative of otherness. But what accounts for human abuses, according to Nietzsche? In most respects, fear and a lack of power. Hatred, for example, stems from fear (*GS* 379), something in the Other that threatens. And hurting people is not an exercise of power because it is "a sign that we are still lacking power, or it shows a sense of frustration in the face of this poverty" (*GS* 13). Blockage of self-development (which means achievement through the overcoming of obstacles) may lie behind abusive behavior because "whoever is dissatisfied with himself is continually ready for revenge, and we others will be his victims" (*GS* 290). Indeed, Nietzsche calls cruel people "retarded" (*HH* 43).

Understanding human abuses does not mean they can be excused or ignored. Political rectification is called for, but Nietzschean psychology warns against vengeful resentment and dwelling on memories of abuse. In fact, the affirmation project of eternal recurrence requires overcoming revenge against "time and its 'it was' " (*Z* II: "On Redemption")—an overcoming specifically identified with will to power in this passage. Harm can either debilitate or provide avenues for overcoming harm meaningfully. The latter, I believe, is implicated in what Nietzsche calls "active forgetting" (*GM* I:1–2). Strong natures who have a sense of power can "forget" injuries. Active forgetting in this manner lets moral offense pass; it does not mean literally forgetting one's injury, nor does it require forgiveness. It is rather a letting go of the psychological effect of being harmed and the retention of offense in one's memory.

Active forgetting can be implicated in dispositions and formats that make democracy possible. Ancient Greek democracy grew in part out of indigenous forces spotlighted by Nietzsche: particularly agonistic modifications of natural violence into rituals of competition (see *HC*).[4] In Greek democracy, voting was expressed as *diaphora*, meaning to divide up or disagree. The outcome of a vote was often described as a "victory" (*nikē*), but in the sphere of speech rather than violence.[5] It became clear to the Greeks that civil war was the ultimate danger to the polis, the turn to violence in the face of disputes that could destroy the political order from within. After the Peloponnesian and civil wars, the restoration of democracy was predicated in part on a conception of "amnesty," on swearing an oath "not to recall past misfortunes" (*mēmnēsikakein*). Such amnesty required a kind of active "amnesia" that would let go past passions and violence in favor of accepting the "victories of speech" in democratic debate, which could always be revisited because the force of language would supplant the terminating force of violence. Consequently, the acceptance of democratic outcomes demanded a capacity to willingly accept defeat, to live under results that could "offend" one's interests. Such offense must be "forgotten" in accepting political defeat.

The capacity to accept defeat in democratic contests is less likely when secure conceptions of the good are in place and when historical memory rules over the ability to suspend offense at past wrongs. The cultivation of moral "suspension" is a *background* force in the development of democratic formats and cannot therefore be guaranteed simply by implementing such formats. Often the conflicts between peoples or groups are irresolvable and prone to violence owing to competing memories held fast in a delusional zero-sum game of vengeance or rectification. Active forgetting can make political coexistence more likely, but it need not involve dismissing the past, nor would it require reconciliation or forgiveness. Historical memory is essential to human life, but an agonistic conception of will to power can exchange a vengeful memory for an incorporation of the past that overcomes offense on behalf of a new future.

## Immigration and Nationalism

In Europe and America there have been growing impulses for political nationalism, which aims to establish, maintain, or recover the identity of a particular nation, often defined along civic, ethnic, linguistic, religious, or economic lines. Nationalism is usually juxtaposed against an external or internal Other, against globalist forces or immigrants perceived to be jeopardizing the national character. Current trends can be traced to a number of causes—especially economic globalism, employment retrenchment, and Islamic terrorism—but in any case, fear, anger, and frustration have brought on scapegoating, compressed allegiances, and various us-them constructions for the sake of identity protection and causal narratives.

It is difficult to actually specify what the character of a "nation" is in nationalism,[6] but today it is more an atavistic attitude that has little objective bearing. Whatever ethnic, linguistic, economic, or religious aspects may have provided some national homogeneity in the past, modern mobility, interpenetration, and technology have pluralized developed nations more and more so that any current promotion of a national identity amounts to a nostalgic fantasy. At times, nationalistic urges mix with socio-cultural complaints about a harmonious, idyllic community that has been lost or ruined by current political conflicts and social disorder. The problem is this: we inhabit many "communities" due to different parts of our personal identity, as we noticed earlier, and whatever homogeneity may have existed in the past was underwritten by the *exclusion* of certain groups from political participation or the mutual *seclusion* of different groups within their own enclaves. Modern mobility and professed inclusiveness produce inevitable stresses on communal identities. That is why the agonistic perspectivism of democratic politics is best able to tolerate and negotiate these modern developments.

## The Good European

Nietzsche poses a challenge to nationalism with his concept of the "good European." In HH 475 he points to the mobility of people in modern Europe, the "nomadic life" of those who do not own land, and the crossing of types bringing a "mixed race" that counters nationalistic tendencies. Accordingly, he says, "one should not be afraid to proclaim oneself simply a *good European* and actively work for the amalgamation of nations." This should not be read as a call for some united European entity because it is fluidity and interpenetration that seems to be the emphasis. One way to understand Zarathustra's call to "remain true to the earth" (*Z* I: "Prologue" 3) and to think with an "earthly head" (*Z* I: "On the Afterworldly") is to recognize Nietzsche's non-territorial "geo-philosophy," which is continually emphasizing actual geographical locales, sea, sun, sky, mountains, animals, plants, and nomadic journeys—all in contrast to culturally imposed borders and denatured political ideals.[7] As I have argued in another work, the meaning of *Übermensch* in *Zarathustra* can be understood as getting "over" the separation of the "human" sphere from its natural habitat, the earth.[8]

In *GS* 377, Nietzsche speaks to "good Europeans" who are "homeless," who are unmoored from current ideals and realities, who are "children of the future," and to whom he commends his "secret wisdom of *gaya scienza*." Homelessness stands for a rejection of humanitarian and cosmopolitan ideals born in the Enlightenment—particularly a "free society" dedicated to equal rights, justice, and concord—and an affirmation of "danger, war, and adventure," which can ward off the effects of egalitarian mediocrity. A pro-Enlightenment critic of this venture against universal rational principles would highlight the danger of regression to ethnic or national identities. Yet in *GS* 377, homelessness includes a repudiation of nationalistic and racial tribalism. Good Europeans "are too diverse and racially mixed in our descent, as 'modern men,' and consequently we are not inclined to participate in the mendacious racial self-admiration and obscenity that parades in Germany today . . . and that is doubly false and indecent among people of 'historical sense.' " Historical sense is linked to an "untimeliness" that includes an open future. But it also involves an admission of having inherited "millennia of European spirit" and even having grown *out of* a Christian righteousness that would sacrifice everything for its faith. Good Europeans also have a faith, a "hidden Yes" in all their rejections and doubts, an affirmative posture that commands them to set sail as emigrants (*Auswanderer*).

Being historical, then, seems to mean exceeding the present by force of an open future and an inherited past. The subtitle of *BGE* is *Prelude to a Philosophy of the Future*. Sections 210–12 of that work reflect on the nature of philosophers and prospects for coming thinkers. Philosophers must be creators and exercise will to power in overcoming the present, whereby they "reach for the future" (*BGE* 211). It seems that philosophers of the future are not philosophers *in* the future but *of* the future—in being oriented toward the future, in bringing forth something new.[9] The philosopher is "*necessarily* a person of tomorrow and the day after tomorrow" (*BGE* 212). True philosophers cannot be compared with typical "philosophical laborers" and yet in the course of their "education" they can benefit from passing through established steps of thought to prepare their ventures.

> Perhaps the philosopher has had to be a critic and a skeptic and a dogmatist and historian and, moreover, a poet and collector and traveler and guesser of riddles and moralist and seer and "free spirit" and practically everything, in order to run through the range of human values and value feelings and *be able* to gaze with many eyes and consciences from the heights into every distance, from the depths up to every height, from the corner onto every expanse. But all these are only preconditions for his task: the task itself has another will, it calls for him to *create values*. (*BGE* 211)

The summary point is that Nietzsche's picture of the good European and the true philosopher renders a spatial and temporal openness, a geographical and intellectual reach beyond borders and established ideals, beyond the present—and yet this is a dynamic emergence *out of* an inherited past that provides bearings for creative ventures.[10] Such a looping structure can help unpack what Nietzsche means by calling upon good Europeans to set sail as emigrants (*Auswanderer*) in *GS* 377. The third section after that, *GS* 380, is titled "The Wanderer Speaks" ("Der Wanderer Redet") and it suggests a departure from one's culture that does not entirely leave it behind (the focus of this section being European morality), which adds a complicated structure to the dynamic of "overcoming" that operates in the will to power. Just as one must overcome the sedimented fixations of one's culture, one must also overcome the polar *opposition* to one's culture that marks the initial gesture of independence.

> If one would like to see our European morality for once as it looks from a distance, and if one would like to measure it against other moralities, past and future, then one has to proceed like a wanderer who wants to know how high the towers in a town are: he *leaves* the town. "Thoughts about moral prejudices," if they are not meant to be prejudices about prejudices, presuppose a position *outside* morality, some point beyond good and evil . . . a freedom from everything "European," by which I mean the sum of imperious value judgments that have become part of our flesh and blood. . . . One must have liberated oneself from many things that oppress, inhibit, hold down, and make heavy precisely us Europeans today. The human being of such a beyond who wants to behold the supreme measures of value of his time must first of all "overcome" this time in himself—this is the test of his strength—and then not only his time but also his prior aversion and contradiction *against* this time (*seiner bisherigen Widerwillen und Widerspruch gegen diese Zeit*), his suffering from this time, his untimeliness. (*GS* 380)

The overcoming of untimeliness here injects ambiguity into the "untimely" character of good Europeans in *GS* 377. If we add a geographical element to the "wandering" images in *GS* 377 and 380, it seems that emigration does not entail abandonment or repudiation of a homeland. How can Nietzsche's call for "good European emigrants" contribute to our discussion of political identity, now geared toward the question of immigration? It must be noted that I am departing significantly from the grand scale of Nietzsche's interest in philosophers as culture creators; nevertheless, I believe the features of his thought sketched in this chapter can well address the contemporary social-political issues at hand.

## The Emigrating Self

I am borrowing from Nietzsche the idea of an "emigrating self," which can cover both the geographical case of immigration and the multi-perspectival character of personal identity, where we are continually "migrating" in a field of different orientations—ethnic, familial, occupational, linguistic, religious, political, and so on—that are often in tension with each other. The "self" cannot be confined to any particular identity because it is an ongoing intersection of identities that is ever open. The notion of agonistic will to power can apply here as intersectional opportunities for self-development in tensional occasions of overcoming. Difference, then, is both a trigger of stress and a stimulant for new possibilities. The advantage here is that difficulties in confronting difference are taken seriously without a turn to separatism. An emigrating self can address both the burden and the promise of modern plurality, mobility, immigration, and integration. Here we bypass binary categories that often operate in such matters: conservatism versus liberalism, tribalism versus universalism, parochialism versus cosmopolitanism, fixed identity versus nomadic disjointure. We advance, rather, a deracinated self that is yet full of open possibilities born from engaging difference *and* sustaining fluid identities—from inhabiting a tensional field of self-creation that does not settle into any single form or aggregate harmony.

Since the Enlightenment, a notable response to identity conflicts has been cosmopolitanism, originally a Stoic notion that Kant emphasized in his *Perpetual Peace*. Modern cosmopolitanism is counterposed to nationalism or any kind of statist ideology, especially when stemming from contingent identities such as ethnicity and religion, which generated much violence in European history. Cosmopolitanism aims to supersede tensional differences by way of universal rationality and a global moral egalitarianism. Shortly I will challenge this standpoint as unduly dismissive of contingent identities. But here I mention an overlapping relationship between cosmopolitanism and enlightenment principles that underwrote or gave cover for decidedly egregious abuses in European and American history.

Nietzsche's thought has become well known for unmasking regimes of power that profess to be impartial advocates of universal ideals or superordinate rationality. Nietzsche's account of the "sovereign individual" (*GM* II:2) has usually been read as bearing on his notion of the free spirit or creative type. I have long challenged this consensus by arguing that the sovereign individual is expressive of the free, rational individual so indigenous to modern morality and political philosophy.[11] It is true that the sovereign individual castigates weaklings who cannot stand by their promises—sounding like Nietzsche's higher type—but the disdain of this individual toward inferiors can betray the dirty little secret of modern liberal rationality: not only its judgment of the inferior status of those who do not exercise autonomous reason—witness Kant's classic critique of "self-imposed tutelage" in *What is Enlightenment?*— but also the very real case of racial and gender biases in modern thinkers who champion "universal" reason while demoting those who do not or cannot live up to this ideal (such as women and non-white peoples). We are now more clearly aware of racist assumptions in various "enlightened" philosophers such as Hume, Kant, and Hegel. Even Mill, who repaired gender biases, still held that the liberty principle could not apply to children (of course) and "barbarians."[12] Contemporary liberal political theory may have moved past these particular categorial judgments, but there remains a continuing generalized judgment of citizens who are not "rational" enough in political life. For Nietzsche, any perspective is energized by overcoming some Other, and so the elitist tone of the sovereign individual can indeed refer to the modern rational subject and also uncover its complicity in paternalistic domination.

Here I am simply following a Nietzschean diagnosis that decodes concealed forms of power in a political perspective that presents itself as a universal model of emancipation, and therefore it does not own up to its own exclusionary or controlling effects. Along these lines I add a few remarks about the contract theory of government. The "state of nature" story supporting this political model emerged in a historical setting that can show it in a different light. The story pictures the formation of government as an act of will on the part of rational individuals who promise to abide by the formation of a state, the punitive force of which will override the fractious state of nature. Government is a rational human artifice, as opposed to the ancient idea that the state emerges out of a natural social condition. The "artificial" construction of the state accorded with and bolstered the ideal of individual autonomy; it could also help make sense out of the apparent contingency of political forms in the face of encountering different social systems in the Age of Discovery. Another consequence of the contractarian alternative was its tacit, if not overt, complicity with colonialism. The artificial willful construction of the political order could underwrite the willful imposition of European models upon the supposed pre-political, "natural" condition of native peoples, especially when their forms of life were deemed "backward," not to mention exploitable.[13] One advantage of Nietzsche's critical challenge is its capacity to put a critical spotlight on such philosophical moments in the contract theory that otherwise might be only dimly seen, if at all. Easier to see is the case of the United States. Americans are rightly proud of their democratic heritage, but we are usually quiet about how our nation was founded on conquest and enslavement. Although we have owned up to the evils of slavery and its aftermath, we are almost completely silent about the fate of Native Americans, which is arguably the worst sustained story of genocide in human history.[14] And we should not ignore how some of the assumptions in our "enlightened" tradition made such atrocities possible, or at least easier to sanitize.

## Ethnic Identity

Let us consider the notion of ethnic identity, by which I mean a loose concept pertaining to often overlapping differences of race, nationality, geography, language, religion, customs, dress, food, and art. From a biological standpoint, racial differences are not substantive, but when surface differences are connected with cultural differences, real diversity obtains at that level. Ethnic identities are therefore anthropologically contingent but existentially genuine forms of life. Such diversity enriches human experience and it should not be downplayed or devalued on behalf of a cosmopolitan ideal.[15] We can employ Nietzsche's idea of unconscious drives to (1) indicate the way in which ethnic identities are imprinted in our makeup from the earliest moments of life, in the manner of cultural habits that become second nature,[16] and (2) help explain seemingly ingrained biases that spawn interethnic prejudice and strife. I take up these two points in what follows.

First, people do not simply wear their ethnic identity like an article of clothing; they are attached to it in deep ways that should be taken seriously and not be demeaned as mere "folk" thinking. I have changed my mind on this matter from personal experience. From early in life I felt disconnected from my family and have always resisted group identifications. I was part of the counterculture in the 1960s but I refused to join my friends at Woodstock because I knew I would be irritated at being swept up in such a large community. In my self-conception I deemed myself an existential hero who belongs nowhere, who is not part of any "herd." My wife is Asian American, and her mother's family comes from Hawaii. She once told me that Hawaii is the only place where she feels truly comfortable because the cultural environment and demographic there so fit her makeup. I was bemused by this, thinking it rather quaint. I am Lebanese-Syrian, but I was born in the 1940s; assimilation was the rule (we were not taught Arabic) and there were few like people in my neighborhood and school. I did grow up with Arabic food and there were many cultural articles at home. Holiday family gatherings were packed with relatives from America and abroad. Arabic language, music, and food enveloped the scene, but I never really paid it much mind. In the late 1990s my wife and I went to Beirut for the first time. After a few days I started to think of family gatherings a lot. I was a smoker at the time, and one day I was having a cigarette on a street corner and a tourist came up to me and asked directions to some place. That struck me, and I stayed for a while on the corner. In time, another tourist came up to me, and then someone spoke Arabic to me. I began to take in the scene—the sights, sounds, smells—and started seeing many faces who looked like my relatives. Damn it, I really felt connected. Later I told my wife about this; I admitted that I understood her now. Beirut was an environment that in a way felt like a huge family gathering. Here is my point: ever since then I have been sensitized to the power of ethnic identities. I was the last person I thought would be susceptible to such feelings. When they came to me in such a strong way, I became convinced that they run deep in the human condition.

Second, ethnic strife and prejudice at a certain level are no less real and understandable. From an evolutionary standpoint, wariness of difference would seem to be a beneficial and selective trait. An animal that regarded any and every new encounter with open arms or indifference would not last long. Human wariness when confronted with difference, then, can be considered instinctive and natural. Nevertheless, human culture has introduced counter-instinctive ethical bearings that can take hold and even become second nature. Openness to difference is a real possibility, especially given a natural capacity for empathy that is first prompted with kin and kind but that can be expanded to wider circles with experience and familiarity.[17] But this should be understood as a *potentiality* in the midst of instinctive bearings that can resist it. In Nietzschean terms, then, openness to difference would be a function of will to power, of overcoming a natural predilection against otherness. In developmental terms and generally, such a process must be understood in light of its overall structure. In other words, human beings are prone to be wary of difference and yet capable of expanding horizons of interest and acceptance—especially if the tensional character of difference is acknowledged rather than castigated and implicated in self-development by way of agonistic creative energy. In view of this complicated environment, proposing a universal love of humanity or unqualified hospitality would be a nonstarter in Nietzschean terms, and perhaps even an ascetic fantasy.[18]

## American Immigration

Even though American democracy was built from Enlightenment ideals, if we consider geographical context and the history of immigration, we might recognize a workshop for the kind of conflicting and emigrating selfhood I have been exploring—with obvious exceptions in American history, to be sure. Both historically and geographically, America was able to define itself as something new and set apart from European traditions—having no long history of cultural fixtures and established institutions—which is why the French Revolution was so much more radical and disruptive. American "pluralism" at first was rather homogeneous (with entrenched racial and gender restrictions) and wedded to Enlightenment reason (with an abstract declaration to "all men"), but its professed openness was appealing to many peoples wanting a fresh start. Immigration patterns from all around the world expanded robustly, particularly in the late nineteenth and early twentieth centuries.

Historically, however, America from the start was predominantly white and Anglo and Protestant. So much so that even today being a WASP is not readily perceived as an ethnic identity, even though it surely is. Moreover, immigration was largely driven by an assimilation ethos, which was embodied by the famous "melting pot" metaphor—not really open and pluralistic in the end because it welcomed different cultural types only to be melted down and poured into an Anglo mold. Although American culture was never purely homogenized, assimilation created a kind of vapid pluralism that has been challenged by multicultural movements, but the movements themselves have generated worries about tribalism.

If we pay heed to the concrete, existential phenomenon of immigration as lived experience, we can see more readily the Nietzschean inflection I have been exploring, which would amount to reciprocal energies of self-development by way of tensional differences and so neither homogeneous nor tribalistic. From the immigrant standpoint, risk and courage are called for. The Nietzschean ideal of "experimentation" (*GS* 319, 324) is endemic to such a venture. The receiving culture, however, can experience immigration as a fearful influx of alien otherness, and of course most immigrant groups coming to America were met with prejudice in various ways. Immigrants and recipients, therefore, necessarily have their identity challenged and disturbed. Indeed, all peoples coming to America, original settlers included, had to go through an "uprooting embarkment" that unsettles normal comforts and familiarities for the sake of something new—of course it goes without saying that Native Americans and enslaved African peoples are a different story altogether.

In any case, immigration in America, ideally understood, makes for frayed identities reaching an "open" space that can receive them all because it is defined by none. Each identity, then, would have to shape a balance between the following conditions: (1) the loss of fixed attachments in one's home culture, (2) an acceptance of basic cultural norms in one's new home, (3) the uprooted remembrance and retention of one's heritage, and (4) a coexistence with other deracinated identities. Native and naturalized citizens, however, would also have to face and learn from the ongoing influx of different peoples. All of this represents an intermingling of identity and difference that is not reducible to any particular identity, a mere aggregate of identities, or a merging of identities—a balancing act best captured by the metaphor of a "stew," wherein the different foods are sustained but the whole is enriched by a mixing of flavors.[19]

## Notes

1. Parts of this chapter are drawn from previous work of mine: *A Nietzschean Defense of Democracy: An Experiment in Postmodern Politics* (Chicago: Open Court, 1995); *Nietzsche's "On the Genealogy of Morality": An Introduction* (Cambridge: Cambridge University Press, 2008); and "Nietzsche on Consciousness and Language," in *Nietzsche's Therapeutic Teaching: For Individuals and Culture*, eds. Horst Hutter and Eli Friedland (London: Bloomsbury, 2013), 191–204.

2. *A Nietzschean Defense of Democracy*, chap. 5.

3. See *Nietzsche's "On the Genealogy of Morality,"* 93–96, 260–64.

4. For a discussion of the connections between Greek democracy and contests, see Jean-Pierre Vernant, *Myth and Society in Ancient Greece*, trans. Janet Lloyd (Sussex, UK: Harvester Press, 1980), 19–44.

5. See Nicole Loraux, *The Divided City: On Memory and Forgetting in Ancient Athens*, trans. Corrine Pache (New York: Zone Books, 2001), chap. 1. I am indebted to this work for the historical points under discussion.

6. See Efraim Podoksik, "What Is a Nation in Nationalism?" *Journal of Political Philosophy* 25, no. 3 (Nov. 2017): 303–23.

7. For an excellent treatment of this facet of Nietzsche's thinking, see Gary Shapiro, *Nietzsche's Earth: Great Events, Great Politics* (Chicago: University of Chicago Press, 2016), esp. chap. 3.

8. See *Nietzsche's Life Sentence: Coming to Terms With Eternal Recurrence* (New York: Routledge, 2005), 55–56.

9. See Alexander Nehamas, "Who Are the 'Philosophers of the Future'? A Reading of *Beyond Good and Evil*," in *Reading Nietzsche*, eds. Robert Solomon and Kathleen Higgins (Oxford: Oxford University Press, 1988), 46–67, esp. 58.

10. Creativity is a complex intersection of freedom and form: certain "fetters" are needed both to prepare cultural departures from purely natural states (*HH* 221) and to give a comprehensible shape to new cultural forms (*WS* 140), See also *BGE* 188.

11. See my *Nietzsche's "On the Genealogy of Morality,"* 75–83.

12. It can be argued that the very idea of "race" was a construction of modern philosophy and that the science of "anthropology" was racially tinged in coming to terms with non-European peoples. See Emmanuel Chukwudi Eze, *Achieving Our Humanity: The Idea of a Postracial Future* (New York: Routledge, 2001), chaps. 1–3.

13. A glance at Locke can be illuminating here. In his *Second Treatise* (V.24–43), Locke framed the social contract in terms of property rights. Each individual is rightfully its own "property," its own self-possession (i.e., a sovereign individual). When through artifice individuals mix their labor with nature, they are entitled to the product as their own property. Locke connects this idea with the divine command to subdue and cultivate the earth, and modern forms of production seem to be the highest expression of following this command. Locke at times mentions American Indians and their primitive production in the midst of vast stretches of uncultivated land. He says that even the smallest parcel of cultivated land in England is superior in value to the largest area of untapped land in America. Revealingly, Locke calls this uncultivated land "waste." Who could fail to notice here the hints of colonialist rhetoric, in the sense that the "state of nature" in discovered lands not only lacks proper political conditions that can be imposed, but it also lacks legally protected property rights that can by right be claimed by productive settlers because nature is wasted by the natives.

14. The effects of nonindigenous diseases, warfare, broken treaties, confinement to reservations, and sanctioned violence of every kind are in a way more heinous for their invisibility to American consciousness.

15. For an attempt to formulate an agonistic sense of cosmopolitanism, see Tamara Caraus, "Towards an Agonistic Cosmopolitanism: Exploring the Cosmopolitan Potential of Chantal Mouffe's Agonism," *Critical Horizons* 17, no. 1 (Feb. 2016): 94–109.

16. For Nietzsche's thinking on second nature, see *HL* 3; *D* 38, 455; *GS* 290.

17. See my discussion in *Ethics and Finitude: Heideggerian Contributions to Moral Philosophy* (Lanham, MD: Rowman & Littlefield, 2000), chap. 6.

18. Derrida's thinking on hospitality is interesting in this regard. See *Of Hospitality*, trans. Rachel Bowlby (Stanford: Stanford University Press, 2000). He recognizes that absolute hospitality is impossible, but it stands as aporetically structured with actual possibilities of hospitality. Beginning with hospitality as such, however, as welcoming the Other without qualification and then claiming the deconstructive paradox of hospitality, is to me an unnecessary and unnatural launch of the question, which comes to haunt every case of hospitality with an impossible measure that can never be met and which in my view is susceptible to a Nietzschean charge of concealed nihilism.

19. Kristen Brown Golden uses the metaphor of curry to make a similar point. See her *Nietzsche and Embodiment: Discerning Bodies and Non-dualism* (Albany: State University of New York Press, 2006), 30–45.

## References

Brown Golden, Kristen. *Nietzsche and Embodiment: Discerning Bodies and Non-dualism*. Albany: State University of New York Press, 2006.
Caraus, Tamara. "Towards an Agonistic Cosmopolitanism: Exploring the Cosmopolitan Potential of Chantal Mouffe's Agonism." *Critical Horizons* 17, no. 1 (Feb. 2016): 94–109.
Chukwudi Eze, Emmanuel. *Achieving Our Humanity: The Idea of a Postracial Future*. New York: Routledge, 2001.
Derrida, Jacques. *Of Hospitality*. Translated by Rachel Bowlby. Stanford, CA: Stanford University Press, 2000.
Hatab, Lawrence, J. *A Nietzschean Defense of Democracy: An Experiment in Postmodern Politics*. Chicago: Open Court, 1995.
———. *Ethics and Finitude: Heideggerian Contributions to Moral Philosophy*. Lanham, MD: Rowman & Littlefield, 2000.
———. *Nietzsche's Life Sentence: Coming to Terms with Eternal Recurrence*. New York: Routledge, 2005.
———. *Nietzsche's "On the Genealogy of Morality": An Introduction*. Cambridge: Cambridge University Press, 2008.
———. "Nietzsche on Consciousness and Language." In *Nietzsche's Therapeutic Teaching: For Individuals and Culture*, edited by Horst Hutter and Eli Friedland, 191–204. London: Bloomsbury, 2013.
Locke, John. *Two Treatises of Government*. Cambridge: Cambridge University Press, 1988.
Loraux, Nicole. *The Divided City: On Memory and Forgetting in Ancient Athens*. Translated by Corrine Pache. New York: Zone Books, 2001.
Nehamas Alexander. "Who Are the 'Philosophers of the Future'? A Reading of *Beyond Good and Evil*." In *Reading Nietzsche*, edited by Robert Solomon and Kathleen Higgins, 46–67. Oxford: Oxford University Press, 1988.
Podoksik, Efraim. "What Is a Nation in Nationalism?" *Journal of Political Philosophy* 25, no. 3 (Nov. 2017): 303–23.
Shapiro, Gary. *Nietzsche's Earth: Great Events, Great Politics*. Chicago: University of Chicago Press, 2016.
Vernant, Jean-Pierre. *Myth and Society in Ancient Greece*. Translated by Janet Lloyd. Sussex, UK: Harvester Press, 1980.

2

# Nietzsche and Tragic Identity

PAUL KIRKLAND

Because he presents human selves as plural and contesting, Nietzsche offers a valuable resource for considering the politics of identity. Rather than presenting the reconciliation of oppositions in the self or a political community, Nietzsche shows the value of ongoing contestation among elements of identity. We can think of identity in two primary ways: as a matter of what is given and as a matter of what is chosen. Those who would form ethical and political theory oriented by autonomy would prioritize the chosen while others would draw us to attend to those circumstances prior to choices. Questions of the politics of identity surrounding race, class, gender, and sexual identity have involved grappling with the relation between the two in considering the political role of such identities. Nietzsche gives us way to think about the politics of identity that does not devolve into either of the extremes or offer a promise of reconciliation. By showing the self as composed of an unsettled mix of competing drives, Nietzsche gives us a way to think about identity that is not fixed, but rather the site of politicized contest.[1] Rather than presenting the multiplicity of the soul as prelude to a determined order, Nietzsche shows the distinct advantages of continued contest and internal enmity. As I will argue in this chapter, he offers a tragic model for composing the psyche, one that allows for retaining conflict in a coherent life.

Aims of recognition, solidarity, and liberation have shaped the politics of identity. Models that turn on questions of recognition look to the public sphere as offering some form of socially mediated reconciliation. Charles Taylor presents the case for an understanding of recognition that connects the politics of differences with that of universal dignity.[2] Others have drawn from the complex sources of political identity to address the crosscutting and contesting features of identity. Kimberlé Crenshaw's development of the notion of intersectionality shows the political salience of contested sources of identity.[3] A liberal and cosmopolitan framework shapes Kwame Anthony Appiah's account of identity and politics that supports plurality. He shows that effort to build individuality draws from multiple sources that are meaningful even though they do not have permanent biological or metaphysical origins behind them.[4] Defending a Millian view of liberty for the sake of diversity, eccentricity, and individuality,[5] Appiah aims to weave together a liberal framework of freedom with an ethical dimension of solidarity into an account of cosmopolitanism that entails making meaning across lines of identity and difference.[6] Michel Foucault's analyses of the histories and sources of the construction of the self takes a more radical approach to identity than one committed to a liberal framework. Foucault surely draws on Nietzsche in his efforts to explore and disrupt the histories and discourses that shape identity, seeking to multiply discourses and liberate those that are marginalized.[7] His approach challenges the stability of sources of identity, tracing the varying sources of the discourses and powers that shape us.[8]

Nietzsche offers a distinct approach to the politics of identity by looking to the conditions of enduring opposition and multiplicity rather than the recognition of fixed identities, the reconciliation of communities, or the liberation of excluded discourses. Nietzsche's insistence on new ways of considering the soul, comparing it to a social structure, prepares the path for identity as contest. By offering a distinctive approach to the matter of identity, Nietzsche's thought allows us to get beyond the conflict between universalistic political claims and particularistic claims grounded in solidarity and rooted identities. It thereby offers political movements linked to notions of identity ways to consider the tensions at play in forming identities and to treat these as dynamic works of artful fashioning. Political movements informed by Nietzsche's tragic view of identity would seek a space in which the contest of the self and the contests of a community can be composed as a tragic artwork. An ongoing dynamic of self-challenging and self-composing tragic identity would make way for a politics of affirmation rather than a politics of recognition, leaving room for competing identities, contests within the self, and contests for the role of identity in community. In this chapter, I present Nietzsche's view of contested identity as a tragic view of identity. Two interrelated views of tragedy are relevant. First, tragedy involves conflicts that do not admit of reconciliation. The second view recognizes that the art of tragedy involves constructing works that hold together just as they show the contradictions at their core.

## Souls in Contest

In his treatment of the soul, calling for a new psychology, Nietzsche makes clear the lack of a unifying source of identity, rejecting both permanence and singularity of soul. His call for a new approach to understanding and enacting human identities requires expelling "the belief which regards the soul as something indestructible, eternal, indivisible, as a monad, as an *atomon*" (*BGE* 12). Rejecting those efforts to find a unity of soul as a source of its permanence, Nietzsche acknowledges, "It is not at all necessary to get rid of 'the soul' at the same time" (*BGE* 12). As he calls for a "new psychologist" and declares psychology "the path to the fundamental" problems, it becomes clear that he aims to offer a psychology of multiplicity. Instead of either losing the soul or accepting the belief in its permanent unity, "the way is open for new versions and refinements of the soul-hypothesis; and such conceptions as 'mortal soul,' and 'soul as subjective multiplicity,' and 'soul as social structure of the drives and affects,'" need consideration (*BGE* 12). Nietzsche welcomes accounts of the soul that treat it as multiplicity, a view that stands as much against reductionist physiology as it does against "soul atomism." In such an approach to identity, subjective experiences will continue to play an important role. Of course, Nietzsche's favored metaphor is that of a social structure or a political body (*BGE* 12, 19). As Nietzsche declares, "our body is a social structure composed of many souls," he rejects those views that would identify with any one of the parts (*BGE* 19). Instead he introduces the question of what sort of social structure the competing souls constitute and shows us that there is a good reason to consider the competing drives of human life as we have regarded souls. Each is animated in a different way, producing results in the lives of individual human beings.

By opening the question of multiplicity in the soul, Nietzsche rejects the metaphysical unity of the soul but also raises the question of whether the task of forming identity involves forging a unity. Using the same analogy as in Plato's *Republic*, Nietzsche proposes a model quite different than one based on hierarchy, unity, and the rule of reason.[9] One might think of unity as artistry under the "constraint of a single taste" (*GS* 290) as Nietzsche presents the aesthetic need in *The Gay Science*. He clearly challenges a model in which the dominance of reason provides order.[10] Some interpretations of Nietzsche's political project have claimed that a Platonic project of domination with a new goal is the best way to understand Nietzsche's effort. For example, Hugo Drochon has argued that Nietzsche's plan for a new Europe involves a Platonic political project.[11] Michael Gillespie has gone so far as to present the object of Nietzsche's project as the domination of a new artist-tyrant of the future who could rule the way Plato's hypothetical philosopher-king would rule.[12] This political goal requires the creation of a figure (*Übermensch*) that could overcome the contradiction between Socrates and tragic culture.[13] Agonistic views of Nietzsche's politics have largely sought to show how his thought might serve a democratic politics,[14] republican or radical.[15] While retaining his objections to democracy, Nietzsche rejects Platonic tyranny, declaring the age of spiritual tyrants, of which Plato is the chief representative, to be over (*HH* 237).

The converse of a new tyrannical order emerges in Foucault's treatment of Nietzsche's work and his own use of a genealogical method. By destroying a realm of absolutes, a privileged position of permanence, "the historical sense" on Foucault's reading, becomes "capable of shattering the unity of man's being."[16] Foucault describes the shattering of metaphysical unity as one "that is capable of liberating divergence and marginal elements."[17] With this claim, Foucault connects the problematic unity of the self with the task of liberation. The liberatory project directs its attention to what has been marginalized, aiming to give a place to suppressed sources of identity. Following Foucault's path, genealogy would lead to the quest for ever more marginalized sources of identity as each newly liberated element left some other part marginalized by new discourses and strategies.[18] The endless multiplication of discourses moves in the direction of cacophony guided by a strategy that is relentlessly self-undermining. Rather than writing of liberation, Nietzsche looks for genuine enemies and full opposition. (See *TI* "Morality" 3; *GM* III:25.) By attending to those forces that would maintain genuine contest, and thus plurality, Nietzsche offers a way to think about identity that differs from both the model of tyranny and the model of endless multiplication.

In *Twilight of the Idols*, Nietzsche is abundantly clear about the problem of psychological tyranny. As Nietzsche describes Socrates as "turning reason into a tyrant" (*TI* "Socrates" 10), he presents such Socratic domination as a forced unity. Nietzsche characterizes this effort as absurd, rooted in self-deception about the roots of reason itself (*BGE* 191). For Nietzsche the tyranny of such Socratism infects Plato, who was really too noble for it (*BGE* 190), setting the course for the domination of a tyrannical effort to forge unity and the rule of those Platonist doctrines against which Nietzsche declares a fight in the Preface of *Beyond Good and Evil*.[19] By sharp contrast with the aim of forging a tyrannical unity, either Platonist or anti-Platonist, Nietzsche values the "spiritualization of enmity" (*TI* "Morality" 3). Embracing "the value of having enemies" (*TI* "Reason" 3), Nietzsche contrasts himself with unifying positions like that of the Church that seek "the destruction of its enemies" (*TI* "Reason" 3). Instead, "we immoralists" embrace the continued existence of the enemy.[20] Nietzsche declares the value of such enmity in spiritual matters, political matters, and psychological matters in the context of explaining this mode of valuing. The contrast with the effort to order the psyche with a unifying commander becomes clear when he announces: "Our attitude toward the 'internal enemy' is no different: here too we have spiritualized enmity [*Fiendschaft*]; here too we have come to appreciate its value. The price of fruitfulness is to be rich in internal opposition" (*TI* "Morality" 3). This formulation gives us the clearest of Nietzsche's most significant and distinctive contribution to our capacity to thinking about identity. The richness in internal opposition announces an aim contrary to settling the final unity of identity and clarifies what is needed to maintain genuine multiplicity and vital tension.

Nietzsche's attention to maintaining opposition springs from the role of futurity and enmity in the life of a genuine philosopher. Having declared that genuine philosopher, by contrast with philosophical laborers such as Kant and Hegel, are commanders and legislators, Nietzsche appears to give us a glimpse of the character of the philosopher of the future to which *Beyond Good and Evil* is offered as a prelude (*Vorspiel*). Yet rather than contrast past philosophers with future philosophers, Nietzsche makes the declaration about all genuine philosophers. It appears that he is prepared to write about the character of philosophy as such and continues to do so, using Socrates as one of his examples. This description invokes futurity and enmity: "More and more it seems that the philosopher, being of necessity a man of tomorrow and the day after tomorrow, has always found himself, and had to find himself, in contradiction to his today: his enemy was ever the ideal of today" (*BGE* 212). Here, Nietzsche makes clear that a philosopher is always of the future and is thereby necessarily in opposition to his own time. He claims a general character of philosophy such that each will appear as an enemy of his time. As times vary, this enmity will appear in very different forms.

In the specific time of modern ideas and specialization, Nietzsche writes that a philosopher "would be compelled to find the greatness of man, the concept of 'greatness,' precisely in his range and multiplicity, in his wholeness in manifoldness" (*BGE* 212). Nietzsche tips his hand, letting his reader know that talk of greatness and nobility are appropriate to an age like that of modern academic specialization. Greatness is offered as an antidote to the character of the time, one useful in establishing a tension with the pursuits of modernity. In addition to the goal of opposition, Nietzsche articulates the grand wholeness of man in terms of multiplicity.

The fullness of humanity is able to emerge when humanity can be experienced as manifold. For this reason, a philosophical task is not that of comprehending its time in thought, but rather opposing what dominates its own time. Establishing such opposition serves the goal of maintaining multiplicity. The valences appropriate to philosophical efforts will vary according to the necessities of establishing such opposition. The example Nietzsche provides shows the role of opposition in his understanding of philosophy. Nietzsche writes first of the age of Socrates: "In the age of Socrates, among men of fatigued instincts, among the conservatives of ancient Athens who let themselves go—'toward happiness,' as they said; toward pleasure, as they acted—and who all the while still mouthed the ancient pompous words to which their lives no longer gave them any right, irony may have been required for greatness of soul" (*BGE* 212). In a case where the claims to nobility have been decayed and claims to greatness have been calcified, undermining these claims could be understood as a proper philosophic aim, even one that might be consistent with greatness of soul. The language of greatness among corrupt Athenians protects something that is not great, Nietzsche suggests, and needs challenging by something in clear opposition to it. In a time like that cutting "into the flesh and heart of the 'noble,' with a look that said clearly enough: 'Don't dissemble in front of me! Here-we are equal'" (*BGE* 212) is fitting for a philosopher oriented by futurity and enmity. Because the claims to nobility and greatness are nothing but a facade for debased pleasure, undermining the basis for those claims is appropriate even if those challenges serve equality. Nietzsche's pronouncements in the name of human greatness cannot then be taken to simply take at face value the assertion of nobility. At best, such self-assurance is partial and one-sided. There is also a place for Socratic questioning of claims to distinction, nobility, and excellence, one that stands opposite to the conservation of rank.

Along with this defense of the timely untimeliness of a Socratic approach to philosophy, Nietzsche declares his contemporary Europe to present a diametrically opposed problem: "Today, conversely, . . . today the concept of greatness entails being noble, wanting to be by oneself, being able to be different, standing alone and having to live independently" (*BGE* 212). With a description that prefigures some of his characterization of nobility in part 9 of *Beyond Good and Evil*, connecting nobility to independence from all external standards, Nietzsche shows that the praise for such a type befits a modern age where claims of universality and equality threaten to blunt all distinctions. In each case, Nietzsche seeks the enemy, the genuine opponent to the dominant value, not simply what has been excluded but what might offer sufficient opposition to the dominant character of the day. The examples Nietzsche proffers identify something like the chief opponents that form the sort of enmity constituting the most manifold human greatness. He sets in opposition noble distinction and Socratic irony, self-assertion and critical undermining.

## Double Descent

When Nietzsche offers a portrait of his own life and an attempt to account for his own wisdom, he presents himself as such an opposition. He describes himself as a product of double descent (*doppelte Herkunft*), linking the duality he attributes to himself to his mother and his father. Instead of accounting for this wisdom with anything singular, his dual descent is the source of wisdom, suggesting that his philosophical life is not the product of resolving the conflict within himself or finding an original identity but living the tension between his conflicting parts. He presents this conflict as one between his mother and his father: "To express it in the form of a riddle, already dead as my father, while as my mother I am still living and becoming old" (*EH* "Wise" 1).[21] Nietzsche makes this a bit more clear as he continues: "This dual descent, as it were, both from the highest and from the lowest rung on the ladder of life, at the same time a decadent and a beginning" (*EH* "Wise" 1). His identity is born of opposition, and he now clarifies the opposition as both beginning and decay. Rather than something purely noble and creative, a part of him, one that enhances his wisdom, includes decadence. His life, as he presents it, moves in two directions at once.

The dual descent allows him to recognize decay and ascent as a matter of experience: "I know both, I am both" (*EH* "Wise" 2). He is not a resolution of a contradiction or a force that has forged a new identity, but wise precisely because he is both. This self-portrait provides a picture of a philosopher that differs drastically than any that would identify philosophy with the singularity of reason. Nietzsche embraces a life that does not resolve the problem of identity, rather it experiences its multiplicity as an advantage. As his mother, he remains ascending and strong, and as his father, he is in decay. The combination of things that would appear irreconcilably opposed shapes the possibility of his life.

The full opposition that makes his life like a work of tragedy includes a significant element of the decadent and dialectical. He writes of this part of his life: "In the midst of torments that go with an uninterrupted three-day migraine, accompanied by laborious vomiting of phlegm, I possessed a dialectician's clarity par excellence and thought through with very cold blood matters for which under healthier circumstances I am not a mountain-climber, not subtle, not cold enough. My readers know perhaps in what way I consider dialectic as a symptom of decadence; for example in the most famous case, the case of Socrates" (*EH* "Wise" 1). Presenting his own character as one that is both decadent and a beginning, Nietzsche describes the merits of the part of himself that is decadent just as he relates it to an unhealthy state. Only in this state, Nietzsche claims, is he able to have the "cold blood" necessary for a kind of "dialectical clarity" not available to him in his moments of greater health. While on the one hand Nietzsche is claiming to be able to diagnose decadence from experience, he is also showing a place in his character for a part quite at odds with the traits he attributes to nobility. While such nobility possess the strength to act without questioning their own actions, to create values by the measure only of themselves (*BGE* 265), and to act in a way that is not a reaction to any outside force, they do not provide an account of their own actions or their own character (see *GM* I:10, *BGE* 287). The capacity to provide such an account distinguishes the complex character of Nietzsche himself from the simple nobles. Because a part of him is decadent, he can see clearly and describe clearly what is healthy and ascending.

The effort to provide such an account runs in a direction that Nietzsche explicitly describes as Socratic. In this anti-Socratic autobiographical narrative Nietzsche reveals the value of a dialectical capacity that is partial rather than dominating. Rather than attributing to the capacity for rigorous questioning and clarity a final authoritative place, Nietzsche presents his partial decadence as a matter of perspective, and ultimately of shifting perspectives. He nonetheless makes abundantly clear that his own subtlety, his psychological insight, and his capacity for clarity can be attributed to decadence. They are the product of a Socratic element within him. Shifting perspectives are the key to the capacity for his clarity: "Looking from the perspective of the sick toward healthier concepts and values and conversely, looking again from the fullness and self-assurance of a rich life down in the secret work of the drive of decadence—in this I have had the longest training, my truest experience; if in anything, I became master of this" (*EH* "Wise" 1). The content of his life, and the experience that accounts for his wisdom, comes from a dual perspective. He claims now that the capacity to see the healthier concepts as clearly as he does comes from the times when he looks at them from a decadent point of view. This is not surprising if we consider the simply account of those nobles who act on instinct and faith (*BGE* 287). Giving an account of such a capacity is quite different from having such a capacity, and those endowed with the simplest kind of strength or nobility would never think to offer an analysis of that capacity. Yet, rather than simply announce the superiority of a contemplative or dialectical consideration of the actions and faiths of others, Nietzsche includes the reverse as part of his distinctive capacity as well. Instead of favoring a detached point of view, he also looks at the drive of decadence from the perspective of the "self-assurance of a rich life" (*EH* "Wise" 1). From that perspective the cold analysis and the dialectical subtlety simply appears to be decadent and weak. Rather than leaving the final word to either perspective, Nietzsche finds in his capacity "to reverse perspectives" his unique ability to offer a "revaluation of values" and a distinct source of his wisdom.

In this way, Nietzsche presents his decadence in sharp contrast with Socratic decadence. In *Twilight of the Idols,* Nietzsche presents Socrates's decadence as the source of the "equation of reason, virtue, and happiness" opposed to all earlier Greek instincts and the destruction of noble taste. Socratic dialectic and decadence is opposed to nobility. In estimating his own case, Nietzsche maintains this opposition between nobility and dialectics, but unlike the case of Socrates, he presents his character as containing both. By contrast, he writes of Socrates: "When one finds it necessary to turn reason into a tyrant, as Socrates did, the danger cannot be slight that something else will play the tyrant" (*TI* "Socrates" 10). Following this,

Nietzsche treats the commitment to rationality as "fanatical, absurd, and pathological" (*TI* "Socrates" 10). The core of this claim is that there is nothing rational about the Socratic commitment to reason. The description is quite telling. Turning reason into a tyrant turns it into an irrational and passionate force. In describing this absurdity, Nietzsche uses the language of tyranny, which he attributes to Plato. Turning reason into a tyrant involves treating reason as a savior to which one will resort at any price. In the effort to forge a unity, such rationality loses sight of itself and becomes a force for tyrannical decadence. Nietzsche's challenge to this view does not entail a rejection of rationality or Socratic dialectics, but rather a challenge to the tyranny of Socratic dialectics. He presents this challenge in the duality of his own identity in *Ecce Homo*.

When Nietzsche asks, "Is it necessary to go on to demonstrate the error in this faith in 'rationality at any price'" (*TI* "Socrates" 11), he makes clear the stakes. First, he treats Socratic rationality as a kind of faith. It is no more rational than any other faith to commit wholly to reason. And treating the Socratic commitment to rationality as a commitment had "at any price" paints it as the kind of tyranny of a singular domination. Moreover, such a faith is "decadent," an attempt to address decayed values with something that is "but another expression of decadence" (*TI* "Socrates" 11). Rather than a recovery of virtue, health, or nobility, it is a further decay, and it clearly exposes itself as a form of decay, Nietzsche argues in its relation to the other instincts: "To have to fight the instincts—that is the formula of decadence: as long as life is ascending, happiness equals instinct" (*TI* "Socrates" 11). This statement is one of Nietzsche's clearest claims about the distinction between ascending drives in contrast to decadent ones. Healthy, noble, ascending drives are self-justifying. Nietzsche describes the "unshakeable faith" of noble souls who do not look beyond themselves for some sort of justification (*BGE* 265). Treating the problem of Socrates as the domination of decadent drives, Nietzsche shows the problematic character of tyrannical philosophy. On one level, the problem is that such a drive is not noble and creative but ultimately only destructive. On a deeper level, the problem is that the decadent questioning mode is self-contradictory. It acts as though it can proceed without "instinct," on the basis of reason alone, never turning to challenge its own rationality. But challenging rationality from the perspective of rationality is either impossible or simply self-destructive. In order to gain any perspective on the drive to rationality at any price, one would need another perspective, one necessarily more akin to the ascending unquestioning self-assured drives Nietzsche sometimes characterizes as noble.

In treating himself, Nietzsche claims to be complex rather than unified and not only decadent: "Apart from the fact that I am a decadent, I am also the opposite" (*EH* "Wise" 2). As if he wanted to expressly defy logic, he asserts that he is something and its opposite. The opposite of decadent is the healthy, instinctive, and certain. Nietzsche claims that he has "always instinctively chosen the right means against wretched states" as he possesses "an absolute instinctive certainty about what was needed" for him to recover health in times of sickness or decay (*EH* "Wise" 2). The hyperbolic language betrays a complexity even in these instinct of health, for along with possessing the right instincts, he also claims to know they are right, a knowledge that would require attaining reflective distance. He foregrounds the recovery of health from times of the literal sickness of migraines and nausea, but he also lets us see that this bears on the relation between noble self-assured drives and decadent questioning ones. Along with decadent and ascendant, or healthy and sick, Nietzsche appears to assert that he is both Socratic and noble. It is the decadence and its dialectical perspective that provide him the critical distance to offer a clear articulation of ultimate health. The dialectical remains part of his toolbox even as he does not allow it to dominate.

Because Nietzsche claims that his capacity to recover from sickness and a cycle of self-questioning is rooted in instincts, he insists that the condition for such recovery "is that one be healthy at bottom" (*EH* "Wise" 2). Nietzsche's claim to be healthy at bottom is not another unification at the level of health, for to be healthy "at bottom" is not to be simply healthy. It is to have a healthy response to one's own sickness.[22] This healthy response to one's own sickness can only come about as result of the experience of sickness. Simple health would be the unproblematic faith of the noble. A healthy response to sickness is also able to include the capacity to understand the health of ascending and noble and affirmative drives. The combination does not follow the Socratic model (as Nietzsche presents it) because the Socratic model, especially as presented by Plato as Nietzsche interprets him, is tyrannical and one-sided, always challenging and seeking to undermine all drives but its own. It nonetheless involves a considerable dose of the Socratic. It is reflective, it challenges itself, and it questions all other drives.

Concluding this section by asserting "I am the opposite of a decadent," he does so without qualification in the manner of one whose health and nobility need no questioning or justification. Yet it seems appropriate to understand this tone as a matter of Nietzsche's changing perspectives. In the section on his great health, he writes in the tone of one who is entirely healthy, yet in the section on his decadence he highlights his capacity to reverse perspectives. He turns from his knowledge of how to reverse perspectives (*EH* "Wise" 1) to his instinct to do so (*EH* "Wise" 2). What appears from one perspective as a matter of knowledge appears again as a matter of instinct. The capacity to know the health of one's own instincts would entail having both perspectives, and the opposition between them, as part of one's character. It involves being not one but a multiplicity, and even an opposition among one's parts.

## Tragic Identity

This opposition leaves a self-portrait that is tragic, and it suggests the capacity for an art of tragedy that does the work of maintaining an identity in dynamic tension.[23] We might conceive of tragedy as an opposition between forces that cannot be reconciled and the art that holds them together. Competing goods, claims, and sources of identity that resist some larger principle of reconciliation set up a tragic conflict. Nietzsche's own early account of tragedy presents this opposition as one between an Apollonian drive to distinction and the Dionysian drive to annihilate all distinction. This appears again in his presentation of the noble as the heroic drive to distinction in *Beyond Good and Evil* (*BGE* 265, 287). In the same context Nietzsche presents the hermit as one who would see absence of grounds behind each of these claims (*BGE* 289). The noble and the hermit are two perspectives on the same human situation. The noble takes the absence of grounds as a spur to find his own faith sufficient while the hermit finds no good reason for any one faith rather than another. Nietzsche reveals a fundamental tension between each individual faith and examination that would undermine every faith.[24] This tension emerges in any effort to fix a final identity. In Nietzsche's examination of the soul, the role of the philosopher, and his own life, this tension has emerged as a tension between noble assertion and dialectical examination. Clarity regarding this opposition and the capacity to hold the tension together involves a perspective akin to that of the tragic artist.

In the cheerful tone of *The Gay Science*, Nietzsche describes the artist's eye as one that allows floating and playing above morality, providing the good will to appearance (*GS* 107). Such a floating artist's eye would make possible a view of the crucial opposition that was not identical with that of a single-minded hero.[25] Nietzsche's claim that style is the most needful thing (*GS* 290) could be understood to point to the need for the perspective of the artist's eye within a complex soul. The artist's eye and the need for style call for giving internal opposition an artistic shape.[26] In light of Nietzsche's presentation of opposition at the core of the self, his claims about self-creation and style can be read in a new light. Rather than tyrannical task of forcing unity upon complex self, the artistic demand to give style to one's character could be understood to involve bringing the parts into a dynamic tension that has shape, as in great works of tragedy. Rather than unity and harmony as an aesthetic aim, Nietzsche's characterization of tragedy and his dual account of himself emphasize the dynamics of conflict.

Nehamas's influential argument that self-creation on a literary model can forge a kind of unity[27] finds its key basis in Nietzsche's claim that the "the constraint of a single style" (*GS* 290) is "the one thing needful." On this reading, Goethe stands as a chief example of a character that has made itself a unity.[28] Instead of using Goethe or any literary character as the model for a coherent identity, Nietzsche offers his readers something new in the possibility of affirming a life lived in contest with itself. Nietzsche offers the model of his own life as one in which continued becoming is possible because continued contest remains possible. Instead, he portrays his experience as one that is both healthy and decadent, one moved by both affirmative instincts and dialectical clarity. The two continue to challenge one another in the life of a tragic philosopher in a dynamic that is capable of affirming itself in contest with itself. If we take the need for style in a tragic vein, the artist element of giving style would entail maintaining a dynamic tension between conflicting elements of the self. Rather than imposing an art that forced the conflicting elements into a larger coherence, we might understand the successful artist to maintain the dynamic of parts that do not admit of easy resolution. Such effort to craft a tragic work of art from the conflicting elements of oneself would add an element that could look upon the elements that are in conflict from a sufficient distance to see their conflict rather than finding a realm in which they can be reconciled. Instead of claiming to eliminate tragic conflict by reconciling elements on a higher plane of the good, Nietzsche's call for style would involve making beautiful the tensions and conflicts that constitute a dynamic self.

The self-portrait Nietzsche offers in *Ecce Homo* offers just such a model in literary form. He depicts his life as a tragedy by presenting himself not as a tragic hero but as one that contains the opposition between health and decay along with an "artists' eye" that can float above the conflict and offer a view of the contest itself. In giving us both the opposition and the artist's perspective, Nietzsche looks upon himself with the gaze of the tragedian.

In the context of such a portrait, he announces his distinct and original achievement as "the first tragic philosopher" (*EH* BT 3). This view of himself is rooted in maintaining the dynamics of his own internal opposition.

By proclaiming that he is first a tragic philosopher, Nietzsche announces his distinction from the precedents offered by all other philosophers and the tragic poets.[29] Here is how he declares his distinctiveness: "Before me this transposition of the Dionysian into a philosophical pathos did not exist: tragic wisdom was lacking" (*EH* BT 3). A "philosophical pathos" distinguishes his accomplishments from those of the tragic poets who present the phenomenon of the Dionysian that Nietzsche has analyzed. Of course, these claims appear in his review of *The Birth of Tragedy*, in which he claims that he was "the first to comprehend the wonderful phenomenon of the Dionysian" (*EH* BT 2). Comprehending the Dionysian, not merely exemplifying the phenomenon, marks a distinctive accomplishment allowing Nietzsche to present himself as the first tragic *philosopher*.

In presenting the accomplishment of *The Birth of Tragedy*, Nietzsche announces that he "was the first to see the real opposition" between antipathy to life and "a Yes-saying without reservation, even to suffering, even to guilt, even to everything that is questionable and strange in existence" (*EH* BT 2). He claims that he sees an opposition more comprehensive than any treated by ancient tragedians or previous philosophers. It is the recognition of both sides of this opposition that allows something new to emerge, and because what it recognizes is an opposition, not a resolution, it becomes clear why Nietzsche would characterize his insight as tragic. More than the tragic poet, Nietzsche claims to see clearly the phenomenon of the Dionysian as "the highest affirmation" and to recognize its true opponent in "Socratism," the source of decadence (*EH* BT 1). His understanding of the Dionysian involves a view of it from a perspective akin to the Socratic rather than one embodying Dionysian creation. This "Socratic" perspective, decadent as it may be, differs substantially form the Socratism that asserts its " 'Rationality' at any price," and in so doing "undermines life" (*EH* BT 1). The singularity of what Nietzsche calls Socratism is its danger.[30] What it needs in order not to undermine life is a real opponent that challenges its supremacy and opposes its singularity. Nietzsche claims to have found this real opponent in a proper understanding of Dionysian affirmation.

It is helpful to read Nietzsche's description of Dionysian philosophy as saying "Yes to opposition and war" (*EH* BT 3) in light of his claim that he saw "the real opposition" between the degenerating and the affirmative (*EH*

BT 2). Both together would constitute tragic philosophy. Tragic philosophy cannot be a one-sided unreflective confidence of the noble individual or the tragic hero, nor can it adopt the Socratism that would analyze all phenomena from the presumption of the comprehensive adequacy of rationality. It would include not only an awareness of the fundamental opposition between the two but also that opposition itself. Tragic philosophy emerges as the full expression of the rich internal opposition and a continually self-contesting identity.

Nietzsche's account of his warlike character further elaborates the importance of maintaining opposition. Nietzsche declares that he is a "warlike philosopher," a character that involves "look[ing] for what resists" (*EH* "Wise" 7). Such a search for real resistance differs sharply from seeking to attack and eliminate opponents. It involves looking for the "real opposition," for the greatest possible opponent, one that will provide sufficient resistance. Nietzsche explains, "The task is not simply to master what happens to resist, but what requires us to stake all our strength, suppleness, and fighting skill—opponents that are our equals" (*EH* "Wise" 7). The warlike spirit Nietzsche describes here is not identical to a conquering spirit. Rather than seeking to dominate or a eliminate enemies (*TI* "Morality" 3), it seeks enemies who are equals. If we take seriously the equality of the enemy, the combat cannot come to an end. Neither of two equal opponents can defeat the other. The goal instead would be the perpetuation of the contest itself. When Nietzsche describes his own recognition of the real opposition, it becomes clear that he seeks those oppositions that cannot be resolved, oppositions that can be understood as tragic. A tragic philosopher composes the opposition and composes himself as an internal opposition. Nietzsche's account of himself as both healthy and decadent as well as capable of recognizing both and assessing each from the reversed perspective composes such a self-contesting identity.

By presenting the real opposition as one between the drives that confidently assert themselves and those that would undermine them, Nietzsche shows the tragic character of an identity rich in internal opposition. The infinite multiplication of voices or the Socratic undermining of claims to distinction would both threaten to swallow all of the drives Nietzsche associates with nobility. Rather than leaving only a one-sided assertion or the singularity of challenges to every possible foundation, Nietzsche offers a portrait of an identity that affirms both, one that takes shape in the dynamic play of instinctive certainty and dialectical challenging. Such a view of the self is tragic, not pessimistic, because it does not resolve the tension between its contesting parts, and, like tragic art, it takes shape in the play among its contesting elements.

Internalizing tragic conflict involves an identity that is never simply settled.

Beyond the multiplicity embraced by more recent authors, such as Crenshaw or Appiah, Nietzsche provides a resource for thinking about identity in unexpected ways. A Nietzschean model for considering identity shows the advantages of affirming the contest rather than seeking reconciliation among competing sources of identity. Rather than looking to ways in which competing sources of identity overlap, Nietzsche shows the value of the contest among them and fosters affirmation of the unsettled and contested character of identity. Keeping Nietzsche's sense of contested identity in play could expand the way we think about identity as a source of solidarity and originality. Construction of dynamic opposition allows for multiple and competing sources of identity to maintain their places in politicized contests of identity and solidarity. Rather than accepting identity as it is imposed or constructing identity as a sovereign self, Nietzsche's tragic view of identity involves holding the two in a contesting relation with one another. Composing oneself as a tragedy would entail neither eschewing those distinctive features one might assert as the grounds of identity and solidarity nor treating them with finality. Instead, each source of identity can assert itself like a noble faith while it also remains open to contestation. Instead of insisting on a unity found in an origin or constructed by a community, Nietzsche's sense of tragic unity would retain the two in an oppositional dynamic with one another. Such a dynamic would leave neither fixed categories nor the complete shattering of all identities. Rather than avoiding challenges to one's own identity, Nietzsche fosters a sensibility that would embrace challenging any defining unity. He encourages seeking genuine opposition in a way that would shape one's own life as a community of contest. His considerations of identity and tragedy teach us that such internal opposition can be the source of the sort of fruitfulness that allows a future open to possibilities not yet determined.

## Notes

1. While some have sought to make the "sovereign individual" the basis for constructing a Nietzschean politics (David Owen, "Nietzsche, Ethical Agency,

and the Problem of Democracy," in *Nietzsche, Power, and Politics*, eds. Herman W. Siemens and Vasti Roodt [Berlin: Walter de Gruyter, 2008], 148; Owen, "Equality, Democracy, and Self-Respect: Reflections on Nietzsche's Agonal Perfectionism," *Journal of Nietzsche Studies* 24 [2002]), Acampora has shown the problems of readings of Nietzsche that take such a "sovereign individual" as an ideal and their insufficient attention to the Nietzsche's view of human beings as pluralities. Christa Davis Acampora, "On Sovereignty and Overhumanity," in *Nietzsche's "On the Genealogy of Morals": Critical Essays*, ed. Christa Davis Acampora (Lanham, MD: Rowman & Littlefield, 2006). See also Richard White, *Nietzsche and the Problem of Sovereignty* (Chicago: University of Chicago Press, 1997). For an examination of Nietzsche's agonistic politics that does not rely on an ideal of the sovereign individual, see Lawrence J. Hatab, *A Nietzschean Defense of Democracy: An Experiment in Postmodern Politics* (Chicago: Open Court, 1995).

2. Charles Taylor, "The Politics of Recognition," in *Multiculturalism: Examining the Politics of Recognition*, ed. Amy Gutmann (Princeton, NJ: Princeton University Press, 1994), 37. Taylor argues that identity is shaped by recognition, which can involve reflecting a demeaning picture of a person or group that does real harm (25). Presenting a dialogic portrait of identity, Taylor connects identity to a defining community (Taylor, *Sources of the Self: The Making of Modern Identity* [Cambridge, MA: Harvard University Press, 1989], 36), and he presents the goal of self-understanding and community as linked to the task of "overcoming of subjectivism" (510). In this effort, Taylor points to Habermas's account of intersubjectivity (512). In defining "action oriented to mutual agreement" as the content of discursive democracy, Habermas argues that communicative rationality is a matter of working out "the dichotomies within reason" against those who find opponents to reason within the self. Jürgen Habermas, *The Philosophical Discourse of Modernity*, trans. Frederick G. Lawrence (Cambridge, MA: MIT Press, 1987), 295, 303. Attending to "situated reason," Habermas argues, can work toward such reconciliation "without paying the price of absolutizing spirit" (304). As the classic source for such dialectic of recognition is of course Hegel's *Phenomenology of Spirit*, attention to immanent sources of reason allows those who follow this path to seek reconciled unity on an immanent plane.

3. In her landmark essay "Mapping the Margins," Crenshaw demonstrates that the intersections of race and gender demand attention to the specifics of Black women's experiences in order to consider and liberate those lives in public discourse. "Mapping the Margins: Intersectionality, Identity, and Violence against Women of Color," *Stanford Law Review* 43 (1991): 1241–1299. She argues for the explicit consideration of identity and outcomes in law, one that attends to the formation of specific identities and attends to the discourse shaping them rather than making an anti-essentialist move against constitutive elements of identity (see also Crenshaw, "Race, Reform, and Retrenchment: Transformation and Legitimation in Antidiscrimination Law," *Harvard Law Review* 101, no. 7 [1988]).

4. Drawing from W. E. B. Du Bois, Appiah argues that norms of identification serve the project of individuality. Kwame Anthony Appiah, *Lines of Descent: W. E. B. Du Bois and the Emergence of Identity* (Cambridge, MA: Harvard University Press, 2014), 151. In *Dusk of Dawn* (1941), Du Bois uses the history of the concept of race to separate it from biological meanings in order to show its socially contestable meaning. *Dusk of Dawn: An Essay Toward the Autobiography of a Race Concept* (New Brunswick, NJ: Transaction, 1995), 116–31. Group relations rooted in claims like those about race or nationality may, Appiah argues, demand solidarity on an ethical level while allowing a moral cosmopolitanism. Kwame Anthony Appiah, *The Ethics of Identity* (Princeton, NJ: Princeton University Press, 2005), 232. In this distinction, Appiah draws from the Hegelian distinction between *Sittlichkeit* and *Moralität*. Appiah's articulation of a two-standpoint approach drawn from Kant provides an account of autonomy in operating "as if" one is free to make choices determining one's own life (56).

5. See John Stuart Mill, *On Liberty* (Indianapolis, IN: Hackett, 1978 [1869]), part 3.

6. Kwame Anthony Appiah, *The Lies That Bind: Rethinking Identity* (New York: Liveright, 2018), 217–18.

7. Michel Foucault, "Nietzsche, Genealogy, and History" in *The Foucault Reader*, ed. Paul Rabinow (New York: Pantheon Books, 1984), 87.

8. See especially Michel Foucault, *The Hermeneutics of the Subject*. Lectures at the College de France 1981–1982 (New York: Picador, 2001) for an account of the procedures at work in the construction of a knowing being. Foucault shows the history of care for oneself, beginning in a demand to know oneself, not to produce a hidden truth behind appearances but a network of fractured appearances (504). See also Michel Foucault, *Lectures on the Will to Know: Lectures a the College de France 1970–1971 and Oedipal Knowledge*, trans. Daniel Defert (New York: Palgrave Macmillan, 2013), 205.

9. Plato, *Republic* 443d.

10. On a literary model of unity, see Alexander Nehamas, *Nietzsche: Life as Literature* Cambridge, MA: Harvard University Press, 1985), 170–99. Even Nietzsche's models for artful unity find strength by incorporating the broadest possible variety (*TI* "Skirmishes" 49).

11. Hugo Drochon, *Nietzsche's Great Politics* (Princeton, NJ: Princeton University Press, 2016).

12. Michael Gillespie, *Nietzsche's Final Teaching* (Chicago: University of Chicago Press, 2017), 176.

13. Gillespie, 110. Gillespie offers a detailed account of the way in which Nietzsche's "musical politics" would "create a harmony of opposites" (118), capable of transforming European civilization (116). Hugo Drochon's recent work on Nietzsche's politics also argues that Nietzsche had a political strategy modeled on that of Plato, a quite different kind of philosophical ruler, but nonetheless one that exerted singu-

larity of command (*Nietzsche's Great Politics*). A unified political hierarchy, such as that described by Bruce Detwiler, would also involve a singularity of rule (*Nietzsche and the Politics of Aristocratic Radicalism* [Chicago: University of Chicago Press, 1990]).

14. Lawrence J. Hatab, "Breaking the Social Contract" in *Nietzsche, Power, and Politics*, eds. Herman W. Siemens and Vasti Roodt (Berlin: Walter de Gruyter, 2008); Hatab, *A Nietzschean Defense of Democracy*.

15. David Owen, "Nietzsche, Ethical Agency, and the Problem of Democracy"; Owen, *Nietzsche, Politics, Modernity* (New York: Sage, 1995). See also Herman Siemens, "Yes, No, Maybe So . . . Nietzsche's Equivocations on the Relation between Democracy and 'Grosse Politik,'" in *Nietzsche, Power, and Politics*, 231–68, for Nietzsche's complex relation to democracy and an account of his rejection of a democratic cultural ideal. Siemens, "Nietzsche's Critique of Democracy (1870–1886)," *Journal of Nietzsche Studies* 38 (2009): 20–37. For a rich account of contest as Nietzsche's aim, see Christa Davis Acampora, *Contesting Nietzsche* (Chicago: University of Chicago Press, 2013).

16. Foucault, "Nietzsche, Genealogy, and History," 87.

17. Foucault, 87.

18. Employing any discourse, genealogical or otherwise, would require challenging that discourse with what it necessarily marginalizes. While Foucault writes of "a multiplicity of discursive elements that can come into play in various strategies" by contrast with a strict dichotomy of accepted and excluded discourse, the liberating aims would seem to demand the endless multiplication of discourses. Michel Foucault, *The History of Sexuality: An Introduction*, vol. 1 (New York: Random House, 1978), 105.

19. See Maudemarie Clark and David Dudrick, *The Soul of Nietzsche's "Beyond Good and Evil"* (New York: Cambridge University Press, 2012) for a thorough account of the tension formed by opposition to Platonism in Nietzsche's account of the soul in *BGE*.

20. For a discussion of spiritualized enmity, see Paul Kirkland, "Nietzsche, Agonistic Politics, and Spiritual Enmity," *Political Research Quarterly* 73, no. 1 (2020): 4–6.

21. Presenting his origins as a riddle evokes Oedipus and points to question about whether a single model for "unriddling" is adequate. Cf. *BGE* 1.

22. For a recent thorough account of the theme of health, its relationship to a revaluation of values, and its role in Nietzsche's 1886 prefaces, see Melanie Shepherd, "'Let Return to Herr Nietzsche': On Health and Revaluation," *Journal of Nietzsche Studies* 50, no. 1 (2019): 135–48.

23. On this point, see Jacqueline Scott "'The Great Seriousness Begins': Nietzsche's Tragic Philosophy and Philosophy's Role in Creating Healthier Racialized Identities" and Jeremy Fortier "'To Affirm while Resisting:' Ralph Ellison and Nietzsche on Overcoming History," both of which are in this volume.

24. I have treated noble faith, the hermit, and philosophy in Kirkland, "Nietzsche, Agonistic Politics, and Spiritual Enmity," 7–9.

25. Foucault writes about Nietzsche's disagreement with Spinoza's placement of knowledge outside the drives of laughter, lamentation, and detesting, that all three operations are "allied first with malice—mockery, contempt, hatred. It does not involve recognizing oneself in things but in keeping one's distance from them." Michel Foucault, *Lectures on the Will to Know: Lectures at the College de France 1970–1971 and Oedipal Knowledge*, trans. Daniel Defert (New York: Palgrave Macmillan, 2013), 205. Yet if we consider the passage Foucault cites from *The Gay Science*, Nietzsche treats the three as "mutually opposed drives" (*GS* 333). The three are in the first place opposed to one another, and the experience of knowing is the behavior of these drives toward one another. Laughter, at least, of the three elements Nietzsche presents in a conception of the experience of knowing entails not only the opposition of struggle and resistance but also the capacity for "floating" and a "freedom above things" (*GS* 107). A capacity to float and dance above things is surely not born of malice. Rather, it involves a lightness that overcomes the weight that we are as human beings.

26. In arguing that this need for style is at the core of Nietzsche's thought, Nehamas presents the task of making one's life like a work of art as one of crafting it into "a controlled and coherent whole" (*Life as Literature*, 227) that produces psychic unity modeled on a harmony among drives that would allow the experience of freedom of the will (187).

27. Nehamas, 170–99.

28. Nehamas, 191. Pointing to Nietzsche's claim in *Twilight of the Idols* that Goethe "disciplined himself to wholeness" (*TI* "Skirmishes" 49), Nehamas finds the construction of unity as the aesthetic aim for one's own character (Nehamas, *Life as Literature*, 188). Yet the self-creation of which Nietzsche writes in *TI* is in some tension with the unity of style articulated in *GS* 290. In the case of Goethe, the greatest possible multiplicity, "taking as much as possible into himself" provides the source of his totality (*TI* "Skirmishes" 49). Even this literary model still falls one step short of Nietzsche's self-description in *EH* as the "*first* tragic philosopher." Nietzsche does not make this claim supposing that there have been no tragedians in the past, and he is quite clear that a great "Yes to life" and "the eternal joy of becoming" is the key to the psychology of the tragic poet (*TI* "Ancients" 5).

29. Explicitly, he reveals his suspicions about Heraclitus among those he once described as philosophers of the "tragic age." He acknowledges feeling warmer in the presence of Heraclitus than anywhere else and includes his "saying Yes to opposition and war" among the reasons for considering Heraclitus a possible precedent (*EH* BT 3).

30. Nietzsche of course also questions whether such a pursuit of rationality is in fact rational and raises questions about whether Socrates really believed it to be. See *TI* "Skirmishes" 23. See *BT* 14 for Nietzsche's discussion of Socratism as a drive behind Socrates.

## References

Acampora, Christa Davis. *Contesting Nietzsche*. Chicago: University of Chicago Press, 2013.

———. "On Sovereignty and Overhumanity." In *Nietzsche's "On the Genealogy of Morals": Critical Essays*, edited by Christa Davis Acampora. Lanham, MD: Rowman & Littlefield, 2006.

Appiah, Kwame Anthony. *The Ethics of Identity*. Princeton, NJ: Princeton University Press, 2005.

———. *The Lies That Bind: Rethinking Identity*. New York: Liveright, 2018.

———. *Lines of Descent: W. E. B. Du Bois and the Emergence of Identity*. Cambridge, MA: Harvard University Press, 2014.

Crenshaw, Kimberlé. "Mapping the Margins: Intersectionality, Identity, and Violence against Women of Color." *Stanford Law Review* 43 (1991): 1241–1299.

———. "Race, Reform, and Retrenchment: Transformation and Legitimation in Antidiscrimination Law." *Harvard Law Review* 101, no. 7 (1988): 1331–1387.

Clark, Maudemarie, and David Dudrick. *The Soul of Nietzsche's Beyond Good and Evil*. New York: Cambridge University Press, 2012.

Detwiler, Bruce. *Nietzsche and the Politics of Aristocratic Radicalism*. Chicago: University of Chicago Press, 1990.

Drochon, Hugo. *Nietzsche's Great Politics*. Princeton, NJ: Princeton University Press, 2016.

Du Bois, W. E. B. *Dusk of Dawn: An Essay Toward the Autobiography of a Race Concept*. New Brunswick, NJ: Transaction, 1995.

Foucault, Michel. *The Hermeneutics of the Subject*. Lectures at the College de France, 1981–1982. New York: Picador, 2001.

———. *The History of Sexuality: An Introduction*. Vol. 1. New York: Random House, 1978.

———. *Lectures on the Will to Know: Lectures at the College de France 1970–1971 and Oedipal Knowledge*. Translated by Daniel Defert. New York: Palgrave Macmillan, 2013.

———. "Nietzsche, Genealogy, and History." In *The Foucault Reader*, edited by Paul Rabinow. New York: Pantheon Books, 1984.

Gillespie, Michael. *Nietzsche's Final Teaching*. Chicago: University of Chicago Press, 2017.

Habermas, Jürgen. *The Philosophical Discourse of Modernity*. Translated by Frederick G. Lawrence. Cambridge, MA: MIT Press, 1987.

Hatab, Lawrence J. "Breaking the Social Contract." In *Nietzsche, Power, and Politics*, edited by Herman W. Siemens and Vasti Roodt. Berlin: Walter de Gruyter, 2008.

———. *A Nietzschean Defense of Democracy: An Experiment in Postmodern Politics*. Chicago: Open Court, 1995.

Kirkland, Paul. "Nietzsche, Agonistic Politics, and Spiritual Enmity." *Political Research Quarterly* 73, no. 1 (2020): 3–14.
Nehamas, Alexander. *Nietzsche: Life as Literature.* Cambridge, MA: Harvard University Press, 1985.
Nietzsche Friedrich. *The Antichrist.* Translated by Walter Kaufmann. In *The Portable Nietzsche.* New York: Viking Press, 1968.
———. *Beyond Good and Evil.* Translated by Walter Kaufmann. New York: Vintage Books, 1989.
———. *The Birth of Tragedy.* Translated by Walter Kaufmann. New York: Vintage Books, 1967.
———. *The Case of Wagner.* Translated by Walter Kaufmann. New York: Vintage Books, 1967.
———. *Ecce Homo.* Translated by Walter Kaufmann. New York: Vintage Books, 1989.
———. *On the Genealogy of Morals.* Translated by Walter Kaufmann. New York: Vintage Books, 1989.
———. "Homer's Contest." Translated by Christa Davis Acampora. *Nietzscheana* 5 (1996): 1–8.
———. *Human, All Too Human.* Translated by Marion Faber. Lincoln: University of Nebraska Press, 1984.
———. *Twilight of the Idols.* Translated by Walter Kaufmann. In *The Portable Nietzsche.* New York: Viking Press, 1968.
———. *Werke.* Critical edition of Giorgio Colli and Mazzino Montinari. New York: Walter de Gruyter, 1967.
Owen, David. "Equality, Democracy, and Self-Respect: Reflections on Nietzsche's Agonal Perfectionism." *Journal of Nietzsche Studies* 24 (2002): 113–31.
———. "Nietzsche, Ethical Agency, and the Problem of Democracy." In *Nietzsche, Power, and Politics,* edited by Herman W. Siemens and Vasti Roodt. Berlin: Walter de Gruyter, 2008.
———. *Nietzsche, Politics, Modernity.* New York: Sage, 1995.
Plato. *The Republic.* Translated by Allan Bloom. New York: Basic Books, 1968.
Shepherd, Melanie. "'Let Us Return to Herr Nietzsche': On Health and Revaluation." *Journal of Nietzsche Studies* 50, no. 1 (2019): 125–48.
Siemens, Herman. "Nietzsche's Critique of Democracy (1870–1886)." *Journal of Nietzsche Studies* 38 (2009): 20–37.
———. "Yes, No, Maybe So . . . Nietzsche's Equivocations on the Relation between Democracy and 'Grosse Politik.'" In *Nietzsche, Power, and Politics,* edited by Herman W. Siemens and Vasti Roodt. Berlin: Walter de Gruyter, 2008.
Taylor, Charles. "The Politics of Recognition." In *Multiculturalism: Examining the Politics of Recognition,* edited by Amy Gutmann. Princeton, NJ: Princeton University Press, 1994.

———. *Sources of the Self: The Making of Modern Identity*. Cambridge, MA: Harvard University Press, 1989.

White, Richard. *Nietzsche and the Problem of Sovereignty*. Chicago: University of Chicago Press, 1997.

3

# Passionate Actors and Wounded Apes
## Nietzsche on Identity Formation

Robert Guay

## Introduction

Nietzsche, over the course of his writings, made a series of cryptic remarks about actors and apes (and the French), their ideals, and questions of conscience. This chapter will suggest, first, that these remarks provide the resources for a discussion of identity formation that can be seen as engaging with contemporary concerns. What I argue is that Nietzsche's discussion of actors and apes is one element of his critique of ideals and idealizing, this particular element is that ideals generate what might be called "bad performativity," and that Nietzsche nevertheless thinks that identity formation is inevitably idealizing. For Nietzsche, then, identity itself is defective: being someone is inherently self-estranging or self-undermining. By appealing to some of Nietzsche's own qualifications, however, and to Wendy Brown's account of "wounded attachments," I point out some conditions for less damaging modes of identity formation. What I try to show is that Nietzsche wishes to acknowledge that identity is ultimately a reactive response to suffering and, nevertheless, to provide grounds for embracing it.

## Actors, Apes, and Ideals

One cannot usually manage to be both cryptic and ambivalent at the same time. Cryptic utterances convey no clear assertoric force, whereas ambivalent ones weakly convey two sets. Yet Nietzsche manages to square this circle in a series of four "questions of conscience" in the opening section of *Twilight of the Idols*. Ambivalence appears in the form of *conscience*, which itself manifests ambivalence, and whose "bite" Nietzsche worries about even as he asks and answers its questions. The questions are cryptic since they lack both an indication of who is being interrogated and an indication of who the questioner is. Perhaps it is Nietzsche, but the questions simply appear, in a section called "Maxims and Arrows," and they do not appear to be maxims. A conscience is something deeply personal, and yet the owner of the conscience in question remains unidentified. Take the second question of conscience, for example: "Are you genuine? Or only an actor? A representative? Or what is represented? In the end you are really only an imitation of an actor . . . *Second question of conscience*" (*TI* "Maxims" 38, ellipses in original).[1] A question of conscience is typically posed to oneself: its force depends on coming from "inside," even as it competes with other, perhaps more powerful, sources of motivation. Here, however, we have reason to think that Nietzsche's conscience is not posing the question to himself: the addressee is condemned without the opportunity to respond or otherwise acknowledge feeling the weight of conscience. The force of the question stands alone, as something that characterizes the sort of concern that conscience presses.

This "question" elides most of the context that would be needed to make sense of it as a philosophical judgment. But even if it does not identify who is being examined and how they fall short, it does at least indicate the nature of a problem. Nietzsche offers a series of contrasts to being "genuine"[2] as being merely an actor, a representative, and an imitator. These contrasting conditions, furthermore, can apparently be embedded in one another, as with being an imitator of an actor. In all of these contrasts, Nietzsche is identifying forms of distance between oneself and what one is doing, or one's social being. If one is "acting" as a performer (*Schauspieler*), one's deeds do not belong to oneself. They belong, instead, to a character, because one is performing or "playing" them rather than simply doing them. To be "merely" an actor suggests further that *nothing* that one says or does belongs to oneself; one's deeds, including even the contriving itself, are a contrivance from which there is no respite. Similarly, being an "imitation of an actor" suggests a performance without a performer. An actor, after all, is a defined social identity that someone occupies, among other roles the same person might take on. An imitation of an actor fails even to occupy that social role or take part in a practice, even as a show is put on, or at least some kind of demonstrativeness takes place: someone is *like* an actor without managing to *be* one. One who *represents* takes on a different kind of distance from one's actions: one makes choices not for oneself but for whoever is being represented. At the same time, however, being represented involves a similar distance, since someone else is making one's choices. Neither being a representative nor being represented seems to be superior; once one falls into that classification, there are no good options. In either case, there is a defective relationship between the activity that takes place and the person whose activity it is supposed to be.

The problem that Nietzsche's interrogator has in mind, then, is that activity can be self-estranging. The questioning implies that there is a natural or "genuine" way in which action proceeds from an agent and then suggests a variety of ways in which that relationship can be contrived or forced such that the deeds cannot align with what they seem to be or who performs them. No specific content is assigned to genuineness here; the rhetorical form of the questioning allows this to be avoided. At the same time, however, the questions can function as accusations against the "you" who might not otherwise be aware that their activity does not properly belong to them. The perlocutionary effect of these accusations, then, is to provoke a conscience that had remained latent. These questions are questions *of conscience* for a pair of complementary reasons. On the one hand, these are conscience's questions: they appeal to the addressee's own concern about a possible gap between what one does and what one should be doing. Nietzsche frames this not in terms of particular moral requirements but in the general ability to take a critical distance from oneself and worry about a pervasive falseness in what one is doing. These questions are thus applicable to, and only carry weight with, a being with a conscience. On the other hand, however, these are also questions of conscience in the sense of a *questioning of* conscience. They provoke a problem that only arises because conscience potentially recognizes a standard of genuineness while at the same time making it impossible for anything to count definitively as meeting this standard.

This latter aspect of the questions of conscience comes into sharper focus with some additional context. Nietzsche elsewhere mentions the role that the actor is playing, or what is being imitated. He does not refer to a specific persona, of course; there are as many actors as persons and even more roles. But he does at least offer a category term for the actor's role, which functions as something like a structural feature of non-genuine personality. Here are three examples from Nietzsche's late works, the first of which immediately follows the second question of conscience:

> I looked for great men, and all I could find were the apes of their ideals. (*TI* "Maxims" 39)

> What? A great man? I always see only the actor of his own ideal. (*BGE* 97)

> The French were just the apes and actors . . . of these ["modern"] ideas. (*BGE* 253)

There are some complexities here: Nietzsche switches between "apes" and "actors," focuses on great men and the French, and, in the third example, replaces "ideals" with the ideas associated with modernity or the eighteenth century. In the overall picture, however, the kind of performance that Nietzsche directs his accusation against involves the performance or imitation of ideals. Nietzsche's suggestion is that those who are considered "great men" appear as such on the basis of living up to ideals, but they are merely imitating or performing them. Since all that he could find were actors and apes, Nietzsche implies that living up to ideals cannot succeed. One can simulate doing so, or put on a show of what it might seem like to do so, but the performance inevitably remains distant from the ideals and the ideals remain distant from the individual's agency. This problem, indeed, must be general enough to sustain the accusation in the question of conscience, where "you are really only an imitation of an actor." This accusation, then, is that ideals provide the conscience's script for genuineness, or more generally the criteria for deeds to stem appropriately from a self, but there is no way to live according to such a script. Even in the case of someone acting out "his own" ideal, acting out ideals and leading one's own life are necessarily estranged.

Nietzsche's discussions of actors and apes thus turn out to be, at least in part, a critique of ideals. This critique—along with the associated critiques of idealism and ideal theorizing—is a widespread feature of Nietzsche's work, and it comes in many different forms. For example, Nietzsche claims that ideals are both empty and psychologically pathological: "But the philosopher despises people with desires, even 'desirable' people—and all desiderata, all human *ideals*. Philosophers would be nihilists if they could be, because as far as they are concerned there is nothing behind any human ideal. Or not even nothing—but unworthy, absurd, sick, cowardly, exhausted things, all the dregs from the *drained* cups of people's lives" (*TI* "Skirmishes" 32). There are a range of other criticisms, too: ideals are based on self-deception and not plausibly connected to human motivation; they are inapplicable to or neglect the concrete, historical conditions of life; they are ideological, in the sense of covertly stemming from and serving dominant interests; they function primarily as an instrument of blame rather than a constructive form of action guidance.[3] But the particular criticism that Nietzsche makes in terms of actors and apes is that ideals produce self-estrangement when one tries to live by them: one can only stand in the relationship to them that an actor does to a role. They represent an aspiration to be a particular sort of person—a "great man," perhaps, or someone else entirely. But there is no way to align oneself to that aspiration, in part because nothing can really count as satisfying it. In part, this is a problem with the content of any such aspiration; for Nietzsche, all the criticisms show that ideals are too underdetermined, contradictory, ideological, and far removed from actual circumstances to mean anything in particular. But a main part of Nietzsche's concern is over what it would mean to adopt any ideal. They function as aspirations by standing outside of one's agency; one can accordingly perform them to show to oneself or others than one is upholding them but not guide oneself by them in a more direct way. To do so would require meeting a standard that both exceeds and does not exist apart from one's performance.

Sartre's famous example of the café waiter can help to illustrate some features of Nietzsche's views. Sartre writes,

> Let us consider this café waiter. His movements are lively and pressing, a little too precise, a little too rapid, he comes toward the customers with a little too lively a step, he leans towards them a little too eagerly, his voice and his eyes express a little too much solicitude for the client's order. . . . All his behavior seems to us a game. He applies himself to linking up his movements as if they were mechanisms that regulated one another; his expressions and his voice even resemble mechanisms; he

gives himself the nimbleness and ruthless speed of things. He is playing, he is amusing himself. But what is he thus playing? It is not necessary to observe for long before realizing: he is playing *at being* a café waiter.[4]

Sartre used this example to illustrate his notion of "bad faith," but for present purposes this helps to show that what Nietzsche was criticizing in terms of "ideals" do not need to be ethereal images of perfection. Part of Sartre's criticism of the waiter here is that he stands at a distance from his own actions because he is "playing at" them rather than simply doing them. In this "playing," the waiter is following an unwritten script, which is all the more potent for being tacit and internalized, for how café waiters act. The script includes affects, bodily comportment, overt shows of solicitousness, and so on; in this case, part of the demonstration is that the movements are so unnatural that they must appear as the fulfillment of particular normative demands rather than as the efficient realization of useful ends. In Nietzsche's terminology, there is an "ideal" in play. This ideal is not an imagined best-of-all-possible-waiters, but nevertheless it imposes demands on what it is to be a waiter.

Social roles that someone might strive to occupy have this status: they present criteria that one can dramatize oneself as meeting, but only mechanically, as it were, or as a game one is playing. The role does not exist apart from its performances, but at the same time, the performer always remains separate from the imagined script; one can never be fully immersed in a role as such. In Sartre's example, the waiter is "amusing himself" by playing the role; he identifies with the one who is amusing or amused rather than the one performing the actions, even though self-distanced amusement is itself part of the performance. The performance is disavowed even as it occupies his whole identity. And this is why Nietzsche's question of conscience seemed to level such a general accusation. Acting out ideals is a general feature of social roles that individuals try to occupy, including even—as Nietzsche suggests in an early work—being a particular self: "But men themselves traffic in very various ways with this higher self of theirs and are often actors of themselves, inasmuch as they afterwards continually imitate that which they are in those moments" (*HH* 624). The language of ideals is missing here, and Nietzsche's perspective is somewhat more hopeful than elsewhere, but his point is similar. Trying to be who we are ends up involving imitating or acting out an image of what we might be, and this seems to leave us "trafficking with" an aspirational, performed self rather than identifying more closely with our deeds.

The objection to ideals that Nietzsche is raising is thus that they generate what might be called "bad performativity." To explain what I mean by this, I will first offer a characterization of performativity in general and then explain how it goes wrong. "Performativity" refers to the kinds of activity that ideals make possible and that in turn give form to the content of ideals. Such kinds of activity can be considered in light of how ideals might shape identity. Individuals can inhabit categories that define them in some way—being a waiter, perhaps, but also categories of race or sexuality, for example. In such cases there are no specific instructions to follow to produce characteristic or uncharacteristic, and yet somehow standards can be applied and expectations are generated, however contentiously. The categories obtain in some meaningful way: people can use them to interpret how someone is acting in light of who they are. Their content is nevertheless dependent on the performed instances of them; the categories are embodied in activities.

These kinds of activity take the form of performances that are imitative or repetitive: the performer attempts to impersonate someone else, reenact a type of action, or recreate a style. Such performances, further, observe regulatory norms, whether tacit or explicit, on how they should be carried out. Enacting these norms constitutes the idealized categories; the performances, by giving concrete, social existence to their scripts—"translating everything into flesh and actuality" (*GS* 301)—bring into being what it is trying to imitate. We can see these features in Judith Butler's treatment of gender: "Such acts, gestures, enactments, generally construed, are *performative* in the sense that the essence or identity that they otherwise purport to express are *fabrications* manufactured and sustained through corporeal signs and other means. That the gendered body is performative suggests that it has no ontological status apart from the various acts which constitute its reality. This also suggests its reality is fabricated as an interior essence."[5] What Butler emphasizes here above all is that the performances are attempts to "express" something that does not exist prior to or apart from the performance; they involve efforts to follow an ideal that is instituted rather than tracked in its pursuit. The agent thus believes that she is pursuing an interior "essence": the "mundane social audience, including the actors themselves, come to believe and perform in the mode of belief."[6] But the convictions of the performance are always out of line with their fabricated effects.

There are many ways in which performativity could go wrong and many phenomena similar to the one that Nietzsche and Butler identify. One very prominent contemporary use of "performative" is to mark off behaviors that are merely symbolic and self-promoting rather than genuine and effective. A typical "performative" behavior, in this sense, would involve participating in a form of activism that involves only an empty expression of allegiance: for example, voicing support for a cause without furthering it in any way, claiming an affiliation without any belonging or sympathetic understanding, or endorsing a view for the purpose of giving a certain impression of oneself.[7] What is sometimes called "virtue signaling" overlaps significantly with this sense of the performative. It is defective in that it is false or insincere, unproductive, and misguided; the very of making a commitment has misfired, and it was the wrong view adopted for the wrong reason anyway. Another related phenomenon is "trolling" as a contemporary form of irony: espousing beliefs that one does not actually hold in order to provoke a reaction. As with performativity, there is a repetitive, stylized, normalizing public performance, as one can see in this discussion of Stephen Miller:

> What's more, the journey from winking provocateur to racist ideologue might be shorter than many imagine. You start out with the goal of provoking the left—and, well, what's more provocative than posting a racist meme on the internet? But with each new like and upvote, an incentive structure forms, a community coalesces, an identity hardens. Before long, the line between performance and principle is blurred beyond recognition, your "true" beliefs buried under so many layers of irony that they've been rendered irrelevant.[8]

Here, as with the other versions of performativity, the public play of speech and action leads to claims of identity, in this case as formed solely around the reactive content of producing a shocking effect. These phenomena thus all share the background condition of taking identity to be constituted at least in part by attempting to pursue norms that are for some reason not available for pursuit. But the problems with virtue signaling and trolling are more partial than the ones that Nietzsche was most interested in. The former involves a small facet of an otherwise established identity, and the latter involves the peculiar constitution of an abhorrent identity. Nietzsche's concern was with the role of ideals in identity formation in general, not just particular aspects or pathological forms of identity.

What I mean, then, by "bad performativity," is the specific way in which ideals are self-estranging. The basic problem with ideals is that they are internalized without anyone knowing what they are or what they might mean to act on them. They are both identified with, as recognizable "internal" features of oneself, and at the same time impossible to identify with, since they are demanding in ways that cannot be fully brought to articulation or reflected on. Butler's analysis of gender is again informative here: "Yet I accept the idea that gender is an impersonation, that becoming gendered involves *impersonating an ideal that nobody actually inhabits*, and that's where I have a certain sympathy with Lacanian discourse. Because symbolic positions—'man,' 'woman,'—are never inhabited by anyone, and that's what defines them as symbolic: they're radically uninhabitable. And yet they have *enormous* force."[9] Butler explains ideals in terms of "symbolic positions," but her basic idea is similar to Nietzsche's. Symbols are puzzling in that they manage to sustain "force" even though their content is inscrutable and thus "uninhabitable." To be who we are, we nevertheless compel ourselves to occupy symbolic positions that we cannot make sense of. Nietzsche did seem to leave out hope that some alternative form of impersonation, a kind of "good" acting, could somehow establish a sound, habitable identity: "Good actors . . . enact themselves, they invent themselves" (*Z* "On Human Prudence"). But we rely on ideals to make sense of who we are, and ideals fails us.

As Nietzsche frames it, then, the problem with ideals is not avoidable. Our ability to construct a sense of who we are and inhabit such an identity depends on ideals; identity is itself idealizing. And since ideals are inevitably self-estranging, identity itself is defective. The problem with identity is not the Schopenhauerian one, of its being painfully, metaphysically unreal, but that it requires accepting self-definitions that one can never come to terms with. As Nietzsche suggests in this passage, there is furthermore no option of abandoning ideals in order to distance oneself from their problems:

> Have we not exposed ourselves to the suspicion of an opposition—an opposition between the world in which until now we were at home with our venerations—and which may have made it possible for us to *endure* life—and another world *that we ourselves are*: a relentless, fundamental, deepest suspicion

concerning ourselves that is steadily gaining more and worse control over us Europeans and that could easily confront coming generations with the terrible Either/Or: "Either abolish your venerations or—*yourselves*!" The latter would be nihilism; but would the former not also be—nihilism?—That is *our* question mark. (*GS* 346)

Here "venerations" take the place of ideals, but Nietzsche's outlook remains the same. Our reverences, although they make life bearable, have come to seem alienating: they are opposed to the "world *that we ourselves are*" and generate a suspicion about ourselves. Removing this opposition between our venerations and ourselves seems to be called for, but there is no such option. Our venerations are inextricably linked with who we are, so the only alternatives are maintaining the opposition and "nihilism."

## Wounded and Idealized Identities

Nietzsche uses the idea of "acting" to convey a problem in the relationship between ideals and identity. It might be impossible to imagine a form of acting so successful that it solves this problem, but one could possibly imagine what a good performativity would be like: constituting oneself and the symbolic space that one comes to occupy, finding that its semantic contours align well with one's desires and dispositions, others arriving at a shared understanding of who one is and what one's effective role in the world should be, and the demands of the role coming to seem fulfilling rather than burdensome. In short, one could spontaneously invent and at the same time play a part that one embraces so fully that it is no longer playing a part. Yet this imaginary completion of identity is not a script that Nietzsche anticipated writing. There are social reasons for this: roles generate expectations from others, for how one represents it to the world, and thus can be alienating. And there are psychological and practical reasons why one's identity can seem ill-fitting and uncomfortable. But part of Nietzsche's suspicion was that such an imaginary completion of identity is itself an ideal that is impossible to live with and thus self-estranging once more. On one hand, it demands to be inhabited so fully that there is no other life to live. And on the other hand, Nietzsche suspects that as ideal it is rooted in disappointment: it expresses anger and vengefulness toward life's failure to provide satisfaction. Nevertheless, Nietzsche held out hope for some formation of identity that neither rested with self-estrangement nor was swallowed up by its own ideality.

As suspicious as Nietzsche was of ideality, one important qualification to this worry was that *moral ideals* are distinctively dangerous. Nietzsche had a wealth of different critiques of moral ideals, of course, but they are dangerous, first of all, psychologically: they stem from instincts that are "hostile to life" (*GS* 335) and that exert a harmful influence even when they are sublimated into a moral form. Dwelling on moral ideals, for Nietzsche, was a way of harboring corrosive drives that obstruct action and weaken one's constitution. They compel, furthermore, misinterpretations of one's life. Moral ideals supplant one's sense of what is important with an orientation to an imaginary "moral world order" (*AC* 25). A complex of beliefs about nature and human personality is needed to sustain confidence in moral ideals, and this leads to a systematic misunderstanding of the conditions of life. Nietzsche also characterizes holding moral ideals as itself a kind of vengeful activity. Through moral ideals one has a way to lash out at others, if only imaginatively, through assignments of blame and viciousness.

This qualification, that it is especially moral ideals that play a harmful role in the constitution of identity, should be of limited comfort, however. The boundary between moral and nonmoral is fluid—there is no essence of the moral as such—and "moral valuations" pervade every aspect of our lives on Nietzsche's historical account. The historical account furnishes even deeper reasons to be suspicious of the role of ideals too. Ideals are part of the process by which grievances are converted not just to particular patterns of belief and action but to fixed, regulated identities. To be sure, in Nietzsche's story these are often moral ideals that distinguish the "good" from the "evil." The historical account, however, identifies a series of processes by which blame is assigned for injuries, injuries are used to articulate a sense of victimization and powerlessness, and the appeal to a shared (and persecuted) experience is used to codify a social position. Membership in this social position becomes self-reinforcing, through collective identification and increasingly refined articulation of shared experiences. In this way an identity is formed: not merely some common features or affinities but a way of being that demands acknowledgment and commitment. And however else this identity is filled out, what binds it together is the perception of grievance and loss.

Wendy Brown borrows from Nietzsche's analysis in her account of "wounded attachments."[10] Brown poses the question, "What kind of political recognition can identity-based claims seek—and what kind can they be counted on to want—that will not resubordinate a subject historically subjugated through identity, through categories such as race and gender that emerged and circulated as terms of power to enact subordination?"[11] Brown arguably extends Nietzsche's analysis of the harms done by politicized identities in two distinguishable ways. One, whereas Nietzsche saw the harm of identity formation primarily in terms of the psychological damage of self-definition through grievance, Brown notes that the actual social functioning of identity can include "resubordination." The social world can respond to the formation of identities and demands for recognition by reimposing conditions of subordination, even when old identities are appropriated for the purpose of emancipation. Two, the interplay of psychic and social factors can lead to identities that are "invested in their own subjection."[12] That is, political identities not only involve wants and desires being shaped in terms of reactions to past injuries, but they also allow an ongoing need to make sense of oneself in terms of relational status. Politicized identity, that is, can become more self-referential than perhaps Nietzsche imagined: once subjection becomes part of identity, it can be inseparable from who one is.

The formation of identity affects what is wanted by and how the world responds to those who belong to such identities; when those identities are based on wounded attachments not only are those wants and the responses to them suspect, but the shaping of ideals of self and possible futures can be corrupted. Identity formation, furthermore, need not wait for wounds to happen; the process can include producing them on its own. Foucault's innovation on the topic of identity formation was to point out that modern institutions, through processes of classification and control, categorize people and "people spontaneously come to fill those categories."[13] To be sure, classificatory discourses attempt to capture distinctions that are already in evidence, but they also have an effect on the persons who come to occupy those categories. And here "historically constituted illness"[14] and idealized identity can coincide. Persons can identify with the categories that have been invented for them, and following, for example, "multiple implantation of 'perversions,'"[15] in Foucault's phrase, define themselves in terms of the desires that come with their role. Identities come in many forms—some of which are shaped by forces that stand far apart from the persons who perform them, mediated by bureaucrats, experts, and professionals of various kinds. Although Nietzsche was worried about homogenous normalizing, it turns out that social institutions can also produce conformity through abnormal and marginalized identities.

Nietzsche's understanding of identity formation was that it was inevitably idealizing and thereby always defective, and subsequent experience has if anything shown this problem to be even deeper than he realized. The final question of this chapter is how to respond to this defect at the heart of identity. One possibility, of course, is to find some way of transcending or moving beyond the investment in woundedness and revenge in the constitution of identity. Even if the imagination of the present is circumscribed by the reactions to current forms of subjection, one can aspire to future goals and ways of self-shaping that strike out in independent ways. This seems to be Wendy Brown's suggestion: "For if I am right about the problematic of pain installed at the heart of many contemporary contradictory demands for political recognition, all that such pain may long for—more than revenge—is the chance to be heard into a certain release, recognized into self-overcoming, incited into possibilities for triumphing over, and hence losing, itself."[16] Identity now defines itself on wounded terms, but it could be possible to forget historical pains and for identity to overcome itself into a non-vengeful form. Frantz Fanon, too, had a similar solution:

> I find myself one day in the world and I acknowledge one right for myself: the right to demand human behavior from the other. And one duty: the duty never to let my decisions renounce my freedom. . . . My life must not be devoted to making an assessment of black values . . . I am not a prisoner of History. I must not look for the meaning of my destiny in that direction. I must constantly remind myself that the real *leap* consists of introducing invention into life. In the world I am heading for, I am endlessly creating myself.[17]

Intermediate stages in the progress of liberation must certainly take account of historical injustices. But the ultimate goal is to transcend all that and take up forms of self-invention free from the burdens of history.

Nietzsche, I do not think, had much to say against transcending resentment and finding new shapes of desire that are not invested in their own subjection. It was not a possibility that he entertained concretely: it belonged to the "beyond" of overcoming morality, asceticism, the shadows of God, justice, and revenge against time. But even if it required an inarticulable, epochal transformation, it was not to be dismissed. In conclusion, however, I want to offer a few Nietzschean words on behalf of the wounded who do not know how to transcend their pasts. That is, I want to present two sets of Nietzschean reasons why identity on idealizing terms—and thus as self-estranging, reactive, defective, and even harmful—could nevertheless furnish meaningful ways of being who we are.

One set of reasons that Nietzsche offers for living with idealized identities and wounded attachments is that performative identity does not require more stability than it provides itself. A possible objection to wounded attachments is that they require an imagination of oneself, or of one's desires, that is in some way untrue to who one really is: the reactive formation of a standpoint supplants a better or more genuine way of being. But there is nothing outside itself that a decentered subject needs to be faithful to. Alan White expresses this in terms of Nietzsche's concept of the virtue of "*Redlichkeit*": "*Redlichkeit* requires insisting on the absence of utterly reliable stabilities or identities."[18] The absence of any stable standard of genuineness that transcends our satisfaction does not entail, of course, that all identities are healthy and good. But the origin of identity in pain, even resentful pain, is not by itself objectionable—especially if Nietzsche is right about ideals, and we are all wounded and make ourselves wounded to shape ourselves. Painful, even resentful modes of self-invention might be the most genuine ways of being who we are.

Another set of considerations that Nietzsche offers in favor of wounded forms of identity formation is that our only perspective on what our liberation might consist in is our own. Even if our ideals are conditioned by complicity with the oppression that we have been subjected to, even if ideals as such are evasions of the pressing demands of political life, they might still constitute our only vision of what could be meaningful for us. Here Wendy Brown offers a critique not of ideals or identity as such but of engaging with political and legal institutions in order to make identity claims: "Rather, it is symptomatic of a feature of politicized identity's *desire* within liberal-bureaucratic regimes, its foreclosure of its own freedom, its impulse to inscribe in the law and in other political registers its historical and present pain rather than conjure an imagined future of power to make itself."[19] The criticism is directed at the "desire" or "impulse" toward employing such means, and the criticism is that it crowds out the ability to imagine what a self-constituting future might consist in. This criticism might indeed be apt: legal tactics and complicity with institutional power could foreclose possible futures. At the same time, it is worth considering Nietzsche's reminder about "this world as it concerns *us*, in which *we* need to love and be afraid, this almost invisible, inaudible world of subtle command, subtle obedience" (*BGE* 226, emphasis in original). Nietzsche's point, I take it, is that self-making has to make sense to us, in our wounded states, by responding to our loves and fears, duties and deferences. For liberation to count as such, it needs to be accessible to us, in thought and affect, as *our* liberation, in light of our remembering. And even if ideals constrain our imagination, and distract and disappoint us, they might still be needed to shape a satisfying view of the future of ourselves.

We can consider this connection between ideals and wounded selves in light of Roy L. Brooks's "atonement model" of reparations for slavery.[20] For Brooks, "racial reconciliation" should be the primary purpose of a reparations program, and this requires both apologies and meaningful, material restitution.[21] The ultimate aim of reparations, or restorative practices in general, can thus be seen in terms of "restoring relationships" that have become damaged through the harms caused by injustice.[22] But in cases of responding to historical injustices, where the perpetrators and victims of the original crimes are long since dead, reconciliation depends on forming both the identities that make apologies possible and forming one in which resentment can be overcome.[23] Apologies alone require background conditions for their success; at a minimum there has to be someone in an appropriate position to make an apology, a meaningful way to express contrition, and someone who is in an appropriate position to accept. Taking on relationships to historical memory and making sense of who we are in terms of these relationships, even when it might seem painful or alienating to do so, can in this way be a requirement for even the possibility of apologies.

## Notes

1. The following translations are used, occasionally with slight modifications: Friedrich Nietzsche, *The Antichrist, Twilight of the Idols, Ecce Homo, and Other Writings*, trans. Judith Norman (New York: Cambridge University Press, 2005); Friedrich Nietzsche, *Beyond Good and Evil*, trans. Judith Norman (New York: Cambridge University Press, 2001); Friedrich Nietzsche, *Human, All-too-human*, trans. R. J. Hollingdale (New York: Cambridge University Press, 1996); Friedrich Nietzsche, *The Gay Science*, trans. Judith Norman (New York: Cambridge University Press, 2001); Friedrich Nietzsche, *Thus Spoke Zarathustra*, trans. Walter Kaufmann (New York: Penguin, 1978).

2. Nietzsche occasionally uses other terms to mark off the positive side. For example, Nietzsche uses "solid" (*fest*) as a contrast with actors (*Schauspieler*) (*GS* 356).

3. These criticisms of ideals also appear in works influenced by Nietzsche. On ideology and abstractness see, for example, Raymond Geuss, *Outside Ethics* (Princeton, NJ: Princeton University Press, 2005); and Geuss, *Philosophy and Real*

*Politics* (Princeton, NJ: Princeton University Press, 2008). On human motivation and blame see, for example, Bernard Williams, "Nietzsche's Minimalist Moral Psychology," in *Making Sense of Humanity and Other Philosophical Papers* (New York: Cambridge University Press, 1995), 65–76; and Williams, *In the Beginning Was the Deed: Realism and Moralism in Political Argument* (Princeton, NJ: Princeton University Press, 2007). On the distance between ideals and actual conditions see, for example, Wendy Brown, *Politics out of History* (Princeton, NJ: Princeton University Press, 2008), esp. 94: "Transcendent ideals in politics—convictions—are, precisely, refusals to allow history and contingency to contour the existing dimensions and possibilities of political life. In this sense, they constitute repudiations of politics, even as they masquerade as sources of redemption. Indeed, we might say that the insistence on the importance of transcendent ideals in politics paradoxically affirms rather than challenges a figuring of the political domain as relentlessly amoral. It places the idealist actor at a distance from politics, thus inevitably disappointed by it and perhaps even prepared to renounce politics because of its failure and compromises vis-à-vis his or her ideals."

4. Jean-Paul Sartre, *L'être et le néant: Essai d'ontologie phénoménologique* (Paris: Gallimard, 1943), 94.

5. Judith Butler, *Gender Trouble: Feminism and the Subversion of Identity* (New York: Routledge, 1990), 136, emphasis in original; cf. 25.

6. Butler, 141. For a similar point, see Erving Goffman, *The Presentation of Self in Everyday Life* (New York: Anchor Books, 1959), 20, on "the cycle of disbelief-to-belief."

7. This sense of "performative" is widespread in nonacademic discourse, but for a nearly Dadaist example, see Rod Dreher, "Against Liberal 'Performative Wokeness,'" *American Conservative* (Jan. 30, 2018), http://www.theamericanconservative.com/dreher/against-liberal-performative-wokeness. For a more thoughtful, contrarian reflection on the category, see Pip Williams, "In Defence of 'Performative' Activism," *Medium*, March 1, 2018, https://medium.com/@pipsuxx/in-defence-of-performative-activism-ff6b475cdafa.

8. McKay Coppins, "Trump's Right-Hand Troll," *Atlantic*, May 28, 2018, https://www.theatlantic.com/politics/archive/2018/05/stephen-miller-trump-adviser/561317/.

9. Judith Butler, "The Body You Want," interview by Liz Kotz, *Artforum* 31 (Nov. 1992), 85, emphasis modified.

10. This is the title of chapter 3 of *States of Injury: Power and Freedom in Late Modernity* (Princeton, NJ: Princeton University Press, 1995), 52–76.

11. Brown, *States of Injury*, 55.

12. Brown, 70.

13. Ian Hacking, *Historical Ontology* (Cambridge, MA: Harvard University Press, 2001), 100.

14. Ian Hacking, *Rewriting the Soul: Multiple Personality and the Sciences of Memory* (Princeton, NJ: Princeton University Press, 1995), 12.

15. Michel Foucault, *The History of Sexuality: An Introduction*, vol. 1, trans. Robert Hurley (New York: Vintage Books, 1990), 37.
16. Brown, *States of Injury*, 74–5.
17. Frantz Fanon, *Black Skin, White Masks*, trans. Richard Philcox (New York: Grove Press, 2008), 204.
18. Alan White, "The Youngest Virtue," in *Nietzsche's Postmoralism: Essays on Nietzsche's Prelude to Philosophy's Future*, ed. R. Schacht (New York: Cambridge University Press, 2001), 76.
19. Brown, *States of Injury*, 66.
20. Roy L. Brooks, *Atonement and Forgiveness: A New Model for Black Reparations* (Berkeley: University of California Press, 2004), 142.
21. Brooks, 141.
22. On the idea of "restoring relationships," see Margaret Urban Walker, *Moral Repair: Reconstructing Moral Relations after Wrongdoing* (New York: Cambridge University Press, 2006), 209.
23. For a discussion of resentment in the context of reparations, see Susan Neiman, *Learning from the Germans: Race and the Memory of Evil* (New York: Picador, 2019), 308.

# References

Brooks, Roy L. *Atonement and Forgiveness: A New Model for Black Reparations*. Berkeley: University of California Press, 2004.
Brown, Wendy. *Politics out of History*. Princeton, NJ: Princeton University Press, 2008.
Butler, Judith. "The Body You Want." Interview by Liz Kotz. *Artforum* 31 (1992): 82–89.
———. *Gender Trouble: Feminism and the Subversion of Identity*. New York: Routledge, 1990.
Coppins, McKay. "Trump's Right-Hand Troll." *Atlantic*, May 28, 2018. https://www.theatlantic.com/politics/archive/2018/05/stephen-miller-trump-adviser/561317/.
Dreher, Rod. "Against Liberal 'Performative Wokeness.'" *American Conservative*, Jan. 30, 2018. http://www.theamericanconservative.com/dreher/against-liberal-performative-wokeness.
Fanon, Frantz. *Black Skin, White Masks*. Translated by Richard Philcox. New York: Grove Press, 2008.
Foucault, Michel. *The History of Sexuality: An Introduction*. Vol. 1. Trans. Robert Hurley. New York: Vintage Books, 1990.
Geuss, Raymond. *Outside Ethics*. Princeton, NJ: Princeton University Press, 2005.
———. *Philosophy and Real Politics*. Princeton, NJ: Princeton University Press, 2008.

Goffman, Erwin. *The Presentation of Self in Everyday Life*. New York: Anchor Books, 1959.
Hacking, Ian. *Historical Ontology*. Cambridge, MA: Harvard University Press, 2001.
———. *Rewriting the Soul: Multiple Personality and the Sciences of Memory*. Princeton, NJ: Princeton University Press, 1995.
Neiman, Susan. *Learning from the Germans: Race and the Memory of Evil*. New York: Picador, 2019.
Nietzsche, Friedrich. *The Antichrist, Twilight of the Idols, Ecce Homo, and Other Writings*. Translated by Judith Norman. New York: Cambridge University Press, 2005.
———. *Beyond Good and Evil*. Translated by Judith Norman. New York: Cambridge University Press, 2001.
———. *The Gay Science*. Translated by Judith Norman. New York: Cambridge University Press, 2001.
———. *Human, All Too Human*. Translated by R. J. Hollingdale. New York: Cambridge University Press, 1996.
———. *Thus Spoke Zarathustra*. Translated by Walter Kaufmann. New York: Penguin, 1978.
Sartre, Jean-Paul. *L'être et le néant: Essai d'ontologie phénoménologique*. Paris: Gallimard, 1943.
Walker, Margaret Urban. *Moral Repair: Reconstructing Moral Relations after Wrongdoing*. New York: Cambridge University Press, 2006.
White, Alan. "The Youngest Virtue." In *Nietzsche's Postmoralism: Essays on Nietzsche's Prelude to Philosophy's Future*, ed. R. Schacht, 63–78. New York: Cambridge University Press, 2001.
Williams, Bernard. *In the Beginning Was the Deed: Realism and Moralism in Political Argument*. Princeton, NJ: Princeton University Press, 2007.
———. "Nietzsche's Minimalist Moral Psychology." In *Making Sense of Humanity and Other Philosophical Papers*, 65–76. New York: Cambridge University Press, 1995.
Williams, Pip. "In Defence of 'Performative' Activism." *Medium*, March 1, 2018. https://medium.com/@pipsuxx/in-defence-of-performative-activism-ff6b475cdafa.

4

# How We Became Who We Are
Retracing Nietzsche's Genealogy of Politicized Identity

ALLISON MERRICK

Nietzsche's autobiography makes it clear that *On the Genealogy of Morality* contains "three decisive preliminary studies by a psychologist" (*EH* "Genealogy"). Assuming that Nietzsche's retrospective assessment of his text is a reliable guide, an important exegetical question arises: Why would a psychologist undertake the genealogical study of morality? Why, to have it another way, does one need to be a psychologist to make plainer the origins of morality? One simple answer readily suggests itself: "A genealogy of moral value judgments . . . consists of an inquiry into their *psychological origin*."[1] Or, to put it differently, we might explain morality's origins by appealing to those "naturally occurring psychological mechanisms—*ressentiment* (*GM* I), internalized cruelty (*GM* II), the will to power (*GM* III)."[2] Taken together, these points offer a tidy, albeit preliminary, answer to the question set above: the psychological and the genealogical investigations come neatly bundled, as it were. To have one, it seems, is to have the other.

If such a picture is broadly accurate and if uncovering the psychological origins of certain forms of life is at least part of what is required to undertake their genealogical investigation, then it is useful to get a clearer picture of the scope and nature of such a relationship.[3] That is, it seems to me that any cogent reconstruction of the genealogical mode of inquiry must account for why it is that a psychologist undertakes the task, what the nature of that domain includes, and why Nietzsche's account is, at least and at a bare minimum, psychologically tenable.[4] This task is, to put it plainly, the aim of this chapter.

To reach such an end, however, it is necessary to have a firm grasp of what "psychology" means to Nietzsche. Since aphorism 23 of *Beyond Good and Evil* lays bare the key features of his view, my first task is to undertake its careful reconstruction. Next, I make use of this account to show its proper place in the exercise of genealogy, as Nietzsche employs it in *On the Genealogy of Morality*. What I show, through presenting the original nobles as an example, is that historical, socio-political conflicts and contexts organize self-experience.[5] Next, I consider and defuse an objection to my view.[6] If my defense holds, and if it is the case that the arguments I offer in the previous sections of the chapter are plausible and persuasive, then another set of questions emerges: How might contemporary philosophers and political theorists expand their uses of this form of inquiry? Beyond excavating our taken-for-granted notions, reclaiming subjugated histories, and demonstrating the simple fact, surely correct, *that* our practices, institutions, and modes of life are contingently constructed, how might this mode of inquiry account for *how* normative dictates organize and order our psychic lives? Further still, why have these psychological dimensions of Nietzsche's genealogical investigations often been underappreciated, even erased, obscured, marginalized, and expunged by contemporary theorists?[7] We can answer these questions—and indeed I do offer some preliminary suggestions in the final section of this chapter—but to do so, I first must set the scene and address that introductory question I posed a moment ago: What does "psychology" mean to Nietzsche? To put it another way, What does he suggest is so distinctive about his account?

## Psychology: Morphology of the Development of Will to Power

In the preceding remarks, I suggested that we can answer the questions I have posed and get a better handle on what Nietzsche means by his use of the term "psychology" by focusing on one key passage from *Beyond Good and Evil*. The section in question begins: "All psychology so far has been stuck in moral prejudices and fears: it has not ventured into the depths. To grasp psychology as morphology and the *doctrine of the development of the will to power*, which I have done—nobody has ever come close to this, not even in thought: this, of course, to the extent that we are permitted to regard what has been written so far as a symptom of what has not been said until now" (*BGE* 23). Here, Nietzsche shows us the shape of his understanding of psychology: it is best understood, he claims, "as morphology and the *doctrine of the development of the will to power*" (*BGE* 23). Clarifying such a characterization is, accordingly, the task of this section and I begin this undertaking as Nietzsche does: by attempting to show how this new form of psychology differs from the other modes—"psychology so far" (*BGE* 23)—that he roundly criticizes.

CONCERNING THE MORAL PREJUDICES OF PSYCHOLOGISTS

Nietzsche provides us with the means of distinguishing his approach: whereas most psychologists are "struck in moral prejudice and fear," Nietzsche's account is markedly unprejudiced; whereas most psychologists are wrecked on the perils of superficiality, Nietzsche ventures to the depths to "open up a *more profound* world of insight"; whereas most psychologists trade in symptomatology, Nietzsche seeks out the underlying etiology (*BGE* 23; cf. *BGE* 12, *BGE* 47, *BGE* 229). If this set of inferences is indeed warranted, and if it is the case that we can distinguish Nietzsche's account because it is not hopelessly marooned by prejudice, what, we might well ask, does it mean precisely to say that "the psychology we have had so far suffered shipwreck" (*BGE* 47)? Where, in other words, has psychology to date run aground?

Nietzsche's answer is plain, and it is this: psychology immobilized itself by placing "itself under the dominion" of customary morality.[8] Customary morality, then, functions as a "prejudgment," as a guiding assumption that supports and undergirds psychological frameworks, even as that faith, that belief, that prejudgment itself remains outside of conscious awareness (*BGE* 47).[9] As people's belief in customary morality shapes their expectations, they are unable to examine, analyze, or question the framework or lens through which they see the world. Hence, they remain, as Nietzsche puts it elsewhere, "under the seduction of morality" and replicate rather than (re) examine or (re)consider customary frameworks (*D* P:3; cf., *BGE* 2, *BGE* 56, *BGE* 186).

The most prominent example of those who "stand under the command of a particular morality, and, without knowing it, serve as its shield-bearers and followers" (*GS* 345) is, undoubtably, the "English psychologists," as

Nietzsche characterizes them in *On the Genealogy of Morality* (*GM* I:1–3). The "superstition" of these psychologists—their pre-reflective commitment to customary morality—leads them to take for granted a connection between the "good" and the "unegoistic," which they then read back onto and into the history of morality (*GM* I:2). Their moral prejudice keeps out of view the historical development of this connection: that such a link "emerged only when aristocratic value judgements *declined*," when it "obtruded itself more and more on the human conscience" (*GM* I:2). Their moral prejudice keeps out of view the relevant psychology, as Nietzsche sees it: the connection between the unegoistic and the good was forged to meet specific psychological needs—to redress feelings of impotence, helplessness, and vulnerability amongst the socially disempowered (*GM* I, passim). Their moral prejudice keeps out of view the critical issue: the question of how the link between the unegoistic and the good psychologically functions for us today—does it similarly help us to keep at bay nagging feelings of powerlessness? Does it ward off our vulnerability? Does it protect us against feelings of helplessness? Might we need it as a "mask," or a "stimulant," or has the value equation itself outlasted its usefulness (*GM* P:6)?

These questions may speak of Nietzsche's commitment to unmooring psychology from moral prejudice; to unlinking psychological studies from their unreflective commitment to and reliance on the dominant evaluative framework as it shapes and orders our affective, which is to say, psychic, lives.[10] To have it another way, and to make use of a terrestrial analogy, these questions indicate that Nietzsche will, in contradistinction to those English psychologists, plumb the depths, undertake that "subterranean" work (*D* P:1), as he calls it, to dig beneath "trust in *morality*" (*D* P:2). This subterranean work reveals the socio-political contests and contexts that shape affective lives as they form senses of self. Indeed, this subterranean work is, in part at least, psychological work: it reveals the frameworks according to which humans have, often pre-reflectively, ordered their cognitive and affective lives; it reveals the concealed organizational structures by which we make sense of ourselves. Nietzsche understands this work in morphological terms: he is keen to make sense of the forms and structures of psychic lives.[11]

Psychology as Morphology

To be interested in what has been occluded from view, or lies beyond the dominant perspective, is to be interested in different organizations of experience, in different forms of life. This helps, I think, to explain why Nietzsche describes his account of psychology as morphology: it implies the study of more than one type, of more than one form, of more than one way of ordering and structuring affective and cognitive experience, which is to say, psychic life. If our moral prejudice locks us into one view, one perspective, one way of ordering things, then a morphological investigation—replete with the suspicion that we can indeed study forms of life—is one way of exploring the systems of evaluation by which we make sense of ourselves, yet which so often remain out of view.

The task of morphology, then, is not simply to consider different psychological organizations but to consider the conditions of their emergence. It is to ask the question: Under what conditions did "their tender feelings and value distinctions" grow? (*BGE* 186). Further, it is to be curious about what makes it necessary to see oneself as good, as beneficent, as benevolent, as altruistic. It is to wonder, yet further still: What are the psychological costs of maintaining such a self-conception? We can answer these questions, as Nietzsche does, by bringing a notable example into view—the psychological organization of the original nobles. We can answer these questions, as I will in the next section, by making plainer a particular form of life as well as the conceptual schemes or systems of evaluation that undergird it.

First, however, if this is persuasive and if we have good reason to be interested in the forms of life that are shaped by historical and socio-political systems, we are still in need of a principle that might help to explain the nature and structure of those reactions. One such principle might be that of psychological hedonism, which would suggest, broadly speaking, that what makes sense of human actions is that people pursue pleasure and avoid pain. Nietzsche's answer, by contrast, is of course the will to power. I shall argue that this largely amounts to claiming that we can understand such varying forms of life by determining how a particular psychic structure is the product of a particular set of resistances that had to be overcome (*BGE* 12; cf. *BGE* 198, 200, 225, 228).

PSYCHOLOGY AS MORPHOLOGY AND THE DOCTRINE OF THE DEVELOPMENT OF THE WILL TO POWER

Nietzsche makes much of the "will to power," going so far as to suggest that "life itself is will to power" ("Leben selbst ist Wille zur Macht") (*BGE* 13) and that "life simply is will to power" ("Leben eben Wille zur Macht ist") (*BGE* 259). He further maintains that the will to power is the "primordial fact of all history" (*BGE* 259). It is the "essence of life" (*GM* II:12) and "the most life-affirming impulse" (*GM* III:18). Furthermore, it shows itself in a wide variety of ways: in "the spontaneous, aggressive, expansive, re-interpreting, re-directing and formative forces" (*GM* II:12), such a "philosophy" is "the most spiritual" of its manifestations (*BGE* 6; cf. *BGE* 227). Nietzsche gives the will to power pride of explanatory place as he employs it to clarify a wide-ranging set of activities and motivational forces.[12] But it remains unclear what, according to Nietzsche, the will to power is, exactly.

Reginster offers a persuasive answer, positing that the will to power is

> the will to the overcoming of resistance. This definition dictates a particular conception of the relation between it and other drives. So defined, the concept of power is, in and of itself, devoid of any *determinate content*. It gets a determinate content only from its relation to a determinate end one desires to realize. For example, a recalcitrant puzzle is an obstacle to the desire to understand, and the strength of an opposing player is resistance against the desire to win. Accordingly, the will to power cannot be satisfied unless the agent has desire for something else than power. . . . The will to power therefore has the structure of a second-order desire: it is a desire whose object includes another (first-order) desire. It is specifically, a desire for the overcoming of resistance in the pursuit of some determinate first-order desire.[13]

For our present concerns, there are two points of significance. On the one hand, we are in possession of an important, albeit negative, claim: the will to power makes no specific or "*determinate content*" claims about *what* it is that we will.[14] Put another way, agents do not, according to such a thesis, primarily desire to dominate, to overpower, or to exploit. To say otherwise—to believe, for example, that one wills power directly in each and every case—would be to furnish the will to power with some particular content. On the other hand, we are in possession of an important positive thesis concerning *how* agents will. The will to power, so understood, is a structural claim, which appears to operate when an agent wills some first-order desire. Thus understood, the will to power is apparent, provided an agent engages in the activity of identifying some resistance and strives to overcome it.

Here it may be tempting to conclude that some first-order desires are better contenders than others, based on how risky, tricky, or otherwise difficult they are to pull off. There is some good textual evidence for making such distinctions; for example, Nietzsche's description of exemplary forms of human agency, such as that of Julius Caesar, whom Nietzsche holds up as "the most magnificent type" (*TI* "Skirmishes" 38). He asks: "How is freedom measured in individuals and in people?" and answers: "It is measured by the resistance that needs to be overcome, by the effort that it costs to stay on top" (*TI* "Skirmishes" 38). So one metric that we can use to evaluate exemplary forms of the will to power is arguably psychic cost, which can be measured in terms of the work that is necessary to maintain that form of life. Nietzsche continues by locating "the highest type of free human being where the highest resistance is constantly being overcome: five paces away from tyranny, right on the threshold, where servitude is a danger" (*TI* "Skirmishes" 38).

For the purposes of this argument, however, I remain agnostic on the issue of which demonstrations are more appropriate candidates and contend that the will to power, as I conceive it, is in operation in both cases. That is—and this is the key to my argument—whether an agent desires to attain some exceptionally challenging goal or whether she desires and indeed surmounts some decidedly more moderate obstacle, *either way* the will to power as a second-order desire is at work. In this way, and in considering the reevaluation of morality that Nietzsche tracks in the first essay of *On the Genealogy of Morality*, we might say that the will to power, as the desire for the overcoming of resistance, is a manifest feature of the revolt even if it does not (since it cannot) serve as the principle of reevaluation.[15] The reason is that an agent, in this case the slave of the first essay, must aim at something other than power, namely at "some determinate first-order desire," such as the desire to experience oneself as efficacious.[16]

Before pressing on to show how Nietzsche draws upon and puts to use this formulation of psychology—understood as morphology of the development of the will to power—in the first essay of *On the Genealogy of Morality*, I shall first consider it against the backdrop of that commonplace way of accounting for human motivation I mentioned at the end of the last section: namely that " 'people strive for happiness' " (*EH* "Books" 5). According to Nietzsche, to say that happiness accounts for human striving is "psychologically absurd" (*EH* "Books" 5). Indeed, he writes: "If you have your '*why?*' in life, you can get along with almost any '*how?*'. People *don't* strive for happiness, only the English do" (*TI* "Arrows" 12). It is an error, Nietzsche argues, to think of happiness as a determinate end or as the aim of action. But why? Martha Nussbaum offers the following answer: "Having feelings of satisfaction as a goal, [Nietzsche] thinks, is a rather base thing, something that he associates with the impoverishment of English culture, as contrasted with German romanticism. Zarathustra, asked whether he is happy, responds, 'Do I strive after happiness? I strive after my works.'"[17] Nussbaum's reference to Zarathustra helps to clarify what constitutes happiness in Nietzsche's view. Willing happiness, like willing power, is a second-order desire that requires one to strive after something else: in this example, one's "works." So Nietzsche's concern, in addition to those worries about "the impoverishment of English culture," is that the very contention that one can seek happiness directly sets us up to stand in the wrong relation to our desires.[18] Indeed, Nietzsche writes: "What is happiness?—The feeling that power is *growing*, that some resistance has been overcome. *Not* contentedness, but more power" (*AC* 2). So "people *don't* strive for happiness," though, of course, it might be the fortunate byproduct of pursing something else, notably the overcoming of some resistance.

I have now cleared some conceptual space and illustrated that psychological inquires must dig deeply to uncover engrained prejudices. I have shown that hedonistic accounts of human motivation are misguided, presenting a more realistic account of human motivation, understood as the longing to feel efficacious. I have also clarified that different forms of life and psychological organizations are possible. I can now turn to substantiating Nietzsche's account by showing how he makes use of it in *On the Genealogy of Morality*, specifically through his account of a particular form of life: that of the original nobles.

## "The Great Revolt Against the Dominance of *Noble* Values" (*EH* "Genealogy"): Revisiting the First Essay of the *Genealogy*

By way of situating this example, let us take note of how Nietzsche describes his objectives in *On the Genealogy of Morality*. In the preface to that work, Nietzsche writes: "We need to know about the conditions and circumstances under which the values grew up, developed and changed (morality as result, as symptom, as mask, as tartuffery, as sickness, as misunderstanding; but also morality as cause, remedy, stimulant, inhibition, poison), since we have neither had this knowledge up till now nor even desired it. People have taken the *value* of these "values" as given, as factual, as beyond all questioning" (*GM* P:6). It is clear that part of the task Nietzsche sets for *On the Genealogy of Morality* is that of excavation: to dig beneath our moral prejudice, our commonplace assumptions about morality—in this case that its *value* has remained constant and that it harbors a privileged status that makes it immune from evaluation—to determine the ways in which that morality has been put to work within varying systems. Nietzsche's inquiry concerns, then, how varying forms of morality function to establish certain modes of life, to prohibit certain actions and foster others (*GM* P:6).

Nietzsche's etymology of "goodness" is an example of such a subterranean enterprise:

> In these words and roots which denote "good," we can often detect the main nuance which made the noble feel they were men of higher rank. True, in most cases they might give themselves names which simply show superiority of power (such as "the mighty," "the masters," "the commanders") or the most visible sign of this superiority, such as "the rich," "the propertied." . . . But the names also show a *typical character* trait: and this is what concerns us here. For example, they call themselves "the truthful." (*GM* I:5)

Three claims, I think, are worth drawing out in detail. First, the etymological evidence shows that the "good" of noble morality is initially linked with cultural and socio-political conditions. Such social arrangements engender "a pathos of distance and nobility" (*GM* I:2) that "grows," as Nietzsche puts it elsewhere, "out of ingrained differences between stations" (*BGE* 257). Accordingly—and this is the second claim—such hierarchical social structures create particular psychic organizations. The reason is that "differences between stations" (*BGE* 257) "made the noble *feel* they were men of higher rank" (*GM* I:5, emphasis added) as those social conditions generated the "predominant *feeling* of complete and fundamental superiority" (*GM* I:2, emphasis added). This provides the "general rule that [for the original nobles, at least] the concept of political superiority always resolves itself into a concept of psychological superiority" (*GM* I:6). Or, as Nietzsche puts it in *Beyond Good and Evil*, "without this pathos, that other, more mysterious paths could not have grown at all, that demand for new expansions of distance within the soul itself, the development of states that are increasingly high, rare, distant, tautly drawn" (*BGE* 257). Third, and finally, these psychic structures are often expressed in the "form of typical character traits," such as honesty; for example, the nobles "call themselves 'the truthful' " (*GM* I:5).

It is worth noting that the account of original nobility in the first essay is indeed complex as it readily trades on socio-political as well as psychological or characterological categories. Reginster describes the master-slave relationship in terms of these categories: "Nietzsche's use of the notions of '(noble) master' and 'slave' is ambiguous. They are now socio-political categories, and now character types. The noble masters value political supremacy qua noble in the socio-political sense, but we will see that their valuing political power is not essential to their possessing a noble character. Nietzsche makes clear that nobility as a type of character is 'the case that concerns us here'" (*GM* I:5; cf. *GM* 6). Accordingly, I will consider the categories of "noble" and "slave" in their socio-political sense as elements in the illustration of an essentially psychological view, which makes use of the same notions to denote specific character types.[19]

Even as the designation "noble" is used by Nietzsche to refer to both social and psychological categories, the account Nietzsche offers is less ambiguous than Reginster lets on. The chronology laid bare in the first essay makes plain the *initial* importance of hierarchical social categories. Indeed, it is such standing that leads to the formulation of the original nobles' psyches (cf. *GM* I:2, 4–6). It is, Nietzsche argues, an essential prerequisite for that other "more mysterious pathos" of distance, namely that of characterological or psychological distance and thereby of self-valuation. We should also not forget that downplaying this feature—Nietzsche claims it is, indeed, a "harsh" truth (*BGE* 257)—is risky, since doing so might very well be another incarnation of that "democratic bias" concerning matters of descent or origins; it would be to overlook the actual history of our moral concepts (*GM* I:4). Of course, it is worth noting that, over time, things become much more complicated as characterological types often become divorced from social class and standing (cf. *BGE* 260).[20]

How does such a reconstruction relate to the arguments I have been advancing thus far concerning Nietzsche's account of psychology? In broad strokes, it shows that if we isolate the original nobles of the first essay, we can see Nietzsche digging beneath our "democratic bias . . . over all questions of descent" to uncover "an *essential* insight into moral genealogy" (*GM* I:4). He demonstrates not simply that the term of valuation, "good," was at one time the primary marker of socio-political positioning (the mighty, masters, commanders, rich or propertied; cf. *GM* I:5), and that such a primary understanding shaped people's sense of self: "good = noble = powerful = beautiful = happy = blessed" (*GM* I:7; cf. *BGE* 260). Further still, it may very well expose our moral prejudice, that there is only one way to order our evaluative lives, and it opens us up to the idea that there may be alternative ways of organizing affective and psychic life.

Yet, it is important to notice that what I have laid out thus far remains only a partial sketch. When Nietzsche's new mode of psychology was introduced in the previous section, it was characterized by three features: (1) it plumbs the depths of traditional morality, (2) it offers an account of how varying psychological types emerge, and (3) it shows how to overcome resistances or, as I have demonstrated, exercise will to power (cf. *BGE* 23). Thus far, I have offered a reconstruction of the first two points, hence a word on how those original nobles surmount obstacles is now in order.

Nietzsche's response on this final element is fairly clear. He writes: "The chivalric-aristocratic value judgments are based on a powerful physicality, a blossoming, rich, even effervescent good health that includes the things necessary to maintain it, war, adventure, hunting, dancing, jousting and everything else that contains strong, free, happy action" (*GM* I:7). Put briefly, the original nobles overcame resistances and developed and fostered a sense of efficacy through activity and action.

## Of Genealogy and Psychology: Williams's Worry

I have so far sought to illustrate Nietzsche's account of psychology (*BGE* 12, 23) and make the argument that its manifest elements are made visible in the case of the original nobles of the First Essay. But this reading is not without its detractors, who worry that because the domain of psychology is idiosyncratic and personal and Nietzsche's account of our moral lives is collective and social, we cannot happily marry the two. Bernard Williams presents the following concern:

> Nietzsche is trying to explain a new kind of collective reason, the shared consciousness of morality, and there is a problem about the role played in this explanation by what is seemingly a type of individual psychological reaction. . . . If we are to see [Nietzsche's] explanation as having force, we shall have to integrate the references to individual psychology with the account of an actual social and historical process, and how exactly this should be done remains a question.[21]

Hence, to put Williams's point another way, it is unclear how the two modes of explanation—the psychological and the historical—might be said to work together, as they operate on different levels of analysis. How might psychological microshifts be used to explain broad, historical macroshifts?

This schema, it seems to me, brings together two issues that ought to be treated separately. It is one thing to ask whether the domain of psychology might be helpful in tracking squarely individual responses, but it is quite another matter to ask whether such psychological responses are sufficiently explanatory to account for wide-ranging and extensive shifts in moral evaluation. This latter point is illustrated by the slave revolt in morality, in which the psychic need to make sense of oneself (*GM* I:13) or to discharge *ressentiment* (*GM* I:10) is said to explain great changes in moral outlook.

In considering the first point, I argue that Nietzsche questions this commonplace individualistic understanding of human psychology, one rooted in intrapsychic conflicts. In its place, and to reiterate my reconstruction of key sections of *Beyond Good and Evil* (cf. *BGE* 23) and *On the Genealogy of Morality* (cf. *GM* I:2, 4–6), Nietzsche's account focuses on interpersonal conflicts, historical socio-political contexts and contests that produce certain forms of life. So, as I have shown, Nietzsche's account of the original noble, for instance, readily draws on certain hierarchical, necessarily socio-political conditions (*BGE* 257; *GM* I:2, 3–5). These circumstances are said to create the psychic space that allows for original nobles to first experience themselves as, or better, to *feel* themselves as noble (*GM* I:2).[22] Forms of psychological organization are shown to be the results of interpersonal conflicts at once socially produced and historically conditioned.[23]

This account has clear implications for issues that operate at the second level of analysis. The psychological and the historical are, thus understood, not seen to be operating on different planes of analysis—one micro, the other macro. Particular socio-political and historical conditions, in the account I have been advancing, instead serve to better explain certain psychic formations and organizations. An example, of course, is Nietzsche's rather subtle account of the affect of *ressentiment*, which trades on these historical, socio-political contexts, to explain why the affect only becomes noxious in certain circumstances (*EH* "Wise" 6).

There are those—and Nietzsche presents Comte de Mirabeau in the First Essay of *On the Genealogy of Morality* as an example—whom *ressentiment* does not "poison," and for whom, more specifically, the affective state does not serve as a recurring way of making sense of oneself or one's experiences (*GM* I:10). There are two explanations, we are told, for why this is the case: first, Mirabeau is strong enough to appropriate the affect and can thereby exhaust the feeling "in an immediate reaction" upon his enemies, his accidents, or his misdeeds (*GM* I:10). Second, the affect simply "fails to appear," which means, more precisely, that someone like Mirabeau, a stand-in for "nobility" in general, does not experience slights as narcissistic wounds (*GM* I:10). In other words, Mirabeau does not regard those who insult or snub him as serious threats or dangers to his sense of self; rather, and crucially, he reveres them. Nietzsche writes: "He desires his enemy for himself, his mark of distinction; he can endure no other enemy than one in whom there is nothing to despise and *very much* to honor!" (*GM* I:10). It is possible, then, to read *GM* I:10 as advancing, and consistent with, the view that *ressentiment* is more than a purely intrapsychic phenomenon, as Williams's argument suggests. In attending, rather, to the interpersonal contexts in which Mirabeau finds himself, we can notice that he is not poisoned by *ressentiment* because he has, among other things, socially and politically permitted and sanctioned "drainage ditches for the affects," as Nietzsche puts it elsewhere (*BGE* 260). Further still, it is possible to read *GM* I:10 as underscoring the appropriative—which is to say the form-giving or shaping—dimensions of Nietzsche's view of psychic life: Mirabeau can incorporate injuries and slights into his sense of self precisely because of the way he shapes his view of an enemy: "A mark of distinction" (*GM* I:10).

## Conclusion

If the arguments of the previous section are persuasive, and if it has become clearer that our psychic lives come to be shaped through historical, socio-political contests, what are some of the implications of this?

First, this analysis goes some way toward showing that because Nietzsche is concerned with making plainer the ways that socio-political positioning shapes psychic life, his account is neither mythic nor quasi-historical.[24] Second, this analysis harbors clear implications for contemporary philosophers and political theorists who wish to produce a genealogical investigation. By way of conclusion, let me spell out this second set of implications.

I am certainly not the first to suggest that the genealogical mode of inquiry can be employed to understand and to redress a number of our most urgent social issues, including racism, sexism, and ableism.[25] I am surely not the first to maintain that this form of inquiry might indeed be utilized to clarify how our most contentious philosophical concepts may be said to function.[26] I may, however, be one of the first to notice that we must also attend to the psychological constraints—to the genealogist as psychologist—and keep this requirement and role plainly in view. That is, in addition to excavating our taken-for-granted notions, reclaiming subjugated histories, and examining how forms of life have been contingently constructed, we can make use of genealogy to understand how our affective, which is to say psychic, lives have come to be ordered and shaped.

Here is one example. When bell hooks went in search of a "blueprint" to aid "the process of decolonization" and "personal and political self-recovery," she staked out "how systems of domination operate."[27] In this way, hooks revealed, clarified, and demonstrated that a system of domination (colonialism) was bound up with forms of power and plainly made use of genealogy, making the "attempt to clarify and intensify the difficulties that enable and disable those [colonial] practices" or forms of life.[28] That is to say, hooks sought to lay bare how the dominant system was constructed. But to leave our reconstruction here, however, would be an error. Indeed, it would be to bypass the psychological dimensions of hooks's account—the ways that she has shown that that "internalized white supremacist thinking" brings with it "self-hatred, low self-esteem."[29] In other words, hooks's blueprint lays bare both *that* systems of domination operate and *how* they come to shape our psychic lives, our view of ourselves, our self-experiences.

More recently, and much more explicitly, Angela Y. Davis, Gina Dent, Erica R. Meiners, and Beth Richie, in their book *Abolition. Feminism. Now.*, have framed their work as a "critical genealogy."[30] The book "proceeds," they maintain, "genealogically to address subjugated histories of organizing that must inform and strengthen our present mobilizations."[31] Hence, in their view, critical genealogies can mobilize feminist abolitionism by attending to the erased political lineages and subjugated histories. This is important, necessary work. It is also work that conspicuously puts to one side the question of *how* these histories come to shape our affective, which is to say, psychic lives.[32] If the arguments of this chapter are compelling, then it seems that Nietzsche's work in *On the Genealogy of Morality* may indeed carry with it a renewed significance for projects of political action: it reminds us that we must assiduously attend to subjugated histories as we concurrently attend to the psychic structures they produce.

## Notes

1. Reginster 1997, 282.
2. Leiter 2002, 173.

3. It is worth remarking that Nietzsche's genealogical mode of inquiry is procedurally overdetermined. That is, Nietzsche tells us quite plainly that his methods, his genealogical inquiries, are governed by a historical criterion (*GM* P:7; *GM* I:1–3; *GM* II:11–12; *GM* III:26), a critical criterion (*GM* P:6; *GM* P:7), and, as we have already seen, a psychological criterion. My aim in this chapter, when seen from this angle, is to make ever plainer the psychological features of this form of inquiry and not to reduce genealogy to simply psychology. On the overdetermined nature of genealogy, see my "Knowing Ourselves: Nietzsche, the Practice of Genealogy, and the Aims of Philosophy" (2021).

4. What is important here is that while I am not the first to notice the three criteria, my work is unique in trying to bring them together. For example, Katsafanas (2011) rightly captures the critical and historical criteria, and Reginster (2021), the psychological and the critical. Yet, there is room for an account that holds all three, of which I offer the preliminary outlines. See my "Concerning the Psychological Type of the Redeemer" (2022).

5. With the proliferation of "genealogical work" (such as Ben-Moshe 2020; Craig 2007; Davis et al. 2022; Erlenbusch-Anderson 2019; Koopman 2013; McWhorter 2009; Srinivasan 2019; or Tremain 2017), I think it is useful to specify that I am in the business of reconstituting Nietzsche's use in particular, which I shall claim does indeed draw on such psychological categories and, for that very reason, is of value to contemporary emancipatory political movements.

6. The objection is plain and is offered by Bernard Williams: Nietzsche traces "a type of individual psychological reaction," so any emphasis on the social-political surroundings is misplaced (2002, 37).

7. Including myself, Merrick 2016; Merrick 2018. I go some way toward redressing that imbalance in my some of my more recent work, Merrick 2021 and Merrick 2022.

8. Here I, like many others, specify Nietzsche's target as Judeo-Christian morality and its secular, largely ascetic, manifestations. See Leiter 2002; Reginster 2021; Janaway 2007; and Robertson 2020.

9. Clark and Dudrick (2012) offer a very helpful reconstruction of what they term "the faith in oppositions of values" (FOV) that runs along these lines.

10. At times Nietzsche questions whether those "new psychologists" can completely free themselves from the trappings of traditional morality. Consider, for example, that in *Beyond Good and Evil*, he writes: "A genuine physio-psychology has to contend with unconscious resistances in the heart of the researcher, it has 'the heart' against it" (*BGE* 23). And, in *On the Genealogy of Morality*, he suggests: "But you will have already understood me:—surely reason enough, do you not think, all in all, why we psychologists of today cannot get rid of a certain mistrust *towards ourselves*? . . . Probably we, too, are still 'too good' for our trade, probably we, too, are still the victims, the prey, the sick of this contemporary taste for moralization, much as we feel contempt towards it,—it probably infects *us* as well. What warning did that diplomat give when he spoke to his peers? 'Above all, gentlemen, we

must mistrust our first impulses!' he said, '*they are nearly always good.*'. . . Every psychologist ought to speak to his peers like that today" (*GM* III:20). Hence, the interpretive question of whether Nietzsche is successful in unmooring his account from moral prejudice is still open.

11. My account, as will already be apparent, differs from others on offer in the secondary literature. Christian Emden has argued, for instance, that "what [Nietzsche] had in mind [in specificizing psychology in this way] was a 'genuine physio-psychology,' that is a morphology of mental forms and intellectual configurations, which is already linked to the material world since it is embedded in the body" (2014, 40). My reconstruction differs insofar as I argue that Nietzsche is keen to make sense of not simply "mental forms and intellectual configurations"—our cognitive lives—as Emden has it, but of our affective lives as well.

12. An objection may be made that the will to power has been given undue attention in Nietzsche studies (Alfano 2019, 26–27). Indeed, Mark Alfano draws on his synoptic quantitative digital humanities approach to argue just that, making the quantitative claim "that the more Nietzsche talks about something, the more he cares about it, and the more we interpreters should pay attention to it" (2019, 4). Even if we may wish to concede (and I'm not sure we ought to make such concessions) to Alfano's argument, we can nevertheless maintain that the will to power is an important explanatory concept regardless of the principle of prevalence.

13. Reginster 2006, 131–32. Ian Dunkle has gone some way toward supplementing this account with the idea of the motivation to grow, which I take to be consistent with what I claim in this section (2020).

14. See, for example, Reginster 2006, 131; Katsafanas 2016, 249.

15. For a discussion of will to power and the project of reevaluation, see Katsafanas 2016.

16. Reginster 2006, 132.

17. Nussbaum 2012, 340.

18. Nussbaum 2012, 340.

19. Reginster 1997, 285.

20. Merrick 2021, 9.

21. Williams 2002, 37–38.

22. Simon May presents an example of an alternative interpretation in the section of his book entitled "'Master' and 'Slave' as Typology Rather Than History," where he claims that "Nietzsche's account of masters and slaves is more interesting as a typology of drives rather than as an account of some original type of person or society" (1999, 51).

23. Similar claims are made elsewhere. In *The Gay Science*, for example, Nietzsche goes so far as to conjecture that "consciousness actually belongs not to man's existence as an individual but rather to the community- and herd-aspects of his nature" (*GS* 354).

24. Contra May 1999; Reginster 2021; Williams 2002.

25. See, for instance, Brown 2001; McWhorter 2009; Scott 2006; Tremain 2017.

26. See, for example, Ben-Moshe 2020; Erlenbusch-Anderson 2018; Williams 2002.

27. hooks 2006, 248.

28. Koopman 2013, 60. See Allen 2016 for a similar account of problematization.

29. hooks 2006, 248.

30. Davis et al. 2022, xiii.

31. Davis et al. 2022, xiii.

32. By contrast, Kaitlyn Creasy (this volume) neatly demonstrates how sexist oppression disempowers women at the level of their emotional lives. In other words, Creasy goes some way toward showing how systems of domination shape and form our affective lives.

## References

Alfano, Mark. 2019. *Nietzsche's Moral Psychology*. Cambridge: Cambridge University Press.

Allen, Amy. 2016. *The End of Progress: Decolonizing the Normative Foundations of Critical Theory*. New York: Columbia University Press.

Ben-Moshe, Liat. 2020. *Decarcerating Disability: Deinstitutionalization and Prison Abolition*. Minneapolis: University of Minnesota Press.

Brown, Wendy. 2001. *Politics out of History*. Princeton, NJ: Princeton University Press.

Clark, Maudemarie, and David Dudrick. 2012. *The Soul of Nietzsche's "Beyond Good and Evil."* Cambridge: Cambridge University Press.

Craig, Edward. 2007. "Genealogies and the State of Nature." In *Bernard Williams*, edited by Alan Thomas, 181–200. Cambridge: Cambridge University Press.

Davis, Angela Y., Gina Dent, Erica R Meiners, and Beth E. Richie. 2022. *Abolition. Feminism. Now.* Chicago: Haymarket Books.

Dunkle, Ian. 2020. "On the Normativity of Nietzsche's Will to Power." *Journal of Nietzsche Studies* 51, no. 2: 181–211.

Emden, Christian J. 2014.*Nietzsche's Naturalism: Philosophy and the Life Sciences in the Nineteenth Century*. Cambridge: Cambridge University Press.

Erlenbusch-Anderson, Verena. 2018. *Genealogies of Terrorism: Revolution, State Violence, Empire*. New York: Columbia University Press.

hooks, bell. 2006. *Outlaw Culture: Resisting Representation*. New York: Routledge.

Janaway, Christopher. 2007. *Beyond Selflessness: Reading Nietzsche's Genealogy*. Oxford: Oxford University Press.

Katsafanas, Paul. 2016. *The Nietzschean Self: Moral Psychology, Agency, and the Unconscious*. Oxford: Oxford University Press.

Koopman, Colin. 2013. *Genealogy as Critique: Foucault and the Problems of Modernity.* Bloomington: Indiana University Press.
Leiter, Brian. 2002. *Nietzsche on Morality.* London: Routledge.
May, Simon. 1999. *Nietzsche's Ethics and His War on "Morality."* Oxford: Oxford University Press.
McWhorter, Ladelle. 2009. *Racism and Sexual Oppression in Anglo-America: A Genealogy.* Bloomington: Indiana University Press.
Merrick, Allison. 2016. "Of Genealogy and Transcendent Critique." *Journal of Nietzsche Studies* 47, no. 2: 228–37.
———. 2018. "'We Need a Critique of Moral Values': Regarding Genealogy and Normativity." In *The Nietzschean Mind*, edited by Paul Katsafanas, 70–82. London: Routledge.
———. 2021."Knowing Ourselves: Nietzsche, the Practice of Genealogy, and the Aims of Philosophy." *Genealogy* 5, no. 2: 41.
———. 2022."Concerning the Psychological Type of the Redeemer: Nietzsche on the Methods of Philosophy." *European Journal of Philosophy* 31, no. 1: 151–62. https://doi.org/10.1111/ejop.12774.
Nietzsche, Friedrich. 1967. *On the Genealogy of Morals* and *Ecce Homo*. Translated by Walter Kaufmann. New York: Vintage Books.
———. 1974. *The Gay Science*. Translated by Walter Kaufmann. New York: Vintage Books.
———. 1989. *Beyond Good and Evil*. Translated by Walter Kaufmann. New York: Vintage Books.
———. 1990. *Twilight of the Idols* and *The Antichrist*. Translated by R. J. Hollingdale. New York: Penguin Books.
———. 1997. *Daybreak: Thoughts on the Prejudices of Morality*. Translated by R. J. Hollingdale. Cambridge: Cambridge University Press.
Nussbaum, Martha. 2012. "Who Is the Happy Warrior? Philosophy, Happiness Research, and Public Policy." *International Review of Economics* 59: 335–61.
Reginster, Bernard. 1997. "Nietzsche on Ressentiment and Valuation." *Philosophy and Phenomenological Research* 57, no. 2: 281–305.
———. 2006. *The Affirmation of Life: Nietzsche on Overcoming Nihilism*. Cambridge, MA: Harvard University Press.
———. 2013. "The Psychology of Christian Morality: Will to Power as Will to Nothingness." In *The Oxford Handbook of Nietzsche*, edited by Ken Gemes and John Richardson, 701–26. New York: Oxford University Press.
———. 2021. *The Will to Nothingness: An Essay on Nietzsche's "On the Genealogy of Morality."* Oxford: Oxford University Press.
Robertson, Simon. 2020. *Nietzsche and Contemporary Ethics*. Oxford: Oxford University Press.
Scott, Jacqueline. 2006. "The Price of the Ticket: A Genealogy and Revaluation of Race." In *Critical Affinities: Nietzsche and African American Thought*, edited

by Jacqueline Scott and A. Todd Franklin, 149–71. Albany: State University of New York Press.
Srinivasan, Amia. 2019. "Genealogy, Epistemology and Worldmaking." *Proceedings of the Aristotelian Society* 119, no. 2: 127–56.
Tremain, Shelley. 2017. *Foucault and Feminist Philosophy of Disability.* Ann Arbor: University of Michigan Press.
Williams, Bernard. 2002. *Truth and Truthfulness: An Essay in Genealogy.* Princeton, NJ: Princeton University Press.

5

# Perspectivism, World-Traveling, and the Multiplicitous Self

## Rereading Nietzsche through Latinx Decolonial Feminist Philosophy

Rebecca A. Longtin

Nietzsche's perspectivism can be a powerful tool for contemporary social and political debates about identity. In general, perspectivism is a philosophical method that roots knowledge in concrete embodied standpoints and their socio-political-cultural contexts. It does not require one unified viewpoint but instead shifts between different perspectives to challenge universal frameworks and dogmatic hegemonies. In Nietzsche's philosophy, perspectivism serves an affective and interpretative role. Our perspectives are flexible and changing because they are grounded in the needs and drives of life, which are rooted in particular contexts and contingent rather than fixed. As a result, this approach introduces a concept of the self that resists rigid or essentialist categories of identity. When read through Latinx decolonial feminist philosophy, Nietzsche's perspectivism can offer tools for contemporary liberatory political theory.[1]

The liberatory potential of Nietzsche's perspectivism becomes more vivid when applied to questions of identity and selfhood in Latinx decolonial feminist theory.[2] Like Nietzsche, Latinx decolonial philosophers question the dominant concepts and categories used to describe identity and explain the need for new interpretative frameworks that can overcome oppressive hierarchies. In "Feminist Border Theory" Elena Ruíz describes the marginalization of Latin Americans as not simply political but also interpretative. She explains how European colonization uprooted indigenous interpretative traditions to forcibly transplant foreign gendered, ethnic, and racial categories.[3] As a result, colonization continues to impact Latin American philosophy through "a sense of inarticulacy"—that is, "the loss of prior social contexts and interpretive alternatives" that make it possible to formulate concepts of identity and selfhood.[4] For Ruíz, the "need to theorize identity based on new social, historical, and epistemic realities thus marks the starting point of Latin American social and cultural theory in general."[5] She notes that these interpretative practices require a more complex concept of the self than the autonomous modern subject and entail a concept of the self as multiplicitous or hybrid.[6] At the same time, many Latin American philosophers throw into relief the difficulty of conceptualizing identity in a way that does justice to marginalized lived experiences without reifying social, racial, and ethnic categories. Omar Rivera explains that one challenge of Latin American philosophy involves the "difficulty of envisioning liberatory programs from the critical positionality of the oppressed without essentializing their identities and those of other groups."[7] Rivera describes Latin American philosophy as encountering a variety of delimitations due to its commitments. Theorizing from a concrete situation requires resistance to the universalizing tendencies of philosophy and a rejection of redemptive metanarratives. In this sense, Latin American philosophy of liberation centers the issue of identity while questioning available concepts, categories, and methods for understanding it. This double commitment requires thinking along the limits or borders of identity,[8] a practice that—following the work of Ofelia Schutte—I will argue requires understanding how to shift between and weave together multiple theoretic, interpretative, and experiential perspectives.

In the seminal book *Cultural Identity and Social Liberation in Latin American Thought*, Schutte describes her philosophical method as "perspectival critical analysis," an epistemological practice that she states is "closest to Nietzsche's idea of perspectivism."[9] For Schutte, perspectival critical analysis is interpretative and nondogmatic. It allows her to distinguish between different theoretical positions on identity while acknowledging her account is not final or absolute.[10] For Schutte, perspectival critical analysis also challenges the modern concept of the self as "an independent, individual subject who is the bearer of various rights and responsibilities in the sociopolitical arena."[11] In contrast to the modern autonomous subject, Schutte understands the identity of the self to be "process-oriented and transformative."[12] While Schutte's use of Nietzsche has been critiqued as contradictory to her feminist and postcolonial projects,[13] her work draws out the social and political applications of Nietzsche's philosophy beyond the possibilities that he could envision during his own time.

This chapter expands on the uses and value of Nietzschean perspectivism. Drawing from Schutte's work, I will highlight resonances between Nietzsche, Gloria Anzaldúa, and María Lugones to recontextualize Nietzsche's perspectivism in relation to Latinx decolonial feminist philosophy. In particular, the concepts of world-traveling and the multiplicitous self as developed by Anzaldúa and Lugones provide new possibilities for interpreting Nietzsche's perspectivism as a philosophical project with liberatory potential. The first section will outline Nietzsche's perspectivism as a method of affective interpretation that, like Anzaldúa and Lugones, emphasizes the significance of concrete, lived perspectives and socio-cultural contexts. The next section connects Nietzsche's praise of perspective-shifting to Lugones's world-traveling and Anzaldúa's border thinking. The final section explains how perspectivism introduces a decentered, multiplicitous concept of the self in Nietzsche, Lugones, and Anzaldúa. The conclusion describes how perspective-shifting allows life-affirming transformations for individuals and communities.

## Nietzsche's Perspectivism as Affective Interpretation

There are many threads to Nietzsche's perspectivism. He discusses perspective explicitly in his middle (*HH, D, GS*) and late writings (*BGE, GM, TI, A,* and *EH*), as well as in the *Nachlass*, and scholars have interpreted his theory and use of perspective in a variety of ways—as perceptual, affective, epistemic, semantic, metaphysical, practical, artistic, and aretaic.[14] Here I will focus on how Nietzsche uses perspective as affective interpretation in *Beyond Good and Evil* and *On the Genealogy of Morals* to question dogmatism and reinterpret values in relation to life.

In "Nietzsche's Affective Perspectivism as a Philosophical Methodology," Mark Alfano uses digital mapping techniques to lay out Nietzsche's usage of perspective (*Perspektive*) and perspectivism (*Perspektivismus*) across his published and authorized texts. Through this digital map, Alfano demonstrates that Nietzsche's discussions of perspective occur most frequently in relation to *life* and second most frequently in relation to *value*. Nietzsche also continually connects perspective to instincts and emotions such as fear, contempt, doubt, and resentment, as well as virtues like curiosity, courage, and justice. These connections suggest that Nietzsche's concept of perspective is affective and evaluative—rather than visual or perceptual—and that perspectivism is integral to Nietzsche's reevaluation of philosophy, morality, and culture.

For Nietzsche, all ideas and values are formed from concrete, lived perspectives—not a universal or absolute position. In *On the Genealogy of Morals*, he states, "There is *only* a perspective seeing, *only* a perspective 'knowing'" (*GM* III:12). Nietzsche calls "objectivity" or "contemplation without interest" a "nonsensical absurdity" and warns us to be "on guard against the dangerous old conceptual fiction that posited a 'pure, will-less, painless, timeless knowing subject'" and "the snares of such contradictory concepts as 'pure reason,' 'absolute spirituality,' 'knowledge in itself'" (*GM* III:12). For Nietzsche, these concepts of the pure subject of knowledge are absurd insofar as they "always demand that we should think of an eye that is completely unthinkable, an eye turned in no particular direction" (*GM* III:12). There is no disembodied eye, no pure subject of knowledge. The eye sees from a given position and, moreover, is pointed in a direction by interest, desire, or will. Like standpoint epistemology,[15] Nietzsche recognizes there is no objective view from nowhere. Knowledge is produced from specific standpoints and socio-cultural contexts. It is interpretative. Nietzsche asserts that it is through "active and interpreting forces" alone that "seeing becomes *something*" (*GM* III:12). Nietzsche rejects the concept of a disinterested, contemplative vantage point for theory and emphasizes the way perspective forms interpretations from multiple interests, feelings, and desires. Part of Nietzsche's work as a genealogist is to show how values that we consider to be pure and rational have a basis in our physiological needs and desires. Nietzsche's perspectivism thus challenges the binary between reason and affect.[16]

For Nietzsche, trying to rid ourselves of affects in order to be more "objective" actually undermines knowledge. The affects are a plurality of relational life forces that dynamically respond to physiological needs within a concrete situation and context. Affects are relational and drive the organism either toward or against something (*GM* III:12). For Nietzsche, the separation of affects and reason in Western philosophy demonstrates why philosophers have struggled with self-knowledge. "We are unknown to ourselves, we men of knowledge—and with good reason. We have never sought ourselves—how could it happen that we should ever *find* ourselves?" (*GM* P:1). For Nietzsche, there is no perception or knowledge without affective interpretation, or perspective. The effort to find a disimpassioned point of view weakens the power of the intellect and our ability to understand life and ourselves.

Moreover, Nietzsche's perspectivism asserts the value of taking on multiple ways of seeing. Nietzsche declares that "the *more* affects we allow to speak about one thing, the *more* eyes, different eyes, we can use to observe one thing, the more complete will our 'concept' of this thing, our 'objectivity' be" (*GM* III:12). We arrive at a more complete understanding by having multiple perspectives. However, it is not simply the multiplicity of perspectives that matters here—it is their mobility, their ability to change and transform. Perspective, as Alfano notes, is deeply connected to Nietzsche's concept of life. In *Beyond Good and Evil*, Nietzsche describes perspective as "the basic condition of all life" (*BGE* "Preface"). Meaning and interpretation reflect the needs and drives of our lives, which are circumstantial and subjective, not universal and unchanging. Life has no fixed nature but instead evolves to meet different challenges and situations posed by a given time and place. As Stegmaier writes, " 'Life' in the philosophical understanding thwarts in its indissoluble contingency and temporality all the attempts to organize it permanently. It is always different from what one can grasp of it; literally, 'life' cannot be 'established' or 'fixated.' "[17] For this reason, a value that is life-affirming will look different across different times and places—it is situational and thoroughly contingent. Nietzsche's *Genealogy of Morals* asserts that "whatever exists, having somehow come into being, is again and again reinterpreted to new ends, taken over, transformed, and redirected by some power superior to it; all events in the organic world are a subduing, a becoming master, and all subduing and becoming master involves a fresh interpretation, an adjustment through which any previous 'meaning' and 'purpose' are necessarily obscured or obliterated" (*GM* II:11). In this sense, all life is perspectival: a process of continual interpretation and reinterpretation in relation to physiological needs.

In *Beyond Nihilism: Nietzsche Without Masks*, Schutte describes the purpose of Nietzsche's perspectival approach as "exposing all 'life-denying' values for what they are, no matter how sacred or well established these may be within a culture" and freeing "the interpretation of life from all forms of ascetic, dualistic, and alienated conceptions of existence."[18] Shifting between multiple perspectives uproots unhealthy dogmatic ideas and values to lay ground for new, healthier ones.

Nietzsche's perspectivism allows the reexamination of long-standing philosophical, ethical, and cultural assumptions in ways that can contribute to feminist and decolonial philosophy. Nietzsche's perspectivism recognizes the way that social practices, culture, and power shape knowledge and values. Approaching perspective as affective interpretation dethrones universalism and questions objectivity in ways that break down hegemonies of knowledge and open up the possibility of creating new ways of thinking. Like Nietzsche, feminist decolonial philosophers also challenge the Western philosophical tradition—including universalism, the opposition between reason and emotion, and mind-body, subject-object, and self-other binaries—and imagine new possibilities. As C. Heike Schotten describes, "both Nietzsche and revolutionary feminism offer what we might call a thoroughgoing critique of everything existing."[19] There is now a large body of scholarship in feminist philosophy and decolonial theory that adopts aspects of Nietzsche's philosophy to critique patriarchal values and colonial frameworks of thinking.[20]

At the same time, Nietzsche's philosophy is limited in its ability to shift perspective because of his attachment to strength as a value and weakness as a lowly state to be overcome. For Schutte, Nietzsche's philosophy cannot overcome nihilism and affirm life because it remains tied to the duality of strength and weakness.[21] Schutte notes two different concepts of will to power in Nietzsche's philosophy: "In one case, power is used in the sense of domination, whereas in the other it is used in the sense of recurring energy."[22] The second concept of will is creative, transformative, and generative in a way that holds promise for overcoming nihilistic dualisms and oppressive binaries. The first concept of will upholds oppressive binaries because it emphasizes strength and encourages dominating the weak and mastering others. In *Beyond Good and Evil*, Nietzsche interprets life as "essentially appropriation, injury, overpowering of what is alien and weaker; suppression, hardness, imposition of one's own forms, incorporation and at least, at its mildest, exploitation" (*BGE* 259). In *Genealogy of Morals*, Nietzsche describes will to power—"the most life-affirming drive"—as a force that subdues others (*GM* III:18). With this concept of life, Nietzsche frequently presents creative growth and transformation in conflict with and at the expense of others.[23] Complicated further by his sometimes misogynistic, xenophobic, anti-Semitic, and anti-Black claims,[24] this binary of strength and weakness demonstrates a willful and arrogant exclusion of perspectives historically associated with dependency and marginalized by those who controlled the means of knowledge production.

In this sense, Nietzsche's perspectivism requires a more radical reworking of perspective. We can find resources for such a reworking in the recent insights of Latinx decolonial feminist philosophy. While Nietzsche articulates how various standpoints have been constructed by value systems and power relations, his version of perspectivism can be deepened and broadened through the phenomena contemporary feminist border thinkers have illuminated through their understanding of perception, power, and identity.

## World-Traveling, Border Thinking, and Relational Perspectivism

Lugones's concept of world-traveling and Anzaldúa's concept of *mestiza consciousness* examine how cultural perspectives shape our worlds and sense of self and offer flexible, relational, and nonhierarchal approaches to shifting between different perspectives.

Lugones develops her notion of playful world-traveling in response to Marilyn Frye's distinction between arrogant perception and loving perception. Like Nietzsche, Frye's essay "In and Out of Harm's Way: Arrogance and Love" investigates optics and aims to provide "general correctives to poor vision."[25] Unlike Nietzsche, Frye defines poor vision as arrogant perception, a patriarchal, white/Anglo worldview that orders everything according to a hierarchical teleology in which man is the telos: "With this world view, men see with arrogant eyes which organize everything seen with reference to themselves and their own interests."[26] Frye explains the role arrogant perception plays in epistemic injustice and systemic oppression through its coercion of objects of perception and then introduces loving perception as its antidote. Whereas the arrogant eye "creates in the space about him a vacuum mold into which the other is sucked and held," the loving eye is attentive and allows the other to be independent.[27] Unlike the arrogant eye, the loving eye recognizes that "one must consult something other than one's own will and interests and feels and imaginations . . . One must look and listen and check and question."[28] Rather than assimilating or simplifying the other, loving perception "knows the complexity of the other as something which will forever present new things to be known."[29] Arrogant perception thus forms an exclusive, unyielding, hierarchical perspective that strives to maintain its position of power by reifying others, while loving perception is responsive to others and open in its mode of creating relations. In relation to Nietzsche's perspectivism, we can see how arrogant perception lacks the ability to shift its perspective, especially in relation to others, while loving perception would allow for movement between many views.

The challenges and stakes of loving perception become more vivid in Lugones's thought. In "Playfulness, 'World'-Travelling, and Loving Perception," Lugones takes up the task of dismantling the structures of arrogant perception by considering how racial and cultural boundaries limit loving perception. As Lugones notes, Frye's essay ignores the role colonialism plays in forming arrogant perception's failure of identification and failure of love. In particular, Lugones explains how often white/Anglo women exercise arrogant perception on women of color.[30] By contrast, working intersectionally and cross-culturally, Lugones reframes loving perception as "playful 'world'-travelling." Lugones describes a *world* not as a collection of things, a definitive place, or a worldview but as a "construction of life."[31] People are constructed differently by different worlds such that moving between worlds changes the construction of self. For this reason, Lugones describes traveling as the "shift from being one person to being a different person."[32] For Lugones, playfulness allows the possibility of traveling and is the antidote to arrogance because "one cannot cross the boundaries with it. One needs to give up such an attitude if one wants to travel."[33] Lugones thus reinterprets loving perception as being able to shift one's self-identity in a way that allows for identification with others.

Lugones's description of loving perception as world-traveling presents a radically intersubjective sense of the self by describing its fluidity between worlds.[34] While Frye emphasizes that the loving eye does *not* see "with the other's eye instead of her own."[35] Lugones describes loving perception as entering into someone else's world. Frye wants to maintain the independence and autonomy of subjects, but for Lugones, "I am incomplete and unreal without other women. I am profoundly dependent on others without having to be their subordinate."[36] Lugones's account of loving perception thus requires a more relational and interdependent concept of the self. Her concept of world-traveling highlights the way that others shape how we see the world and understand ourselves, which lends itself to a more intersubjective and relational framework for shifting perspective than Nietzsche's perspectivism, which often excludes or dominates the other.[37]

Perspective-shifting is also important for Anzaldúa's feminist border thought (*pensamiento fronteriza feminista*). Anzaldúa thinks through borders as both geopolitical spaces that divide territories and psychic spaces, or perspectives, from marginal positions of exclusion. She examines the relationship between these different meanings of borders in *mestiza consciousness*—the viewpoint of mixed-race (*mestiza*) Chicana women who find themselves between cultures and between worlds.[38] For Anzaldúa, *la mestiza* sees the world through multiple perspectives at once and since "we perceive the version of reality that our culture communicates," she is pulled between different points of view simultaneously.[39] Being American, Mexican, and indigenous brings together conflicting cultures and perspectives, particularly between the oppressor and oppressed, the colonizer and colonized. When multiple cultural perspectives come together—especially between oppositional positions like oppressor and oppressed—it causes *un choque*, or "cultural collision."[40] She describes this plurality as a "clash of voices" with opposing messages that result in "mental and emotional states of perplexity," insecurity, and indecisiveness.[41] For this reason, *la mestiza* experiences perspectivism as a struggle: "Cradled in one culture, sandwiched between two cultures, straddling all three cultures and their value systems, *la mestiza* undergoes a struggle of flesh, a struggle of borders, an inner war."[42]

For Anzaldúa, it is important that these multiple perspectives maintain their tension and do not resolve into a coherent unity. She emphasizes the importance of *divergent* thinking that, unlike the *convergent* thinking of traditional Western philosophy, does not try to resolve conflicting points of view and instead allows ambiguities and contradictions: "Rigidity means death. Only by remaining flexible is she able to stretch the psyche horizontally and vertically. *La mestiza* constantly has to shift out of habitual formations; from convergent thinking, analytical reasoning that tends to use rationality to move toward a single goal (a Western mode), to divergent thinking, characterized by movement away from set patterns and goals and toward a more whole perspective, one that includes rather than excludes."[43] Convergent thinking erases differences and conflict to bring everything into a unified whole. It frames everything in black and white, as either/or. In doing so, it silences and marginalizes anything that does not fit within its framework. This type of thinking is common to universalism and other tools of oppression that have been used in Europe's colonization of Latin America. By contrast, divergent thinking provides complex, hybrid categories and nonhierarchical ways of relating.[44] For Anzaldúa, divergent thinking offers a broader, more inclusive perspective that can embrace contradictions and ambiguities, rather than reducing everything to a unified whole.

*La mestiza* has a more highly attuned capacity to see the world from many perspectives than those who occupy dominant positions because it is often demanded of them. In *Borderlands/La Frontera*, Anzaldúa describes *la facultad*, a shift in perception that outsiders experience in liminal spaces or places where they do not feel a sense of safety or belonging—for example, hyperawareness of danger in one's environment or a heightened ability to detect potential violence in someone's body language. While everyone has this ability to see the everyday differently, those who are in between worlds feel it more acutely and develop this awareness, sometimes unknowingly, to survive. Yet this shift in perception is more than a survival instinct—it is a mode of revealing the world. Anzaldúa describes it as a heightened sensitivity that deepens perception, making it possible to see through the surface of things. *La facultad* allows one "to see in surface phenomena the meaning of deeper realities, to see the deep structure below the surface."[45] It is an altered state of perception that "causes a break in one's defenses and resistance," "takes one from one's habitual grounding," and "causes the depths to open up."[46] Being in between worlds makes *la mestiza* vulnerable to reversals of perspective. However, it is this vulnerability that creates a new, deeper understanding of the world.

The use of multiple perspectives in Latinx decolonial feminist thought is about more than questioning objective concept-formation and examining how knowledge is situated in concrete socio-cultural contexts. It is also about forming a new understanding of the self as multiple. How one sees the world and how one sees oneself are intimately tied together, and for *la mestiza* both are both constantly undone, redone, shifted, and reinterpreted. The next section will explain how perspectivism calls for a different concept of the self than the modern subject.

## Perspective and the Multiplicitous Self

Perspectivism not only shatters the idea that there is one ideal vantage point that can establish objective truth; it also challenges the unity of the subject. This section will explain how Nietzsche, Anzaldúa, and Lugones challenge the modern concept of the self through perspectival interpretative frameworks that decenter and fracture subjectivity to provide a more complex, multiplicitous, and transformative concept of the self. Each philosopher employs perspective to challenge the modern concept of the self as a unified, rational agent or *res cogitans* that can stand apart from the world and look on it through disinterested contemplation.

For Nietzsche, perspectivism is not simply the idea that there are many possible viewpoints, but also that viewpoints are formed from multiple drives (*Triebe*), affects (*Affekte*), instincts (*Instinkte*), feelings (*Gefühlen*), and desires (*Begierden*). Perspectivism allows many ways of seeing, thinking, and feeling, and more importantly, resists the modern concept of subjectivity as a pure, autonomous intellect. For Descartes, the subject is a thinking thing (*res cogitans*), the "I think"—an ego that stands apart from the world and reasons from their subjective experiences with the goal of achieving objectivity. For Kant, the self is a transcendental ego, a necessary reference point for experience that forms its unity and coherence. In both cases, the subject serves as the unified center of experience and knowledge. Nietzsche challenges this concept of the subject and questions the unity and identity of the self. In *Genealogy of Morals*, he explains that "there is no such substratum; there is no 'being' behind doing, effecting, becoming; 'the doer' is merely a fiction added to the deed—the deed is everything" (*GM* I:13). For Nietzsche, this fiction comes from grammar, which requires a subject-verb structure that privileges the subject as the source of the action. The philosophical assumption that there must be a well-defined subject behind an action is merely "a seduction of language" (*GM* I:13). As Christoph Cox describes, "Nietzsche comes to regard the self as merely a grammatical habit that supports a moral fiction."[47] In *Beyond Good and Evil*, Nietzsche rejects the very idea of a substantive, pre-given subject, which he says is simply a newer, more sophisticated version of the soul hypothesis (*BGE* 12). He repudiates the idea of "soul atomism," which he describes as the belief in a "soul as something indestructible, eternal, indivisible, as a monad, as an *atomon*" (*BGE* 12). He states that the idea of the "I" as a "synthetic concept" is a product of thought rather than its cause, and he uses the term "subject-multiplicity" instead (*BGE* 19, 12). As Cox notes, Nietzsche reverses the way we typically think of the subject by "arguing that what is primary are actions, deeds, accidents, and becomings, rather than subjects, doers, substances, or beings."[48]

The perspectival self is a plurality without a center. Scholars such as Walter Brogan and João Constâncio have referred to this aspect of Nietzsche's philosophy as *decentered subjectivity*, a fractured and multiple sense of the self that rejects modern, metaphysical concepts of the subject because it that does not form a unified, coherent whole.[49] To describe Nietzsche's decentered subjectivity, Brogan points toward Nietzsche's fragmentary style of writing—aphorisms and contradictions that can be difficult to reconcile—as well as his identification with Dionysius, the twice-born god who was dismembered and reconstituted and who represents transgression, disruption, and excesses that break through order.[50] Along similar lines, Constâncio uses the phrase *decentered subjectivity* to describe the lack of center within Nietzsche's "subject-multiplicity," which is characterized by fragmentation, disintegration, and contradictoriness. Examining Nietzsche's critiques of the modern subject in *Beyond Good and Evil* and *The Gay Science*, Constâncio emphasizes how Nietzsche questions "immediate certainties" about consciousness and instead describes it in terms of the herd or species—both of which challenge subjectivity that is centered on the "I" (*BGE* 16; *GS* 354). Yet rather than being an impediment to action, this decentered, multiplicitous self is connected to the drives and instincts that are a part of life.

Like life, the self is a continual process of becoming. In *Thus Spoke Zarathustra*, Nietzsche presents the idea that the self must continually give birth to itself: "For the creator himself to be the child new-born he must also be willing to be the mother and endure the mother's pain. Truly, I have gone my way through a hundred souls and through a hundred cradles and birth-pangs" (*Z* II "On the Blissful Islands"). Self-becoming is not a passive process, but an activity.[51] As Nehamas reads Nietzsche, the self is a work of art that each person creates: "The unity of the self, which therefore also constitutes its identity, is not something given but something achieved, not a beginning but a goal."[52] Nietzsche's philosophy teaches us that the self is not given and instead must be constructed—a process frequently involving radical, disorienting transformations that break from what is comfortable and familiar. This concept of the self allows more radical transformations of perspective because it is fluid. Moreover, shifting one's perspective is not only necessary—it is a passionate, creative, and transformative activity. Perspectivism and the multiplicity of the self thus express what Nietzsche values: life-affirming transformations that expand one's horizons.

Like Nietzsche, Lugones and Anzaldúa present a comparatively decentered account of the self because they recognize how radically one transforms in traveling between different worlds. Lugones notes that she may enact some qualities, like playfulness, in one world but not in another. She is able to say that she is playful and that she is not playful—both are true of her identity. As Lugones explains, "I am different persons in different 'worlds' and can remember myself as both as I am in the other. I am a plurality of selves."[53] She is playful and she is not playful—she is and she is not—and this contradiction unearths the multiplicity of her identity. Lugones argues that traveling between worlds shows us "we are not fixed in particular constructions of ourselves" but instead "we are *open to self-construction*."[54] For Lugones, the capacity for self-construction allows us to see objects of arrogant perception not as victims but as "subjects, lively beings, resistors, constructors of visions even though in the mainstream construction they are animated only by the arrogant perceiver."[55] The capacity for self-construction shows that the self lacks a definitive nature or center in a way that allows creative resistance to oppression. Thus loving perception also recognizes the multiplicity of the self that, in line with Nietzsche, deconstructs the modern subject.

In *Borderlands/La Frontera* and "Geographies of the Self—Reimagining Identity," Anzaldúa explains the need for a plural sense of self that goes beyond the traditional categories of identity based on history, biology, and nationality. She writes, "Conventional, traditional identity labels are stuck in binaries, trapped in jaulas (cages) that limit the growth of our individual and collective lives. We need fresh terms and open-ended tags that portray us in all our complexities and potentialities."[56] Instead of these cages, Anzaldúa sees identity as expansive and "interconnected with its surroundings" like the "subterranean webs" of interconnected tree roots.[57] Anzaldúa describes identity as a web, something that "we weave (tejemos), and are woven into."[58] The sense of identity here is thoroughly relational. Anzaldúa's descriptions of the self emphasize how one can simultaneously have multiple identities (the new *mestiza*) and explore the meaning of crossing boundaries and occupying spaces that are in-between (*la nepantla*). Anzaldúa turns to those "dwelling in liminalities" who inhabit "the cracks between the worlds."[59] *Nepantlera* comes from the Nahuatl word *nepantla,* a border space. Anzaldúa describes *nepantilism* as "torn between ways."[60] She writes, "These tensions between extremes create cracks or tears in the membrane surrounding, protecting and containing the different cultures and their perspectives. Nepantla is the place where at once we are detached (separated) and attached (connected) to each of our several cultures."[61] The self, as understood through Anzaldúa's new *mestiza* and *nepantlera* is "a multiplicity that is transformational" with many identities that are woven together in complex ways.[62] Anzaldúa describes the *multiplicitous self* as constructing a unified sense of herself through *amasamiento,* or kneading the various parts of oneself together. "*Soy un amasamiento*, I am a kneading, of uniting and joining that not only has produced both a creature of darkness and a creature of light, but also a creature that questions the definitions of light and dark and gives them new meanings."[63] Indeed, everyone has multiple aspects of their identity that contradict and come together in complex ways, but the new *mestiza* experiences this plurality to a greater degree through the nuances of a multicultural heritage and through learning to navigate different spaces with different norms, practices, and expectations. As Mariana Ortega explains, *la nepantlera*, someone who crosses borders and travels between worlds, "constantly experiences ruptures in her everyday experiences that lead to a more thematic or reflective orientation toward activities."[64] Ortega explains that the marginalized and oppressed experience their multiplicity in a way that is *sharper* and *thicker*. The world-traveler's sense of self is continually built, undone, and rebuilt in traveling between worlds—a process that is full of anxiety and alienation, as well as creativity and openness, as some possibilities are opened and others are closed in ways that are not always within one's control. The new *mestiza* recognizes in her multiplicity both that she is a continual process of construction and that she must create herself within a world in relation to others.

Ortega's book *In-Between* brings Anzaldúa's work into conversation with the history of existential phenomenology to explain how Latina feminism opens up a new understanding of the self. As Ortega emphasizes, the multiplicitous self undermines subject-object duality and instead draws out the interweaving of the self and world. The qualities a person can exhibit, activities one can do, and relations one can build are all situational, which means the construction of the self is never done in isolation or on some transcendental plane outside of our concrete material, social, political conditions. Since situations continually change, Ortega describes the multiplicitous self as *flexible* and *mobile*, which for Ortega means "recognizing this self's decenteredness, or not having an *a priori* central identity."[65] Like Nietzsche, Ortega describes the self as lacking any a priori identity and instead as being radically open to self-transformation. But unlike Nietzsche, who uses the *Übermensch* as the ideal of self-construction, Latina feminist philosophers like Anzaldúa and Ortega consider the lived experiences of historically marginalized women to think through the concrete challenges and costs of such transformations. As Anzaldúa explains in *Luz en lo Oscuro*, "To be healed we must be dismembered, pulled apart. The healing occurs in disintegration, in the demotion of the ego as the self's only authority."[66]

In *Nos/Otras*, Andrea Pitts explains how across the history of both philosophy and political projects of nation-building, heterogeneity has been understood as chaos and something to be tamed. Multiplicity frustrates those who seek to "render the entirety of an otherwise ostensibly incongruous world into smooth layers of understanding and classification. In this way, multiplicity has appeared threatening and in need of order."[67] By contrast, Pitts and other decolonial Latinx feminist philosopher see multiplicity as "a constant and reassuring glimpse into the promise of the future."[68] Multiplicity expresses the flourishing of diverse forms of life. It emphasizes interdependencies. It acknowledges the complicated relationships people can have to places and histories. It recognizes the shared role we play in making meaning. For these reasons, Anzaldúa's relational concept of identity has played an important role in coalitional politics.[69]

The new *mestiza* not only helps us to consider the self as multiplicitous, flexible, and transformational, but also, as Ortega explains, "Through shifting and being able to see multiple views or perspectives and comparing them, *la nepantlera* is thus more capable of transformation, and of developing alternative interpretations that are key to forging a critical stance."[70] As Butler explains in *Undoing Gender*, Anzaldúa does more than show the social meaning of mediating between worlds. Rather, "[Anzaldúa's] point is more radical. She is asking us to stay at the edge of what we know, to put our own epistemological certainties into question, and through that risk and openness to another way of knowing and of living in the world to expand our capacity to imagine the human."[71] The new *mestiza* thus lives and embodies the ability to continually shift perspectives, which Nietzsche praises so highly.

In each of these accounts, the formation of the self becomes a complex, creative act, rather than a passive, natural, or teleological process to be taken for granted. There is no essential human nature. We are responsible for creating humanity.

## Perspectivism, Pluralism, and Liberation

In comparing Nietzsche, Lugones, and Anzaldúa, I attempt to weave a narrative of perspectivism that travels between worlds. One takeaway of the narrative I have constructed is the enduring significance of perspectivism, particularly if we want to theorize in intersectional ways that do justice to multiple standpoints and worldviews. Moreover, understanding the self beyond the binaries of traditional categories requires the ability to incorporate a variety of perspectives. It is a practice that lends itself not only to pluralism but also to a plural sense of the self. If Nietzsche's perspectivism is meant to be an expansive mode of questioning values and learning how to be human, it must learn to cross borders, weave together multiplicities, and stay open to other ways of seeing.[72]

## Notes

1. An earlier version of this paper appeared as an essay for the *Women in Philosophy* series on the *Blog of the American Philosophical Association*. It was written for a general audience and emphasizes the differences between Nietzsche, Anzaldúa, and Lugones more than their connections. Longtin 2021.

2. See Lugones 2010 for an explanation of decolonial feminism, which is distinct from feminist philosophy because it recognizes how European colonialism has shaped concepts of gender. Lugones states that "the coloniality of gender is still with us; it is what lies at the intersection of gender/class/race as central constructs of the capitalist world systems of power" (Lugones 2010, 746).

3. Ruíz 2011, 350.

4. Ruíz 2011, 350.

5. Ruíz 2011, 350.

6. Hybridity is important to Latin American theories of identity (Canclini 1995). Linda Alcoff describes Latinx as a hybrid race and ethnicity, or *ethnorace* (Alcoff 2000 and 2006).

7. Rivera 2019, 1.

8. *Border thinking*, as Ruíz describes, "can be very broadly understood as a socio-political perspective or organizing concept around which complex narratives of displacement associated with multi-ethnic identity, migratory life, and multicultural citizenship can be theorized" (Ruíz 2011, 351). She distinguishes between Mignolo's border thinking and Anzaldúa's feminist border thought, which I will discuss later in this chapter.

9. Schutte 1993, 5.

10. Schutte 1993, 5.

11. Schutte 1993, 5.

12. Schutte 1993, 6.

13. Alcoff argues that Schutte decontextualizes Nietzsche's metaphysical, epistemological, and metaphysical tools for purposes they were not intended to serve and questions whether it is possible to use the form of Nietzsche's thought without the content, which expresses misogynistic and colonial attitudes at certain times (Alcoff 2004).

14. The scholarship on Nietzsche's perspectivism takes a range of interpretative positions, especially in terms of the role perspective plays in Nietzsche's philosophy as a whole. Welshon describes perspectives as "regulative fictions" (Welshon 2009), Danto sees perspectivism as asserting an interest-relative account of truth (Danto 1965), Reginster explains perspectivism in relation to freedom of spirit (Reginster 2000), Janaway and Katsafanas offer different semantic interpretations (Janaway 2007; Katsfanas 2016), and Clark discusses it as an anti-foundationalist position (Clark 1990).

15. Feminist and decolonial philosophers both utilize standpoint epistemology to situate knowledge and point out marginalized perspectives.

16. See Creasy 2020 for a more thorough explanation of Nietzsche's concept of affects and their importance in his philosophy. See also Creasy (in this volume) "Sexism Is Exhausting: Nietzsche and the Affective Dynamics of Sexist Oppression."

17. Stegmaier 2015, 95.

18. Schutte 1984, 39.

19. Schotten 2006, 303.

20. See *Womanizing Nietzsche* (Oliver 1995), *Feminist Interpretations of Friedrich Nietzsche* (Oliver and Pearsall, 1998), and *Nietzsche, Feminism and Political Theory* (Patton 1993) for feminist interpretations and applications of Nietzsche's thought.

21. Schutte 1984, 193.

22. Schutte 1984, 76.

23. See Kaufman 1998 for a longer explanation of Schutte's distinction between two wills and its meaning for feminist philosophy.

24. When this concept of will to domination is considered alongside some of his comments about Africans, colonization, slavery, and cruelty, it can be difficult to imagine how his philosophical methods can bolster philosophical projects of liberation. Scholars debate the extent to which Nietzsche supported colonization and slavery. Bernasconi explains that Nietzsche's commentary on Africans can be read as racist without having an essentialist concept of race (Bernasconi 2017). Bamford situates Nietzsche's comments on colonialism in *Dawn* within his concern about the effects of industrialization on workers (Bamford 2014).

25. Frye 1983, 53.

26. Frye 1983, 67.

27. Frye 1983, 69.

28. Frye 1983, 75.

29. Frye 1983, 76.

30. Lugones 1987, 7.

31. Lugones 1987, 10.

32. Lugones 1987, 11.

33. Lugones 1987, 16.

34. Multiple thinkers have offered concerns with and critiques of Lugones's description of world-traveling. Bowman explains why world-traveling is not enough to overcome white ignorance and can lead to an attitude of tourism (Bowman 2020). A forthcoming paper by Shelbi Nahwilet Meissner provides an overview of different critiques and amendments to Lugones's description of world-traveling. See Shelbi Nahwilet Meissner, "'World-Traveling in Tule Canoes: Indigenous Philosophies of Language & An Ethic of Incommensurability." Forthcoming in *Hypatia*.

35. Frye 1983, 74.

36. Lugones 1987, 8.

37. Certain aspects of Nietzsche's philosophy suffer from arrogant perception. Kaufman notes that one of Nietzsche's concepts of will to power—the will to dominate—is hostile to alterity and otherness. This concept of the will emphasizes the need to dominate others in order to avoid atrophy and diffusion. She explains

116 | Rebecca A. Longtin

that the will to dominate "gains its vitality through sublimation and negation" and treats "an other as a mirror" in order to maintain the stability of the self. For this reason, "any genuine alterity threatens the self, which is constituted through this strategy. The self is hostile to epistemological pluralism and must constitute for itself a dominated and silenced other" (Kaufman 1998, 65). The self maintains its coherence and unity by resisting relating to others.

38. Anzaldúa's use of "mestiza" is not meant to essentialize race or ethnicity. Anzaldúa scholars often interpret her use of mestiza as a queer, feminist reworking of traditional cis-het masculine descriptions of mestizaje. As Andrea Pitts explains, "Mestizaje is more than a simple cultural or biological mixture, it is a claim, at an agential and ontological level, regarding the *locatedness* and boundaries of self and other, and between identification and othering" (Pitts 2021, 36). See Arrizón 2006; and Pitts 2021, 34–36.

39. Anzaldúa 1987, 78.
40. Anzaldúa 1987, 78.
41. Anzaldúa 1987, 78.
42. Anzaldúa 1987, 78.
43. Anzaldúa 1987, 79.

44. Schutte's perspectival analysis of Latin American cultural identity is an example of divergent thinking that demonstrates the issue with convergent thinking. She explains that "the standpoint of identity adopted here refers ultimately to a differential reality, not to a centrally regulated force. The 'identity' of which I speak here is not derived from a fixed origin, but is a result of multiple configurations always in the process of reorganizing and redefining themselves. In terms of liberatory theory, such identities-in-the-making result from a process of endangered or forgotten differences and bringing them to a public attention. This involves breaking through the silence imposed on some forms of thought and only subsequently trying to 'position' such differences within the general purview of the culture for the enrichment and benefit of all" (Schutte 1993, 15).

45. Anzaldúa 1987, 38.
46. Anzaldúa 1987, 39.
47. Cox 1997, 279.
48. Cox 1997, 280.

49. Brogan 1991; Constâncio 2015. Some Nietzsche scholars disagree with this interpretation of Nietzsche's concept of the self as fractured and multiple and see it as a temporary or undesirable state of existence that can be overcome. However, in the passages that point toward this possibility, Nietzsche reintroduces aristocratic or heroic values that emphasize domination, which makes this concept of the self less relevant for the purpose of this paper. Gemes suggests a troubling interpretation of Nietzsche's higher unity of the self: not everyone has the strength to achieve this unity and be counted as a "person" (Gemes 2001, 340–44). While this is not the only way to interpret Nietzsche's concept of self-creation, there is ample evidence that

it reasserts structures of domination. See Whitmire 2009; Thiele 1990; and Gemes 2001 for an account of the higher unity of the self in Nietzsche. See Kaufman 1998 for a feminist critique of Nietzsche's masculine heroism.
   50. Brogan 1991, 420, 428.
   51. See Homan's discussion of Nietzsche's concept of self-becoming in chap. 4, "Becoming Who We Are: A Conversation" (Homan 2020).
   52. Nehamas 1985, 182.
   53. Lugones 1987, 14.
   54. Lugones 1987, 16.
   55. Lugones 1987, 18.
   56. Anzaldúa 2015, 58.
   57. Anzaldúa 2015, 58.
   58. Anzaldúa 2015, 60.
   59. Anzaldúa 2015, 61.
   60. Anzaldúa 1987, 78.
   61. Anzaldúa 2015, 56.
   62. Anzaldúa 2009, 246.
   63. Anzaldúa 1987, 81.
   64. Ortega 2016, 50.
   65. Ortega 2016, 76–77.
   66. Anzaldúa 2015, 29.
   67. Pitts 2021, 1.
   68. Pitts 2021, 1.
   69. Pitts 2021, 20–23.
   70. Ortega 2016, 38.
   71. Butler 2004, 228.
   72. I am grateful for the feedback provided by Lauren Guilmette, Omar Rivera, Allison Merrick, Rebecca Bamford, and C. Heike Schotten on earlier drafts of this chapter.

# References

Alcoff, Linda Martín. 2000. "Is Latina/o Identity a Racial Identity?" In *Hispanics/Latinos in the United States: Ethnicity, Race, and Rights*, edited by Jorge J. E. Gracia and Pablo De Greiff, 23–44. New York: Routledge.
———. 2004. "Schutte's Nietzschean Postcolonial Politics." *Hypatia* 19: 144–56.
———. 2006. *Visible Identities: Race, Gender, and the Self*. Oxford: Oxford University Press.
Alfano, Mark. 2019. "Nietzsche's Affective Perspectivism as a Philosophical Methodology." In *Nietzsche's Metaphilosophy*, edited by Paul Loeb and Matthew Mayer, 127–45. Cambridge: Cambridge University Press.

Anzaldúa, Gloria. 1987. *Borderlands/La Frontera: The New Mestiza*. San Francisco: Aunt Lute Books.
———. 2009. "(Un)natural Bridges, (Un)safe Spaces." In *The Gloria Anzaldúa Reader*, ed. Ana Louise Keating. Durham, NC: Duke University Press.
———. 2015. *Light in the Dark / Luz en Lo Oscuro: Rewriting Identity, Spirituality, Reality*. Durham, NC: Duke University Press.
Arrizón, Alicia. 2006. *Queering Mestizaje: Transculturalism and Performance*. Ann Arbor: University of Michigan Press.
Bamford, Rebecca. 2014. "The Liberatory Limits of Nietzsche's Colonial Imagination in *Dawn* 206." In *Nietzsche as Political Philosopher*, edited by Barry Stocker and Manuel Knoll, 59–76. Berlin: De Gruyter.
Bernasconi, Robert. 2017. "Nietzsche as a Philosopher of Racialized Breeding." In *The Oxford Handbook of Philosophy and Race*, edited by Naomi Zack, 54–64. Oxford: Oxford University Press.
Bowman, Melanie. 2020. "Privileged Ignorance, 'World'-Traveling, and Epistemic Tourism." *Hypatia* 35: 475–89.
Brogan, Walter. 1991. "The Decentered Self: Nietzsche's Transgression of Metaphysical Subjectivity." *Southern Journal of Philosophy* 29.4: 419–30.
Butler, Judith. 2004. *Undoing Gender*. New York: Routledge.
Canclini, Nestor García. 1995. *Hybrid Cultures: Strategies of Entering and Leaving Modernity*. Minneapolis: University of Minnesota Press.
Clark, Maudemarie. 1990. *Nietzsche on Truth and Philosophy*. Cambridge: Cambridge University Press.
Constâncio, João. 2015. "Nietzsche on Decentered Subjectivity." In *Nietzsche and the Problem of Subjectivity*, edited by Branco and Constâncio, 279–316. Berlin: De Gruyter.
Cox, Christoph. 1997. "The 'Subject' of Nietzsche's Perspectivism." *Journal of the History of Philosophy* 35: 269–91.
Creasy, Kaitlyn. 2020. *The Problem of Affective Nihilism in Nietzsche: Thinking Differently, Feeling Differently*. New York: Palgrave Macmillan.
Frye, Marilyn. 1983. "In and Out of Harm's Way: Arrogance and Love." In *The Politics of Reality*, 52–83, New York: Crossings Press.
Gemes, Ken. 2001. "Postmodernism's Use and Abuse of Nietzsche." *Philosophy and Phenomenological Research* 62.2: 337–60.
Homan, Catherine. 2020. *A Hermeneutics of Poetic Education: The Play of the In-Between*. Lanham, MD: Lexington.
Janaway, Christopher. 2007. *Beyond Selflessness: Reading Nietzsche's Genealogy*. Oxford: Oxford University Press.
Katsafanas, Paul. 2016. *The Nietzschean Self: Moral Psychology, Agency, and the Unconscious*. Oxford: Oxford University Press.
Kaufman, Cynthia. 1998. "Knowledge as Masculine Heroism or Embodied Perception: Knowledge, Will, and Desire in Nietzsche." *Hypatia* 13: 63–87.

Kofman, Sarah. 1993. *Nietzsche and Metaphor*. Translated by Duncan Large. Stanford: Stanford University Press.
Longtin, Rebecca. 2021."Relational Perspectivism in Anzaldúa and Lugones Contra Nietzsche." *Blog of the American Philosophical Association*. https://blog.apaonline.org/2021/11/17/relational-perspectivism-in-anzaldua-and-lugones-contra-nietzsche/.
Lugones, María. 1987. "Playfulness, 'World'-Travelling, and Loving Perception." *Hypatia* 2: 3–19.
———. 2003. *Pilgrimages/Peregrinajes: Theorizing Coalition against Multiple Oppressions*. Lanham, MD: Rowman & Littlefield.
———. 2010. "Toward a Decolonial Feminism." *Hypatia* 25: 742–59.
Meissner, Shelbi Nahwilet. " 'World-Traveling in Tule Canoes: Indigenous Philosophies of Language & An Ethic of Incommensurability." Forthcoming in *Hypatia*.
Nehamas, Alexander. 1983. "Immanent and Transcendent Perspectivism in Nietzsche." *Nietzsche-Studien* 12: 473–90.
———. 1985. *Nietzsche: Life as Literature*. Cambridge, MA: Harvard University Press.
Nietzsche, Friedrich. 1961. *Thus Spoke Zarathustra: A Book for Everyone and No One*. Translated by R. J. Hollingdale. New York: Penguin Books.
———. 1966. *Beyond Good and Evil: A Prelude to a Philosophy of the Future*. Translated by Walter Kaufmann. New York: Random House.
———. 1989. *On the Genealogy of Morals and Ecce Homo*. Translated by Walter Kaufmann and R. J. Hollingdale. New York: Vintage Books.
Oliver, Kelly. 1995. *Womanizing Nietzsche: Philosophy's Relation to the "Feminine."* New York: Routledge.
Oliver, Kelly, and Marilyn Pearsall, eds. 1998. *Feminist Interpretations of Friedrich Nietzsche*. University Park: Pennsylvania State University Press.
Ortega, Mariana. 2016. *In-Between: Latina Feminist Phenomenology, Multiplicity, and the Self*. Albany: State University of New York Press.
Parkes, Graham. 1994. *Composing the Soul: Reaches of Nietzsche's Psychology*. Chicago: University of Chicago Press.
Patton, Paul, ed. 1993. *Nietzsche, Feminism and Political Theory*. New York: Routledge.
Pitts, Andrea J. 2021. *Nos/Otras: Gloria E. Anzaldúa, Multiplicitous Agency, and Resistance*. Albany: State University of New York Press.
Reginster, Bernard. 2000. "Perspectivism, Criticism and Freedom of Spirit." *European Journal of Philosophy* 8: 40–62.
Rivera, Omar. 2019. *Delimitations of Latin American Philosophy: Beyond Redemption*. Bloomington: Indiana University Press.
Ruíz, Elena. 2011. "Feminist Border Theory." In *The Routledge International Handbook of Contemporary Social and Political Theory*, edited by Gerard Delanty and Stephen Turner, 350–61. New York: Routledge.
Schotten, Heike C. 2006. "Revolutionary Futures: Nietzsche, Anzaldúa, and Playful 'World'-Travel." *Human Architecture* 4: 303–20.

Stegmaier, Werner. 2015. "Subjects as Temporal Clues to Orientation: Nietzsche and Luhmann on Subjectivity." In *Nietzsche and the Problem of Subjectivity*, edited by Branco and Constâncio, 487–510. Berlin: De Gruyter.

Thiele, Leslie Paul. 1990. *Friedrich Nietzsche and the Politics of the Soul: A Study of Heroic Individualism*. Princeton, NJ: Princeton University Press.

Tuana, Nancy, and Charles Scott. 2020. *Beyond Philosophy: Nietzsche, Foucault, Anzaldúa*. Bloomington: Indiana University Press.

Welshon, Rex. 2009. "Saying Yes to Reality: Skepticism, Antirealism, and Perspectivism in Nietzsche's Epistemology." *Journal of Nietzsche Studies* 27: 23–43.

Whitmire, John F., Jr. 2009. "The Many and the One: The Ontological Multiplicity and Functional Unity of the Person in the Later Nietzsche." *Pluralist* 4: 1–17.

Part II

# Elitism and Political Hierarchies

# 6

# Shame, Humiliation, and *Whiplash*

## The Case of the Ascetic Priest

DANIEL CONWAY

We must count the ascetic priest as the predestined savior, shepherd, and advocate of the sick herd: only thus can we understand his tremendous historical mission. *Dominion over the suffering* is his kingdom.

—Friedrich Nietzsche, *On the Genealogy of Morality*

*Increscunt animi, virescit volnere virtus.* [The spirits increase, vigor grows through a wound.]

—Friedrich Nietzsche, cited without attribution, *Twilight of the Idols*

## Introduction

Of the myriad figures and characters profiled by Nietzsche, none is more enigmatic than the *ascetic priest*. According to Nietzsche, the priest is impotent, yet formidable; noble, yet subordinate; zealous in his demand for purity, yet ashamed of his own impurity; desirous of isolation, but dependent on community; contemptuous of the lower orders, but solicitous of their welfare; oriented by doctrine to the otherworldly, yet tethered in practice to the worldly; bent on secular dominion, yet committed to a strategy of mutual assured destruction; allegiant to the ascetic ideal, but indirectly productive of rival ideals; committed to the one true morality, yet unwittingly destined to promote the emergence of variant moralities.[1]

After encouraging his readers to receive the ascetic priest as the arch-villain of his genealogical tale, Nietzsche reveals that he and the priest are in fact kindred agents in the service of life itself. Notwithstanding the priest's central role in fomenting the "slave revolt in morality," on the strength of which he transformed aimless sufferers into self-policing sinners, Nietzsche attributes to the ascetic priest a "tremendous [*ungeheure*] historical mission" (*GM* III:15), counting him "among the greatest *conserving* and yes-creating forces of life" (*GM* III:13). Apparently, that is, they play for the same team, even if they play very different (and in fact antagonistic) positions. At the same time, however, Nietzsche envisions no positive role for the ascetic priest in the post-Christian epoch they have been jointly tasked to inaugurate.

While various features of the priestly type might command our attention and warrant our scrutiny, my aim in this chapter is to explore the priest's ingenious use of *shame* to pacify (and later weaponize) the sufferers entrusted to his care. By teaching them to be ashamed of their debts and misdeeds (and, later, of the fallen nature to which their debts and misdeeds attest), the priest both saves and sickens them.[2] He does so, moreover, while simultaneously advancing (and aggrandizing) his own political position, which ultimately exceeds the ambit of his control. As a purveyor of shame, in other words, the priest is responsible for producing multiple politicized (and re-politicized) identities, including *one*—that of the "*new philosopher*" (*GM* III:10)—that he neither anticipates nor welcomes.

In *Daybreak*, Nietzsche unspools a speculative anthropological account of the origin of the "contemplative" type, of which he considers the priest a particularly influential variant. Like other contemplatives, "whose lives were melancholy and poor in deeds" (*D* 42), the priests were defined from the outset by their condition of diminished power and vitality. Compensating for their physical impotence with a fevered imagination, the priests managed to stoke fear in those who otherwise would prefer to banish them from their midst (*D* 42). Securing for themselves a liminal haven on the periphery of the human community, they succeeded in presenting themselves as potentially valuable (or at least tolerable) sources of wisdom and prophecy. Capitalizing on their fluid identity and their penchant for introspection, they specialized in drawing and policing the shifting boundaries that divide citizens and strangers, gods and men, right and wrong, saved and damned, clean and unclean, and so on. Mobilizing their innate talents for language and learning, while attesting credibly to otherworldly sources of power and patronage, the priests were "despised to just the extent they were not dreaded" (*D* 42).

In *GM* we are reintroduced to the priests as the ultimate insiders outside: Notwithstanding their noble birth, the priests were relegated by the warriors of the knightly-aristocratic caste to a second-class status. Assigned to mind the lowest orders of society, and to quell the agitations of the rabble collected therein, the priests dared not challenge the wishes of their knightly-aristocratic kin. Despite their contempt for the lower orders, which was compounded by their obsession with cleanliness and purity, the priests had no choice but to deliver the motley sufferers and criminals entrusted to their care from the danger they posed to themselves as would-be antagonists of the knightly-aristocratic nobles (*GM* III:15). The priests' signal innovation toward this end was their formation of a docile, misery-loving *herd*, wherein self-destructive fantasies of personal revenge were displaced by a concern for the welfare of the unassuming collective. Convincing their charges to seek the cause of their suffering not in their uncaring tormentors but in their own shameful, debt-ridden selves, the priests succeeded thereby in "alter[ing] the direction of *ressentiment*" (*GM* III:15).

Although physiologically inferior to the warrior nobles and, as a result, understandably reluctant to challenge them in contests of physical strength or martial prowess, the priests were not without recourse. According to Nietzsche, they patiently waged a war of "cunning" [*List*] (or "spirit" [*Geist*]), which the warrior nobles recognized as such only when they were too late to defend themselves (*GM* III:15). Having pacified the lower orders, which pleased the knightly-aristocratic caste and seemingly confirmed its unchallenged superiority, the priests quietly experimented with the use of shame to secure the terms of their revenge. Already alert to the power of shame to form and bind a docile collective, the priests soon discovered that further amplifications of shame would grant them a measure of political power that was otherwise unavailable to them. As the instigators and arbiters of shame, the priests eventually learned how to weaponize their herds and flocks, dispatching them to sow doubt and self-reproach throughout the knightly-aristocratic caste of nobles.[3]

That the priests have prevailed, Nietzsche observes, is indisputable (*GM* I:16). But what is their endgame strategy? Will they persevere to the bitter end, ultimately destroying the very conditions of the political power and secular authority they have amassed? In *The Antichrist*, Nietzsche strongly suggests that there is no place for the priestly type in the post-theistic European epoch he intends to inaugurate (*A* 52). Having survived, barely, the rearguard assault masterminded by the priests, the "good Europeans" whom Nietzsche rallies must proceed with their legislations in full awareness of the destructive power of the priesthood. In his cheeky "Decree Against Christianity," which he apparently meant to append to *The Antichrist*,[4] Nietzsche goes so far as to declare that "the priest is *our* chandala—he should be condemned, starved, and driven into every desert."[5]

While perhaps understandable, Nietzsche's enmity for the priests may strike us as overstated, especially if he is interpreted as imputing to the priests a fixed, unchangeable (and irremediably toxic) nature, which would render them permanently inimical to the new European order he envisions and lightly sketches. Is it not possible that the priests, too, may be encouraged (or expected) to evolve? That their predilection for shame-throwing might be optimized by the canny lawgivers whose arrival on the scene, or so Nietzsche promises, is imminent? Is it not possible, for example, that their talent for pacifying the lower orders could be appropriately circumscribed and their political ambitions effectively constrained? Or is it the case that the priests are simply too powerful, albeit in their besetting impotence, to be granted a place in the new European order? The irony here is that this is precisely the impression that the priests have been so successful, traditionally, in cultivating in their likely nemeses. Has Nietzsche fallen captive to their spell?

In order to evaluate Nietzsche's various attempts to politicize the figure and role of the priest, I wish to develop an interpretation of the 2014 Damian Chazelle film *Whiplash*, which tells the story of a sadistic music teacher, Terence Fletcher (played by J. K. Simmons, who received an Academy Award for his performance), and his talented protégé, Andrew Neiman (played by Miles Teller). On the one hand, the film graphically confirms Nietzsche's deepest reservations about the place of the priests in the post-theistic society he envisions for himself and his best readers. Fletcher is abusive, manipulative, relentlessly critical, and prone to cruel displays of gratuitous humiliation. Desperate to win Fletcher's approval, Andrew sacrifices nearly everything to become an elite jazz drummer. Their relationship is volatile, destructive, and beyond toxic. After a particularly humiliating episode, which concludes Andrew's otherwise promising apprenticeship at the fictional Shaffer Conservatory, third-party interventions are required to disentangle him from Fletcher, though they later manage to find one another once again.

On the other hand, Fletcher's abuse is presented in the film as responsible for escorting Andrew to his most promising incarnation as a jazz drummer. In the climactic scene of the film, Andrew turns the tables on his tormenter, leveraging his own experience of humiliation to compel Fletcher's approval. Ever allegiant to the music, Fletcher has no choice but to conduct Andrew through his epic, show-stopping solo. While it is undeniable that Fletcher has mistreated Andrew, we also are led to conclude—or at least consider—that his campaign of soul-scorching humiliation was ultimately productive of genius.

Viewers of *Whiplash* are left with several nagging questions: Is the shame endured by Andrew justified by the virtuosity he eventually displays? Is Fletcher a master teacher after all, doing "whatever it takes" to coax his underperforming protégé toward greatness, or is he a garden variety sadist? Is whiplash, whether literal or figural, an acceptable price of admission for those who aspire to enter the ranks of the all-time greats? Considered more generally: Is anyone ever warranted in risking *everything*—either of one's own or another's—in pursuit of a singular expression of virtuosity?

According to most philosophers, of course not. But according to Nietzsche? Here, in fact, the case is not so clear. Nietzsche boasted of being an "immoralist" and famously cheered the exploitation of entire peoples in the pursuit of the larger or greater end they might be made to serve (*BGE* 126). As he rallied his best readers to the "task" reserved for them, in fact, he implored them *not* to be deterred by the objections that were certain to be directed toward their cruelty-laced displays of "extravagant honesty" ["ausschweifende Redlichkeit"] (*BGE* 230). He furthermore believed that the production of genius, by whatever means, should never be taken lightly. His primary objection to the Reich, after all, was that it revered politics, rather than culture, as the supreme expression of the power of an ascendant people or nation (*TI* "Skirmishes" 39). Finally, as William Pamerleau has observed in the context of his own treatment of *Whiplash*, "Nietzsche does, indeed, endorse the infliction of suffering, on ourselves and others, in order to promote individual development. As biological organisms, violence and struggle are integral to the workings of nature. The process of self-overcoming, even among cultured human beings, requires violence of a sort, as Nietzsche's frequent use of the warrior metaphor suggests."[6]

From a Nietzschean point of view, we know, one conclusion is irresistible: a setting in which shame is mobilized as an instrument of elevation is certainly more interesting (if also more grotesque) than a setting in which no one suffers the pain of self-reproach.[7] If we value the profusion of Bird-like virtuosity, moreover, we may find ourselves inclined toward a setting in which shame is allowed (and even encouraged) to perform the upbuilding labor attributed to it in *Whiplash*. According to Nietzsche, after all, a civilization, or people, that fails (or refuses) to encourage the flowering of exotic genius is destined to wither and fade.

## Tough Talk = Tough Love?

In the first act of *Whiplash*, Chazelle introduces us to the principal figures in the drama. Andrew Neiman is talented, ambitious, and socially maladjusted. Chafing under the burden of mediocrity that he associates with his family and birthright, he longs to distinguish himself as a jazz drummer. As luck would have it, Andrew is discovered and flattered by renowned studio band leader Terence Fletcher, on whom he becomes increasingly and dangerously reliant for the validation he seeks. Along the way, Andrew meets and woos Nicole, a vulnerable young woman whom he subsequently (and rashly) decides is a potential—and, so, disposable—distraction from his single-minded pursuit of greatness. As this last point confirms, the first act of the film leads us from the motherless, conventionally bourgeois world in which Andrew feels stifled and trapped to the cruel, homoerotic world of Terence Fletcher's studio band.

The second act of the film corroborates the wisdom of those who eschew the use of shame as a tool of moral instruction.[8] Fletcher is an unusually cruel taskmaster, and Andrew quickly becomes the favored target of his wrath. As a teacher and mentor, Fletcher is in fact every parent's nightmare. The "tough-love" humiliation he dispenses is both seductive and disorienting. Falling under Fletcher's spell, Andrew gradually cuts himself off from all other attachments and interests. Practicing so long and hard that his hands begin to bleed, Andrew finally earns his spot as the core drummer in Fletcher's studio band.

As the second act of the film comes to a close, however, it is evident that Andrew has been depleted by the physical toll of his nonstop practicing and by the psychological toll of Fletcher's abuse. Upon arriving at the competition venue for a high-profile performance, Andrew discovers that he has misplaced his drumsticks. After Fletcher threatens to replace him with an understudy, Andrew rushes off to retrieve his sticks. Determined to return in time to join the band on stage, Andrew, driving too fast and obviously distracted, is involved in a traffic accident. Bloodied, disheveled, whiplashed, but remarkably undeterred, he abandons his wrecked rental car and returns on foot to the performance hall.

Desperate to prove himself to Fletcher, Andrew insists on taking his hard-earned place in the band, even after suffering multiple injuries. Fletcher somehow allows him to do so, despite his visible wounds, lack of focus, and obvious disorientation. His performance is predictably wretched, and Fletcher, ever the sadist, publicly shames him before removing him from the ensemble. At this point Andrew finally snaps under the weight of the accumulated humiliation. Intent on causing physical harm, he lunges toward Fletcher and tackles him. His education at the Shaffer Conservatory is over, as is Fletcher's career there. Whiplash begets whiplash.

The centerpiece expression of Fletcher's sadism is his oft-rehearsed rendition of his favorite anecdote, wherein legendary drummer Jo Jones is said to have launched a cymbal at the head of a not-ready-for-prime-time Charlie Parker. (Apparently imagining himself in the role of Jones, Fletcher at one point unexpectedly heaves a folding chair at Andrew. He proceeds to berate and slap Andrew before banishing him from the studio.) The point of this anecdote, as rendered by Fletcher, is that the crashing cymbal awakened Charlie Parker from his underachieving doldrums, inflicting the "whiplash" that motivated him to become the creative, innovative genius who is now universally praised as the Bird.

That Fletcher consistently misconstrues this anecdote, drawing from it an unearned and distinctly cruel lesson, is presented in the film as beside the point.[9] Fletcher's guiding credo is as chilling as it is simple: the ends justify the means, and the only end that matters is the production of virtuosity on the once-in-a-lifetime scale of a Charlie Parker. (If you are not a jazz aficionado, simply exchange the surpassing genius of your choice for the Bird.) If Fletcher can make a virtuoso of Andrew, as Jones supposedly did of Parker, then all is or will be forgiven (if not forgotten). A crucial element of Fletcher's preferred rendition of this anecdote is his emphasis on the sheer vulnerability of the young Charlie Parker. Jo Jones wounded Charlie Parker, humiliating him and reducing him to tears, because he cared about the music.[10] Determined never to be laughed at again, or so Fletcher claims, Charlie Parker practiced as no one before him had ever practiced. As idealized by Fletcher, that is, Jones inflicted Parker with the wound that healed him.[11]

When he returned a year later to the stage at the Reno, Parker produced what Fletcher describes as "the best motherfucking solo anyone had ever heard." This element of the anecdote bears noting inasmuch as it conveys Fletcher's unapologetic justification of the abuse he dispenses. To treat a talented protégé with anything less than the fury that Jo Jones hurled at Charlie Parker, Fletcher insists, would be unjust. As Fletcher tells it, moreover, his abusive approach is foolproof in its capacity to separate the contenders from the pretenders. When asked by Andrew if he worried about possibly discouraging the next Charlie Parker, Fletcher replied, "the next Charlie Parker never would be discouraged." Mere mortals might give up and slink away, but Fletcher has no use for them. He is determined to raise the next Charlie Parker, a god among men. The sissies and wannabes he culls from his cutthroat ensemble are but collateral damage in his unimpeachable campaign to fledge artistic genius.

Escalating the drama surrounding this teachable moment is Fletcher's moving encomium to a former protégé, Sean Casey, who, he claims, was killed in an automobile accident. As Fletcher remembers him to his current band, Casey was the perfect pupil: hard-working and driven, summoned on this occasion to assure Andrew (and perhaps others) of the merits of Fletcher's abusive teaching methods. According to Fletcher, Casey was hired at Lincoln Center by Wynton Marsalis and was awarded first chair by the end of his first year with the orchestra. As memorialized by Fletcher, Casey thus represents the elusive payoff the band members nervously await, cementing in them the feelings of shame and self-reproach that urge them onward. As we later learn, of course, Sean Casey did not die in an auto accident (though Andrew nearly did). In fact, Casey hanged himself, the victim, or so claimed the lawyers engaged by his family, of Fletcher's incessant humiliation.[12]

In many respects, of course, this is a straightforward, textbook case of predatory abuse. Andrew may be poised on the cusp of adulthood, but he also finds himself on the vulnerable end of an unbalanced power relationship. Fletcher is the recognized authority figure in the room, and he should know better than to humiliate the students who have been entrusted to his care. There is little ambiguity here, and we certainly would not want to blame Andrew, who is clearly the victim of Fletcher's predation, even if we wish he had displayed better judgment.

## A Final Lesson in Therapeutic Whiplash

The third act of the film validates the wisdom of those who see the potential value of self-reproach.[13] From this point forward in the story, the shame in question is (or should be) entirely *self*-directed, as Andrew, estranged from Fletcher and separated from the conservatory, endeavors to pick up the pieces of his life. Indeed, the entire context has shifted: Andrew is no longer a student or protégé, and Fletcher, fired from his position at the conservatory, is no longer a teacher. The relevant authorities and authority figures have stepped in, and a banal order has been restored to Andrew's life. He has received the professional treatment and parental nurture he needed, and he is half-heartedly weighing the equally dreary options that will commence the next chapter in his life.

A chance meeting between the former antagonists would seem to confirm the establishment of a new, more equitable balance of power. Passing by a jazz club where Fletcher is playing the piano, Andrew stops of his own volition to listen. In our (and perhaps Andrew's) first glimpse of Fletcher as a musician in his own right, we are struck by his surprisingly gentle touch on the keys. When he invites Andrew to stay for a drink, Fletcher manifests a mellow, perhaps even chastened, aspect. Has he changed? Grown? Mended his ways? Not exactly. Initiating what we later recognize to be an insidious confidence game, Fletcher unburdens himself. As it turns out, he too is misunderstood and underappreciated, his gruff exterior sheltering a heart of gold. As he confides to Andrew, "Truth is, I don't think people understood what it was I was doing at Shaffer. I wasn't there to conduct . . . I was there to push people beyond what's expected of them. I believe that is an absolute necessity. Otherwise we're depriving the world of the next Louis Armstrong, the next Charlie Parker." Charlie Parker. The Bird. The ultimate justification for those high-intensity teaching techniques that philistines predictably condemn as cruel and unusual. After being humiliated by Jo Jones, or so Fletcher insists, "Charlie Parker practiced with one goal in mind: never to be laughed at again." And if Jones had not humiliated Parker, if he had uttered a perfunctory platitude along the lines of "good job"? "End of story. No Bird. That, to me, is an absolute tragedy."[14]

To all appearances, the mystery of Terence Fletcher has been solved. He simply wants to bequeath to the world its next jazz luminary, and he is not about to apologize for the depth of his devotion to this tragedy-defying objective. He is sufficiently convincing,[15] in fact, that when he unexpectedly invites Andrew to sit in with his new ensemble, Andrew may very well think that this is simply a gig. Foolishly believing that his testimony against Fletcher has remained strictly confidential, which is what the lawyers promised him, he may surmise that he finally has won over his former nemesis. As Andrew soon learns, however, Fletcher knows about his testimony and is bent on revenge. As we soon learn, moreover, Andrew is not finished with Fletcher. He too can deliver a healthy dose of whiplash.

Anyone who witnessed only this final performance might be moved to praise Fletcher as the teacher and conductor who finally unlocked the enormous potential that lay unrealized in Andrew Neiman. We might not be surprised, in fact, if Andrew himself were to concur with this assessment, for he finally becomes the drummer *and the person* he always wanted to be. In this moment, in fact, the eminently sensible plans he had begun to make for himself vanish into thin air. What had he been thinking as he suffered therapists, lawyers, and other cookie-cutter authority figures to alienate him from his *eros* and plot for him a safer course through life? In their own ways, these well-intentioned third parties were nearly as toxic as Fletcher, and infinitely less compelling. Indeed, who was he kidding as he prepared to resign himself, like the cousins he loathed, to the familiar routines of a normal existence? He was born to be "one of the greats," and he wanted for himself nothing less than what this moment promised him. To borrow the familiar schoolyard rendition of Nietzsche's famous aphorism: in the end, Fletcher's abuse did not kill Andrew; *therefore*, it made him stronger. Is this not what every teacher and mentor seeks to accomplish?

## Nietzsche's Profile of the Ascetic Priest

Nietzsche is of interest here not only for his pithy aphorism but also for his astute psychological profile of the ascetic priest, which is useful to us in our efforts to understand shame-throwing sadists like Terence Fletcher. According to Nietzsche, the genius of the ascetic priest lay in his capacity to ascribe meaning to the suffering of those for whom meaningless suffering was literally unbearable (*GM* III:11). Urging them to scan their underdeveloped souls for flaws and defects, the ascetic priest led them to discover within themselves the cause or origin of their suffering (*GM* III:15).

The shame they were made to feel was both real and devastating, but it was counterbalanced by the meaning they were able to derive from their efforts to police their shameful—and, eventually, *sinful*—selves. In what appears to be his seminal insight into the psychology of the ascetic priest, Nietzsche observes that "[The ascetic priest] brings salves and balms with him, no doubt; but before he can act as a physician he first has to wound; when he then stills the pain of the wound *he at the same time infects the wound*—for that is what he knows [how] to do best of all, this sorcerer and animal-tamer, in whose presence everything healthy necessarily grows sick, and everything sick tame" (*GM* III:15). This potent combination not only inures the priest's followers to his ministry but also grooms them for their eventual role in his more overtly political machinations. Exploiting their expanded capacity to feel meaningfully ashamed, he recruits them for his own campaign of revenge against his sworn enemies, the knightly-aristocratic caste of nobles.

The important point for our present purposes is that Nietzsche diagnoses the ascetic priest as a "healer" who sickens those to whom he tends (*GM* III:17). According to Nietzsche, moreover, the priest performs this divided office involuntarily and in absolute confidence of the healing powers at his disposal. Focused narrowly on his efforts to protect his clients from their self-destructive impulses, he never pauses to consider the possibility that his unorthodox methods *also* cause harm. He bullies and goads his "herd" toward its optimal configuration by manipulating their personal feelings of shame and humiliation. He does so to their immediate advantage, to be sure, redirecting their resentment and encouraging them to identify themselves with the improving prospects of the docile collective he has formed (*GM* III:15). In securing their immediate advantage, however, he also escalates the threat of their (undetected) peril (*GM* III:17). In teaching them to feel shame, after all, he does nothing more than initiate them into *his* way of life, which is made meaningful (if not pleasant) by an unending drama of self-loathing and self-recrimination. Despite his defining impotence (*GM* I:7), that is, the priest is able to reproduce himself via the asexual mechanism of replication.[16]

Notwithstanding his preferred self-assessment, however, the ascetic priest does not cure his followers of the suffering that propels them into his care (*GM* III:17). He treats only their symptoms, prescribing the kind of "affect medication" that simply numbs or masks their pain. This limitation is the occasion for Nietzsche's "most fundamental objection to priestly medication" (*GM* III:17), and not simply because the priest is guilty of false advertising. As his clients become ever more dependent on the shame he both triggers and relieves, the priest explores the full extent of the power he enjoys over them. When he senses their potential usefulness for his personal pursuit of vengeance, he prescribes what amounts to a debilitating overdose of shame, which, despite temporarily blotting their consciousness and inducing a blissful experience of *ataraxia*, only further exacerbates their illness (*GM* III:20). Having previously shamed them for what they have and have not done, he now causes them to feel ashamed of *themselves*, that is, of their fallen nature, to which they are encouraged to trace the provenance of their various misdeeds.[17] In exchange for their experience of shame (poison), that is, he produces in them the ecstatic "orgies of feeling" that grant them a transient release from their suffering (balm) (*GM* III:20).

## Terence Fletcher: The High Priest of Jazz Virtuosity

Duly armed with this profile of the ascetic priest, let us return to our analysis of *Whiplash*. Perhaps the first thing we notice about the world of Terence Fletcher is that it is a very male world, in which procreation, idealized in the film as the birth of artistic genius, takes place via cloistered and often obscene male mediations.

As if to punctuate Andrew's descent into the dark, sickly underworld of jazz musicianship, the second act of *Whiplash* features a scene in which he makes a tough-guy show of dumping his sort-of girlfriend, ostensibly so that he may focus exclusively on his music. Having pledged himself to the priestly, hyper-masculinist world over which Fletcher holds dominion, Andrew now has no time for Nicole, the confused, homesick college student he had been courting. Her incredulous response, which is entirely justifiable and on point, is the final expression of sanity that Andrew hears (and predictably ignores) before embarking upon the *katabasis* scripted for him by Chazelle.

Here we detect the invisible power of Fletcher's priestly influence over Andrew: without asking him to make this or any other particular sacrifice, Fletcher silently compels his protégé to conclude that the girl is the real enemy. Never mind that they barely know one another, or that Andrew is presumptuous in ending their incipient relationship. In fact, Nicole is correct in her summary judgment of him: there *is* something wrong with him. As a function of his fealty to Fletcher, he has become a coward, not only for ending a romance of as-yet-undetermined intensity, but also for pretending that she stands in the way of the achievement he desires for himself. By closing this symbolic door on the world of heterosexual pleasure and, at its limit, sexual reproduction, Andrew enters in earnest the (or at least this) exclusively male world of jazz musicianship.[18] In this world, there will be no distractions, no temptations, not even a hint of heterosexual titillation. (The irony, of course, is that the product and supposed point of their collaborations is the stereotypically heterosexy music they provide for their appreciative audiences.)

According to Fletcher, virtuoso musicians must be birthed the old-fashioned way, via military-grade discipline, excruciating humiliation, and homophobic degradation.[19] Unable to create and nurture new life, and deathly afraid of the women who might partner with them in doing so, the men who navigate this world must coax new life from other males, by whatever means are necessary. Just as Jo Jones fledged the Bird by launching a cymbal at the head of an unprepared Charlie Parker, so Terence Fletcher aims to midwife the birth of Andrew Neiman as the core drummer in the Shaffer Conservatory studio band. Under Fletcher's stern supervision, women are neither needed nor wanted.[20]

That Fletcher wields a priestly authority over his flock is perhaps obvious. As his surname may be meant to convey, he is unquestionably the dominant male in a highly charged homoerotic context. Alternately dispensing poison and balm, he molds these "worthless" musicians into a tightly coordinated studio band.[21] Allegiant to the higher power he assigns to the music, as exemplified by the patron saint of jazz, Charlie Parker, Fletcher commands admiration and respect for his single-minded dedication.[22] Desperate to please him and, thereby, to earn his blessing, the musicians endure unrelenting storms of abuse. Of course, Fletcher also looks the part: his black vestments, shaved head, and trim, calorie-starved physique all suggest a scrupulously curated asceticism. Finally, as we have seen, he betrays not even a hint of interest in women. He is all about the music, which means, to him, that he is all about the young men entrusted to his ministry.

The second thing we notice about the world of Terence Fletcher is its pervasive sickness, as evidenced by his aggressive inversion of values. Here, too, Nietzsche's profile of the ascetic priest is instructive. Although the priest is both ingenious and successful in his efforts to mobilize the demotic orders to which he ministers, he remains dependent on these orders and, as a result, unacceptably proximate to (and implicated in) their ignoble, unclean way of life. Despite his noble birthright, that is, the priest is now more closely associated with the rabble than with his natural peers among the warrior caste. Even as he exacts his revenge, moreover, he is relegated to a dominion he did not choose and does not admire. The world he has remade in his hateful image, he knows, is not a world worthy of his nobility. Much like the figure of the "lord" in Hegel's influential account of dialectical contestation, the priest has created an arrangement in which he does not value, and cannot accept, the only recognition he is likely to receive. He will gain his revenge, but he will not regain his nobility.

What this means for viewers of *Whiplash* is that the world ruled by Terence Fletcher is shadowed by the compensatory, displaced nature of his dominion. He may strut and curse like a drill sergeant,[23] but he certainly is no warrior. Despite his tough-guy persona, in fact, his own claim to greatness is derivative, indirect, insecure, and ultimately dependent on the improbable emergence of the Bird-like genius whom, he admits, he has not yet managed to produce. Here two points are relevant. First, he is but a teacher, which in itself counts as a kind of failure for an aspiring jazz musician.[24] Second, by his own estimation, he is as yet a failed teacher. Even when the band plays well, or prevails in a competition, he can scarcely savor the moment, for it only serves to remind him of what he has not yet accomplished. Like the priestly nobles who are assigned to mind the lowest orders of an aristocratic society, Fletcher resents his demotion in status and prestige. The smallish world of competitive studio band is not the domain he chooses to rule but the domain over which he *may* and *can* rule. As a result, he cannot affirm either the adoration or the hatred he elicits from his protégés, for he knows that both responses reflect the artificial conditions of his dominion.

Just moments after speaking sweetly to the young daughter of a colleague or former student, for example, Fletcher treats his band to a salty, vulgar, homophobic pep talk. They go on to win the competition, with Andrew on drums, which of course only serves to remind Fletcher that he is but a teacher—a *successful* teacher, to be sure, on the studio band circuit, but pathetic nonetheless when compared to the jazz greats whose ranks he once longed to join. Hence his fanatical pursuit of the purity of jazz virtuosity: fledging the next Bird would allow him not only to atone for his own personal failure but also to strike back at *his* teachers, whom he blames, presumably, for failing *him*, for not doing everything in their power to develop *his* musical talent, for saying "good job" when his best efforts had been merely adequate.

At some level, we suspect, Fletcher must realize that his version of the Sean Casey incident is an utter fabrication. To be more precise, however, this is something that he both does and does not know about himself. The centerpiece insight of Nietzsche's diagnosis of the priestly type is that the priest doubts *everything*, including his own self-doubt. This incurable duality, or double consciousness, is emblematic of the pious self-recriminations that are the priest's stock in trade. Fletcher is not so much inauthentic or hypocritical in any traditional sense as he is permanently at war with himself and ineluctably self-divided. We might go so far as to say of Fletcher that he is *authentically inauthentic*: there simply is no true self or stable identity that he might be said to hide, cleverly or poorly, from view. His outward displays of abuse may be calibrated to hasten the production of genius, but they are also repercussions of the psychological torment he heaps upon himself. Pushing away his most promising students, a distancing gesture that Andrew replicates with his family and Nicole, is the single most effective way for him to maintain plausible deniability with respect to his own (dismal) prospects for redemption.

His sole source of consolation is his unflinching commitment to his ideal. He may not have fledged a Bird-grade virtuoso, but at least he has not allowed potential genius to lie fallow. (To borrow his terminology, he has averted *possible* tragedies, whatever that may mean, but he has not averted any *actual* tragedies, for he has not yet produced a jazz luminary.) Whether he knows it or not, he thus acquires an incentive to alienate all (but the very best) of his students. By driving his students away, moreover, he defers the moment of reckoning at which he will be obliged to pronounce himself an utter failure. And although his wretched treatment of his students may distract them (and their parents) from the magnitude of the judgment that awaits him, Fletcher himself is painfully aware of his failure thus far. As Nietzsche astutely observed, the priest demands purity of others because he is all-too-conscious of the filth he harbors and cannot discharge.

In his own estimation, and perhaps also in reality, Fletcher is a phony, a showman, a *Schauspieler*, to borrow one of Nietzsche's preferred terms of derision.[25] The affectations of the master teacher—the too-hip-for-his-age black wardrobe, the suspiciously supercharged misogyny and homophobia, the overstated respect for the purity of the music, the cloying piety of his oft-repeated anecdote about Jo Jones and Charlie Parker, the just-for-show biceps—everything about Fletcher is ever so slightly offbeat and out of tune. What we come to suspect is that his volcanic rage is meant to distract its targets from the fact that *he* is a habitual failure, a condition he tends to misplace behind his eminently understandable failure thus far to fledge the next Charlie Parker. In truth, it is Fletcher who is always either rushing or dragging. He hates himself in either event, even while accusing (and slapping) Andrew for similar lapses.

Fletcher is distinctive, that is, not by virtue of his accomplishments as a teacher of tyrants but by virtue of his surpassing aspiration and commitment. "I really tried," he explains to Andrew in his own defense, vainly hoping that the tiresome adverb he wields will magically endow his admittedly thin resumé with an ersatz (or promissory) achievement. This is the same Fletcher, by the way, who routinely ridiculed his protégés for *trying* rather than *achieving*, as if the cruel, results-oriented cosmos he pretended to channel were somehow partial, in his case, to the labor theory of value.

The inescapable brute fact of his own failure, on his own terms at least, also may account for his hair-trigger paranoia. Responding to Andrew's tendency to rush the tempo, which, he regularly reminds them, is *his* tempo, Fletcher floats the suspicion that Andrew may mean to take him down: "If you deliberately sabotage my band, I will fuck you like a pig."[26] In the next scene, Fletcher once again launches the accusation that someone may "deliberately sabotage [his] band," when he banishes the trombonist Metz for failing to know whether or not he was in tune. He was, but his ignorance was sufficient in Fletcher's estimation to warrant his dismissal from the ensemble.[27] It never occurs to the band that Metz was in fact a casualty of Fletcher's poor teaching methods.

The third distinctive feature we notice about this inverted world is its permanent suspension of the most familiar moral concerns pertaining to the cultural tasks associated with reproduction, education, and benefaction. In this world, encapsulated for us in Terence Fletcher's rehearsal hall, only the results matter. Propriety, politesse, reciprocal respect, manners, and civil discourse all fall by the wayside. No measures are considered too extreme or too cruel if they even vaguely promise success. As Fletcher confides, the real tragedy is not that his brand of abusive pedagogy might discourage the next Charlie Parker from becoming the next Bird but that lesser instructors might not be sufficiently vehement in their exhortations. The only possible failure Fletcher will acknowledge is the one that he is likely never to experience: biting his tongue, issuing faint or false praise, accepting mediocrity, cosseting those who need to have cymbals or chairs thrown at them.

And in the off chance that a gifted protégé will not be turned away? Immediately following Andrew's promotion to core drummer, we gain a glimpse of what Andrew appreciates about the narcissism of Fletcher's inverted world. With the extended family gathered around the dining table, Andrew attempts to communicate to them the magnitude of his success thus far at Shaffer Conservatory. Invariably, however, the table talk and the praise return to the exploits of his dim cousin, who is something of a stud in Division III college football. Despite his increasingly snarky efforts to offer an alternative assessment of the relative merits of their respective levels of achievement,[28] Andrew is painfully aware that he simply cannot compete in this setting. On the commonly accepted scale of dinner-table machismo, even a dopey football player outranks an elite jazz drummer.

Exasperated by the bourgeois philistinism on display in his extended family, Andrew boldly claims to prefer the grim fate of Charlie Parker—"dying broke and drunk and full of heroin at the age of thirty-four," as his father puts it—to that of his cousins as he imagines they will turn out. In doing so, of course, he publicly pledges his allegiance to the hip, bizarro world of Terence Fletcher, a fantasy world in which cerebral percussionists lord over small college halfbacks, a world in which a real hero does not get the girl because he already has thrown her away. So long as he does not allow Fletcher to bully him into leaving this world, he may cling to his dream of taking his place among the greats.

And all the while, the door leading out of Fletcher's chamber of horrors is clearly marked, unlocked, and unguarded. Fed-up musicians may leave at any time, and they are not required to ring a bell or otherwise acknowledge that they have washed out. They need simply exit this underground world for good, never to return. And yet Andrew does not leave, even when invited and inveigled to do so. Nor is he held in place by the usual sorts of obligations and conventions. No one requires or even invites him to continue. As we know, in fact, Fletcher has no qualms about auditioning potential replacements for the drummers whom he routinely drums out of his ensemble. In short, Andrew may leave whenever he likes, but he never does. Even in the wake of his public humiliation as Fletcher's whipping boy, it is the school that breaks up with him. Is this a sign of psychological abuse? Of unresolved Oedipal torments? Of course. But such is the lifeblood of the inverted world that Andrew has voluntarily entered and is determined to conquer.

## A Dual Metamorphosis

In setting up the much-admired conclusion of *Whiplash*, Chazelle is careful to address (and allay) most of the standard moral concerns we have considered. Finally exposed as a serial abuser, Fletcher has been fired from his teaching position at the conservatory. For his part, Andrew has received the care he needs from responsible adults. After a stay in the hospital, he begins the long, painful process of reassembling his life. To a certain degree, he is successful in doing so. He even reaches out to Nicole, who, having wisely moved on, is understandably cautious and reserved. When he accepts Fletcher's invitation to sit in, that is, he does so (more or less) as a consulting adult in full possession of the "perspective" he needs to make an informed decision. There is no obvious sense in which he is coerced to accept Fletcher's invitation, and he presumably is under no illusions about the kind of person Fletcher is. With eyes wide open, he arrives at Carnegie Hall on time, unbloodied, and with drumsticks firmly in hand. As we soon learn, however, he cannot shake the dream of becoming "one of the greats," which, in his mind, is inextricably linked to the dream of finally compelling Fletcher's respect.

Fletcher's apparent role in unlocking Andrew's virtuosity finds a fairly direct parallel in Nietzsche's speculations on the future of the ascetic priest. Thus far, as he explains, the ascetic priest has provided the cover for the philosopher to develop and flourish. Unwelcome and mistrusted in their own right, philosophers have managed to survive by posing, often unwittingly, as variants or offshoots of the "contemplative" type (*GM* III:10). Perfecting the priestly tactic of encouraging others to leave them alone (*GM* III:10), philosophers have managed to carve out for themselves a modest cultural niche, wherein they have been free to adapt the ascetic ideal to suit their extra-ascetic needs and nature. The catch, of course, is that philosophers have been most convincing in their performance of this role when they have ceased simply to pretend. Obliged to "*believe* in [the ascetic ideal] in order to be able to represent it" (*GM* III:10), philosophers have tended to fall captive to their own performances, thereby forfeiting the potential advantages pertaining to a strategic (i.e., conditional) embrace of the ascetic ideal.

This final point bears noting, for it clouds the prospect that Nietzsche is keen to promote, namely that of the emergence of the *new* philosopher from the "gloomy caterpillar form" that is furnished by the "wraps and cloak" of the ascetic priest (*GM* III:10). Those philosophers who sincerely believe in the ascetic ideal and have come to regard themselves as priests will take wing only if they are prompted to do so by a world that is "sunnier, warmer, brighter" than our own (*GM* III:10). As Nietzsche grimly surmises, however, there may not yet be "sufficient pride, daring, courage, [and] self-confidence available today . . . for 'the philosopher' to be henceforth—*possible* on earth" (*GM* III:10). In other words, Nietzsche both foretells the emergence of the new philosopher and cautions us that the desired metamorphosis [*Verwandlung*] is not likely to transpire any time soon. Here too we glimpse his ambivalence toward the ascetic priest,[29] whom he presents but cannot fully endorse, as a possible (if unlikely) sponsor of the new philosopher. Having labored to portray the ascetic priest as "impotent," as capable of reproducing only by replicating his hatred in others (*GM* I:7), Nietzsche is understandably reluctant to entrust the future to the nurture and protection afforded the new philosopher, supposedly, by the unsuspecting priest.

Nietzsche's ambivalence notwithstanding, his blueprint for redemption is fairly clear: this new species of philosopher will emerge only by asserting its independence from the ascetic priest and by pledging its strategic (i.e., conditional) allegiance to the ascetic ideal. This transformation will come as a surprise, no doubt, to the priests in question, who believe themselves to be grooming the next generation of guardians of the ascetic ideal. In that event, and here I pick up the speculative thread of Nietzsche's narrative, the priests in question will not take kindly to such a brazen act of betrayal. They will cling to their authority until it is forcibly wrested from them, or until they have no choice but to acknowledge the comparative advantage afforded the emergent philosopher by his evolved relationship to the ascetic ideal. In other words, the betrayed priests will either fight to the death *or* learn from the conditional asceticism of the new philosopher.

Just such a scene crowns the climactic third act of *Whiplash*. After flattering Andrew and inviting him to sit in, Fletcher slyly revises the set list, leaving Andrew unprepared and humiliated in front of his fellow musicians and a knowledgeable audience. As expected, Andrew exits the stage in shame, whiplashed once again by the master abuser. This time around, however, things are different. After huddling briefly with his suddenly supportive father,[30] Andrew returns to the stage and, preempting Fletcher's remarks to the audience, opens the familiar introduction to "Caravan," which he proceeds to develop into an unscheduled drum solo. The ensuing reversal is both startling and unmistakable. Turning the tables on his tormentor, Andrew ignores Fletcher's repeated demands to relinquish the direction of the music. When Fletcher screams, "Andrew, what are you doing, man?," Andrew responds: "I'll cue you." Reflecting the metamorphosis that is now underway, Chazelle's direction of the scene shifts the spotlight to Andrew, leaving Fletcher literally and figuratively in the dark. Andrew's soaring drum solo announces his liberation from the "gloomy caterpillar form" manifested by the black-clad Terence Fletcher.

## Timely Interventions: Nietzsche and Chazelle

Compounding (and ultimately resolving) the drama of the third act of *Whiplash* is the timely reappearance of Andrew's father, who, like most parents, both does and does not want his son to follow his *eros*. Widely acknowledged as a failure in his own right, Jim Neiman understands (and perhaps still feels) the draw of virtuosity in artistic expression. A onetime jazz prodigy in his own right, he chose to travel the safe, well-worn path of bourgeois conformity. Indeed, when he reminds Andrew of the unfavorable conditions under which the Bird eventually fell to earth, he comes across as a frightened scold. His son does not respect his choices and, truth be told, neither does he.

Jim knows, in short, that Andrew has unfinished business with Fletcher, and with jazz more generally. He also realizes that Andrew will not move resolutely forward until this business is finished, one way or the other. Splitting the difference between protecting and encouraging his son, Jim decides to attend the performance and lend Andrew his moral support. After comforting his humiliated son, Jim gently (and perhaps inadvertently) delivers one final healing wound. In offering to drive Andrew home, Jim reminds his son of the secondhand life that awaits him if he retreats once again from the troll who blocks his path. Duly whiplashed by the prospect of abandoning his dream, and of retracing the timid trajectory of his father's regret-filled life, Andrew returns to the stage to confront (and vanquish) his nemesis. As we shall see, this (quiet) intervention is crucial to the uplifting conclusion that Chazelle crafts for the film.

Chazelle's introduction of a third-party mediating figure prompts us to reconsider Nietzsche's metamorphosis narrative. Although this narrative features no third party—and so, no mediating agent—it may be the case that Nietzsche means for *his* intervention (viz. his telling of the story in *GM*) to jumpstart the stalled emergence of the new philosopher. Just as the reappearance of Andrew's father serves to join the two worlds that Andrew and Fletcher have been determined to keep separate, thereby blurring the divisions they have drawn for themselves and each other, so Nietzsche's telling of the story blows the cover of the new philosopher, thereby alerting the ascetic priest to the betrayal that awaits him. Displaying a credible (if limited) allegiance to both parties, Nietzsche apparently means to force an issue that, in his opinion, now (or very soon) must be resolved. In short, his intervention in Essay III of *GM* is intended to compel (or accelerate) the emergence of the new philosopher.[31]

That Nietzsche is not content simply to chronicle this metamorphosis, as if he were a patient, disinterested observer of the process, is fairly clear from his penchant for rhetorical digressions and interjections. From the very first words of *GM*, in fact, we are aware of his dissatisfaction with the status quo: those "knowers" whom he counts among his target readership can no longer afford the luxury of remaining "unknown" to themselves (*GM* P:1).[32] He thus takes it upon himself to rouse them from their oblivion, precisely so that they may become the intrepid "free spirits" they (mistakenly) take themselves to be.[33] His plan to awaken his best readers culminates, as it must, in his efforts to insert himself into the metamorphosis narrative that he relates in *GM*. No longer willing to suffer the new philosopher to emerge and take flight on his preferred schedule, Nietzsche seeks to inflict a healing wound. In divulging the secret of the new philosopher's impending emergence, he not only models to his best readers the disruptive practice of truth-telling he recommends to them (*BGE* 230), but he also deprives the new philosopher of the comfort and security he derives from the patronage of the unsuspecting ascetic priest. Nietzsche does so, in fact, by (figuratively) launching a cymbal at the head of the not-ready-for-prime-time new philosopher-in-waiting, shaming him for relaxing into the seductive status quo of the ascetic ideal. For his part, the new philosopher-in-waiting must decide if he is a priest after all, just as he has pretended all along, or if he is something more, something transcendent, something destined for an as yet undetermined index of human (or overhuman) excellence. Duly whiplashed, or so Nietzsche hopes, the new philosopher may finally take flight.

In what is certainly the most uplifting scene in *Whiplash*, Fletcher voluntarily cedes to Andrew the direction of the music. Despite being publicly humiliated by a rogue percussionist, Fletcher does not react as we might have expected.[34] Presumably, he could have responded to Andrew's insubordination by shaming him once again, smugly apologizing to yet another audience of jazz connoisseurs for the wretched performance of his core drummer. That he refrains from doing so in this instance confirms that his sadism in fact admits of a *limit*, which is both reached and illuminated by the fledging of Andrew's Bird-like virtuosity.

If Fletcher is humiliated by Andrew's star turn, he does not show it. Visibly intrigued by this unexpected turn of events, Fletcher removes his jacket—thereby shedding the chrysalis of his priestly authority—and begins to conduct Andrew's uninvited drum solo. Unlike most bullies, as it turns out, Fletcher actually can take the abuse that he is better known for dishing out. Removed from the crucible of the studio they once shared (and trashed) together, Andrew and Fletcher are both free to live up to their professed (but only now confirmed) devotion to the music. In apparent admiration of the results of their unplanned collaboration, these former antagonists actually exchange a knowing look and smile. Indeed, we apparently are meant to understand that Andrew's brazen display of insubordination has inflicted upon Fletcher a healing wound of his own. At this moment, Fletcher does not need to win, prevail, dominate, shame, or humiliate. He simply needs to be part of history, just as he has claimed all along. Unlike Zarathustra, whose preferred disciples remain persistently (and suspiciously) MIA, perhaps because he insists on calling them his "children" (*Z* IV:20), Fletcher basks in the satisfaction of the teacher whose wreath has been cleanly plucked by a worthy disciple. Unlike Zarathustra, that is, Fletcher actually welcomes the healing wound (or whiplash) that will allow him, finally, to "go under."

Is this the procreative, tragedy-averting vindication that Fletcher has long anticipated? Earlier, we know, he saw fit to play Jo Jones to Andrew's Charlie Parker, throwing a folding chair rather than a cymbal. Now, as Andrew asserts himself, drumming to a tune made famous by none other than Jo Jones, Fletcher willingly adjusts his direction of the music to accommodate the cues he receives from Andrew. What formerly was *his* tempo, as he never tired of reminding his band, is now Andrew's tempo. Of course, "Caravan" is also the tune that Andrew botched, not surprisingly, following his traumatic automobile accident. Redemption beckons.

As we know, Nietzsche's blueprint for the emergence of the new philosopher makes no provisions for the post-betrayal future of the ascetic priest. If the priest is as rigid and unyielding as Nietzsche suggests, however, it will be difficult to frame the envisioned conflict between priests and philosophers as anything but a zero-sum contest. As he explains, in fact, it is not clear that the priest will survive the betrayal that awaits him: "The ascetic priest possessed in [the ascetic] ideal not only his faith but also his will, his power, his interest. His *right* to exist stands or falls with that ideal: no wonder we encounter here a terrible antagonist—supposing we are antagonists of that ideal—one who fights for his existence against those who deny that ideal" (*GM* III:11). As described, the priest identifies himself strictly and categorically with the ascetic ideal. Refusing to acknowledge any goals or objectives other (or higher) than that of self-denial, he no doubt will condemn the philosopher's conditional, tactical reliance on ascetic techniques and practices.[35] But how will he respond when the emergent philosopher finally takes wing, demonstrating the viability of an unanticipated vector of human development, over which the ascetic ideal shall have no dominion?

What is at stake in this conflict is nothing less than the future of the ascetic ideal: Will the future of humankind (or Western civilization) continue to be shaped by the priest's slavish, non-negotiable devotion to this ideal, or will the course of human (and post-human) development be guided by the philosopher's selectively instrumental relationship to the ascetic ideal? While Nietzsche clearly favors the latter vision of an extra-moral epoch in European history, going so far as to describe the prankish new ideal twinkling on the horizon (*GS* 382), the emergence of the new philosopher would seem to leave no room for the priestly type.[36] Does this mean that the priest is destined, like his knightly-aristocratic kin, to occupy an evolutionary cul-de-sac?[37]

Chazelle sees things differently. Chancing a giant Hollywood leap beyond the stalled developmental process described by Nietzsche, Chazelle authorizes Andrew to conduct Fletcher through a parallel process of metamorphosis. Having relinquished the spotlight and shed his black jacket, Fletcher appears supportive, vulnerable, and almost human, especially as he smiles appreciatively at Andrew. The intriguing suggestion here, which Nietzsche did not explicitly consider in his metamorphosis narrative, is that the emergence of the new philosopher actually might have a similarly liberating effect on the priest. Apparently, that is, a world "sunnier, warmer, brighter" than our own might bring out the best in both philosophers and priests (*GM* III:10).

In that event, or so Chazelle encourages us to speculate, the philosopher's betrayal of the priest would be understood to inflict a healing wound. No longer obliged to maintain his slavish fidelity to the ascetic ideal, the priest would be free to renegotiate the terms and conditions of his asceticism, for example, by dialing back his self-hatred and withdrawing his vitality-draining investments in otherworldly sources of meaning and value.[38] Much as the metamorphosis of Andrew Neiman lifts the burden of failure from the shoulders of Terence Fletcher, so the rise of Nietzsche's new philosopher may succeed in drawing the priest aloft. Even if the liberated priest does not fly so high as the liberated philosopher, he nevertheless may succeed in escaping the cramped, face-to-the-ground perspective that has defined (and constrained) his earthbound existence. On Chazelle's depiction of the ideal *agon*, the process of self-overcoming eventuates in the liberation of all contestants, including those who formerly found themselves locked in a zero-sum death match. The key here, as we have seen, is that both parties suffer and survive the healing wounds they receive.

Too good to be true? Probably. Too Hegelian in its orchestration of an improbably dialectical win-win solution? Certainly for Nietzsche's taste.[39] Chazelle's Hollywood ending nevertheless raises an important question about Nietzsche's blueprint for the emergence of the new philosopher.[40] Is the priestly type correctly and faithfully characterized by its devotion-to-the-death allegiance to the ascetic ideal? Are the priests simply unable to engage *at all* in the kind of selective, situational asceticism that Nietzsche attributes to the new philosophers? Are the priests impervious to the kinds of healing wounds that spur spiritual growth in their clients and victims?

In all (or most) other respects, we might note, the priests whom Nietzsche describes manifest an unusually resilient capacity to adapt to changing and unwanted circumstances. Burdened by self-directed doubt and suspicion, chronically uncertain of their identity and authority, prone to resentment and excessive self-loathing, obliged to wring power from their defining impotence, the priests may strike us as a good bet to survive the betrayal coming their way. As we know from Nietzsche's genealogical tale, the priests were able to tolerate (and eventually exploit) their humiliating assignment to mind the unclean lower orders of society. Are we supposed to believe that these same priests (or their successors in the lineage) would not tolerate the "sunnier, warmer, brighter world" in which the buoyant philosopher declares (and enacts) his independence from the ascetic ideal?

## Conclusion

If we apply Chazelle's version of the metamorphosis narrative to Nietzsche's unfinished story, we may conclude that the priest need not be undone by the betrayal-cum-apostasy of his former protégé. Even in his humiliation, the whiplashed priest may take pride in (and credit for) this unforeseen development as a novel and potentially welcome advance in the ongoing elaboration of the contemplative type. Following the flighty lead of the emergent philosopher, contemplatives of all stripes now may experiment with ascetic techniques of varying duration and intensity, with an eye toward adopting only those techniques that are likely to serve their larger, extra-ascetic ends. In other words, the priest eventually may come to understand that he has received the same kind of healing wound that he typically inflicts on others. If so, he may allow and even encourage the new philosopher to establish a healthier relationship to the ascetic ideal, going so far, perhaps, as to ease himself into a similarly renegotiated relationship. In doing so, after all, the priest would stand to reap the benefits afforded him by ascetic techniques while liberating himself from the leaden seriousness of the ascetic ideal. Transcending the limitations of his earthbound, caterpillar form, he may learn to enjoy the "sunnier, warmer, brighter world" he now inhabits.

And why not? Is this not *his* metamorphosis, and *his* liberation, as well? After all, he has provided the nurture, cover, and training that have prepared the new philosopher to launch himself skyward. (Or, if we prefer the creepy compensatory drama scripted by Nietzsche, the priest is responsible for birthing, or midwifing, the new philosopher.) Their eventual separation will be devastating for the priest, but need it be lethal as well? Can the priest not take pride in the independence of his progeny? Might he not be surprised (and even gratified) to discover that his reproductive options are not exclusively limited to replications of his hatred and self-contempt?

Thus the question becomes: Is the priestly type permanently tethered to the ascetic ideal, destined, like Major T. J. Kong (Slim Pickens) astride a nuclear warhead, to ride it out to the bitter end? Or is the priestly type defined only historically (i.e., contingently) by its dependence on the ascetic ideal? Is it not possible that the priest has been fooling himself all along, pledging his allegiance to the ascetic ideal without actually considering alternative (and potentially more effective) vehicles for his contemplative pursuits? Might he not find himself awakened and invigorated by the whiplashing he has received from his erstwhile ward and protégé?

One final thought: Is it possible, as Aaron Ridley has suggested, that Nietzsche *needs* the priests to be inflexibly allegiant to the ascetic ideal, constitutionally opposed to their own prospects for adaptation?[41] Is this a requirement—and so, an internal weakness—of his narrative? If so, will his best readers, like Ridley, need to address this weakness as they pluck his wreath and continue his work? To his credit, Nietzsche foresaw this very possibility, even if he did not present it as indicative of his own fate: "There is a point in every philosophy when the philosopher's 'conviction' [*Überzeugung*] appears on the stage—or to use the language of an ancient Mystery: *Adventavit asinus / Pulcher et fortissimus* [The ass arrives, beautiful and most brave] (*BGE* 8)."[42]

## Notes

1. Here I follow Staten, *Nietzsche's Voice*, 56–65; and Ridley, *Nietzsche's Conscience*, 61–63. See also Conway, *Reader's Guide to Nietzsche's "On the Genealogy,"* 112–22.

2. My understanding of the psychology of shame is indebted to Williams, *Shame and Necessity*, esp. 75–85.

3. Here I follow Ridley, *Nietzsche's Conscience*, 57–63.

4. Nietzsche says as much in his draft letter to Brandes in Dec. 1888 (*Sämtliche Briefe* 8, no. 1170: 502).

5. Shapiro, *Nietzschean Narratives*, 146.

6. Pamerleau, "The Cost of Greatness," 7. In his concluding remarks, Pamerleau notes that "Nietzsche never explicitly claims that there should be no limit to

the pursuit of greatness, but he never offers a positive theory that would establish one. Either he thinks there is no limit—which *Whiplash* shows is problematic—or there is but he never worked it out" (16).

7. Rawls, *A Theory of Justice*, 420–25.

8. See, for example, Rawls, 422. See also Cavell, *Conditions Handsome and Unhandsome*, 16–21; and Conway, *Nietzsche and the Political*, 52–60.

9. According to Gene Ramey, as recounted to Parker's biographer Stanley Crouch in *Kansas City Lightning*, the episode in question unfolded as follows: " 'Bird had gotten up there and got his meter turned around,' Ramey remembered. 'When they got to the end of the thirty-two-bar chorus, he was in the second bar on that next chorus. Somehow or other he got ahead of himself or something. He had the right meter. He was with the groove all right, but he was probably anxious to make it. Anyway, he couldn't get off. Jo Jones hit the bell corners—*ding*. Bird kept playing. *Ding. Ding.* Everybody was looking, and people were starting to say, 'Get this cat off of here.' *Ding!* So finally, finally, Jo Jones pulled off the cymbal and said '*DING*' on the floor. Some would call it a crash, and they were right, a *DING* trying to pass itself as under a crash. Bird jumped, you know, and it startled him and he eased out of the solo. Everybody was screaming and laughing. The whole place' " (154). As Richard Brody sums up the episode, what Jo Jones did was "not attempted murder but rather musical snark; a humiliation but not an oppression." "Getting Jazz Right in the Movies," *New Yorker*, Oct. 13, 2014.

10. Crouch confirms Fletcher's assessment of the depth of Parker's humiliation following his botched solo (*Kansas City Lightning*, 154–55).

11. In the "Aftersong" with which he concludes *Beyond Good and Evil*, Nietzsche attributes this peculiar brand of beneficence—malevolent, sinister, and absolutely necessary—to the kind of "friend" who appears at just the right time [der Freund zur rechten Stunde] to deliver the blow that will renew one's forward progress.

12. That Casey also may have been grateful to Fletcher is suggested by the inscription on the CD Fletcher plays for his band: "To Dr. Fletcher—Sean."

13. See Cavell, *Conditions Handsome and Unhandsome*, 33–50.

14. See also the analysis by Pamerleau, "The Cost of Greatness," 10–11.

15. When asked to comment on this scene, Chazelle remarks, "At that point, you've spent over an hour watching the character be just an absolute monster—we were trying to make *the* most unforgiveable bastard ever—and then having him deliver a piece of philosophy in such a compelling, charismatic and intelligent way, you could see people almost forget what a psycho he is" (Chazelle, "Director Damien Chazelle Reveals").

16. Those in whom Fletcher replicates his self-contempt are seemingly destined to pay it forward. In particular, abusive yelling is contagious: Carl rages at Andrew for misplacing the drum music folder. Fletcher registers some grudging respect for Andrew when he plays "Whiplash" by heart (i.e., no sheet music) and they win

first place at the Overbrook Jazz Competition. Pamerleau offers the intriguing suggestion that Fletcher himself may have pilfered the folder entrusted to Andrew by Carl ("The Cost of Greatness," 12).

17. Here I follow Ridley, *Nietzsche's Conscience*, 50–57; see also Conway, *Reader's Guide to Nietzsche's "On the Genealogy*,*"* 128–34.

18. On the theme of "jazz hate," see Ratliff, "Jazz Hate."

19. In his biography of Parker, *Kansas City Lightning*, Stanley Crouch confirms Fletcher's account of the hypercompetitive environment at the Reno: "The early-morning Reno jam session was the big time, and if you weren't ready, you didn't come expecting to do anything more than listen. It was highly competitive, a place to out-think, out-execute, and out-swing the opposition. This, as Ralph Ellison has pointed out, was the jazz musician's 'true academy,' where the novice learned his trade . . . and eventually became one of the professionals, a player whose individuality and flexibility combined for an artistic personality worthy of serious consideration" (151–52).

20. Although Fletcher conducts (and apparently prefers) an all-male ensemble, we know that the Shaffer Conservatory enrolls (some) female students. When scouting for promising talent in the (lesser) Nassau Band at the conservatory, Fletcher informs a female saxophone player that she has the first chair only because she is "cute." When Fletcher introduces Andrew to his studio band, he calls him a "squeaker" and asks, "Isn't he cute?"

21. If Fletcher may be said to fit Nietzsche's profile of the ascetic priest, it is possible that he is both a "mean-spirited bully" and a teacher "dedicated to producing greatness," to borrow the language favored by Pamerleau ("The Cost of Greatness," 1).

22. A. O. Scott refers, appropriately, to the "cult of perfection" over which Fletcher presides. Scott, "Drill Sergeant in the Music Room."

23. Scott, "Drill Sergeant in the Music Room."

24. That Jim Neiman, too, is both a former (= failed) musician and now a teacher—"teacher of the year," according to Aunt Emma—is an important element of the Oedipal drama in which Andrew is entangled. Fletcher will turn out to be the better mentor (or "father") only if he succeeds in fledging Andrew as a virtuoso drummer. According to Chazelle, as we shall see, a successful resolution of the Oedipal drama requires both of these father figures to contribute—each in his own way—to the elicitation and expression of Andrew's genius.

25. The most obvious comparison is with Richard Wagner, whom Nietzsche exposes as "this old magician, this Klingsor of all Klingsors" (*CW* PS:1). See also Conway, "The Case of Wagner," 294–99.

26. In his *Empire* interview with Ali Plumb, Chazelle explains, "It's 'if you deliberately sabotage my band I will fuck you like a pig' in the film, but in the trailer it's 'gut you like a pig.' It was originally written as 'gut you like a pig' but J. K. subbed

it with 'fuck,'" which I preferred. So yeah, it's 'fuck you like a pig in the movie, but when they were cutting the trailer they were trying to find scary, outrageous lines to give a taste of the film, and I know we had the 'gut' option in our back pocket."

27. Chazelle may mean for this to be an ominous moment for Andrew. Watching the anti-Semitic Fletcher bully a Jewish bandmate may have unsettled Andrew, whose surname and father, played by Paul Reiser, attest to a Jewish heritage that the film only indirectly confirms.

28. See the analysis by Pamerleau, "The Cost of Greatness," 9–10.

29. Here I follow Staten, *Nietzsche's Voice*, 56–60; and Ridley, *Nietzsche's Conscience*, 52–63.

30. According to Chazelle in his *Empire* interview with Ali Plumb, the role of Andrew's father in the final act was initially meant to be more substantial: "There was still some rejiggering in terms of what Andrew's dad did, and at the end there used to be much more of a moment between them off stage, and that got pared down both in the writing and the edit. We did shoot more stuff of them off to the side of the stage that was very creatively edited out to turn it into a look between them instead of a whole scene."

31. I am indebted here to Shapiro, *Nietzsche's Earth*, 102–10. See also Conway, "Does That Sound Strange to You?," 89–98.

32. See Havas, *Nietzsche's Genealogy*, 155–60; and Conway, "Wir Erkennenden," 116–21.

33. See Conway, *Reader's Guide to Nietzsche's "On the Genealogy,"* 135–47.

34. Earlier, we recall, Fletcher vowed to "fuck . . . like a pig" anyone whom he suspected of sabotaging his band.

35. The distinction between the ascetic *ideal* and ascetic *procedures* (or, in my wording, *techniques* and *practices*) is persuasively drawn by Ridley, *Nietzsche's Conscience*, 57–63.

36. See Shapiro, *Nietzschean Narratives*, 146.

37. Nietzsche suggests as much when he implies that the priests will have exhausted their service to life once they have unwittingly contributed to the production of those "immoralists" among whom Nietzsche presumes to place himself and his best readers (*TI* "Morality" 6). Having affirmed the priests for their role in catalyzing his self-overcoming, Nietzsche suggests that he is now authorized (by life itself) to issue and act on a negation [*Verneinung*] of the priestly type (*EH* "Destiny" 4).

38. For an instructive attempt to account for the affects and attitudes that may be associated with the prescribed emigration "beyond selflessness," see Janaway, *Beyond Selflessness*, chap. 14.

39. Notable among Nietzsche's complaints about his "first-born" (viz. *The Birth of Tragedy*) is his observation that its proffered resolution of the Apollonian and Dionysian impulses "smells offensively Hegelian" (*EH* BT:1).

40. Here I follow Staten, *Nietzsche's Voice*, 48–60; and Ridley, *Nietzsche's Conscience*, 57–63.

41. Ridley, 63.

42. Earlier versions of this chapter were presented at the meetings, respectively, of the Western Political Science Association (2016) and the Eastern Division of the American Philosophical Association (2021). I am grateful to both audiences for the comments I received.

## References

Brody, Richard. "Getting Jazz Right in the Movies." *New Yorker*, Oct. 13, 2014.

Cavell, Stanley. *Conditions Handsome and Unhandsome: The Constitution of Emersonian Perfectionism*. Chicago: University of Chicago Press, 1990.

Chazelle, Damien. "Director Damien Chazelle Reveals 9 Whiplash Secrets." Interview by Ali Plumb. *Empire*, Oct. 28 2015, at 12:53. https://www.empireonline.com/movies/features/damien-chazelle-whiplash-secrets/.

———, dir. *Whiplash*. 2014; Culver City, CA: Sony Pictures Worldwide.

Conway, Daniel. "*The Case of Wagner* and *Nietzsche contra Wagner*." In *A Companion to Friedrich Nietzsche: Life and Works*, edited by Paul Bishop, 285–307. Rochester, NY: Camden House, 2012.

———. "Does That Sound Strange to You? Education and Indirection in Essay III of *On the Genealogy of Morality*." In *Nietzsche, Nihilism, and the Future of Philosophy*, edited by Jeffrey Metzger, 79–101. London: Continuum, 2009.

———. *Nietzsche and the Political*. London: Routledge, 1997.

———. *Reader's Guide to Nietzsche's "On the Genealogy of Morals."* London: Continuum Books, 2008.

———. "Wir Erkennenden: Self-referentiality in Zur Genealogie der Moral." *Journal of Nietzsche Studies* 22 (2001): 116–32.

Crouch, Stanley. *Kansas City Lightning: The Rise and Times of Charlie Parker*. New York: Harper Collins, 2013.

Havas, Randall. *Nietzsche's Genealogy: Nihilism and the Will to Knowledge*. Ithaca, NY: Cornell University Press, 1995.

Janaway, Christopher. *Beyond Selflessness: Reading Nietzsche's Genealogy*. Oxford: Oxford University Press, 2007.

Nietzsche, Friedrich. *The Antichrist*. In *The Portable Nietzsche*, edited and translated by Walter Kaufmann. New York: Viking Penguin, 1982.

———. *Beyond Good and Evil: Prelude to a Philosophy of the Future*. Translated by Walter Kaufmann. New York: Random House/Vintage Books, 1989.

———. *Daybreak*. Translated by R. J. Hollingdale. Cambridge: Cambridge University Press, 1982.

———. *The Gay Science*. Translated by Walter Kaufmann. New York: Random House/Vintage Books, 1974.

———. *On the Genealogy of Morals*. Translated by Walter Kaufmann and R. J. Hollingdale; *Ecce Homo*. New York: Random House/Vintage Books, 1989.

———. *Sämtliche Briefe: Kritische Studienausgabe in 8 Bänden*. Edited by G. Colli and M. Montinari. Berlin: dtv/De Gruyter, 1986.

———. *Sämtliche Werke: Kritische Studienausgabe in 15 Bänden*. Edited by G. Colli and M. Montinari. Berlin: dtv/De Gruyter, 1980.

———. *Twilight of the Idols*. In *The Portable Nietzsche*, edited and translated by Walter Kaufmann. New York: Viking Penguin, 1982.

Pamerleau, William. "The Cost of Greatness: A Nietzschean Analysis of Whiplash." *Film and Philosophy* 20 (2016): 1–18.

Ratliff, Ben. "Jazz Hate." *Slate*, Dec. 15, 2016. https://slate.com/culture/2016/12/la-la-lands-cliched-confused-depiction-of-jazz.html?pay=1692548666688&support_journalism=please.

Rawls, John. *A Theory of Justice*. Cambridge, MA: Harvard University Press, 1971.

Ridley, Aaron. *Nietzsche's Conscience: Six Character Studies from the Genealogy*. Ithaca, NY: Cornell University Press, 1998.

Scott, A. O. "Drill Sergeant in the Music Room." *New York Times*, Oct. 9, 2014. https://www.nytimes.com/2014/10/10/movies/in-whiplash-a-young-jazz-drummer-vs-his-teacher.html?_r=1.

Shapiro, Gary. *Nietzsche's Earth: Great Events, Great Politics*. Chicago: University of Chicago Press, 2016.

———. *Nietzschean Narratives*. Bloomington: Indiana University Press, 1989.

Staten, Henry. *Nietzsche's Voice*. Ithaca, NY: Cornell University Press, 1990.

Williams, Bernard. *Shame and Necessity*. Berkeley: University of California Press, 1993.

7

# Freedom against Equality
## Nietzsche's Aristocratic Politics

Rebecca Aili Ploof

What values should we value most and why? How should we evaluate values and what metric of assessment would we use to do so? Versions of these questions feature prominently in *On the Genealogy of Morality* and, indeed, seem to have preoccupied Nietzsche for quite some time. In the preface to this text, Nietzsche recalls that his younger years were spent poring over questions like "under what conditions did man invent those value judgments good and evil?"; what value do such judgments *"themselves have?"*; and have they "inhibited or furthered human flourishing up until now?"[1] Nietzsche's earlier writings examined these same concerns too. *Human, All Too Human*, for one, investigates the "value and origins of ascetic morality," troubling Schopenhauer's elevation of ascetic ideals to the level of "values in themselves" (*GM* P:4, P:5).

The *Genealogy*'s first treatise zeroes in on a similar line of thought. In the conclusion to this opening essay, Nietzsche affirms that values are only ever valuable relative to goals. Asking whether now commonplace notions of morality have any value—or any utility as some of Nietzsche's interlocuters put it—only begs the question "Value relative *to what end*?" (*GM* I:17). The value of any given moral framework, in other words, can only be determined in relation to a broader value claim. Although moral frameworks may readily supply their own implicit answers to the question of value, Nietzsche resolves that ideally it would be the philosopher's task to "solve the problem of value" and "determine the order of rank among values" (*GM* I:17). In a sense then, Nietzsche suggests, it is the job of philosophy to discern what matters most. The philosopher asks, What value should we prioritize above all others? And in asking this question the philosopher always *also* asks, What end should we care most about furthering?

Here Nietzsche's text poses a second-order question, the *Genealogy*'s answer to which is the focus of my intervention: If one of philosophy's charges is to grapple with and solve the problem of value, what resolution to this problem does Nietzsche himself offer? What value does the *Genealogy* champion and *"to what end"*? (*GM* I:17). Focusing on this work of Nietzsche's, I argue that the value prized above all others in the *Genealogy* is freedom and that such a solution to the problem of value is consonant with what others have described as Nietzsche's aristocratic politics more generally.[2] Freedom furthers the end of "human flourishing," or affirmation of life, which is elseways stymied by the proliferation of democratic values like equality. It is the ontological freedom to become otherwise—which is to say the potential to create and recreate human being—that enables the human condition in its current, unhealthy ascetic form to be overcome. Where freedom supports such self-transformation, Nietzsche contends, equality threatens and undermines it. Not only has the democratization of ascetic ideals contributed to the ascetic form's rise to near unquestioned dominance but appeals to equality have entrenched it: by delegitimating the drive to become more and better than, equality licenses stasis. As such the *Genealogy* advances an argument for the cultivation of freedom over and against equality, stipulating, finally, that such cultivation is for the benefit of an aristocratic few. Only an elite handful of "creative spirit[s]" will be capable of actively exercising the freedom to become otherwise, leaving behind the ascetic form and adopting instead a healthier overhuman identity (*GM* II:24). Realizing this new form of human being for themselves, these aristocratic few ought not worry, Nietzsche argues, about any parallel transformation among the many. Freedom is the most valuable value because it equips noble individuals to achieve a more life-affirming, overhuman way of being in the world.

In developing a reading of the *Genealogy* that in this way emphasizes its aristocratic features and commitments, I depart from countervailing efforts to identify a democratic dimension to Nietzsche's thought. Typically conceding that Nietzsche was not himself a democrat, interpretations in this vein take various aspects of his philosophy to be either productive of or reconcilable with democracy. Lawrence J. Hatab, for instance, argues that despite Nietzsche's antipathy to equality, the "spirit of his own thinking" is entirely compatible with the contentious as well as meritocratic aspects of democratic politics.[3] Echoing Hatab's view, Alan Schrift reads Nietzsche's account of perspectivalism, his deconstruction of the subject, and his embrace of agonism as "conceptual resources for working out a politics of radical democracy."[4] Likewise responding to readings such as Hatab's, Maudemarie Clark paints yet a different portrait of a democratic Nietzsche: values like hierarchy and inequality were for him congruent with and reproducible through democratic institutions, the rise of which Nietzsche accepted as effectively "irresistible."[5]

In fact, modern political thought evinces deep disagreement over equality's relationship to freedom generally and over the relationship democracy in particular tends to cultivate between these two values. For some modern thinkers, freedom and equality were simply two sides of the same coin. Jean-Jacques Rousseau, for example, theorized freedom and equality as mutually reinforcing principles both of which were integral to self-rule by the demos.[6] For others, however, in addition to being decidedly antagonistic values, democratic life had a dangerous propensity to privilege equality at the expense of freedom. According to Alexis de Tocqueville, for one, the equalizing forces of modern democracy threatened to stifle freedom both through the homogenization of thought and through the tyrannical exercise of popular sovereignty.[7] Voicing a related set of anxieties, John Stuart Mill sought to defend freedom from modern democracy's legalistic and customary encroachments, arguing that among its many advantages, liberty was essential to the growth of human knowledge and understanding.[8]

My reading of the *Genealogy* positions Nietzsche as contributing to this conversation. Like Tocqueville and Mill, Nietzsche endeavors to rescue freedom from the oppressive effects of equality, either unleashed or enshrined by modern democratic life.[9] Doing so is important for Nietzsche, however, not simply because freedom provides a bulwark against tyrannical majorities or because it protects creative thought and innovation. Instead, freedom is ontologically valuable. Equipping a select group of individuals to transcend the ascetic human form, freedom supports the achievement of a healthier, overhuman way of being in the world, albeit one inaccessible to most. If ontological freedom was historically discovered and deployed by an aristocratic class, Nietzsche maintains, then recovering it will be the challenge, and reward, of elites as well: overhuman becoming is the prerogative not of the many but of the few.

## Activating Ontological Freedom

I begin by reconstructing what Nietzschean freedom is, pinning its origins and discovery to what the *Genealogy* terms the slave revolt in morality. A conceptual battle waged between and among aristocrats, the slave revolt in morality activates the freedom to become otherwise. It brings into existence a new identity and form of human being molded in accordance with ascetic ideals and characterized by bad conscience. I then trace how, typified by pain, guilt, and torture, this new form of human being is profoundly unhealthy and, ironically, unfree.

The *Genealogy* presents humanity—although not all humans—as uniquely capable of self-creation and self-recreation.[10] Ontological freedom, or the capacity to create and recreate human being, is a distinct feature of the human condition, even if it is not accessible to everyone. Put differently, human nature is for Nietzsche open-ended and subject to change. This is why he describes humanity as a "path" or "bridge" to be traversed and overcome: it entails the ontological freedom to alter and transcend its very form of being (*GM* II:16). Moreover, that humanity contains this potential means that even less than ideal self-formulations can nevertheless give rise to improved forms of human becoming. Thus, bad conscience, for example, is for Nietzsche a kind of "sickness" only in the way that "pregnancy" is: the discomfort of being pregnant and pain of giving birth carries with it the promise of a new human life (*GM* II:19). The ontological freedom to become otherwise means that good things can emerge even out of the worst stages of human development, such that perhaps even the ascetic human form might ultimately be redeemed through radical self-transformation.

Notably, however, freedom of this sort has historically been, and I argue below remains for Nietzsche, the privilege of a specific class or type.[11] The slave revolt in morality—through which humanity was in part pressed into its current shape—was advanced, as Nietzsche tells it, by two warring factions of elites. Referring neither to an actual group of slaves nor a discrete moment in time, Nietzsche distinguishes between an active, "knightly-aristocra[cy]" and their inactive, "priestly" counterparts, positioning the slave revolt in morality as a product of conceptual infighting between these two blocs (*GM* I:7).

Arguing that the right to name things always follows from privilege and power, Nietzsche surmises that this intra-elite conflict can be traced through an exercise in comparative etymology (*GM* I:2). Out of careless contempt for those of lesser rank and a generative yes-saying to themselves, active knightly aristocrats across cultures long ago developed the binary language of good/bad. Reflected in languages as varied as Sanskrit and Greek, "good" on this logic was what was noble, happy, truthful, and beautiful while bad was what was base, unhappy, deceitful, and coarse (*GM* I:2, I:5). Embracing their own power and force, Nietzsche associates these knightly aristocrats with the image of a "blond beast."[12] Found in "Roman, Arab, Germanic, Japanese nobility, Homeric heroes, [and] Scandinavian Vikings," the "blond beast . . . roams about lusting after booty and victory" and this image in the *Genealogy* celebrates the knightly-aristocrats' drive to physically express and assert themselves through violence and domination (*GM* I:11).[13]

By contrast, Nietzsche reasons, out of calculated hatred and reactive no-saying to this knightly group, a "*priestly* caste" of aristocrats developed instead the binary language of good/evil (*GM* I:6, I:11). This linguistic shift began when priestly aristocrats started to frame the original idea of good and bad as a distinction between pure and impure. Good in this account was what was pure and bad was what was impure. Fixated on purity, the "priestly aristocracy," turned away from the physical, sensual world, which it came to see as tainted and unclean (*GM* I:6). Yet this rejection of worldly endeavors ultimately diminished the relative power of the priestly elite, breeding among them a poisonous hatred of and *ressentiment* toward the active "warrior caste" (*GM* I:7, I:10). Out of a desire for revenge, then, inactive priestly aristocrats tried to subvert the values of those holding active political power. This was achieved, Nietzsche writes, by turning the logic of good/bad on its head in order to contend that only the miserable, powerless, and lowly were good, while the powerful were not just bad but evil. Going so far as to damn their knightly brethren before God, the priestly aristocracy took "spiritual revenge" on the political power of their opponents (*GM* I:7).

Advanced by priestly elites the world over, slave morality draws on ascetic self-denial and free will to refashion human being. Alleging that the powerful are evil, slave morality requires us to suppress all outward expression of power, promising instead to control our aggressive impulses, and be good. The *Genealogy*, however, argues that this kind of self-denial is unhealthy and self-harming: when we refuse ourselves all outward expression of power, the impulse to aggression is simply discharged inwardly and experienced as bad conscience.[14]

This is reflected in poor psychological health and in the manner in which the ascetic form of human being, committed to slave morality, is constructed.[15] Capable of promising to be good, remembering that pledge, and feeling obliged to uphold it, this new human form marks an incredible break with humanity's otherwise more primal, animalistic past. Naturally forgetful and unable to feel guilt or shame, the ascetic devotee of slave morality is forged only through pain, torture, and abuse.[16] The ability to remember, for example, must be seared into us. "'One burns something in,'" Nietzsche writes, "'so that it remains in one's memory. Only what does not cease *to give pain* remains in one's memory'" (*GM* II:3). It is by either experiencing or witnessing brutal punishments, like stoning, flaying, and breaking on the wheel, that human beings come to remember the rudimentary prohibitions of collective life. As such, the ability to remember, and with it all the higher cognitive functions that depend on memory, are underwritten and made possible by bodily pain.

It is one thing to remember one's promises and another to feel guilty about breaking them, yet the genesis of guilt is a grim story as the *Genealogy* tells it too. Here Nietzsche begins with the relationship between buyer and seller, or creditor and debtor. This is a relationship he takes to be so fundamental to human sociability as to inform the most elemental ways in which we think about collective life (*GM* II:8). Where communities are traditionally thought of as creditors, who provide peaceful protection to their members, the constituents of any given community take on the role of debtors who must repay their common creditor for such security. Those who shirk repayment are "criminals" and are punished in equivalence to their outstanding debt. Because "seeing-suffer feels good" and "making-suffer" feels even better, in punishing debtors the communal creditor is repaid an amount of sadistic pleasure equivalent to what it is owed (*GM* II:6).

As it happens, Nietzsche argues, people come to think of themselves as indebted to their present community as well as to an ancestral community long since passed (*GM* II:19). Our flourishing in the present is thought to be possible only by dint of the sacrifices and achievements of those who have come before us, yet as long as these gifts continue to bear fruit, our ancestral debt to the past grows. Expanding exponentially, this debt becomes unpayable, and as this happens our fear of and guilt before the eldest elder multiples. It multiples to the point where this ancestor of all ancestors becomes, in our minds, a god (*GM* II:19). In this way, those who promise to contain their aggression, abide by the rules of communal life, and repay all debts experience irremediable psychological discomfort and pain in the form of guilt before the divine.

This thought, found across all formulations of slave morality but perfected by Christianity in particular, "becomes an instrument of torture" for its adherents (*GM* II:22). The *Genealogy* dramatizes this by comparing such a psychological condition to that of a caged and abused wild animal. Denied all outward expression of power, the ascetic human condition chains and confines the "blond beast" within. Encouraged to feel guilt and shame, the primal "animal-self" is subjected, so to speak, to "vivisection and cruelty" (*GM* II:24). Battered into domesticated submission, this creature in turn inflicts pain on itself, "beating" its body "raw on the bars of its cage" (*GM* II:16). Slave morality, in short, gives rise to a tortured and self-torturing new identity.

In this way the aristocratic battle over good, bad, and evil births a new mode of human being: one that, committed to slave morality, experiences the world through bad conscience. This is a testament to the actuality of ontological freedom. Yet this new way of being is not itself free just as it is not productive of human flourishing. Distinguished by the anguish of pain, guilt, and torture, the ascetic human form championed and imposed by the priestly elite supports not freedom and well-being, or even their possibility, but instead illness and constraint.

## Arresting Ontological Freedom: Asceticism Democratized

It is the democratization of slave morality and asceticism that gives rise to this limiting and confined human form. In this section, I contrast the *Genealogy*'s account of the ways in which asceticism can be genuinely life-affirming in discrete contexts with the ways in which its universalization is otherwise life-denying and inhibitive of ontological freedom. I examine how the ascetic priest popularizes ascetic ideals, cementing through their universalization a static, unhealthy form of human being inconducive to future becoming. I then turn to Nietzsche's suggestion that in the contemporary world, science and democracy now reproduce and entrench ascetic principles, further impeding the realization of ontological freedom.

The *Genealogy* associates asceticism with two archetypal figures: the philosopher and the priest. For the philosopher, it is asceticism's rejection of sensuality that makes it deeply appealing. Sensuality threatens to undermine the philosopher's commitment to intellectual inquiry by creating relationships of dependence that distract from it. In order to be free to engage in such inquiry, Nietzsche explains, the philosopher seeks to avoid any and all forms of reliance. "Abhorring marriage," for this reason, the philosopher would prefer to say " 'no' to all unfreedom," wandering off "into some sort of *desert*" in pursuit of the solitary life of the mind (*GM* III:7). As such, the *Genealogy* argues, asceticism is appropriate for philosophers: it sanctions and supports the particular way of life they seek.

Yet just because asceticism is suitable for philosophers does not make it necessarily life-affirming for anyone else. This is the problem, the *Genealogy* contends, with the second archetypal character invested in asceticism: the ascetic priest who democratizes earthly withdrawal by preaching asceticism for all. The ascetic priest—a relative of the priestly aristocrat touched on above and a persona often adopted by philosophers in disguise—treats life itself as a "wrong path" that should be traced back and rejected (*GM* III:10, 11).[17] While devaluing human being full stop, and yearning for "an entirely different kind of existence," the ascetic priest nevertheless denies the very freedom that would otherwise support humanity's healthy self-transformation (*GM* II:11). Abhorring the this-worldly, physical nature of our existence, the ascetic priest perpetuates a degraded and debased form of human being.

How does the ascetic priest do this? Among adherents of slave morality, who are tortured by bad conscience, many are in search of an explanation for their psychological discomfort and despair (*GM* III:15). The ascetic priest offers such an explanation, telling any and all who will listen that they themselves are to blame for their own suffering. We are the agents of our own pain, the ascetic priest counsels, not because we have made ourselves this way, as the *Genealogy* contends, but because as human beings we are innately "sinful" (*GM* III:16). Our lives are harrowing and wretched because we were born in and live in sin. Responding in this way, the ascetic priest further ingrains bad conscience by turning the outward search for aggression-cum-blame inward, while also revealing himself to be just as guilt-ridden and unwell as his followers. In this respect, Nietzsche analogizes, the ascetic priest is like a physician who suffers from the same disease as the patients he attends (*GM* III:17). Yet in prescribing forms of palliative care that only distract from and anesthetize pain, the ascetic priest succeeds merely in prolonging his congregants' suffering.

Thus democratizing ascetic withdrawal from this-worldly life, the ascetic priest universalizes the philosopher's otherwise sui generis retreat from sensuality. Unlike the philosopher, however, the priest's many followers are not so much buoyed and affirmed by this denial as they are made to feel worse by it. Popularizing a set of ideals that entrench the ascetic human form and, for most, amplify bad conscience, the ascetic priest works at cross purposes to freedom and human flourishing.

Where the ascetic priest's efforts are centuries upon centuries old, modernity has introduced new avenues through which asceticism maintains its hold on thought and being. The first, and more remarked upon of these avenues in the *Genealogy*, is modern science. Nietzsche himself argues that, like asceticism, modern science denigrates sensual subjective experience, over and above which it places objectivity on a pedestal. Modern science believes in objective truth, he contends, affirming that it exists—pure and eternal—outside of the messy world of human beings. Ideally, modern science would even like to think that such truths are discernable absent the contamination of a subjective human interpreter (*GM* III:24). By celebrating pure objectivity, then, the scientist or "truthful one," like the ascetic priest, "*affirms another world* than that of life, nature, and history" (*GM* III:24). In so doing, both figures turn their back on this world, which cannot help but be complicated by human sensuality and subjectivity. In this way a "hiding place for . . . bad conscience," science merely reinscribes the ascetic human form, obscuring and impeding the realization of any identity or "ideal above" and beyond it (*GM* III:23).

Modern democracy, another avenue in the contemporary world through which asceticism maintains its chokehold on freedom and human flourishing, similarly disinclines striving for anything more or better. Indeed, Nietzsche associates it with scientism for precisely this reason (*GM* III:25).[18] Promoting the "reduction and equalization" of all, democratic social and political order effectively silences that which "wishes to become greater" (*GM* I:12). Delegitimating stratification, modern democratic appeals to equality encourage a downward regression to the "mediocre" mean, rejecting on principle all aspiration to anything higher (*GM* I:12). In this way both scientism and democratization reflect a stubborn disinterest in and disregard for that which is not already fact or status quo. Accepting the world as it is, both take for granted and make it difficult to alter the now dominant ascetic form of human being. As such, popularized asceticism in its spiritual, scientific, and socio-political manifestations poses a threat to ontological freedom and improved human becoming.

## Recovering Ontological Freedom

In imagining how such freedom might be recovered, the *Genealogy* lays out at least three potential antidotes to asceticism. By recuperating physical sensuality, turning to art, and embracing laughter, it may be possible to recover the ability to become otherwise yet again. However, I argue, Nietzsche frames each as an incredibly difficult pursuit. In this way he makes the achievement of healthier ways of being in the world available to none save an elite few. Moreover, he stipulates, these higher spirits ought not concern themselves with the trickle-down transformation of the many. What was long ago activated by a handful of enterprising aristocrats must be reclaimed by and for the few once more.

Asceticism, in the forms of slave morality and bad conscience, demands the suppression of physical power, creating an internal, self-harming discharge of energy. Nietzsche suggests that the reaffirmation of our material being may counteract this. This is the analytical function of the *Genealogy*'s many animal metaphors.[19] Unlike ascetic human beings, animals enjoy a positive orientation toward their own physicality. To be an animal, in other words, is to be unbothered by the natural, outward expression of physical drive. An ascetic "bird of prey," for example, that beats itself up for being a bird of prey and forbids itself to hunt any more "lambs," is unthinkable (*GM* I:13). As such, Nietzsche's animal metaphors encourage the rehabilitation of "life, nature, and history" in contradistinction to asceticism's denigration of the this-worldly here and now (*GM* III:24).

This is perhaps best captured by the animal image through which Nietzsche presents the hybrid ascetic priest-philosopher. "Until the most recent time the *ascetic priest*," he writes "has functioned as the repulsive and gloomy caterpillar-form in which alone philosophy was allowed to live and in which it crept around. . . . Has this really changed? Has the colorful and dangerous winged animal, the 'spirit' that this caterpillar concealed within itself . . . finally been unfrocked after all and let out into the light?" (*GM* III:10). Daring, cheerful, and new, the possibility of a butterfly exists within the caterpillar's dull and dreary form. Philosophers who have cloaked themselves in the trappings of ascetic priesthood should shake off their caterpillar skins, enter into the cocoon, and reclaim the chrysalid capacity to become new creatures again.

Art, Nietzsche suggests, is another means though which asceticism can be thwarted. Art has this potential because, unlike science, it makes no pretense to objectivity or truth. Entirely compatible with subjective views and aims, art readily embraces truth's opposite: "Art, in which precisely the *lie* hallows itself, in which the *will to deception* has good conscience on its side, is much more fundamentally opposed to the ascetic ideal than is science" (*GM* III:25). Of course the artist's lie consists not in the use of deceit but of artifice. The work of art is always a fabrication and as such invites a subjective rather than objective response. Even if a work of art resonates with those who encounter it as somehow "true," its fabricated quality means it is not committed, in the way science is, to the value and principle of truth. Art does not elevate truth above and beyond "life, nature, and history" and this is what allows it to function as a counterweight to asceticism (*GM* III:24).

Associated by Nietzsche with both physicality and art, laughter is yet a third mechanism through which asceticism can be challenged.[20] Where asceticism esteems pain, *ressentiment*, and gloom, the affective pleasure of laughing—at, for example, the tragicomedy of the ascetic condition itself—instead paves the way for transformative becoming. It is for this reason that the *Genealogy* identifies the "real enem[ies] and *injurer*[s]" of asceticism as those "comedians of th[e] ideal" (*GM* III:27). Nietzsche connects laughter, especially laughing at oneself, with great artistry. "Every artist" he writes "only arrives at the final pinnacle of his greatness when he is able to see himself and his art *beneath* him—when he is able to *laugh* at himself" (*GM* III:3). In coming to see one's condition as laughable, one begins to see it as something to be left behind and overcome. In fact, laughter is compatible not just with artistry but with physicality. As a pleasurable bodily experience, it cheerfully returns us to our physical, this-worldly selves.

That artistry and physicality should be essential to beating back asceticism, and recovering ontological freedom, is further reflected in the otherwise puzzling image with which Nietzsche closes the *Genealogy*'s preface. Here he warns readers that for his writing to be intelligible, an "art of interpretation" must be brought to bear on it (*GM* P:8). "Admittedly," he allows, "to practice reading as an *art* in this way one thing above all is necessary, something which these days has been unlearned better than anything else . . . something for which one must almost be a cow and in any case *not* a 'modern man': *ruminating*" (*GM* P:8). The animal's positive orientation to its own embodiment, and the artist's embrace of subjectivity, disrupt and push against ascetic ideals. This is what allows Nietzsche's call to overcome asceticism to be heard and taken up. The cow-like reader, able to engage the *Genealogy* as a work of art, will be Nietzsche's co-combatant in the fight to reclaim ontological freedom, and by way of such freedom, human flourishing.

Yet none of these prescriptive recommendations is widely practicable. To read ruminatingly, and fully understand the *Genealogy*, for example, one must not only disband with the modern habitus but also have already mastered Nietzsche's other texts. The *Genealogy* will be comprehensible to those who have "first read [Nietzsche's] earlier writings," and indeed, have "spared" little "effort in the process," for these themselves are "not easily accessible" (*GM* P:8). Moreover, the ability to laugh at oneself in the manner Nietzsche advocates is possible only for those who have already achieved a remarkable level of accomplishment. It is, after all, the "artist" who has ascended to the "final pinnacle of his greatness" who can begin to "laugh at himself" (*GM* III:3). Finally, the kind of healthy, embodied self-transformation Nietzsche calls for is presented in incredibly challenging terms as well. The metamorphosis undertaken by the hybrid ascetic-priest philosopher requires "pride, daring, bravery, [and] self-assuredness" (*GM* III:10). Approachable only through "enough will of the spirit, will to responsibility, [and] *freedom of the will*," such transmutation may be available to the caterpillar, but it is hardly universal (*GM* III:10). Where the first and second of these prescriptive suggestions entail the challenging cultivation of a difficult skill, this final recommendation appears to rest instead on a particular inbuilt capacity.

Recalling the way in which ontological freedom was first activated through aristocratic activity, the *Genealogy* makes clear that the work of reclaiming such freedom will fall to an elite few as well.[21] So too, however, will its great promise: a healthier, more life-affirming identity productive of human flourishing. Although it is not inconceivable that this becoming, like its ascetic forebear, might in turn be passed down to or even imposed on the many, Nietzsche is emphatic that these "creative spirits" not trouble themselves with such considerations. Because the elite few are "alone the *guarantors* of the future"—able to do that which "no sick person" ever could—it would be a "grave mistake" for them to serve as mere "physician, comforter, [or] savior" to the unwell masses (*GM* III:14). The "higher," Nietzsche stresses, "*must* not degrade itself" as a "tool of the lower" (*GM* III:14). Enjoying a "right to exist . . . a thousandfold greater" than these others, such higher spirits must be allowed to run free, across the "bridge" that is humanity, toward a form of being that is instead provocatively vibrant and new (*GM* III:14; II:16).

## Conclusion

Politics, of course, is about power and, as the *Genealogy* highlights, the ways in which power shapes and manifests in the world through the creation and imposition of values. Nietzsche's formulation, then, of the "problem of value" and the way in which the *Genealogy* itself approaches this problem is inescapably political. In formulating a response to the question of what value we should value most and why, philosophy cannot help but supply a political answer, and Nietzsche's text is no exception.[22]

My contention has been that the *Genealogy* advances a solution to the problem of value that prioritizes freedom for the few over and against equality for the many. Affirming that the "welfare of the majority and the welfare of the few are opposing value viewpoints," the *Genealogy* presents the recovery of ontological freedom for these few as a necessary means to the end of "human flourishing" (*GM* II:17). Equality has imperiled the freedom to become otherwise, entrenching—first through the universalization of ascetic ideals and now through scientism and democracy—a form of human being that is self-harming and unwell. Historically activated and realized through aristocratic struggle, ontological freedom must be reclaimed and exercised by those with enough strength and "will of spirit" to contest and subvert this unhealthy state of affairs. Demanding "pride, daring, [and] bravery," only an elite handful of great individuals—artists and philosophers among them—will find themselves worthy of meeting this challenge and enjoying its bountiful rewards (*GM* III:18).

What implications might the *Genealogy's* solution to the "problem of value" hold for democratic practices and identities today? How, for instance, might a Nietzschean notion of freedom productively challenge contemporary democratic political forms and subjectivities? If answers to twenty-first-century questions such as these are elusive, Nietzsche's location within the history of political thought is clearer. Endeavoring to invigorate freedom and protect it from equality, Nietzsche joins the ranks of other nineteenth-century theorists concerned with the threat modern democracy posed to freedom. Nietzsche's innovation, however, is to connect this alleged danger to ontological change and possibility: freedom is the most valuable value because it enables the transformation of human being itself. Empowering a select few to slough off the ascetic human form, it enables the rarified among us to approach a healthier, overhuman identity and way of being in the world.

## Notes

1. Friedrich Nietzsche, *On the Genealogy of Morality*, trans. Maudemarie Clark and Alan J. Swenson (Indianapolis, IN: Hackett Publishing, 1998), P:3. Hereafter referred to as *GM*.

2. On Nietzsche's "aristocratism" and "elitism," see for example Ruth Abbey and Fredrick Appel, "Nietzsche and the Will to Politics," *Review of Politics* 60, no. 1 (1998): 83–114; Keith Ansell-Pearson, *An Introduction to Nietzsche as Political Thinker* (Cambridge: Cambridge University Press, 1994), 39–44; Wendy Brown, "Nietzsche for Politics," in *Why Nietzsche Still? Reflections on Drama, Culture, and Politics*, ed. Alan D. Schrift (Berkeley: University of California Press, 2000), 205–23; Sheldon Wolin, *Politics and Vision: Continuity and Innovation in Western Political Thought* (Princeton, NJ: Princeton University Press, 2006), 489–90.

3. Lawrence J. Hatab, *A Nietzschean Defense of Democracy* (Chicago: University of Chicago Press, 1995), 3.

4. Alan D. Schrift, "Nietzsche *For* Democracy?," *Nietzsche-Studien* 29 (2000): 222.

5. Maudemarie Clark, "Nietzsche's Antidemocratic Rhetoric," in *Nietzsche on Ethics and Politics* (New York: Oxford University Press Online, 2015), 12.

6. Jean-Jacques Rousseau, *The Social Contract and Other Later Political Writings*, trans. Victor Gourevitch (Cambridge: Cambridge University Press, 1997), 78.

7. Alexis de Tocqueville, *Democracy in America*, trans. Harvey C. Mansfield and Delba Winthrop (Chicago: University of Chicago Press, 2000), 268–73.

8. John Stuart Mill, *On Liberty, Utilitarianism, and Other Essays* (Oxford: Oxford University Press, 2015), 62–64.

9. Paul Franco argues that Tocqueville and Nietzsche share a concern about the threat democracy poses to human greatness, stemming from the fact that both adopt "the distinctive standpoint of aristocracy." See "Tocqueville and Nietzsche on the Problem of Human Greatness in Democracy," *Review of Politics* 76, no. 3 (2014): 439–67. Highlighting only Nietzsche's "aristocratism," Gerald Mara and Suzanne Dovi identify a common opposition in both his and Mill's work to democracy's suffocation of "individual creativity and self-development." See "Mill, Nietzsche, and the Identity of Postmodern Liberalism," *Journal of Politics* 57, no. 1 (1995): 2.

10. In developing this view, I follow Ridley's argument that fatalism and the possibility for self-creation are not antagonistic but rather compatible strands

of Nietzsche's thought. See Aaron Ridley, "Nietzsche, Nature, Nurture," *European Journal of Philosophy* 25, no. 1 (2016): 129–43. In defense of a related reading, see also Robert C. Solomon, *Living with Nietzsche: What the Great "Immoralist" Has to Teach Us* (Oxford: Oxford University Press, 2003), 181–83. Cf. Brian Leiter, "The Paradox of Fatalism and Self-Creation in Nietzsche," in *Willing and Nothingness: Schopenhauer as Nietzsche's Educator*, ed. Christopher Janaway (Oxford: Oxford University Press, 1998), 217–57.

11. In this sense there is indeed an important, fatalistic quality to Nietzsche's account of self-creation and self-recreation: only some are, at bottom, equipped to exercise ontological freedom.

12. On the term "blond beast" and the ways in which this phrase is frequently misconstrued, see Gerd Shank, "Nietzsche's 'Blond Beast': On the Recuperation of a Nietzschean Metaphor," in *A Nietzsche Bestiary: Becoming Animal Beyond Docile and Brutal*, eds. Christa Davis Acampora and Ralph R. Acampora (New York: Rowman & Littlefield, 2004), 140–55.

13. Ontological freedom, then, should not be confused with the "will to power." What Nietzsche refers to in the *Genealogy* with the phrase "will to power" is not the self-transformation of being but the untrammeled expression of vitality. In this way—while laying the groundwork for ontologically transformative priestly reaction—Nietzsche's knightly aristocrats and blond beasts actualize their "will to power" or "*instinct for freedom*" sans the transcendence of being (*GM* II:17; *GM* II 18).

14. See also Acampora, "On Sovereignty and Overhumanity: Why It Matters How We Read Nietzsche's *Genealogy* II: 2," in *Nietzsche's "On the Genealogy of Morals": Critical Essays*, ed. Christa Davis Acampora (New York: Rowman & Littlefield, 2006), 147–61.

15. To be clear, Nietzsche cautions against "forming a low opinion" of this development *merely* because it is "ugly and painful from the outset" (*GM* II:18).

16. On memory and forgetting in Nietzsche's thought, see also Christa Davis Acampora, "Forgetting the Subject," in *Reading Nietzsche at the Margins*, eds. Steven V. Hicks and Alan Rosenberg (West Lafayette, IN: Purdue University Press, 2008), 34–56.

17. Historically, Nietzsche notes, the philosopher regularly adopted the outward appearance of the priest because it afforded more safety and protection. On the hybridity and interplay of these two archetypal figures, see also Mark Migotti, "Sensuality and Its Discontents," *Journal of Nietzsche Studies* 44, no. 2 (2013): 315–28.

18. Babette Babich identifies an even stronger affinity between modern science and democracy in Nietzsche's other work. See Babette Babich, "Ex aliquo nihil: Nietzsche on Science, Anarchy, and Democratic Nihilism," *American Catholic Philosophical Quarterly* 84, no. 2 (2010): 231–55.

19. On Nietzsche's use of animal imagery more broadly, see Acampora and Acampora, *A Nietzschean Bestiary: Becoming Animal Beyond Docile and Brutal* (New York: Rowman & Littlefield, 2004); Vanessa Lemm, *Nietzsche's Animal Philosophy:*

*Culture, Politics, and the Animality of Human Being* (New York: Fordham University Press, 2009); and T. J. Reed, "Nietzsche's Animals: Idea, Image, and Influence," in *Nietzsche: Imagery and Thought*, ed. Malcolm Pasley (Berkeley: University of California Press, 1978).

20. The function of laughter, humor, and comedy in Nietzsche's work has attracted sustained scholarly interest. See for instance Charles Boddicker, "Humour in Nietzsche's Style," *European Journal of Philosophy* 29, no. 2 (2021): 447–58; Lawrence J. Hatab, "Laughter in Nietzsche's Thought: A Philosophical Tragicomedy," *International Studies in Philosophy* 20, no. 2 (1988): 67–79.

21. Emphasizing the ways in which Nietzsche's use of rhetoric works to persuade the elite few to take up the task of transforming moral values, Janaway offers a compatible reading of the *Genealogy*. See Christopher Janaway, *Beyond Selflessness: Reading Nietzsche's "Genealogy"* (Oxford: Oxford University Press, 2007), 14–15.

22. On this point, see Robert Guay, "Passionate Actors and Wounded Apes: Nietzsche on Identity Formation," in this volume.

# References

Abbey, Ruth, and Fredrick Appel. "Nietzsche and the Will to Politics." *Review of Politics* 60, no. 1 (1998): 83–114.

Acampora, Christa Davis. "Forgetting the Subject." In *Reading Nietzsche at the Margins*, edited by Steven V. Hicks and Alan Rosenberg. West Lafayette, IN: Purdue University Press, 2008.

———. "On Sovereignty and Overhumanity: Why It Matters How We Read Nietzsche's *Genealogy* II: 2." In *Nietzsche's "On the Genealogy of Morals": Critical Essays*, edited by Christa Davis Acampora. New York: Rowman & Littlefield, 2006.

Acampora, Christa Davis, and Ralph R. Acampora, eds. *A Nietzschean Bestiary: Becoming Animal Beyond Docile and Brutal*. New York: Rowman & Littlefield, 2004.

Ansell-Pearson, Keith. *An Introduction to Nietzsche as Political Thinker*. Cambridge: Cambridge University Press, 1994.

Babich, Babette. "Ex aliquo nihil: Nietzsche on Science, Anarchy, and Democratic Nihilism." *American Catholic Philosophical Quarterly* 84, no. 2 (2010): 231–55.

Boddicker, Charles. "Humour in Nietzsche's Style." *European Journal of Philosophy* 29, no. 2 (2021): 447–58.

Brown, Wendy. "Nietzsche for Politics." In *Why Nietzsche Still? Reflections on Drama, Culture, and Politics*, edited by Alan D. Schrift. Berkeley: University of California Press, 2000.

Clark, Maudemarie. *Nietzsche on Ethics and Politics*. New York: Oxford University Press Online, 2015. https://doi.org/10.1093/acprof:oso/9780199371846.001.0001.

Franco, Paul. "Tocqueville and Nietzsche on the Problem of Human Greatness in Democracy." *Review of Politics* 76, no. 3 (2014): 439–67.

Hatab, Lawrence J. "Laughter in Nietzsche's Thought: A Philosophical Tragicomedy." *International Studies in Philosophy* 20, no. 2 (1988): 67–79.

———. *A Nietzschean Defense of Democracy*. Chicago: University of Chicago Press, 1995.

Janaway, Christopher. *Beyond Selflessness: Reading Nietzsche's "Genealogy."* Oxford: Oxford University Press, 2007.

Leiter, Brian. "The Paradox of Fatalism and Self-Creation in Nietzsche." In *Willing and Nothingness: Schopenhauer as Nietzsche's Educator*, edited by Christopher Janaway. Oxford: Oxford University Press, 1998.

Lemm, Vanessa. *Nietzsche's Animal Philosophy: Culture, Politics, and the Animality of Human Being*. New York: Fordham University Press, 2009.

Mara, Gerald M., and Suzanne L. Dovi. "Mill, Nietzsche, and the Identity of Postmodern Liberalism." *Journal of Politics* 57, no. 1 (1995): 1–23.

Migotti, Mark. "Sensuality and Its Discontents." *Journal of Nietzsche Studies* 44, no. 2 (2013): 315–28.

Mill, John Stuart. *On Liberty, Utilitarianism, and Other Essays*. Oxford: Oxford University Press, 2015.

Nietzsche, Friedrich. *On the Genealogy of Morality*. Translated by Maudemarie Clark and Alan J. Swenson. Indianapolis, IN: Hackett Publishing, 1998.

Reed, T. J. "Nietzsche's Animals: Idea, Image, and Influence." In *Nietzsche: Imagery and Thought*, edited by Malcolm Pasley. Berkeley: University of California Press, 1978.

Ridley, Aaron. "Nietzsche, Nature, Nurture." *European Journal of Philosophy* 25, no. 1 (2016): 129–43.

Rousseau, Jean-Jacques. *The Social Contract and Other Later Political Writings*. Translated by Victor Gourevitch. Cambridge: Cambridge University Press, 1997.

Schrift, Alan D. "Nietzsche *For* Democracy?" *Nietzsche-Studien* 29 (2000): 220–33.

Shank, Gerd. "Nietzsche's 'Blond Beast': On the Recuperation of a Nietzschean Metaphor." In *A Nietzschean Bestiary: Becoming Animal Beyond Docile and Brutal*, edited by Christa Davis Acampora and Ralph R. Acampora. New York: Rowman & Littlefield, 2004.

Solomon, Robert C. *Living with Nietzsche: What the Great "Immoralist" Has to Teach Us*. Oxford: Oxford University Press, 2003.

Tocqueville, Alexis de. *Democracy in America*. Translated by Harvey C. Mansfield and Delba Winthrop. Chicago: University of Chicago Press, 2000.

Wolin, Sheldon. *Politics and Vision: Continuity and Innovation in Western Political Thought*. Princeton, NJ: Princeton University Press, 2006.

8

# Masters, Slaves, "Terrorists"

## On Elitism and Existential Threats

C. HEIKE SCHOTTEN

Nietzsche's critique of slave morality in *On the Genealogy of Morals* (1967 [1887]) is among the most well-known and, as Allison Merrick observes, critically well-trodden parts of his philosophical corpus.[1] This is perhaps due in part to the fact that Nietzsche here seems to be at his clearest, laying out an argument that proceeds, if not entirely linearly, then at least in a single general direction. The argument of the book unfolds over the course of three numbered essays (rather than, say, getting dispersed among a series of aphorisms only apparently organized by theme, as in many of his other works) and seems, by the end, to issue in an overall and relatively clear conclusion; namely, the diagnosis of modern nihilism. All this is reassuring to those of us who have been professionally trained to locate arguments and aim to transmit that same skill set to undergraduates in our classrooms.

There is another reason, however, for the well-troddenness of this particular philosophical ground in Nietzsche, which is not simply its seeming straightforwardness, but also the straightforward way in which, despite numerous asides, diversionary diatribes, and dialogues with unnamed interlocutors, Nietzsche nevertheless seems to lay out with some perspicuity his critique of what we might, anachronistically, call liberatory or anti-oppression politics.[2] Indeed, in an even narrower subset of very famous and well-worn pages in Essay I, Nietzsche offers a critique of what he calls slave morality. A clear rejection of Christianity and its modern derivatives, this critique also has the very real and obvious potential to function as a more general dismissal of any progressive politics that would object to inequality, a politics he suggests should not be understood as righteous but rather the vengeful path to power taken by weak and contemptible people who cannot survive or flourish any other way. My suspicion, then, is that readers and critics return to this part of Nietzsche over and over again not simply because of its (relative) clarity, but also because of the difficult and provocative character of the argument he advances there. Nietzsche seems clearly to criticize not just modernity's "sacred cow,"[3] equality, but also any social or political movement that might seek to advance it. Given modernity's still relatively undisturbed self-identification as the era of progress, democracy, and egalitarianism, not to mention our own self-identifications (however conscious or unconscious) as liberal, progressive, or even radical commentators and critics, Nietzsche's challenge here—mercilessly articulated, bracingly written, and unambivalent in its disparagement of "slavishness"—cuts to the core of what we think about ourselves, the world, and how we live, not to mention the value and worth of our movements for justice and liberation.

Despite this seeming contradiction or challenge, then, it is noteworthy that, for the most part, the influential readings and applications of Nietzsche's critique of slave morality—most if not all of which are penned by self-identified left, progressive, or otherwise "critical" critics—have not tried to prove him wrong. Instead, they have maintained his argument largely intact and, instead, used it to criticize left or progressive social movements as contemporary versions of slave morality. The most famous version of this argument is Wendy Brown's still widely cited essay, "Wounded Attachments,"[4] which remains a definitive statement of left Nietzscheanism and is referenced to this day as an important and relevant critique of so-called identity politics. Variations of this critical use of Nietzsche abound, however, particularly with regard to feminism.[5] Although a perhaps valiant effort on the part of left commentators to engage in self-criticism, I nevertheless find the prominence of Brown's essay and the proliferation of its derivatives troubling. Given the dearth of what I would call liberatory scholarship or critique within Nietzsche studies, it seems that this interpretive self-criticism sets an unfortunate precedent that only left movements—or, perhaps, only feminism—should be subjected to this particular Nietzschean analysis, a significant if unavowed critical consensus that reflects rather than challenges conservative and anti-feminist tendencies in Nietzsche studies, not to mention academic philosophy and political theory more broadly. Why has this conservatism become the disciplinary legacy and political afterlife of (this part of) the *Genealogy*? Why would otherwise self-identified progressive, left, and/or feminist commentators like Brown seek to solidify such readings of our movements or our shared, political world?[6]

The issue here may simply be a more straightforward interpretive one, at least to the extent that Nietzsche himself was certainly no "progressive" or left-leaning thinker. His critique of slave morality is, in essence, a claim that the undeserving many have taken the reins of power to the detriment of the exceptional few. This is, in broad strokes, Corey Robin's definition of "reactionary"[7] and therefore may mean that applying this criticism to politics somehow requires that one take a conservative position. However, quite a bit rides on what it means to understand Nietzsche as "conservative" or as advancing a critique of a so-called progressive modernity. I would suggest that, whether or not we read Nietzsche's critique of slave morality as "conservative" or "progressive," it is crucial to recognize that it is a critique presented from the perspective of those in power—whether we want to call them the oppressor or the ruling class or, to use his language, the "masters," the elite, the great, or the few.[8] Nietzsche would of course never call these latter entities "the oppressor"; such language already indicates a break with the position and argument he is advancing. That, however, is precisely the point. What is at stake in the difference between these terminological choices is less an interpretive question regarding what exactly Nietzsche said than a matter of political commitment in how Nietzsche is taken up and used by us, his readers. In other words, this issue of perspective explicitly raises the question of an *interpreter's* commitment to the notion that there are (or are not) significant, widespread hierarchies of social power that structurally disempower, disenfranchise, and subordinate most people(s) to the benefit of an elite few, much less if and how such hierarchies are legitimate.

Of course, Nietzsche very much does believe that there are widespread social power imbalances that disenfranchise some—this is one of his major complaints about modernity. But those disenfranchised ones, in his view, are the superior and the few (who are the latter because they are the former). This elite should not be marginalized because, unlike the great masses of modern men[9] who are little better than "herd animals" and for whose ideas, talents, and aspirations Nietzsche has little respect, these superior few are more deserving (precisely how or in what way has been analyzed by Nietzsche scholars for decades). In short, however, Nietzsche is both a reactionary and an elitist. This is (or should be) neither a controversial nor necessarily derogatory statement; it is, rather, simply an acknowledgment of Nietzsche's political commitments and the perspective from which he advances them. It does mean, however, that using his critique of slave morality to understand or critique contemporary political formations risks not only colluding with this conservatism and elitism, but also reproducing it by failing to sever it from its commitment to naturalized hierarchy and situatedness as a critique "from above."

This is an approach that I, at least, do not wish to reproduce. My approach in this chapter, then, will be different from that more traditionally pursued and applied in political theory interpretations of Nietzsche. Rather than reprimanding either feminism or the Left for its fearfulness about power, as Brown does,[10] I think it is both more accurate as well as more liberatory to use Nietzsche's critique of slave morality to diagnose the misplaced resentment of the Right—of, for example, neoconservatives who shore up American greatness via recourse to demonization of communist, "totalitarian," or Muslim enemies; white supremacists who publicly proclaim, in an anxious and defensive performance of their own derivative self-affirmation, "Jews will not replace us"; or trans exclusionary feminists who seek to protect "women" from the ostensible threat posed by trans people. Far from an accurate or relevant diagnosis of so-called left or progressive identity politics, I argue instead that slave morality better describes the trials and tribulations of the embattled and beleaguered white guys (and gals) of the world and synopsizes one of the predominant mainstream explanations for the surprise 2016 presidential election of Donald Trump.[11] The sort of hamstrung, reactionary rage that Trump orchestrates and right-wing groups in affinity with him exhibit is the politics of resentment plain and simple, much more so than anything "identity politics" has ever mustered. The extraordinary moral panics about trans people—in particular, trans children—and the paranoid public outrage about trans people using public restrooms, participating in team sports, or accessing healthcare belie a fabrication of threat seemingly unparalleled in magnitude and absurdity, leveraged solely to produce regimes of intense surveillance and punishment—if not outright elimination—of trans people.[12]

This seemingly academic question of Nietzsche interpretation is thus also a timely and urgent question of political praxis, not only for his readers but also for those of us committed to liberatory social movements for justice and liberation. In this chapter, therefore, I too return to those battered few pages of the first essay of Nietzsche's *Genealogy* and, like Brown and her derivatives, largely endorse the argument he makes about slave morality there. However, breaking with Brown and similar commentators, I do not read and apply this bit of Nietzsche from the perspective from which he advances it. That is, I refuse to reproduce the reactionary elitism that governs his critique of slave morality. This move is crucial not only for Nietzsche studies but also for any critical political theory that aims to have something of relevance to contribute to the people and movements being quashed by the current global ascendance of the fascist and reactionary far Right. By contrast with Nietzsche, I take the existence of widespread socio-political oppressions—in particular, white supremacy, cis-hetero patriarchy, capitalist exploitation, settler conquest, colonial/imperial expansionism, and the multitude of their interlocking manifestations—for granted. I consequently refuse his seeming conflation of weakness and subordination with contemptibility and slavery. Reading and adopting Nietzsche's critique of slave morality from the perspective of the oppressed allows for a separation to be made between the "slave's" slavishness, on the one hand, and weakness or political powerlessness, on the other. Nietzsche's critique of slave morality can therefore be applied to those whom it more accurately characterizes: the reactionary right-wing powerholders ascendant in our current moment (which is also, in some sense, every moment hitherto in the existence of these so-called United States[13]).

My specific right-wing focus will be twenty-first-century "terrorism" discourse, which I will argue is both fundamentally moralizing and a weapon of the strong. Although for Nietzsche, moralism is a weapon of the weak, which is how and why it is objectionable, I will argue that, as evidenced in Essay I, there is no reason to believe that there is any necessary coincidence among slavishness, weakness, and political powerlessness. Indeed, Nietzsche's critique of slave morality is a critique of both morality and slavishness, which I would suggest are mutually definitionally implicated for him: to be slavish is to be a moralizer, and to moralize is to act like a slave. But that is not the same as saying that only weak people moralize, or only subordinated or oppressed people are slavish. Rather, moralizing is the primary activity or trait of slavishness and what, specifically, Nietzsche finds contemptible—*not* oppression, subordination, or political abjection per se. Analyzing both the historical development and contemporary deployment of the category of "terrorism" from this angle reveals that this morally overloaded term gets used not to leverage weakness into strength but, rather, to (continue to) secure the indefinite power of US empire and US and Israeli settler colonialism. "Terrorism" is thus a weapon of the strong to be sure, but it is no less slavish—and, thus, contemptible—for all that.

This chapter proceeds in three parts. First, I argue for the disaggregation of Nietzsche's critique of slave morality from his elitism, a move that authorizes the use and application of his critique for otherwise dominant or hegemonic political positions. Next, I offer a brief historical examination of the development of the term "terrorism" as it has come to be used in contemporary US popular and political discourses, arguing that the entrenched moralism of this category explains the recalcitrance of Islamophobia and anti-Muslim racism. Finally, I clarify how and why this moralism constitutes the effective movement of slave morality, emerging as it does from the manufactured existential angst of otherwise globally dominant colonial and imperial powers, specifically the US and Israel. My overall argument is that, once severed from his elitist commitments, the moralism of slave morality to which Nietzsche objects better captures the false fears of the dominant than the allegedly reactive complaints of the oppressed. This resonance is exemplified in "terrorism" discourse, which was and continues to be constructed by those holding the global levers of power in their hands, but who nevertheless insist on mischaracterizing themselves as the righteous victims of an overpowering and impossible-to-comprehend evil threat. The championing of life, freedom, and democracy that seemingly commonsensically anchors the moralizing discourse on "terrorism" is, therefore, not an unmarked or somehow universal valuing of these things, but rather a championing of the lives and well-being of Americans and Israeli Jews in an alliance all too often construed as simply "the West" or "democracy." This civilizationalist vision of life entails that any refusal of its imperial imperatives is construed as everything that "terrorism" is understood to be in both right-wing and popular discourses alike: unthinkable, annihilatory, anti-life, irrational, "savage," and evil. This is the colonial moralism specific to "terrorism" discourse, and it purchases the innocence of "the West," the existential threat posed by "terrorism," and, consequently, its moral intractability as what must be unconditionally opposed by decent, upright, innocent people.[14] However politically powerful this discourse and its popularizers may be, it is nevertheless wholly slavish in Nietzsche's sense; that is, it is a form of vengeful, mendacious moralizing.

## Masters and Slaves

In this section, I offer two points about Nietzsche's critique of slave morality in Essay I of the *Genealogy*.[15] First, there is no reason to think that the categories of "master" and "slave" correspond to political categories of "powerful" and "powerless" or "oppressor" and "oppressed." Second, despite how he presents things in Essay I, it is not actually or necessarily the case that master and slave morality arise dialectically or in response to one another. What this means is that although the categories of master and slave for Nietzsche are clear designations of value and/or worth(lessness) for him, they are not necessarily straightforward mappings of sites or situations of political power. Even if they were, and we were legitimately able to conflate mastery with "the powerful" or "the oppressor [class]" and slavery with "the weak" or "the oppressed [class]," it is not necessarily the case that the slavishness, weakness, or oppression of the slaves comes about *because of* the imposition, power, or oppression of the masters. Indeed, although Nietzsche relishes presenting slavishness as a specific reaction to the imposition of the masters, there is nothing else in his account (aside from rhetorical delight) that suggests the necessity of this relationship. Taken together, these two observations make it possible to sever Nietzsche's critique of slave morality from his elitism and thus render its analysis of *ressentiment* an apt description of reactionary, conservative politics.

In section 10 of the first essay of *On the Genealogy of Morals*, Nietzsche claims that the slave revolt in morality is the by-product of persons or groups who have somehow been prevented from acting and must therefore resort to other means in order to live and flourish. Reactive from the outset, Nietzsche notes that slave morality always requires a "hostile external world" in order to exist at all; "its action is fundamentally reaction."[16] Moreover, this reactivity is essentially negative: slave morality says "no" to that hostile external world, to what thwarts its own activity and expenditure. The slavish type, then, comes to exist only via reference to an imposed external (set of) force(s) and can only understand and affirm itself through negation of that imposition: "slave morality from the outset says No to what is 'outside,' what is 'different,' what is 'not itself' " (*GM* I:10). Nietzsche calls this negative activity *ressentiment*; its mightiest production and primary weapon is the concept of evil: "picture 'the enemy' as the man of ressentiment conceives him—and here precisely is his deed, his creation: he has conceived 'the evil enemy,' 'the Evil One,' and this in fact is his basic concept, from which he then evolves, as an afterthought and pendant, a 'good one'—himself!" "Evil" is used to limit, judge, and punish those deemed to have brought about the original imposition that has so bitterly limited the activity of the weaker. This production of evil is accomplished via the fabrication of the responsible subject, an actor with the ability to do otherwise, who thus may be held accountable—and punished!—for his (mis)deeds. Incapable of acting themselves, impotent to strike back at their aggressors, and condemning the aggressors' imposition as the very definition of evil, slavish types valorize their own weakness and produce the unwieldy apparatus responsible-subject/moral-opprobrium/political-punishment to restrain the activity of the strong. Nietzsche is clear about the effectiveness of this weapon (*GM* I:7–8) and equally clear that it is not a weapon the strong deserve to have wielded against them. For imposition is the character of life itself. It is erroneous to think such fatality comes at one's own expense or vengefully demand that life be otherwise. Rather, "to be in capable of taking one's enemies, one's accidents, even one's misdeeds seriously for very long—that is the sign of strong, full natures in whom there is an excess of power to form, to mold, to recuperate and to forget" (*GM* I:10).

Noble morality, by contrast, does not emerge as the result of any necessary relationship to any other person or set of forces. Instead, noble morality is cast by Nietzsche as the anti- or non-morality; it might be characterized as unselfconscious self-affirmation: "the 'well-born' *felt* themselves to be 'happy'; they did not have to establish their happiness artificially by examining their enemies, or to persuade themselves, *deceive* themselves, that they were happy (as all men of *ressentiment* are in the habit of doing)" (*GM* I:10). Unlike the slavishness of slave morality, masters regard encounters with foreign elements as at best unremarkable, at worst a negative confrontation so fleeting or light that it is quickly forgotten or otherwise dispensed with:

> [The noble mode of valuation] acts and grows spontaneously, it seeks its opposite only so as to affirm itself more gratefully and triumphantly—its negative concept "low," "common," "bad" is only a subsequently-invented pale, contrasting image in relation to its positive basic concept—filled with life and passion through and through—"we noble ones, we good, beautiful, happy ones!" When the noble mode of valuation blunders and sins against reality, it does so in respect to the sphere with which it is not sufficiently familiar, against a real knowledge of which it has

indeed inflexibly guarded itself: in some circumstances it misunderstands the sphere it despises, that of the common man, of the lower orders; on the other hand, one should remember that, even supposing that the affect of contempt, of looking down from a superior height, *falsifies* the image of that which it despises, it will at any rate still be a much less serious falsification than that perpetrated by its opponent—in *effigie* of course—by the submerged hatred, the vengefulness of the impotent. There is indeed too much carelessness, too much taking lightly, too much looking away and impatience involved in contempt, even too much joyfulness, for it to be able to transform its object into a real caricature and monster. (*GM* I:10)

What becomes clear from this discussion is that mastery and slavishness register not so much the difference between the powerful and the powerless (or the oppressor and the oppressed), but rather something we might call an ethical disposition, the content of which is twofold: (1) the order (first or second) and character (affirmative or deceptive) of self-recognition, and (2) the resulting activity in response to this self-recognition (nothing at all or revenge). So the masterful type, for instance, recognizes himself first and the other second, if at all. Indeed, "recognition" is not really the correct word here, for the masterful type is self-affirmative without reference to any other being or standard. He is first insofar as he is good and he is good insofar as he is first. The two entail and are inextricable from one another, leaving any other person, force, or thing secondary if not irrelevant, and rendering the "first" of this formulation an erroneous or solely retrospective attribution.

While the masterful type is largely indifferent to the existence of others, the slavish type, by contrast, takes his existence to be founded upon and in reaction to the existence of other(s) to whom he responds with both negation and hostility:

> This, then, is quite the contrary of what the noble man does, who conceives the basic concept "good" in advance and spontaneously out of himself and only then creates for himself an idea of "bad"! This "bad" of noble origin and that "evil" out of the cauldron of unsatisfied hatred—the former an after-production, a side-issue, a contrasting shade, the latter on the contrary an original thing, the beginning, the distinctive *deed* in the conception of slave morality—how different these words "bad" and

"evil" are, although they are both apparently the opposite of the same concept "good." (*GM* I:11)

Therefore, these two types have very different behavioral responses to their encounter with an/other: the masterful type is indifferent—having no reaction at all—or else is harmlessly destructive, carelessly removing obstacles to his own existence and flourishing, which he thoughtlessly calls "bad." The slavish type, by contrast, because of his derivative existence, resorts to vengefulness and resentment for the alleged hostility or aggression he experiences at the hands of the other. Destruction and revenge, then, respectively constitute the distinctive forms of activity for the masterful and slavish type.[17]

Reading master and slave morality in this way makes clear that what Nietzsche condemns about slavishness or weakness is the fact that slavish types understand themselves only residually, as afterthoughts, secondary to a hostile (set of) force(s) deemed primary and domineering, if not outright oppressive. They wage war on these forces, condemning them for their "injustice," seeking to triumph over them by criminalizing their activity, without which they could not exist and against which they have come to understand themselves, if only as a negation. Ironically, then, slaves need the external phenomena from which they claim to suffer, for without these constraints they themselves are nothing. In either case, however, slaves leverage an indirect and ignoble form of power—lying, self-hatred, and vengefulness—in order to take down those who are somehow "stronger" or "better" by declaring them to be "evil" and deserving of punishment. It is by means of these ignoble practices that the lesser-off, the worse, the weaker, and the undeserving come to dominate and rule. Their foremost aspiration (aside from achieving hegemony for this moralized worldview) is punishment of the "evil" ones. Indeed, punishment is slave morality's raison d'etre.

Yet it is not necessarily the case that these slaves or slavish types who seek to punish the instigators of the "oppression" or injury from which they suffer are themselves "the oppressed," or somehow subordinate or "weaker" in a socio-political sense. It is true that Nietzsche tends to suggest in Essay I that master and slave morality arise in a historical, dialectical relationship with one another, such that the "others" whom the master encounters are necessarily the slaves, while the "others" so hated and vilified by the slaves are necessarily the masters who have imposed the constraints against which the slaves protest. Yet there is no necessity that this is so. First, as already argued, the master sees virtually *all* external phenomena, insofar as they are not-himself, as what is lower or not to be affirmed—

regardless of whether that not-himself is strong or weak, a slave, or even, perhaps, another master. Second, it is simply not the case that the "hostile external world" to which the slave objects and against which he reacts is necessarily the existence, imposition, or violence of the master. In other words, just because the slave *perceives* the external world as hostile does not mean that the external world actually *is* hostile. As Nietzsche notes, "This inversion of the value-positing eye—this need to direct one's view outward instead of back to oneself—is of the essence of *ressentiment*: in order to exist, slave morality always first needs a hostile external world; it needs, physiologically speaking, external stimuli in order to act at all—its action is fundamentally reaction" (*GM* I:10). Looking at this important sentence more closely, I would argue that there is quite a bit of difference between needing "external stimuli" and needing a "hostile external world." Indeed, given the overall dishonesty of slavish types, it seems plausible that the "hostility" of these external stimuli may not be intrinsic to the phenomena themselves, but rather an act of projection. A slavish type understands and experiences himself as under siege, but that does not mean he *is* under siege—this is a fact about the slave, not the external world, much less the master. Indeed, even if the slave *were* under siege, and *by* the master no less, the slave would still not be under siege in the purposive or systemic sense associated with the word "oppression."

All this is to say that Nietzsche rhetorically conflates categories that are analytically distinct. Here, those conflations are "mastery" with strength or power or superiority, on the one hand, and "slavery" with weakness or powerlessness or inferiority, on the other. Yet what is superior about mastery is its unselfconscious self-affirmation, and what is inferior about slavishness is its derivative, conservative, self-preservative vengefulness. Dissatisfied with their position at the bottom, slavish types compensate for this low standing by blaming those above them for having caused it, rather than their own weaknesses or inadequacies. Successfully punishing those on top *for being on top* thus constitutes the slave's revenge. However, there is no reason to presume that those with political power are masterful in this specific way or that those on the bottom of socio-political hierarchies are slavish in this specific way. Indeed, recognizing these analytical distinctions allows us to escape Nietzsche's elitism while maintaining his critique of moralism intact. Moralizing may be slavish but, as it turns out, it is a better description of the activity of those who fear the decay of their hitherto unquestioned position of power and attempt to leverage this fear in the familiar and pity-inducing forms of innocence, victimhood, and existential threat.

## "Terrorism"

In 2011 and 2015, the liberal Center for American Progress (CAP) released two reports on what it calls the Islamophobia Network in America. The first, entitled *Fear, Inc.*, documented a small group of seven wealthy foundations that funded "five key people and their organizations" to the tune of some $40 million from 2001 to 2009. These five people and organizations produced demeaning and stigmatic misinformation about Muslims (e.g., that President Obama was one, or that he was controlled by them, or that Muslims were seeking to take control of the US government through the implementation of Shari'a law) and Islam (e.g., that it is a "totalitarian" doctrine, that it requires lying and violence), misinformation that ascended to national prominence "through effective advocates, media partners, and grassroots organizing."[18] Their second report, *Fear, Inc. 2.0*, documented the continued existence of the Islamophobia Network and the transformation of its discourse during the Obama era in anticipation of the 2016 presidential election, including the anti-"terrorism" training of US police officers and media coverage of the Boston Marathon bombing.[19]

Based entirely on publicly available records and tax returns, the information provided in the CAP reports and its description of this Islamophobia Network is both credible and persuasive. Hardly a conspiracy theory, CAP isolates the Islamophobia Network's key players, debunks the misinformation it spreads, and shows the connections between and among its big foundation donors, online bloggers and journalists, academic "experts," political pundits, and government officials. As Moustafa Bayoumi importantly points out, however, the CAP reports do not explain how or why the rhetoric and misinformation of the Islamophobia Network has such traction in US public discourse. Why, in other words, does the Network's Islamophobia work so well? What is it about this discourse that so successfully influences public opinion, generates campaign contributions, and turns people out to the polls? The CAP reports offer a careful assessment of the political goals and interests of the few folks who run it. But what about those who are swayed by its rhetoric? As Bayoumi writes, "*Fear, Inc.* . . . makes a convincing case, but it also assumes that people can be directed to act by the network and not by their own desires or for their own reasons."[20]

Bayoumi suggests that Islamophobia works because it plays on white Christian Americans' fears of becoming, sooner or later, a minority in "their own" country. Surely correct, this analysis names without further exploring the full psychic and emotional resonance of Islamophobia with

American mass publics. This existential fear that Bayoumi aptly names is seized upon and amplified in the moralism of "terrorism" discourse, which is always in close proximity to Islamophobia and discourse about Islam. Indeed, as Junaid Rana has argued, at this point it is no longer necessary to say "Muslim" when one says "terrorist"; the equivalence is both implicit and presumed.[21] The reason, then, that the racist lies of the Islamophobia Network work so well is because of their proximity to "terrorism" and the prospect of annihilation it portends, which Bayoumi acknowledges in the form of demographic threat. In either case, however, the fear is of eradication, annihilation, or nonexistence in the face of a threat perceived as overpowering, difficult to understand, and perhaps impossible to contain.[22]

Far from an accurate understanding of either Islam or political violence, however, this Islamophobic "terrorism" discourse is instead an ideological determination used to insulate US settler-empire from critique, render its victims deserving of its abuses, and delegitimize any resistance to it as unthinkable and perverse.[23] It is a weapon of the strong deployed to secure that power and preserve it from erosion by those deemed by its framework to be "evil," immoral, or wicked. The (im)moralization of Islam into "terrorism," an impossible-to-comprehend category of nihilist evil that devalues life, is thus an important reminder that "terrorism" is not the name of a particular form of political violence so much as a premiere ideological tool by which resistance to empire and colonization is illegitimated out of existence.

"Terrorism's" status as a definitionally fraught, morally overdetermined category did not begin with 9/11, even if the US's more official "War on Terror" did. As Nadine Naber argues with regard to Arab American history, in a point that is also apposite to the problem of "terrorism," 9/11 did not constitute "an essential break or rupture" with a prior, unmarked past but is, rather, better understood "as an extension if not an intensification of a post-Cold War US expansion in the Middle East."[24] "Terrorism's" Cold War roots extend to both the US's imperial ventures in Latin America and its self-proclaimed struggle against "totalitarianism."[25] The emergence of "terrorism" as a prominent term in the discourse of Western/capitalist states was concomitant with the rise of anti-colonial nationalist movements throughout the rest of the globe.[26] Central to arguments taking place at the United Nations at this time, for example, was the status of the political violence committed by both parties to such conflicts: the violence committed by national liberation movements, which the Western/capitalist states by and large wanted to condemn as terrorism, and the violence committed by colonial and Western/capitalist powers, which the Soviet and unaligned states wanted to condemn as terrorism. Hence, from the very beginning of its explicit emergence into both American and international political discourse, "terrorism" functioned as a crucial arbiter of the line between legitimate and illegitimate violence, domination and oppression versus resistance and liberation.

Enter Benjamin Netanyahu, a longstanding Israeli politician who has built his career in part on a dogged promotion of the anti-"terrorism" platform.[27] In 1979, Netanyahu hosts an influential international conference on "terrorism" in Jerusalem, "convened to begin the formation of an anti-terror alliance in which all the democracies of the West must join."[28] Such an alliance was necessary because the conference's participants were dissatisfied with the "easy moral relativism" characterizing the UN debates happening at this time, wherein "One man's terrorist is another man's freedom fighter."[29] The conference therefore set out to establish that "a clear definitional framework exists, regardless of political view,"[30] proclaiming that terrorism is "the deliberate, systematic murder, maiming and menacing of the innocent to inspire fear in order to gain political ends."[31] This definition of terrorism, conference-goers maintained, makes clear its fundamental alliance with both tyranny and totalitarianism, its constitutive "abhorrence of freedom and a determination to destroy the democratic way of life,"[32] and makes it, as Netanyahu's father insisted, "an offshoot of Nazi philosophy."[33] "Terrorists" refuse to distinguish between civilians and non-civilians, and they usurp political power via anti-democratic means. They are thus threats to the Western and democratic way of life and explicit attacks on that way of life. According to Netanyahu Jr., at the conference, this definition "was shown persuasively to be, beyond all nuance and quibble, a moral evil"[34] or, as Paul Johnson put it, "intrinsically evil, necessarily evil and wholly evil."[35]

While Netanyahu Jr. is incorrect to say that this definition is not political or influenced by a particular point of view, he is wholly correct to note that its clear association with and overdetermination by moralism diminishes its ability to mean more than one thing, a semantic debilitation that might be seen as this conference's central purpose. Moralism, in other words, was the crucial tool by which refusal of or resistance to US/Israeli political and economic dominance was rendered the proper domain of "terrorism" and thus disqualified as anti-colonial, anti-imperial, nationalist, or liberatory, while the lives of US and Israeli citizens were classified as "innocent." Of course, such moralization erases the role and relevance of US and Israeli policy to the phenomenon of "terrorism," de-historicizing and tarnishing any resistance to such policies with the taint of illegitimacy and inhumanity.

Thus, by 1984, the year of Netanyahu's second international conference on "terrorism," he could credibly argue that "The root cause of terrorism lies not in grievances but in a disposition toward unbridled violence. This can be traced to a world view which asserts that certain ideological and religious goals justify, indeed demand, the shedding of all moral inhibitions. In this context, the observation that the root cause of terrorism is terrorists is more than a tautology."[36] Lisa Stampnitzky has carefully documented the transformation whereby "terrorism" has today become an identity that provides its own explanation, a characteristically immoral act committed by a specific type of immoral person.[37] The roots of this view are evident here, in 1984. The "disposition toward unbridled violence" that Netanyahu claims is the cause of terrorism marks the term's rise as both an identity category and a form of savagery or barbarism; the "more than" tautology of his observation signals the premier definitional attribute of terrorism—its evil. As Netanyahu explains, it is not just that terrorism is an evil act or behavior, but rather that terrorists are themselves evil, presumably either as representatives of an evil principle at work in the human order (a metaphysical and potentially theological claim) or followers of an evil ideology that subordinates everything—morality in particular—to its own aims (a psychologizing political claim). Regardless, the only way that the statement "the cause of terrorism is terrorists" is not an empty tautology is if it is also an ontological statement about the existence of evil itself, which becomes flesh in the body of the "terrorist."[38] Netanyahu's father, again a contributor to the second conference, puts it the most starkly of anyone:

> The terrorist represents a new breed of man which takes humanity back to prehistoric times, to the times when morality was not yet born. Divested of any moral principle, he has no moral sense, no moral controls, and is therefore capable of committing any crime, like a killing machine, without shame or remorse. But he is also a cunning, consummate liar, and therefore much more dangerous than the Nazis, who used to proclaim their aims openly. In fact, he is the perfect nihilist.[39]

The terrorist here is both pre-moral and pre-civilization, thus in effect pre-human. But, despite this seeming primitiveness, the terrorist is in fact very advanced, more cunning and dangerous than even the Nazis, who at least made plain their genocidal intent. Unlike Nazis, terrorists lie about their deeds, mendaciously suggesting they pertain to national liberation or ending colonialism. Terrorists therefore know full well they are committing murder, but they couch it in liberatory rhetoric to deceive good and innocent people. Perhaps alluding to Nietzsche, Netanyahu Sr. concludes that the terrorist is thus the "perfect nihilist."

By the time of this second conference, not only has the "terrorist's" evil been firmly established vis-à-vis the innocence and uprightness of the settler state and its citizens, but his ineffable Muslim-ness is coming into view, side by side with a distinct US-Israeli alliance in the shared cause of democracy and "the West." Although the instigating role played by the Soviet Union in orchestrating international "terrorism" remains a prominent theme continued forward from the first conference, its power in this regard is now rivaled by "Arab nationalism" and "Islamic fundamentalism" as the premiere "wellspring" of terror; hence, Netanyahu Jr. now asserts in 1984 that "terrorism is thus uniquely pervasive in the Middle East, the part of the world in which Islam is dominant."[40] Notably, the term "totalitarian" is still in use, primarily by the American contributors, albeit this time to link Arab and Muslim countries with the communism of the Soviet Union and, therefore, by definitional association, the Nazism of 1940s Germany. By the time of the second conference, then, terrorism's "ideological source,"[41] political culmination, and ultimate beneficiaries have all become identical: Communist totalitarianism. Terrorism is totalitarian both in its refusal to acknowledge distinctions between civilians and non-civilians and in its use of violence as a "first resort"[42] for resolving conflict. As well, terrorism is the premier tool of totalitarian regimes and sponsored by totalitarian regimes, specifically the Soviet Union, its satellites (such as Cuba and North Korea), and the emergent Arab states (Libya, Syria, and, although not Arab, Iran). Hence the "fiercely anti-West" PLO comes in for special scrutiny throughout the second conference as a kind of culmination and exemplar of the totalitarian Communist/Arab terrorist threat, "the pivotal link" between "the Soviet Union and the Arab World."[43] As then Secretary of State George Schulz put it, "If freedom and democracy are the targets of terrorism, it is clear that totalitarianism is its ally."[44] In Senator Daniel Patrick Moynihan's words, "The totalitarian state is terrorism come to power."[45] Or, as Netanyahu sums up, "Modern terrorism has its roots in two movements that have assumed international prominence in the second half of the twentieth century, communist totalitarianism and Islamic (and Arab) radicalism."[46] In short, "terrorist" states are "built on the foundations of Marxism and radical Islam."[47]

The moralized fight against totalitarianism that effectively defined twentieth-century Cold War discourse in the US thus broadens and expands in collaboration with Israeli powerbrokers to include Arab and Muslim countries and people, exporting the civilizationalism of anti-totalitarianism to a new global battle, the fight against "terror." The discursive slide from totalitarianism to terrorism—evident in George W. Bush's famous fake phenomenon "Islamo-fascism" (itself derived from neoconservative opinion-makers who played a significant role in consolidating civilizationalist anti-totalitarianism in the US) transfers and transforms the conjoined Nazi/communist threat of totalitarianism to the new Arab/Muslim threat of "terrorism." So, for example, in his address to the nation on Sept. 20, 2001, President Bush said of Al-Qaeda, "We have seen their kind before. They're the heirs of all the murderous ideologies of the 20th century. By sacrificing human life to serve their radical visions, by abandoning every value except the will to power, they follow in the path of fascism, Nazism, and totalitarianism."[48] Note again the allusion to Nietzsche in the invocation of "the will to power." The implication is that, like Nietzsche (and, of course, Nazis), "terrorists" are anti-morality or "beyond good and evil," a nihilism that the civilized world must necessarily reject. Distinctive as Bush's rhetoric of good and evil may have seemed, then, in the wake of an unprecedented act of violence against the United States, the discourse he employed to explain and characterize it was in fact the result of decades of conservative and neoconservative attacks on communism, decolonization, "totalitarianism," and the new Left within the US, as well as an Israeli-led effort to delegitimize anti-colonial violence as by definition evil and immoral. Such immoralism was, however ironically, associated all too frequently with Nietzsche himself.[49]

In arguing that "terrorism" is both the premier tool of totalitarian regimes and the means of bringing new totalitarian regimes into existence, "terrorism" becomes the new Nazi threat—to Europe, to America, to Jews, indeed to the entirety of the West and its civilization. This project consolidates the US-Israeli alliance as part of a shared democratic and Western civilization that are equally menaced by the same threat, a threat that even Netanyahu Jr. acknowledges is "a seemingly bizarre collaboration between Arab and Islamic radicalism and communist totalitarianism."[50] A conflagration of evil and anti-civilizational movements, ideologies, and people, America and Israel are threatened by, alternatively and yet strangely simultaneously, totalitarianism, Communism, and "terrorism." As Netanyahu cunningly sums up,

> The antagonism of Islamic and Arab radicalism to the West is frequently misunderstood. It is sometimes explained as deriving from American support for Israel. But the hostility to the West preceded the creation of Israel by centuries, and much of the terrorists' animus is directed against targets and issues that have nothing to do with Israel. Indeed, the relationship is most often the other way around. Middle Eastern radicals did not develop their hatred for the West because of Israel; they hated Israel from its inception *because it is an organic part of the West.* That is, because Israel represents for them precisely the incarnation of those very traditions and values, foremost of which is democracy, which they hate and fear.[51]

It is not, then, that "terrorists" are responding to or resisting US empire and Israeli colonization. It is rather that "terrorists" hate Israel because it is, like the United States, "*an organic part of the West*"; that is, because it is democratic and civilized. And terrorists hate democracy and civilization because (as we have seen) they are evil. Indeed, this is what evil effectively means. Emptying political violence and resistance of any meaning whatsoever, "terrorism" becomes another word for savagery and nihilism, for the negation of the West and everything it ostensibly stands for: freedom, democracy, and the American way. The interchangeability of "terrorism" with Nazism illustrates this most dramatically; as Jin Haritaworn, Tamsila Taquir, and Esma Erdem note, the frequent conflation of Islam with Nazism in European and American political discourse creates "a basic equivalence between 'Muslim = Nazi' and 'Muslim = Evil,' in which specific persons, relationships and events appear ultimately interchangeable."[52] This is the most distinctive moral and civilizationalist slander offered to smear the Muslim/Arab figure of "terrorism": not only mendacious or tyrannical, the "terrorist" represents the West's exceptional example of annihilation par excellence—the Holocaust—a figuration that casts the West as victims of unprecedented oppression and simultaneously reinforces the ostensible solidarity between "Western civilization" and Israel as emblem of the Jewish people, who are themselves cast as eternal victims of genocidal violence.[53]

## Elitism and Existential Threat

It is worth noting that, despite these power brokers' frequent invocations of Nietzsche as a nihilist or immoralist par excellence, their reversal of strong and weak, transmogrification of these categories into oppressor and oppressed, and vengeful vilification of these "oppressors" into figures of "terrorist" evil actually exemplifies the logic of slave morality he so trenchantly critiques. In the case of the production of "terrorism," in other words, we have a case study in the separability of the different components of Nietzsche's critique of slave morality as well as a field of application of his critique that need not reproduce his elitism but can instead be used to disrupt it. First, of course, although it should not be necessary to point this out, both the United States and Israel are among the richest and most powerful countries in the world, with staggering military might and nuclear arsenals at their disposal. Moreover, they have achieved this status at least in part due to their character as settler colonial states—states that came into being via conquest of lands belonging to indigenous peoples whom they have removed, transferred, segregated, massacred, and/or exterminated.[54] The "terrorism" about which these powers complain, then, is far from the tyrannical or "totalitarian" threat they present it as. Rather, the intermittent emergence of violence against these oppressor states by its subject peoples—which might more accurately be characterized as *resistance*—is the "imposition" about which the slavish type complains and which Nietzsche notes this type nevertheless requires in order define his existence. Proving not only their derivative selfhood but also their reactionary inability to give up on the existence of their enemies, whom they need if they are to survive as noble, heroic, innocent, and worthy of value, the US and Israel work tirelessly to produce a false and contorted image of the evil "terrorist" in order to sanctify their own colonial and imperial expansionism, which they define as the noble project of democracy, security, and freedom.[55]

There is, therefore, as Nietzsche's analysis suggests, no necessary connection between political power and nobility or mastery, just as there is no necessary connection between political weakness or subordination and slavishness. In the case of "terrorism" discourse, this non-coincidence is on full display. It is the most powerful parties—the world's unipolar hegemonic settler colonial and imperial power, the United States, along with its adjunct, Israel, an illegally occupying and settler colonial power—who are generating a mendacious discourse of victimization that is ridiculous on its face but nevertheless wholly necessary to preserve their identity as innocent victims; justify their regimes of surveillance, targeting, disappearance, incarceration, torture, targeted killing, drone strikes, massacres, lethal weapons experimentation on civilian populations, starvation, and extrajudicial assassination; and preserve their own unaccountability for the violence they perpetrate in the name of democracy, freedom, civilization, security, and humanity. Indeed, in its most extreme iterations, "terrorists" are narrated as having the capacity to destroy "Western civilization" as "we" know it. It does not take too much reflection or evidence, however, to remind ourselves of the global realities of economic and political power that render such melodramatic narratives fictitious at best. This "clash of civilizations" thesis[56] is better understood as the beleaguered victim narrative of still dominant, still hegemonic, and still profoundly destructive so-called Western, colonial, and imperial powers.

In this discourse, "terrorists" are the enemies of "civilization" because they both represent and portend the unthinkability of total destruction and the elimination of everything known, valued, sanctified, and secure. This is a disintegration that is existential, generating a panic other and deeper than the fact of mortality. It is a destruction that cannot be borne by the living, threatening a disarticulation so total that it exceeds the cessation of biological life typically connoted by the word death, a nihilism so baffling it can only be described by its detractors in the supernatural language of evil. The existential horror marshaled by this moralization, however, cannot be extricated from the question of perspective—that is, the question of *whose* existence, exactly, is so threatened—if we are capably to distinguish between Right and Left, oppression and liberation. The extinction phobia marshaled by the US and Israel in "terrorism" discourse emerges clearly as the worldview of the few, the powerful, the elite. Their existential anxiety about the annihilation of that privilege (or power, class, race, caste) is the bedrock upon which the conservative viewpoint is built: conservatives are acutely aware of "the fragility of a civilization" and that it can be "destroyed by malign forces."[57] Their consequent impulse toward preservation—which requires the annihilation of enemy threats—disperses itself ideologically as a moralized insistence on elite survival at the expense of everyone else as the only thinkable and credible political position, a moralism that stigmatizes, punishes, and eliminates those who reject this survivalist framework because such rejection constitutes an attack on their own and their worldview's mortality. As I have argued elsewhere, this is the fundamental mechanism not simply of slave morality, but also of settler colonial, imperial, and heteronormative ideologies as well.[58]

This slave morality of the powerful continues in the current ascendance of what some have called the alt-right, others describe as a global wave of neo-authoritarianism, and still others view as the reemergence of global fascism. The structure of the argument, however, remains the same. As Mark Bray writes,

Both Trump and the alt-right have managed to tap into a widespread white conservative anxiety about the rapid demise of "traditional" white America—an anxiety about the fact that they are losing the demographic "battle" and will no longer constitute a majority of the population in a generation, that they are losing the culture war as gay marriage has become legal, that the notion of white privilege is gaining currency, that the black struggle is ascendant, that "rape culture" is being targeted, and transgender identity and rights are increasingly legitimated.[59]

While white supremacy, empire, (settler) colonialism, and cis-hetero patriarchy are foundational to the United States, Donald Trump's presidency eroded the governing norms of liberal respectability politics (however inadequate these were in themselves) that previously prevented mainstream politicians from voicing such sentiments so nakedly. The result has been that the most extreme ideological manifestations of the historical founding of this country have come out of the woodwork, making themselves known, proclaiming pride in their existence, recruiting new members, and openly threatening—when not succeeding at perpetrating—violence and harm to women, Black and indigenous people and people of color, immigrants, Muslims, refugees, Jews, queer and trans people, and their allies. In this sense, the January 6 "insurrection" is better understood as an attempted restoration—an attempt, as Trump promised, to make American great again.[60]

The notion, however, that Black and indigenous people, people of color, queer and trans people, immigrants, refugees, and Muslims are somehow victimizing either "the American people" or the US government is not just implausible but an outright falsehood used to manufacture a posture of victimization, without which the identity of "the American people" and the US government as emblems of freedom and democracy threaten to disintegrate and/or become legible for what they really are: paragons of whiteness and institutions of white supremacy. Any emancipatory response to the discourse of "terrorism," then, must be sharply attuned to the false politics of victimhood and the racialized politics of punishment that comprise it and so much other reactionary discourse about loss: the loss of innocence and democracy, of national security and peace, or—to be Nietzschean about it—of power, stature, or greatness in the face of the many impediments embodied and imparted by the inferior masses. To sympathize with this loss and existential angst is to grant legitimacy to the elitist configuration of power and social worth conservatism both advocates and represents. As Corey Robin explains,

> The conservative, to be sure, speaks for a special type of victim: one who has lost something of value, as opposed to the wretched of the earth, whose chief complaint is that they never had anything to lose . . . this brand of victimhood endows the conservative complaint with a more universal significance. It connects his disinheritance to an experience we all share—namely, loss—and threads the strands of that experience into an ideology promising that the loss, or at least some portion of it, can be made whole.[61]

This conservative cry is the lament of Nietzschean *ressentiment* and a reactionary morality of survival. It functions as a wall against dissent and the means by which dissent is evacuated of political content by characterizing it as insupportable threat—as unreasonable, corrupt, immoral, unthinkable, indefensible, evil, or perverse. Such moralization makes "terrorists"—Muslims, Arabs, and all those who "look like" them—deserving of elimination by definition. It produces queer and trans people as threats—to "women," the public, and the health and safety of children. This "right-wing annihilationism"[62] is the consequence of elitist extinction phobia and why it is so important to be critically attuned to the actual, material conditions of power and powerlessness that attend any assertion of political oppression or victimization. As Robin makes clear, the Right continually borrows from the Left's vision, philosophy, and rhetoric of emancipation, but it does so to advance the cause of hierarchy rather than freedom (a political formation he calls "upside-down populism"[63]).

Recognizing with Nietzsche, then, that *all* slave moralities are contemptible, let's refuse to sign on to the moralizing project of condemning "terrorism" in the name of the further advancement of US empire and its settler colonial permutations. The construal of Islam, "terrorism," or, sometimes, "Islamic terrorism," as fundamentally the enemy of civilization, an instantiation of nihilism, and the embodiment of evil are all wrapped up together. The moralism of this category explains the purchase of Islamophobia in the hearts and minds of so many, and the hidden hierarchy underpinning the term's genealogy makes clear that it is the beleaguered cry of the powerful, not the oppressed. Leaving Nietzsche's naturalized, elitist hierarchy behind, let's nevertheless follow his embrace of mastery by affirming the unthinkable monstrosity of the "impositions" generated by the wretched of the earth. In a masterful act of self-affirmation and self-affirmative solidarity, let's recognize that the "hostile external world" to which these influence peddlers object is, in fact, the cause of the oppressed, who are neither slaves nor contemptible but, rather, the unwitting victims of the gratuitous and expansionist violence of the world's hegemonic global powers, which they triumphantly whitewash with hackneyed morality tales about evil "terrorists" and their "innocent" victims.

## Notes

1. Merrick, "'What Renders our Sores Repugnant': Revisiting Nietzsche on *Ressentiment*," in *European-Supra-European: Nietzsche's View from Afar*, eds. Marco Brusotti, Herman Siemens, Corinna Schulbert, and Michael McNeal (Berlin: De Gruyter, 2020).

2. See Schotten, "Reading Nietzsche in the Wake of the 2008–09 War on Gaza," in *The Digital Dionysus: Nietzsche and the Network-Centric Condition*, eds. Nandita Biswas-Mellamphy and Dan Mellamphy (New York: Punctum, 2016).

3. Wendy Brown, "Democracy Against Itself: Nietzsche's Challenge," in *Politics out of History* (Princeton, NJ: Princeton University Press, 2001), 126.

4. Brown, "Wounded Attachments," in *States of Injury: Power and Freedom in Late Modernity* (Princeton, NJ: Princeton University Press, 1995).

5. See, e.g., Daniel W. Conway, "*Das Weib an Sich*: The Slave Revolt in Epistemology," in *Feminist Interpretations of Nietzsche*, eds. Kelly Oliver K and Marilyn Pearsall (University Park: Pennsylvania State University Press, 1998); Rebecca Stringer, "'A Nietzschean Breed': Feminism, Victimology, *Ressentiment*," in *Why Nietzsche Still? Reflections on Drama, Culture, and Politics*, ed. Alan Schrift (Berkeley: University of California Press, 2000); Marion Tapper, "*Ressentiment* and Power: Some Reflections on Feminist Practices," *Nietzsche, Feminism and Political Theory*, ed. Paul Patton (New York: Routledge, 1993). For an updated version of this Brown-esque critique of feminism, albeit in the realm of legal theory rather than philosophy or political theory, see Janet Halley, *Split Decisions: How and Why to Take a Break from Feminism* (Princeton, NJ: Princeton University Press, 2008).

6. For a fuller critique of Brown's argument in "Wounded Attachments" as shoring up naturalized hierarchy by reprimanding oppressed people for the slavishness of their resistance to it, see Schotten, "Wounded Attachments? Slave Morality, the Left, and the Future of Revolutionary Desire," in *Nietzsche and Critical Theory*, ed. Michael Roberts (Leiden, NL: Brill, 2020).

7. See Corey Robin, *The Reactionary Mind: Conservatism from Edmund Burke to Donald Trump*, 2nd ed. (New York: Oxford, 2018).

8. See Schotten, "Nietzsche and Emancipatory Politics: Queer Theory as Anti-Morality," *Critical Sociology*, 45.2 (2019): 213–26.

9. I use "men" here (and male pronouns for the singular throughout) because I think this is literally to whom Nietzsche is referring. For justification, see my *Nietzsche's Revolution: Décadence, Politics, and Sexuality* (New York: Palgrave, 2009), "A Note on Citations" and chaps. 4–5.

10. See Brown, "Wounded Attachments," 70, but also the essays that comprise *States of Injury* more broadly.

11. Thus, as Jeffrey Nealon has pointed out, Nietzsche's critique of slave morality may be a better analysis of reactionary conservatism than left-wing identity politics; see Nealon, "Performing Resentment: White Male Anger; or, 'Lack' and Nietzschean Political Theory," in *Why Nietzsche Still?* edited by Alan Schrift. Berkeley: University of California Press, 2000: 274–292.

12. On the Right's use of moral panics around sex/gender/sexuality in order to institute punitive and repressive social orders, see Gayle Rubin, "Thinking Sex: Notes for a Radical Theory of the Politics of Sexuality," in *Pleasure and Danger: Exploring Female Sexuality*, ed. Carole Vance (Boston: Routledge and Kegan Paul, 1984). On trans exclusionary feminisms and the broader "extinction phobia" that drives this (and other) reactionary politics to pursue an agenda of "right-wing annihilationism," see Schotten, "TERFism, Zionism, and Right-Wing Annihilationism: Toward an Internationalist Genealogy of Extinction Phobia," in *TSQ: Transgender Studies Quarterly* 9.3 (Aug. 2022): 334–64.

13. Nikhil Pal Singh, *Race and America's Long War* (Oakland: University of California Press, 2019).

14. In this sense, it is a premier example of what Silvia Posocco calls "wounded whiteness," an identificatory phenomenon through which subjects "make whiteness suddenly appear wounded," thereby "displacing the object and subject of racist aggression." Posocco, "(Decolonizing) the Ear of the Other: Subjectivity, Ethics and Politics in Question," in *Decolonizing Sexualities: Transnational Perspectives, Critical Interventions* (Oxford, UK: Counterpress, 2016), 259. On the coloniality of "terrorism" discourse, see Rabea M. Khan, "Race, Coloniality and the Post 9/11 Counterdiscourse: Critical Terrorism Studies and the Reproduction of the Islam-Terrorism Discourse," *Critical Studies on Terrorism* 14.4 (2021): 498–501.

15. I make both these points in Schotten, "Reading Nietzsche," from which this section draws. The next section, "Terrorism," is adapted from chapter 5 of my *Queer Terror: Life, Death, and Desire in the Settler Colony* (New York: Columbia University Press, 2018.

16. Friedrich Nietzsche, *On the Genealogy of Morals: A Polemic*, ed. and trans. Walter Kaufmann (New York: Vintage, 1967 [1887]); *GM* I:10.

17. It is true that, at times, Nietzsche undermines this seemingly clear-cut distinction, noting that action and reaction are both versions of reactivity and

conceding that masterful types sometimes experience *ressentiment* (*GM* I:10). That said, he also eagerly recuperates these caveats for his overall thesis, arguing that the "deeds" of the masterful type constitute the "true [*eigentlich*] reaction" (as opposed to the false or weak reaction of the slavish type, presumably) and insisting that "*Ressentiment* itself, if it should appear in the noble man, consummates and exhausts itself in an immediate reaction, and therefore does not *poison*" (10).

18. Wajahat Ali, Eli Clifton, Matthew Duss, Lee Fang, Scott Keyes, and Faiz Shakir, *Fear, Inc.: The Roots of the Islamophobia Network in America* (Washington, DC: Center for American Progress, Aug. 2011).

19. Matthew Duss, Yasmine Taeb, Ken Gude, and Ken Sofer, *Fear, Inc. 2.0: The Islamophobia Network's Efforts to Manufacture Hate in America* (Washington, DC: Center for American Progress, Feb. 2015). For more on the Islamophobia Network, its funding, and its deep co-implication with Zionism and the Israeli government, see IJAN: the International Jewish Anti-Zionist Network, *The Business of Backlash: The Attack on the Palestinian Movement and Other Movements for Justice* (2015) and Donna Nevel and Elly Bulkin, *Islamophobia and Israel* (New York: Route Books, 2014).

20. Moustafa Bayoumi, *This Muslim American Life: Dispatches from the War on Terror* (New York: New York University Press, 2015), 161.

21. Junaid Rana, "The Racial Infrastructure of the Terror-Industrial Complex," *Social Text* 34.4 (Dec. 2016), 111–12. On the racialization of "the terrorist" as a conglomeration of "persons who appear 'Middle Eastern, Arab, or Muslim,'" see Leti Volpp, "The Citizen and the Terrorist," *UCLA Law Review* (June 2002); see also Sohail Daulatzai, *Fifty Years of "The Battle of Algiers": Past as Prologue* (Minneapolis: University of Minnesota Press, 2016).

22. In this sense, "terrorism" discourse is a form of extinction phobia; see Schotten, "TERFism, Zionism, and Right-Wing Annihilationism."

23. On "settler-empire" and conceptualizing the United States not as a nation-state but, more accurately, an "empire-state," see Moon-Kie Jung, *Beneath the Surface of White Supremacy: Denaturalizing U.S. Racisms Past and Present* (Stanford, CA: Stanford University Press, 2015); and Singh, *Race and America's Long War*.

24. Nadine Naber, *Arab America: Gender, Cultural Politics, and Activism* (New York: New York University Press, 2012), 61; as Naber elsewhere observes, "the attacks of September 11, 2001 [were] a turning point, as opposed to the starting point, of histories of anti-Arab racism in the United States." Introduction to *Race and Arab Americans Before and After 9/11: From Invisible Citizens to Visible Subjects*, eds. Amaney Jamal and Nadine Naber (Syracuse, NY: Syracuse University Press, 2008), 4. See also Mahmood Mamdani, *Good Muslim, Bad Muslim: America, the Cold War, and the Roots of Terror* (New York: Pantheon, 2004).

25. For critical analysis of "totalitarianism" as a largely manufactured phenomenon used by (proto-)neoconservatives to foment US exceptionalist, racist, anti-communist, and Zionist fervor in postwar US culture, see, e.g., Benjamin

Balint, *Running Commentary: The Contentious Magazine that Transformed the Jewish Left into the Neoconservative Right* (New York: Public Affairs, 2010); Abbot Gleason, *Totalitarianism: The Inner History of the Cold War* (New York: Oxford University Press, 1995); William Pietz, "The 'Post-Colonialism' of Cold War Discourse," *Social Text* 19/20 (Autumn 1988): 55–75.

26. See Rémi Brulin, "Compartmentalization, Context of Speech, and the Israeli Origins of the American Discourse on 'Terrorism,'" *Dialectical Anthropology* 39.1; and Brulin, "Defining 'Terrorism': The 1972 General Assembly Debates on 'International Terrorism' and Their Coverage by the *New York Times*," in *If It Was Not for Terrorism: Crisis, Compromise, and Elite Discourse in the Age of War on Terror*, eds. Banu Baybars-Hawks and Lemi Baruh (Newcastle upon Tyne, UK: Cambridge Scholars, 2011).

27. Brulin, "Compartmentalization"; Edward Said, "The Essential Terrorist," in *Blaming the Victims: Spurious Scholarship and the Palestinian Question*, eds. Edward Said and Christopher Hitchens (London: Verso, 2001 [1984]).

28. Benjamin Netanyahu, foreword to *International Terrorism: Challenge and Response*, ed. Benjamin Netanyahu (New Brunswick, NJ: Transaction, 1981).

29. Netanyahu, Preface to Opening Session on "The Face of Terrorism," in *International Terrorism*, 1.

30. Netanyahu, 1.

31. Netanyahu, 1.

32. Netanyahu, 1.

33. Benzion Netanyahu, "Chairman's Opening Remarks," in *International Terrorism*, 5.

34. Benjamin Netanyahu, Preface, *International Terrorism*, 1.

35. Johnson, "Seven Deadly Sins," in *International Terrorism*, 15. The broader context of Johnson's remark is this: "When I say that terrorism is war against civilization, I may be met by the objection that terrorists are often idealists pursuing worthy aims—national or regional independence, and so forth. I do not accept this argument. I cannot agree that a terrorist can ever be an idealist, or that the objects sought can ever justify terrorism. The impact of terrorism, not simply on individual nations, but on humanity as a whole, is intrinsically evil, necessarily evil and wholly evil, and it is so for a number of demonstrable reasons." Those reasons are, as Johnson's title indicates, the "Seven Deadly Sins" of "terrorism."

36. Benjamin Netanyahu, "Terrorism: How the West Can Win," in *Terrorism: How the West Can Win*, ed. Benjamin Netanyahu (New York: Avon, 1986), 204.

37. Stampnitzky, *Disciplining Terror: How Experts Invented "Terrorism"* (Cambridge: Cambridge University Press, 2013); see also Liaquat Ali Khan, "The Essentialist Terrorist," *Washburn Law Journal* 45.1 (Fall 2005).

38. Referencing not Netanyahu but the rhetoric of Donald Rumsfeld in justifying indefinite detention at Guantánamo Bay, Judith Butler writes: "When Secretary Rumsfeld was asked why these prisoners were being forcibly restrained and held without trial, he explained that if they were not restrained, they would kill again.

He implied that the restraint is the only thing that keeps them from killing, that they are beings whose very propensity is to kill: that is what they would do as a matter of course. Are they pure killing machines? If they are pure killing machines, then they are not humans with cognitive function entitled to trials, to due process, to knowing and understanding a charge against them. They are something less than human, and yet—somehow—they assume a human form." *Precarious Life: The Powers of Mourning and Violence* (London: Verso, 2004), 73–74. Cf. Darryl Li's description of the "secular demonology" otherwise known as the literature on "jihadism": a "discourse on monsters who are actually human but whose monstrousness must nevertheless be reasserted." Li, "A Jihadism Anti-Primer," *Middle East Research and Information Project* 45 (Fall 2015): http://www.merip.org/mer/mer276/jihadism-anti-primer. See also Khan, "The Essentialist Terrorist."

39. Benzion Netanyahu, "Terrorists and Freedom Fighters," in *Terrorism: How the West Can Win*, 29–30.

40. Benjamin Netanyahu, "Terrorism and the Islamic World," in *Terrorism: How the West Can Win*, 61–62.

41. Benjamin Netanyahu, "Terrorism and Totalitarianism," in *Terrorism: How the West Can Win*, 39.

42. Jeane Kirkpatrick, "The Totalitarian Confusion," in *Terrorism: How the West Can Win*, 56.

43. Benjamin Netanyahu, "The International Network," in *Terrorism: How the West Can Win*, 86.

44. George Shultz, "The Challenge to the Democracies," in *Terrorism: How the West Can Win*, 20.

45. Daniel Patrick Moynihan, "Terrorists, Totalitarians, and the Rule of Law," in *Terrorism: How the West Can Win*, 41.

46. Benjamin Netanyahu, "Defining Terrorism," in *Terrorism: How the West Can Win*, 11–12.

47. Netanyahu, 12. The strong emergence of a neoconservative position in this analysis—anti-communism, anti-totalitarianism, rejection of the New Left, moralized American exceptionalism, and prioritization of Israel in US foreign policy—much less the presence of the earlier generation of neocons at these conferences (e.g., Moynihan, Kirkpatrick) suggests that the relationship of US neoconservatism with the formation of "terrorism" discourse is an area worthy of further study; see, e.g., Cemalettin Hasimi, "Neoconservative Narrative as Globalising Islamophobia," in *Thinking Through Islamophobia: Global Perspectives*, eds. S. Sayyid and AbdoolKarim Vakil (London: Hurst, 2010). The recurrent worry about so-called totalitarianism suggests that the relationship between Hannah Arendt, the term's most distinguished and well-known originator, and US neoconservatism, is also an area worthy of further study; see, e.g., Balint, *Running Commentary*, 188.

48. "President Bush Addresses the Nation," *Washington Post*, Sept. 20 2001, http://www.washingtonpost.com/wp-srv/nation/specials/attacked/transcripts/bushaddress_092001.html.

49. Nietzsche's connections to Nazism—and fascism more broadly—is a sore that continues to fester at least in part because, with the exception of his sister, most people who see connections between the two condemn the association. But acknowledging this association is the exception to the unspoken rule in Nietzsche studies that we are otherwise not to comment on Nietzsche's politics or attempt to classify his political positions, especially if and as far as they might be considered reactionary (an exception I would trace to the generalized Holocaust Exceptionalism [Schotten, 2018] that informs much of Euro-American philosophy). A few Nietzsche commentators insist on the errors of reading, interpretation, and historiography that lead readers to see connections between Nietzsche and fascism, suggesting our interest in this "Bad Nietzsche" is a misplaced presentist concern anachronistically projected onto him (see e.g., Hugo Drochon, "The Return of the Bad Nietzsche," *New Statesman* Aug. 31–Sept. 6 2018). Yet Nietzsche's consistent and undeniable (if too often sidelined or disavowed) championing of naturalized, elitist hierarchy is a political commitment that is fully compatible with fascistic ideology, even if it is not a program for any particular fascist regime or a blueprint for the Final Solution. There is, in other words, an essential continuity between conservatism and fascism—and, therefore, Nietzsche, who is also a conservative—insofar as they share a "vision of the connection between excellence and rule," which unites "the libertarian, with his vision of the employer's untrammeled power in the workplace; the traditionalist, with his vision of the father's rule at home; and the statist, with his vision of a heroic leader pressing his hand upon the face of the earth." Robin, *The Reactionary Mind*, 1. As Daniel W. Conway puts it, Nietzsche "may not have been the father of fascism, but he certainly was in and of the family." "*Ecce Caesar:* Nietzsche's Imperial Aspirations," in *Nietzsche, Godfather of Fascism? On the Uses and Abuses of a Philosophy*, eds. Jacob Golomb and Robert S. Wistrich (Princeton, NJ: Princeton University Press, 2002), 174. Seeking to delink Nietzsche from fascism without fully confronting his commitment to naturalized, elitist hierarchy thus only reinforces it by rendering it innocuous, if not altogether illegible. See, e.g., Drochon, "The Return of the Bad Nietzsche"; Drochon, "Nietzsche and the Alt-Right: Further Adventures in the Art of Missing the Point," *Philosopher* 107.2 (Spring 2019). However, as the previous statements from Bush and the Netanyahus make clear, the political problem here is not acknowledging Nietzsche's compatibility with fascism, but rather using Nietzsche as an emblem of Nazism in order to veil one's own oppressive and fascistic agendas by trumpeting moral indignation at the Holocaust. Nietzsche is a convenient bogey to invoke the specter of fascism—Nazism in particular—in order to strike a righteous pose against it. But these sorts of invocations of Nazism and the Holocaust (and antisemitism more broadly) instrumentalize fascism and Nazism to manufacture a false victim narrative for those who are, in fact, firmly lodged in the seat of power, masking their own investment in the exact same eliminationist elitism that Nietzsche himself at times explicitly endorsed. On Zionism and/as slave morality, see Schotten, "Reading Nietzsche in the Wake of the 2008–09 War

on Gaza"; on Holocaust Exceptionalism and the instrumentalization of the Nazi genocide of Jewish people to advance anti-Muslim racism and the War on Terror, see Schotten, *Queer Terror.*

50. Benjamin Netanyahu, "Terrorism and the Islamic World," 63.

51. Netanyahu, 62–63, original emphasis.

52. "Gay Imperialism: Gender and Sexuality Discourse in the 'War on Terror,'" in *Out of Place: Interrogating Silences in Queerness/Raciality*, eds. Adi Kuntsman and Esperanza Miyake (York, UK: Raw Nerve Books, 2008), 81; see also Khan, "The Essentialist Terrorist."

53. Of course, it was only once the kind of eliminatory violence visited upon the colonies was "brought home" to Europe that it was finally considered beyond the pale of all human reason, comprehension, dignity, or decency. See Aimé Césaire, *Discourse on Colonialism*, trans. Joan Pinkham (New York: Monthly Review Press, 2000 [1955]); Mamdani, *Good Muslim, Bad Muslim*. As Mark Bray notes, "Fascist ideological, technological, and bureaucratic innovations created a vehicle for the imperialism and genocide that Europe had exported around the world to bring its wars of extermination home." *Antifa: The Anti-Fascist Handbook* (Brooklyn, NY: Melville House, 2017), 132.

54. See, e.g., Noura Erekat, "The Sovereign Right to Kill: A Critical Appraisal of Israel's Shoot-to-Kill Policy in Gaza," *International Criminal Law Review* 19 (2019); Jodi Byrd, *The Transit of Empire: Indigenous Critiques of Colonialism* (Minneapolis: University of Minnesota Press, 2011); Jung, *Beneath the Surface of White Supremacy*; Shira Robinson, *Citizen Strangers: Palestinians and the Birth of Israel's Liberal Settler State* (Stanford: Stanford University Press, 2013); Singh, *Race and America's Long War.*

55. As Erekat notes, e.g., "Palestinians in Gaza, like those in other areas of historical Palestine, are constructed as inherently dangerous subjects, 'terrorist' 'nonhuman' others, their lives constituted, regulated, and thus overdetermined by racialised ideologies that reduce them to unwanted bodies that can be eliminated and killed with impunity." "The Sovereign Right to Kill," 790.

56. Samuel P. Huntington, "The Clash of Civilizations?" *Foreign Affairs* (Summer 1993); cf. Bernard Lewis, "The Roots of Muslim Rage," *Atlantic* (Sept. 1990).

57. Paul Johnson, "The Seven Deadly Sins of Terrorism," in *International Terrorism*, 12–13. In these same pages, Johnson notes that "It is almost impossible to exaggerate the threat which terrorism holds for our civilization."

58. See Schotten, *Queer Terror.*

59. Bray, *Antifa*, 111–12.

60. I owe this insight to Dylan Rodríguez, who made this comment during discussion of the January 6 riot at one of the many panels at the "White Supremacy, Misogyny, and the 'New' Terrorism" conference, convened by Verena Erlenbusch-Anderson at Syracuse University, June 23–25, 2022.

61. Robin, *The Reactionary Mind*, 55–56.

62. Schotten, "TERFism, Zionism, and Right-Wing Annihilationism."
63. Robin, *Reactionary Mind*, 30–31; cf. Bray, *Antifa*, 138–39.

## References

Ali, Wajahat, Eli Clifton, Matthew Duss, Lee Fang, Scott Keyes, and Faiz Shakir. *Fear, Inc.: The Roots of the Islamophobia Network in America*. Washington, DC: Center for American Progress, Aug. 2011.

Balint, Benjamin. *Running Commentary: The Contentious Magazine that Transformed the Jewish Left into the Neoconservative Right*. New York: Public Affairs, 2010.

Bayoumi, Moustafa. *This Muslim American Life: Dispatches from the War on Terror*. New York: New York University Press, 2015.

Bray, Mark. *Antifa: The Anti-Fascist Handbook*. Brooklyn, NY: Melville House, 2017.

Brown, Wendy. "Democracy Against Itself: Nietzsche's Challenge." In *Politics out of History*. Princeton, NJ: Princeton University Press, 2001.

———. "Wounded Attachments." In *States of Injury: Power and Freedom in Late Modernity*. Princeton, NJ: Princeton University Press, 1995.

Brulin, Rémi. "Compartmentalization, Context of Speech, and the Israeli Origins of the American Discourse on 'Terrorism.'" *Dialectical Anthropology* 39.1 (March 2015): 69–119.

———. "Defining 'Terrorism': The 1972 General Assembly Debates on 'International Terrorism' and Their Coverage by the *New York Times*." In *If It Was Not for Terrorism: Crisis, Compromise, and Elite Discourse in the Age of War on Terror*, edited by Banu Baybars-Hawks and Lemi Baruh. Newcastle upon Tyne, UK: Cambridge Scholars, 2011.

Butler, Judith. *Precarious Life: The Powers of Mourning and Violence*. London: Verso, 2004.

Byrd, Jodi. *The Transit of Empire: Indigenous Critiques of Colonialism*. Minneapolis: University of Minnesota Press, 2011.

Césaire, Aimé. *Discourse on Colonialism*. Translated by Joan Pinkham. New York: Monthly Review Press, 2000. Originally published 1955.

Conway, Daniel W. "*Ecce Caesar*: Nietzsche's Imperial Aspirations." In *Nietzsche, Godfather of Fascism? On the Uses and Abuses of Philosophy*, edited by Jacob Golomb and Robert S. Wistrich. Princeton, NJ: Princeton University Press, 2002.

———. "*Das Weib an Sich*: The Slave Revolt in Epistemology." In *Feminist Interpretations of Nietzsche*, edited by Kelly Oliver K and Marilyn Pearsall. University Park: Pennsylvania State University Press, 1998.

Daulatzai, Sohail. *Fifty Years of "The Battle of Algiers": Past as Prologue*. Minneapolis: University of Minnesota Press, 2016.

Drochon, Hugo. "Nietzsche and the Alt-Right: Further Adventures in the Art of Missing the Point." *Philosopher* 107, no. 2 (Spring 2019).

———. "The Return of the Bad Nietzsche." *New Statesman* (Aug. 31–Sept. 6 2018).
Duss, Matthew, Yasmine Taeb, Ken Gude, and Ken Sofer. *Fear, Inc. 2.0: The Islamophobia Network's Efforts to Manufacture Hate in America*. Washington, DC: Center for American Progress, Feb. 2015.
Erekat, Noura. "The Sovereign Right to Kill: A Critical Appraisal of Israel's Shoot-to-Kill Policy in Gaza." *International Criminal Law Review* 19 (2019).
FBI Intelligence Assessment. "Black Identity Extremists Likely Motivated to Target Law Enforcement Officers." Aug. 3, 2017. https://vault.fbi.gov/black-identity-extremist-bie-intelligence-assessment-august-3-2017/black-identity-extremist-bie-intelligence-assessment-august-3-2017-part-01-of-01.pdf/view.
Gleason, Abbot. *Totalitarianism: The Inner History of the Cold War*. New York: Oxford University Press, 1995.
Halley, Janet. *Split Decisions: How and Why to Take a Break from Feminism*. Princeton, NJ: Princeton University Press, 2008.
Haritaworn, Jin, Tamsila Tauqir, and Esma Erdem. "Gay Imperialism: Gender and Sexuality Discourse in the 'War on Terror.'" In *Out of Place: Interrogating Silences in Queerness/Raciality*, edited by Adi Kuntsman and Esperanza Miyake. York, UK: Raw Nerve Books, 2008.
Hasimi, Cemalettin. "Neoconservative Narrative as Globalising Islamophobia." In *Thinking Through Islamophobia: Global Perspectives*, edited by S. Sayyid and Abdool Karim Vakil. London: Hurst, 2010.
Huntington, Samuel P. "The Clash of Civilizations?" *Foreign Affairs* (Summer 1993).
IJAN: the International Jewish Anti-Zionist Network. *The Business of Backlash: The Attack on the Palestinian Movement and Other Movements for Justice*. 2015. http://www.ijan.org/resources/business-of-backlash/.
Jung, Moon-Kie. *Beneath the Surface of White Supremacy: Denaturalizing U.S. Racisms Past and Present*. Stanford: Stanford University Press, 2015.
Khan, Liaquat Ali. "The Essentialist Terrorist." *Washburn Law Journal* 45.1 (Fall 2005).
Khan, Rabea M. "Race, Coloniality and the Post 9/11 Counterdiscourse: Critical Terrorism Studies and the Reproduction of the Islam-Terrorism Discourse." *Critical Studies on Terrorism* 14.4 (2021): 498–501.
Lewis, Bernard. "The Roots of Muslim Rage." *Atlantic Monthly* (Sept. 1990).
Li, Darryl. "A Jihadism Anti-Primer." *Middle East Research and Information Project* 45 (Fall 2015).
Mamdani, Mahmood. *Good Muslim, Bad Muslim: America, the Cold War, and the Roots of Terror*. New York: Pantheon, 2004.
Merrick, Allison. "'What Renders Our Sores Repugnant': Revisiting Nietzsche on Ressentiment." In *European-Supra-European: Nietzsche's View from Afar*, edited by Marco Brusotti, Herman Siemens, Corinna Schulbert, and Michael McNeal. Berlin: De Gruyter, 2020.
Naber, Nadine. *Arab America: Gender, Cultural Politics, and Activism*. New York: New York University Press, 2012.

Naber, Nadine, and Amaney Jamal, eds. *Race and Arab Americans Before and After 9/11: From Invisible Citizens to Visible Subjects*. Syracuse, NY: Syracuse University Press, 2008.

Nealon, Jeffrey. "Performing Resentment: White Male Anger; or, 'Lack' and Nietzschean Political Theory." In *Why Nietzsche Still? Reflections on Drama, Culture, and Politics*, edited by Alan Schrift. Berkeley: University of California Press, 2000: 274–292.

Netanyahu, Benjamin, ed. *International Terrorism: Challenge and Response*. New Brunswick, NJ: Transaction, 1981.

———, ed. *Terrorism: How the West Can Win*. New York: Avon, 1986.

Nevel, Donna, and Elly Bulkin. *Islamophobia and Israel*. New York: Route Books, 2014.

Nietzsche, Friedrich. *On the Genealogy of Morals: A Polemic*. Edited and translated by Walter Kaufmann. New York: Vintage, 1967. Originally published 1887.

Pietz, William. "The 'Post-Colonialism' of Cold War Discourse." *Social Text* 19/20 (Autumn 1988): 55–75.

Posocco, Silvia. "(Decolonizing) the Ear of the Other: Subjectivity, Ethics and Politics in Question." In *Decolonizing Sexualities: Transnational Perspectives, Critical Interventions*. Oxford, UK: Counterpress, 2016.

Rana, Junaid. "The Racial Infrastructure of the Terror-Industrial Complex." *Social Text* 34.4 (Dec. 2016).

Robin, Corey. *The Reactionary Mind: Conservatism from Edmund Burke to Donald Trump*. 2nd ed. New York: Oxford University Press, 2018.

Robinson, Shira. *Citizen Strangers: Palestinians and the Birth of Israel's Liberal Settler State*. Stanford: Stanford University Press, 2013.

Rubin, Gayle. "Thinking Sex: Notes for a Radical Theory of the Politics of Sexuality." In *Pleasure and Danger: Exploring Female Sexuality*, edited by Carole Vance. Boston: Routledge and Kegan Paul, 1984.

Said, Edward. "The Essential Terrorist." In *Blaming the Victims: Spurious Scholarship and the Palestinian Question*, edited by Edward Said and Christopher Hitchens. London: Verso, 2001. Originally published 1984.

Schotten, C. Heike. *Nietzsche's Revolution: Décadence, Politics, and Sexuality*. New York: Palgrave, 2009.

———. "Reading Nietzsche in the Wake of the 2008–09 War on Gaza." In *The Digital Dionysus: Nietzsche and the Network-Centric Condition*, eds. Nandita Biswas Mellamphy and Dan Mellamphy. New York: Punctum, 2016.

———. *Queer Terror: Life, Death, and Desire in the Settler Colony*. New York: Columbia University Press, 2018.

———. "Nietzsche and Emancipatory Politics: Queer Theory as Anti-Morality." *Critical Sociology* 45.2 (2019).

———. "Wounded Attachments? Slave Morality, the Left, and the Future of Revolutionary Desire." In *Nietzsche and Critical Theory*, edited by Michael Roberts. Leiden, NL: Brill, 2020.

———. "TERFism, Zionism, and Right-Wing Annihilationism: Toward an Internationalist Genealogy of Extinction Phobia." *TSQ: Transgender Studies Quarterly* 9.3 (Aug. 2022): 334–64.

Singh, Nikhil Pal. *Race and America's Long War*. Oakland: University of California Press, 2019.

Stampnitzky, Lisa. *Disciplining Terror: How Experts Invented "Terrorism."* Cambridge: Cambridge University Press, 2013.

Stringer, Rebecca. "'A Nietzschean Breed': Feminism, Victimology, *Ressentiment*." In *Why Nietzsche Still? Reflections on Drama, Culture, and Politics*, edited by Alan Schrift. Berkeley: University of California Press, 2000.

Tapper, Marion. "*Ressentiment* and Power: Some Reflections on Feminist Practices." In *Nietzsche, Feminism and Political Theory*, edited by Paul Patton. New York: Routledge, 1993.

Volpp, Leti. "The Citizen and the Terrorist." *UCLA Law Review* (June 2002).

Part III

# Emancipatory Possibilities

9

# Nietzsche and Feminine Subjectivity

ELİF YAVNIK

It is a peculiar experience for a woman to read Nietzsche: one oscillates between feelings of enthusiasm and disappointment. On the one hand, grounds for valuable feminist insights are immediately recognizable in Nietzsche's work, for instance in its anti-essentialism, its genealogical approach, and its challenges to the mind/body and nature/culture dualisms. Yet on the other hand, one cannot help hearing Nietzsche's work address itself to a male audience, or running into a sentence like "when a woman has scholarly inclinations, then usually something is wrong with her sexuality" (*BGE* 144). The delight one finds in reading Nietzsche's work notwithstanding, one seems to keep receiving the message: thinking, creating, even existing is a boy's game, and you cannot join.

It is possibly this experience of attraction/repulsion that induces Luce Irigaray to *talk back* at Nietzsche[1] and Kelly Oliver to ask what it means for a woman to read Nietzsche.[2] Of course Nietzsche is not at all alone in the history of philosophy in excluding or marginalizing women. His case, however, is a particularly interesting one given his overtly misogynistic remarks and those aspects of his thought that make it impossible to make such remarks, as well as the fact that many women thinkers have consistently engaged with and found useful resources in Nietzsche's philosophy.[3]

Two of the ways in which women readers have approached the question of women in Nietzsche interrogate (1) whether Nietzsche's thought is essentialist with regard to "women," and (2) whether it allows feminine subjectivity, that is, whether it is compatible with positing non-masculine valuations, norms, forms, articulations, concepts, ways of being, agencies, selves, and so on. I should note that I use the word "feminine" here without commitment to any binary order, while endeavoring not to lose sight of the fact that it is an attempt to refer to something that is not yet, something that is yet to come. I use "feminine" to refer to something that is not permeated with masculine forms, and not to refer to what is other-than-masculine, that is, neither to what is fantasized as "the feminine" in a masculine order nor to anything imagined in reaction to, in reference to, or in any way secondary to the masculine order. In what follows I focus mainly on this second question about feminine subjectivity. Approaching that question in a productive way, however, requires having answered the first question in the negative, since on the face of things, it appears that Nietzsche denies feminine subjectivity on essentialist grounds.

In the following section, I provide an overview of the discussions preceding the question of feminine subjectivity in Nietzsche. I consider the debate on Nietzsche's essentialism concerning the category of women, and I agree with those scholars who have provided a negative answer. In the next second section of my chapter, I group and examine the answers given to the question of feminine subjectivity in Nietzsche from three positions. In the last section, I conclude by proposing a fourth position that discusses yet unconsidered possibilities in Nietzsche's work to approach the question of feminine subjectivity. Here I maintain that Nietzsche's thought extends itself to the feminine in a half-conscious gesture, and that responding to this call, by engaging, encountering, and countering, does not make a woman un-Nietzschean at all. Indeed, on the contrary, for such a reader there is a lot in the Nietzschean text to befriend, and by means of which to embark together with Nietzsche on a journey beyond "man" and the masculine order.

## Toward the Question of Feminine Subjectivity in Nietzsche's Work

Regarding the issue of his misogynistic remarks, Nietzsche's contemporary women readers manifest a forgiving attitude on the one hand and express disillusionment on the other. They sometimes attempt to explain these remarks as traceable to Nietzsche's "unfulfilled desire for a suitable partner"[4] or to his general ignorance about women.[5] This of course does not amount to an acceptance of these remarks. Hedwig Dohm for example, a contemporary and compatriot feminist, expresses her disillusionment, saying: "Friedrich Nietzsche! You, my greatest writer of the century, why is your writing on women so utterly beyond the good? A deep, deep heartache for me. It makes me even more lonely . . . even more of an outsider."[6] Nevertheless, as will other women later on, they do not easily dismiss Nietzsche's work.

Throughout most of the twentieth century, a relative silence about Nietzsche's statements about women prevails, due for the most part to Walter Kaufmann's contention that these statements are "philosophically irrelevant."[7] This changed in the last quarter of the century when Jacques Derrida's *Spurs: Nietzsche's Styles* and Sarah Kofman's "Baubô: Theological Perversion and Fetishism" appeared, rendering it impossible from then on to disregard the question of women in Nietzsche's work. In light of these works, women interpreters manifested less of a forgiving attitude and maintain that Nietzsche's statements on women should be given serious consideration just like any other aspect of his work. Linda Singer and Ofelia Schutte have pointed out that Nietzsche's remarks on women are neither accidental nor merely autobiographical. They maintain that these remarks are continuous with his thought and should be understood for what they are.[8] Toward the end of the twentieth century and into the twenty-first century, therefore, Nietzsche's work has been increasingly challenged owing to the views on women that it incorporates.

Before focusing on the question of feminine subjectivity in Nietzsche, I will briefly review the discussions around his essentialism, since that debate has implications for the question at hand.

Linda Singer and Ofelia Schutte both hold that Nietzsche has an essentialist conception of women, which they find problematic from the point of view of the question of feminine subjectivity. Singer holds that Nietzsche has an essentialist conception of women as he places women on the side of nature to be defined primarily by their biological functions, rather than on the side of history where struggles of wills are at work. As she writes, women "do not make themselves. . . . The adventures of self-creation that Nietzsche glorifies are explicitly denied them."[9] Thus according to Singer, in Nietzsche's work women are denied the status of being primary actors in history who create their own values, their own interpretations, and their own selves: they are denied subjectivity. Schutte examines

Nietzsche's essentialism with regard to his notions of the "order of rank" and of "higher" and "lower" individuals, and she views his opposition to the political emancipation of women in this light. She holds that Nietzsche, in positing an essential dualism of higher and lower individuals despite his attempt to keep the categories of higher/lower empty, makes it "quite clear what groups are by 'nature' or 'destiny' higher and what lower."[10] Based on his "domination model" of self-actualization, women, who are destined to appear in the lower rank, are denied subjectivity in Schutte's view. As she notes, "Nietzsche claimed that woman is incapable of anything but obedience and superficiality."[11]

However, in response to the question of whether Nietzsche has an essentialist view of women, Jacques Derrida, Sarah Kofman, Maudemarie Clark, Babette Babich, and Lynne Tirrell answer in the negative. Derrida explains that there is no "essence" to woman in Nietzsche, that "woman" is a name for the "untruth of truth," that woman is the undecidability that "all of ontology" conceals.[12] Kofman holds that we should not hastily declare Nietzsche misogynist, as there is no essential "woman" in his writing that he can be said to deprecate; on the contrary, there is a plurality of women figures in Nietzsche's text, one of which is Baubô, the figure of the fecund, cruel, eternal affirmation of life.[13] Clark, too, reasons that there can be no essential woman, no "woman in herself" for Nietzsche as there is no "thing in itself," and that therefore it is difficult to read his remarks on women as misogynistic or anti-feminist.[14] She holds that his apparent misogyny is at the level of sentiment, not belief, and she emphasizes that Nietzsche makes this explicit. Focusing on *BGE* 231 (which I too will take up in the last section of this chapter), Clark argues that Nietzsche means for his remarks to be taken as "his truths," as expressing his will to truth.

Babich draws attention to the metaphoricity of the questions of women and truth in Nietzsche, explaining that the logic of his text makes it impossible to conceive woman as anything more than an empty, "pure fantasy."[15] Tirrell emphasizes the existentialist nature of Nietzsche's notion of the self, and she states that "put anachronistically, Nietzsche holds 'woman' to be a socially constructed category."[16] She holds that Nietzsche's work anticipates Beauvoir's discussion of man as Self and woman as Other. Tirrell claims that Nietzsche correctly identifies the situation of man being the subject that defines the woman, but that that does not prompt him to call for a transformation, to promote the search for the possibilities of feminine subjectivity: "He was not willing or perhaps able to take the sort of feminist stance that is nascent here."[17]

I agree that Nietzsche's claims about women are not to be taken as endorsing an essentialist category of "women," as that would contradict one of the broader aims of his work, namely revealing the dynamics behind supposedly fixed categories. (And while contradiction is characteristic of his work, the contradictions that Nietzsche embraces are productive and not blatant ones.) If Nietzsche is not essentialist with regard to the category of "women," then it cannot be held that he understands "women" as fixed through masculine discourse and that he closes off feminine possibilities on those grounds. It is then meaningful to ask whether his thought allows feminine subjectivity. At the same time, I strongly agree with Singer and Schutte that Nietzsche's remarks on women have to be accounted for. Here, therefore, I intend to advance work that accounts for Nietzsche's remarks on women in relation to the question of feminine subjectivity.

## The Question of Feminine Subjectivity in Nietzsche's Work

Derrida understands Nietzsche's and his own thought as performing a "feminine operation" in writing by giving up the claim to *authority* and marking the "undecidable."[18] He holds that Nietzsche's anti-feminism was directed at a feminism that expressed an aspiration to be "like a man" and "resemble the masculine dogmatic philosopher" by abandoning those valuable aspects of existence that women have traditionally been associated with, such as the body and organic life in general.[19] Derrida himself appears to side with this "anti-feminism" whose operation he does not find "feminine."

There are multiple problems with this view. It persists in conceiving the feminine as primarily what is other than the masculine; it claims to know how a feminine operation may be brought about better than those who experience being feminine every day; and it assumes that, as Kelly Oliver explains, "men can perform the feminine operation, an operation that no 'real' woman can perform, yet women cannot take up the subject position, traditionally masculine, without being derided as 'feminists' just trying to emulate men."[20] In approaching the question of feminine subjectivity in Nietzsche, it is necessary to beware of these attempts to predetermine answers to it. As Cynthia Kaufman reminds us, being valorized as the "other of reason" has little effect on the lives and expressive possibilities of actual living and breathing women.[21] And as Irigaray and Oliver argue, Nietzsche and Derrida do not at all give up authority in writing, much less the position of the subject: on the contrary, their alleged "feminine operation" amounts to an attempt to occupy whatever space might be discovered for the feminine.[22] Hence Irigaray and Oliver hold that, tension between his disparaging remarks about women and the insight his thought offers for challenging patriarchal structures aside, Nietzsche's work appears to be ultimately misogynist in that it does not allow feminine subjectivity.[23]

It is possible to categorize the views offered on the question of whether Nietzsche's thought allows for feminine subjectivity into three broad positions: (1) Nietzsche's thought does not allow for feminine subjectivity, and that is a problem (that of Luce Irigaray and Kelly Oliver); (2) it does allow for feminine subjectivity, yet still there are problems (that of Lewis Call and Tamsin Lorraine); and (3) it does allow for feminine subjectivity, so there is no problem (that of Kristen Brown and Debra B. Bergoffen). I will discuss each of these in turn, and then, in the final section of the chapter, I shall propose a fourth view: that Nietzsche's thought does not allow for feminine subjectivity, and that this denial is not only *not* a problem but it constitutes an important possibility for the emergence of feminine subjectivity.

Luce Irigaray and Kelly Oliver adopt the first position. In *Marine Lover of Friedrich Nietzsche*, Irigaray both calls Nietzsche out and calls out *to* him in revolt, in compassion, and in hope: "If within yourself you no longer find the strength to live, might it not be time to listen to the other, rather than tear holes in her body and drain her blood drop by drop? It is voices from beyond the grave who take such food, is it not?" (Irigaray 1991, 18). Addressing herself to Nietzsche, the marine lover reminds him of immemorial waters, of femininity, and of the mother to which he is doing violence in forgetting, and in forgetting whom he is paving the way to nihilism. The feminine, the mother, forgotten and appropriated "drop by drop" by the masculine subject of discourse, becomes an absence; she becomes an absence between man and man and within man himself, an invisible absence that escapes any perspective, an absence that "threatens the stability of all values."[24] Irigaray explains that the masculine discourse resists this element by reducing and confining it to its own terms, albeit in a guise of elevation, and positing it as the "other of the same": "She would be the privileged trustee of the secret of the truth—and of her non-truth—in that she serves to constitute the identity of the same."[25] The "male (same)" is thus sealed tight to women, except to receive their support: the denial of women and their acceptance into the intelligible order only as idols of phantasy is the sacrifice that continually reinforces and reinstates the masculine order of discourse. Valorized as the "other" of reason, women are denied the position of subjectivity, and their part is played by masculine subjects "mimicking her, perfecting her artistically."[26] However, Irigaray reminds Nietzsche that the advent of the future philosophers he is heralding is not possible without a loving relation with this other, and she claims that "only through difference can the incarnation unfold without murderous or suicidal passion," and that "passage from one era to the other" in spiritual history happens through a relation over "sexuate difference."[27]

Kelly Oliver follows Irigaray's claim that Nietzsche's thought, while attempting to open philosophy up to its others—to other voices, to the body, to nonmeaning—still does not open it up to the feminine body. She too holds that Nietzsche covers over sexual difference by presenting it as an accidental characteristic of a neuter (male) subject, thus reducing all sexuality to the masculine. Disregarding the feminine body results in failing to conceive subjectivity through bodily realities such as pregnancy and childbirth. Nietzsche's work, while claiming to be a "writing with blood," does not consider a feminine experience of bleeding, thus occluding the possibilities of interpretation that this would enable.[28] In this effort to open philosophy up to the body, Oliver shows that feminine bodily experiences are not included among the paradigmatic ones.[29] Oliver emphasizes the importance of keeping the space open for the possibilities of the other, and she claims that this is possible only through concrete engagements with the other, even when, or especially when, the other threatens the status quo: "At our moment in the history of philosophy, it is the feminine other that threatens to make its presence known to philosophy," and that is why "philosophy's survival depends on the feminine."[30] Irigaray and Oliver agree that (1) Nietzsche, that most promising philosopher to challenge the foundations of philosophy, does not allow feminine subjectivity, and that (2) there is no way out of nihilism without engaging with the feminine.

The interpreters who adopt the second position maintain that while Nietzsche's work does allow feminine subjectivity, there still are reasons to worry about the possibilities of this subject for social and political agency. Lewis Call, reminding us that Nietzsche's critique of the Western philosophical tradition is at the same time a critique of the subjectivity forged in that experience, and that his attacks on women who want to be "like men" is continuous with that critique, finds this position productive since the postmodern subject for whom it paves the way, he claims, has the possibility of being "female and feminist."[31] He points out that Nietzsche's work has more to offer for feminist politics than Derrida acknowledges, emphasizing that Nietzsche's contestation of the category "woman," like his contestation of "truth," is not a reactive thinking, but it rather aims at opening those spaces for new affirmations: "Nietzsche . . . uses the metaphor of woman to deny the existence of truth in the conventional sense, but he does so to open a broad space for new affirmations, new kinds of truth."[32] Nevertheless, Call acknowledges that the question remains as to how these possibilities are to be taken up for feminist politics.

Tamsin Lorraine also voices the criticism that "representing and valorizing life as the feminine undecidable . . . does nothing for women in their struggle for recognition and respect."[33] She considers women's experiences of reading *Thus Spoke Zarathustra*, examines four possible positions that they might identify with, and shows that none of them are suitable grounds on which to conceive feminine subjectivity. Even the representation of women as Life itself, coy and unfaithful, which at first look may appear celebratory, is a depiction of women in relation to men. Lorraine asks, "What if Life is bored with all the attempts to win her favor and would much rather have a conversation? What if Life has other projects of her own," pointing out once again the lack of recognition of feminine subjectivity.[34] According to Lorraine, this, however, is not a reason to reject the work, for "women are used to finding their ways into texts that would exclude them."[35] Lorraine finds her way into the text and into subjectivity in Zarathustra's own words, which teach that the only way to redeem the past and its determinations in the present is through forming the future, affirming, positing, imposing one's own values. In light of this suggestion, Lorraine describes a Zarathustra who is a strong woman "in keeping with [her] own taste for the future,"[36] and in doing so she fashions a new position of subjectivity from Nietzsche's text.

Kristen Brown and Debra Bergoffen adopt the third position. Brown disagrees with Oliver's claim that Nietzsche's thought opens Western philosophy up to only the masculine body on grounds that there is no place for a "natural" woman in Nietzsche's thought, as his understanding of biology does not rest on a dualism and is neither static nor teleological. To illustrate her point, Brown shows how Nietzsche's conception of the body is compatible with a phenomenon related to menstruation: (pre)menses. She explains that biological phenomena arise through an exchange across ideational, psychosomatic, and socio-physical planes; that women's physical experiences of (pre)menses is related to cultural valuations; and that where a negative valuation is attributed to menstruation, (pre)menses will be experienced as painful and disease-like. This analysis, Brown explains, is compatible with how Nietzsche conceives cultural valuations as inscribed into one's experience of their body and moral valuations, definitive valuations, and psychosomatic constitutions as co-constituting and as *relata*, rather than reified things.[37] Brown agrees that Nietzsche's thought, "although beginning to introduce the other qua body into Western philosophy, introduces primarily the symbolically masculine body"; however, she holds that "the being of such a body, constituted by and co-participant in a moving constellation of partnering forces may be, if not feminine, feminist," if we keep it in mind that for Nietzsche bodies are not simply biological or symbolic but are constituted through an exchange across planes, through an exchange with values, ideas, experiences of others, and so on.[38] She holds that, given its conception of biology and the body, it is not possible for Nietzsche's work to exclude any *body* and the emergence of subjectivity on that basis. In this way, Brown holds, Nietzsche's ideas "stretch towards a feminist reappropriation."[39]

It should be noted here that Oliver and Brown agree that they are answering different questions. Oliver acknowledges that the biological and the social are mutually constitutive, and she does not base her claims on a presupposition that Nietzsche argues otherwise.[40] And Brown maintains that Nietzsche's corporeality is "laden with symbolism traditionally linked with masculine body."[41] Oliver's criticism rather is that Nietzsche does not acknowledge feminine embodied experiences as resources to draw from. This is different than the question of whether Nietzsche's views on the body may be made to apply to feminine bodies as well. Where Oliver and Brown differ is therefore the grounds on which to approach the issue of feminine body and subjectivity in Nietzsche.

Debra Bergoffen agrees with many that although Nietzsche is definitely "no feminist," his ideas can nevertheless provide important resources for feminist thought.[42] She holds that in Nietzsche's thought, from the other side of the traditional discourse of "truth" that has been articulated by masculine voices, a feminine skepticism arises, and for women who "refuse to live their feminine skepticism passively, transvaluation can become a political strategy."[43] Bergoffen exemplifies this political strategy with the silent protests of the Madres de la Plaza de Mayo and the Abuelas de la Plaza de Mayo in Argentina for the disappearance of their relatives. These mothers and grandmothers, she explains, were making demands from the state not as citizens but as the silenced mothers, which is the position accorded to them by the patriarchy—however, by appropriating and trans-valuing it. In so doing, Bergoffen says that they catch the authoritarian regime "off guard," and they revaluate the value and the meaning given to them by the dominant discourse. The Madres and the Abuelas de la Plaza de Mayo make a claim from the state, from public life, in the name of the family, the private. Bergoffen recalls the alignment of men with the public, the production, transcendence, historical consciousness, and linear time, and of women with the private, family, reproduction, immanence, and circular time. She interprets Nietzsche's Eternal Return as a critique of Western historical consciousness *and* an affirmation of feminine temporality.[44] Her claim is not that Nietzsche is simply proposing to replace the linear time of historical consciousness with the repetition of the familial: "feminine" temporality cannot itself be the answer as long as it remains unhistorical.[45] Eternal Return is rather a new temporality, one that "refuses to allow public time to appropriate all value to itself and refuses to allow private time to be reduced to inertia."[46] Eternal Return, Bergoffen holds, breaks the boundaries of traditional categories of male and female, and it necessarily involves affirming the feminine.[47] Thus Bergoffen locates the possibility of feminist intervention in politics and ethics in the conceptual space opened up by Nietzsche's critique of truth and in his idea of Eternal Return. With these, Bergoffen intimates, Nietzsche's thought paves the way for a transformation of subjectivity.

Three positions, then, are available concerning the question of feminine subjectivity in Nietzsche: Irigaray and Oliver hold that his thought does not allow feminine subjectivity, thereby putting itself at an impasse and failing to take philosophy to its new frontiers. Call, Lorraine, Brown, and Bergoffen, on the other hand, think that Nietzsche's thought does allow feminine subjectivity in some way. Call and Lorraine agree that Nietzsche's thought *can be* put to work to allow feminine subjectivity, but a lot of work is required before it can become politically, concretely fruitful. Brown and Bergoffen find less trouble in showing how Nietzsche's thought is compatible with feminine subjectivity. Brown accounts for this compatibility through a discussion of Nietzsche's dynamic understanding of the body. Bergoffen opposes Irigaray's view that Nietzsche's thought is based on a *forgetting* of the feminine, emphasizes that Nietzsche's Eternal Return involves a continual recalling of the unhistorical into historical consciousness, and finds in that movement possibilities for affirming feminine forms.

## Nietzsche's Summoning of Women

As I already noted, in response to the question of whether Nietzsche's thought is welcoming of feminine subjectivity, I propose the following answer: no, but this attempt at exclusion is more productive than problematic because it is an integral part of a much more genuine and deeper summoning of the feminine. I agree with the position that Nietzsche's work does not allow biological essentialism or any exclusion of the feminine body on that basis. But I also agree that we expect from a groundbreaking philosophy such as Nietzsche's more than what seems like a half-hearted acceptance: we expect it to be not only compatible with feminine subjectivity but also to recognize feminine embodied experiences as resources in the philosophical imaginary. Nietzsche clearly does not make space for articulations of feminine bodily experiences to be counted as constitutive of our conception of subjectivity. Yet (as Lorraine remarks and Bergoffen exemplifies with the Madres and the Abuelas de la Plaza de Mayo) women *are* used to finding their ways into texts that would exclude them. I maintain, in a similar vein, that it is possible to read Nietzsche's texts not just to find a nook there for women but rather to take root in them, and nourished by their resources, to grow out of them—all in a Nietzschean spirit.

Nietzsche's thought visibly excludes feminine subjectivity. But Nietzsche does not just let this exclusion happen, as most thinkers tend to do; he performs it loud and clear. It then becomes necessary to interpret this noisy performance. I read in it both a despising of civilized and shallow invitations to women and a profound summoning of the feminine, coming from the heart of his work.

To explain how, I will focus on two moments in Nietzsche's texts. The first one is Nietzsche's intriguing preface to his series of insults to women in *Beyond Good and Evil* where he writes,

> Learning transforms us; it does what all nourishment does that also does not merely "preserve"—: as physiologists know. But at the bottom of us, way "down there," there is indeed something unteachable, a granite of spiritual *fatum*, of predetermined decision and answer to predetermined selected questions. In every cardinal problem an immutable "this is I" can be heard; about man and woman, for instance, a thinker cannot relearn but only finish learning—only discover to the end what about this is "established" in him already. At times we find certain solutions to problems that inspire strong faith even in *us*; perhaps henceforth we call them our "convictions." Later on—we see in them only the footsteps of our self-knowledge, sign-posts to the problem that we *are*—more correctly to the great stupidity we are, to our spiritual *fatum*, to what is *unteachable* way "down there."—After

the abundant niceness I have just extended to myself, perhaps
I will more easily be permitted to announce a few truths about
"woman in itself," assuming that it is known from the outset
now how very much these are only—*my* truths.—(*BGE* 231)[48]

In this passage, Nietzsche expresses several things at once. He states
(1) that there is a "granite" bottom of our thought, a calcified, solidified
precipitate; (2) that this granite formation is essentially constitutive of us,
of *who we are*; (3) that no amount of education would be able to stir up
this sediment—it is where the mind is passive, it is our *stupidity*; (4) that
the best we can hope for is to see this rock bottom for what it is; (5) that
the question of man and woman belongs here; and (6) that in his remarks
about women he is speaking out of this granite bottom. He holds that
with the "cardinal problem'" of man and woman we are at the end of our
wit, our possibilities of thinking, and of who we are: we are face to face
with the in-itself of our being, which, like all "in-itself," is "stupid" (*GM*
III:7). And with this, Nietzsche not only prefaces his derogatory remarks
that follow, but he also renders visible the grounds and the natural limits
of the philosophical claims on this question.

That Nietzsche does not *argue against* the prevalent views on women
is no surprise. Nietzsche's work in general aims not at refuting or weeding out some idea or another but at understanding and transforming the
grounds on which they grow. And in our "spiritual fatum" he recognizes a
foundation, a calcified substrate of our "convictions," a ground where no
intellectual intervention is possible and that turns all attempts to approach
it into "sign-posts" indicating the route to oneself. It appears that Nietzsche
believes it is possible to take this route, not by trying to *deny* what nourishes
one's thought and one's self but through giving voice to them by bringing
out into the open one's deep-seated convictions, preconceptions, and forms
of violence.

This, however, does not manifest in Nietzsche's work by mindlessly
giving vent to one's prejudices under the guise of frankness. Nietzsche's
thought does not deny subjectivity to women in a commonplace and shallow way. Rather, in its self-awareness, it *performs*, embodies, and renders
loud that denial, that stupidity. It warns women against contracting the
"masculine stupidity" (*BGE* 239)[49] and at the same time insists that the
"abysmal antagonism" (238) between the sexes must not be forgotten; in so
doing, it reveals the impossibility and the irreducible hypocrisy of extending
a polite invitation to, or a civil recognition of, the feminine by masculinist

discourses, as this would manifestly entail the destruction of the inviter and of their world.[50]

Nietzsche therefore does not advocate a project to transform the existing power relations between the sexes, nor is he interested in making space for feminine interventions. Nietzsche's call to the feminine does not come as an invitation; rather, Nietzsche *makes manifest* his inability to extend an invitation, finding in that inability sign-posts to his own grounds. The integrity of his thought then works to voice a profound summoning of the feminine: a summoning that marks sign-posts into and beyond the masculinist author's grounds of possibility.

The second moment I want to focus on involves the figure of the old woman, also the figure of Life and Wild Wisdom, which is traced throughout *Thus Spoke Zarathustra* in three encounters.

> "Much has Zarathustra spoken to us women too, yet he has never spoken to us about woman."
>
> And I replied to her: "About woman one should talk only to men."
>
> "Talk to me too about woman," she said; "I am old enough to forget it straight away." (*Z* I.18)

On their first meeting, Zarathustra is thus challenged into having a genuine relation with this feminine figure. In reply, he gives her his naive views on women, to which she listens and jokingly says are charming for those who are "young enough for them" (*Z* I.18), advising him to not forget to "take the whip" when going to women. Their second encounter is told, *to young women*, in a dance-song about Life and Wisdom. The song expresses Zarathustra's enchantment with Life and his profound lack of knowledge of her; it tells how she thwarts all his attempts to know and how he finds himself in an utterly ambivalent position with regard to her: "From the ground up I love only Life—and verily, most of all when I hate her!" (*Z* II.10). Their last encounter is just before the climax of the book at the end of the third part. Here, exhausted with trying to keep up dancing with her, now finding and now losing her, Zarathustra attempts to aggressively make Life dance to the rhythm he keeps with his whip. But Life engages him in dialogue, and they communicate. In this encounter, Zarathustra is at the end of his wit and of himself: he is about to *leave* Life at the end of the third part. His interlocutor is clearly not one who can appear in his world, she is not one with whom he can communicate without being undone himself; yet it is this interlocutor for whom he yearns the most.

It does not escape women's eyes that "a woman, an old woman . . . continuously haunts Nietzsche's text";[51] that "out of all the characters in the book, Zarathustra seems to take Life and his Wild Wisdom (also characterized as a woman) most seriously . . . it is with Life that Zarathustra seems to be most anxious to have a relationship";[52] and that "the philosophers who follow Nietzsche have not perceived the seriousness of his quest for a feminine companion."[53] While Zarathustra addresses himself above all to men, his ultimate interlocutor appears to be a woman, or rather a plural figure who is at the same time a woman, Life, and Zarathustra's Wild Wisdom. Irigaray is on point when she mentions "the tragic appeal of Nietzsche to a feminine companion in order to become capable of crossing the bridge toward new humanity."[54] She does not however seem to appreciate fully the "tragic" aspect of this appeal, this summoning. Irigaray thinks through the Indian divine image of Şiva and his relationship with feminine companions that shape the destiny of the world and treats Nietzsche's appeal for feminine companionship as part of a dialectic of spiritual history.

Irigaray states that Nietzsche "acknowledges that he needed a feminine companion in order to be able to pursue his work."[55] It is important, however, to realize that the acknowledgment comes from the work and not from the author, the person in whom all the "stupidities" of history are entrenched and who cannot realistically expect to have a relationship with a feminine companion, as *he* is not to survive that contact. Failing to recognize this would occlude Nietzsche's keen appreciation of the profundity of the transformation that the coming of the feminine signifies. Summoning the feminine in the way Nietzsche does (i.e., despite oneself) is truly a tragic appeal. Unlike quests for companions that do not deeply disturb one's *self*, or polite invitations that offer to make space in what inevitably remains one's *home*, such a yearning expresses a need to be fundamentally transformed, together with a strong resistance to that possibility. It is a call to the other to come, to revaluate, and to give new names and meanings.

At our moment in the history of philosophy, it is the feminine other that "threatens to make its presence known to philosophy,"[56] to recall Oliver. The feminine other is both a threat to philosophy and a promise for its survival. Femininity is a defining characteristic of the new species of philosophers, of the future philosophers who are to transform the order of the same through self-affirmations and revaluations. "Metaphysicians of all times" (*BGE* 2), "philosophers, insofar as they are dogmatists" (*BGE* 1), rest their beliefs on a binary valuation along the axis of good and evil and on the supreme value and the impeccable origin of truth. "Supposing truth is a woman" (*BGE* 1), failing to understand the dynamics of one's will, and naming that which it finds itself directed at truth, they clumsily attempt to follow it the way they do with a similarly constructed fantasy, "woman." "What is certain," however, according to Nietzsche, "is that she has not allowed herself to be charmed:—and every kind of dogmatism stands there today with a gloomy and despondent look. *If* it stands at all anymore!" (*BGE* 1). Moving beyond the nihilistic impasse will not be possible without the new species of philosophers. Nietzsche says he unriddles these future philosophers "insofar as they allow themselves to be unriddled—for it belongs to their nature to want to remain riddles at some point" (*BGE* 42). It appears that he could not unriddle them to the point of recognizing their femininity. Women, however, have an idea: as Frances Nesbitt Oppel explains, women readers' positions are "ironically privileged by their exclusion as narrates and actors in the text," and as readers from outside the narrative, they are the ones "most likely to solve its riddles."[57]

Women's participation in public life and feminist interventions in philosophy, social thought, law, and politics, among others, have indeed been questioning and transforming our ways of living, our modes of existing, and the sense we make of the world.[58] Yet this is merely the beginning stages of the needed alteration. The feminine is still *to come*, she is still on her way, and only as she thus materializes will it be possible to speak with other tongues, through other bodies, and have different subjectivities emerge. Feminine words, meanings, revaluations render possible new conceptions and new ways of being. Understanding, for example, "body," "power," "work," or "selfhood" in novel ways would entail radical transformations in medicine, politics, economy, and law, among other areas, which would give rise to possibilities of being related to others and to oneself in new ways. Non-reductive conceptions of the body and of biology would provide further theoretical grounds to support the current queer and trans movements, while moving beyond the binds of masculine forms liberate possibilities of queer subjectivities. We can of course only guess what such transformations would involve. But going by what we have already seen, we can expect them to liberate human existence in significant ways from modes in which it is stuck. One example would be women's demand for maternity leave growing into demands for paternity leave and for parental leave, as the significance of professional and personal lives are reconsidered and men and nonbinary people are also able to reconceptualize themselves vis-à-vis these aspects of their lives. Such a reorganization offers new conceptual, emotional, and material possibilities to relate to one's children, one's partner, and oneself; it allows generations to grow with diverse experiences of bonding in their childhood, thereby transforming future humanity.

The Nietzschean summoning of the feminine is thus a summoning of possibilities of being and living differently. It is a call to have the familiar landscape of reality transformed, to be dislocated as the paradigmatic subject, and to have one's comfort of living through forms that are continuous with one's bodily experiences, interrupted. It is to open oneself up to living in a world that is shaped also by other experiences, other bodies, other sensibilities; to hearing hitherto muted aspects of one's self; to experiencing oneself differently; to having to be other than "man."

One main claim of *Thus Spoke Zarathustra* is that "man is something that shall be overcome." I find it appropriate to use the translation "man" here instead of "human," since as is the case with Nietzsche, it is indeed a gendered human existence that is to be overcome. Being gendered down to its grounds, this existence needs the feminine other to be overcome; it needs the feminine other to come, and through self-affirmations, to revaluate, rename, and transform human existence. This self-affirmation does not consist in "finishing learning" certain "predetermined decisions and answers to predetermined questions." Nothing about this self-affirmation is predetermined, and the self, or the subjectivity, here is to appear only *through* the affirmations. Nietzsche's thought cannot be essentialist with regard to women, because properly speaking, for Nietzsche, women are *not yet*. Nietzsche's thought reveals the profound sense in which the feminine is not yet; it reveals how profoundly human existence is closed off to it. And while manifesting the yearning of the existing masculine consciousness for this other, it at the same time testifies to the impossibility of extending civil invitations to her. Zarathustra says, "Woman is not yet capable of friendship" for being "for far too long" as slave or a tyrant (*Z* I.15). Being for far too long able to enter the masculine order only as determined primarily by a relation of domination, women do not properly figure in it, and it is impossible to have a mutual relationship with one who does not appear, does not materialize: one cannot invite them to friendship in honesty. Yet one can call out, summon, make oneself a *sign-post*. Nietzsche's thought then becomes a sign-post to the profundity of the intervention that the coming of women is to human existence: it becomes a sign-post to the place where we are over man.

## Notes

1. Irigaray 1991.
2. Oliver 1995. One is of course never only a woman, and one never reads Nietzsche as only a woman. Joanne Faulkner, for example, examines Kofman's reception of Nietzsche through her Jewish and feminine identities (Faulkner 2008). Since it is possible to perceive Nietzsche as offending on a broad spectrum, his thought offers multiple interesting intersections from which to read his work. Here I focus on the perspective of the feminine reader.
3. See also Creasy (in this volume) "Sexism Is Exhausting: Nietzsche and the Emotional Dynamics of Sexist Oppression."
4. Ellen Key, in *Krummel: Nietzsche und der deutsche Geist* 2:90, 116. Quoted in Helm 2004, 70. Later, Maudemarie Clark and Luce Irigaray also consider possible effects of Nietzsche's personal relation to women on his work. Clark says she used to not find Nietzsche's misogyny very interesting as she tended to read it as a reflection of his anger at Lou Salomé (Clark 1998, 188–89). And Irigaray claims that Nietzsche "acknowledges that he needed a feminine companion in order to be able to pursue his work, a companion whom he did not find, and we know the exhaustion of energy that, at least in part, resulted from such a lack" (Irigaray and Marder 2016, 67). I return to Irigaray's consideration of the subject later in the chapter.
5. Kathleen J. Wininger relates that Malwida von Meysenbug, the German writer and advocate of women's emancipation who introduced Nietzsche to several intellectual women (and had invited him to Sorrento together with Paul Rée), recommended Nietzsche to drop the subject of women as he does not know many and does not understand them (Wininger, 1998, 238). This interestingly recalls the old woman's remark in *Thus Spoke Zarathustra* that Zarathustra does not know women (Z I.18).
6. Dohm 1898, 534–43. Quoted in Diethe 1996, 143.
7. Kaufmann 2013, 84.
8. Singer says that "the irresponsible things he said about women should be clearly disclosed as irresponsible" (1998, 174) and Schutte states that "the weeding out of the least attractive elements in Nietzsche's work amounts to either self-deceit or censorship, and . . . in any case . . . keeps us from understanding the whole of Nietzsche's vision" (1984, 186). And interpreters like Kofman, Clark, and Graybeal, even when they relate this aspect of Nietzsche's thought to his personal experiences, do that in a way that is not dismissive of the ideas but rather seeks their coherence with and significance in the broader portrait of the author (Kofman 1998; Kofman 1994; Graybeal 1998; and Clark 1998).
9. Singer 1998, 175.
10. Schutte 1984, 187.

11. Schutte 1984, 178.
12. Derrida 1979, 103.
13. Kofman 1994.
14. Clark 1998, 192.
15. Babich 1996, 14.
16. Tirrell 1998, 207.
17. Tirrell, 1998, 219–20.
18. Derrida 1979, 65.
19. Derrida 1979, 65.
20. Oliver 1995, 32.
21. Cynthia Kaufman 1998.

22. Note that Kelly Oliver also states that she does not think deconstruction of the subject makes it impossible to talk about political or ethical agency. The problem, according to her, is that there is no space in these "feminine operations" for feminine subjectivity to appear, even as this deconstructed subject.

23. On this point, Babich disagrees. While she too holds that Derrida manifests a "very masculine self-absorption," she maintains that those who interpret Nietzsche as a misogynist (including Irigaray and Oliver) miss the metaphoricity of woman in Nietzsche (Babich 1996, 7). I examine Irigaray's views on Nietzsche and feminine subjectivity mainly based on her *Marine Lover*. Her position that Nietzsche does not allow feminine subjectivity is not revised in her later work, *Through Vegetal Being*. However here she emphasizes the significance of Nietzsche's profound quest for a feminine companion for his work in general. As I explain in the final section of this chapter, I agree that this quest, or yearning, deeply marks Nietzsche's text and that it is in fact one of the key moments to keep in view in order to understand its position on feminine subjectivity.

24. Irigaray 1991, 118.
25. Irigaray 1991, 117–18.
26. Irigaray 1991, 189.
27. Irigaray 1991, 188; Irigaray and Marder 2016, 70.
28. "What would it mean for a woman to write and read with her blood? . . . Although Nietzsche advocates writing and reading as bloodletting in the manly warrior, he forgets about women's blood that flows into new life. . . . Perhaps interpretation can be of the body and fecund without also being violent. The image of a woman reading and writing with her blood promises a creativity that is neither sadistic nor masochistic" (Oliver 1995, 24).
29. Oliver 1995.
30. Oliver 1995, 199; Oliver 1995, xi.
31. Call 1995, 113.
32. Call 1995, 125.
33. Lorraine 1998, 126.
34. Lorraine 1998, 125.

35. Lorraine 1998, 121.
36. Lorraine 1998, 127.
37. Brown 2006, 56. Tirrell (1998) makes a similar point with regard to Nietzsche's contention that women have an instinct for a secondary role (*BGE* 145). She explains that instincts have an aspect of being learned, that they are "that part of our thought which we have ceased to scrutinize; they are the lessons we have learned too well" (Tirrell 1998, 208). She notes however that this does not make Nietzsche a reductive monist who holds that conscious thought can be reduced to instinct. Nietzsche, she explains, does not embrace the existence of a duality to be reduced, that he "attacks the very legitimacy of the opposition" (204). Thus Tirrell also emphasizes the significance of the nondualistic and nonreductive nature of Nietzsche's conception of biology as grounds on which to view his claims on women.
38. Brown 2006, 42.
39. Brown 2006, 7.
40. Oliver 1995, 188.
41. Brown 2006, 28.
42. Bergoffen 1998, 225.
43. Bergoffen 2004, 162–63.
44. Bergoffen 1989, 78.
45. Bergoffen 1989, 84.
46. Bergoffen 1989, 85.
47. Bergoffen 1989, 87.
48. Jacques Derrida (1979) and Maudemarie Clark (1998), among others, point to this passage, especially to his expression "my truths," to show that Nietzsche is not pretending to make universal claims here. I agree that the passage is significant, and below I explain a way in which it is further revelatory concerning Nietzsche's stance with regard to women.
49. I agree with the interpretation that Nietzsche's anti-feminism was directed at a feminism that held onto masculine models for self-expression. At the same time, I do not find it acceptable that those who do not experience silencing on the basis of their femininity unproportionally occupy the space where strategies for attaining subjectivity are negotiated. Relatedly, I do not hold that Nietzsche's understanding of women as closer to nature is an essentializing view. Where civilization and the modes of life are fashioned through masculine forms, women are bound to appear closer to nature. Stating this, however, does not amount to claiming that there is anything essential about the feminine that keeps her closer to nature. I believe that we find the former claim in Nietzsche and not the latter.
50. As Cynthia Kaufman puts it, "The true otherness of women, the realization of which destroys the thinker's autonomy, must be guarded against by maintaining one's distance from woman, just as the flux of reality must be guarded against by reifying it into an organized, predictable, and controllable framework for understanding experiences" (Kaufman 1998, 76).

51. Kofman 1998, 23.
52. Lorraine 1998, 124.
53. Irigaray and Marder 2016, 67.
54. Irigaray and Marder 2016, 67.
55. Irigaray and Marder 2016, 67.
56. Oliver 1995, 199.
57. Oppel 2005, 138.
58. A popular example could be the recent Me Too movement, which was one instance where it became visible how the transformation of conceptual frameworks redetermine which experiences could be articulated, heard, and conceived.

## References

Babich, Babette E. 1996. "The Logic of Woman in Nietzsche: The Dogmatist's Story." *New Political Science* 18: 7–17.

Bergoffen, Debra B. 1989. "On the Advantage and Disadvantage of Nietzsche for Women." In *The Question of the Other: Essays in Contemporary Continental Philosophy*, edited by Arleen B. Dallery and Charles E. Scott: 77–88. Albany: State University of New York Press.

———. 1998. "Nietzsche Was no Feminist . . ." In *Feminist Interpretations of Friedrich Nietzsche*, edited by Kelly Oliver and Marilyn Pearsall, 225–35. University Park: Pennsylvania State University Press.

———. 2004. "Engaging Nietzsche's Women: Ofelia Schutte and the Madres de la Plaza de Mayo." *Hypatia* 19, no. 3: 157–68.

Brown, Kristen Golden. 2006. *Nietzsche and Embodiment: Discerning Bodies and Non-dualism*. Albany: State University of New York Press.

Call, Lewis. 1995. "Woman as Will and Representation: Nietzsche's Contribution to Postmodern Feminism." *Women in German Yearbook* 11: 113–29.

Clark, Maudemarie. 1998. "Nietzsche's Misogyny." In *Feminist Interpretations of Friedrich Nietzsche*, 187–98.

Derrida, Jacques. 1979. *Spurs: Nietzsche's Styles*. Translated by Barbara Harlow. Chicago: University of Chicago Press.

Diethe, Carol. 1996. *Nietzsche's Women: Beyond the Whip*. Berlin: De Gruyter.

Dohm, Hedwig. 1898. "Nietzsche und die Frauen." In *Die Zukunft*, 534–43. Quoted in Diethe 1996, 143.

Faulkner, Joanne. 2008. "Keeping It in the Family: Sarah Kofman Reading Nietzsche as a Jewish Woman." *Hypatia* 23, no. 1: 41–64.

Graybeal, Jean. 1998. "*Ecce Homo*: Abjection and 'the Feminine.'" In *Feminist Interpretations of Friedrich Nietzsche*, 152–69.

Helm, Barbara. 2004. "Combating Misogyny? Responses to Nietzsche by Turn-of-the-Century German Feminists." *Journal of Nietzsche Studies* 27 (Spring): 64–84.

Irigaray, Luce. 1991. *Marine Lover of Friedrich Nietzsche*. Translated by Gillian C. Gill. New York: Columbia University Press.
Irigaray, Luce, and Michael Marder. 2016. *Through Vegetal Being: Two Philosophical Perspectives*. New York: Columbia University Press.
Kaufman, Cynthia. 1998. "Knowledge as Masculine Heroism or Embodied Perception: Knowledge, Will, and Desire in Nietzsche." *Hypatia* 13, no. 4: 63–87.
Kaufmann, Walter A. 2013. *Nietzsche: Philosopher, Psychologist, Antichrist*. Princeton, NJ: Princeton University Press.
Kofman, Sarah. 1998. "Baubô: Theological Perversion and Fetishism." In *Feminist Interpretations of Friedrich Nietzsche*, 21–49.
Kofman, Sarah. 1994. "A Fantastical Genealogy: Nietzsche's Family Romance." Translated by Deborah Jenson. In *Nietzsche and the Feminine*, edited by Peter J. Burgard, 35–52. Charlottesville: University of Virginia Press.
Lorraine, Tamsin. 1998. "Nietzsche and Feminism: Transvaluing Women in *Thus Spoke Zarathustra*." In *Feminist Interpretations of Friedrich Nietzsche*, 119–29.
Nietzsche, Friedrich. 2005. *Thus Spoke Zarathustra*. Translated by Graham Parkes. New York: Oxford University Press.
———. 2014. *Beyond Good and Evil / On the Genealogy of Morality*. Translated by Adrian Del Caro. Stanford, CA: Stanford University Press.
Oliver, Kelly. 1995. *Womanizing Nietzsche: Philosophy's Relation to the "Feminine."* New York: Routledge.
Oppel, Frances Nesbitt. 2005. *Nietzsche on Gender: Beyond Man and Woman*, Charlottesville: University of Virginia Press.
Schutte, Ofelia. 1984. *Beyond Nihilism: Nietzsche without Masks*. Chicago: University of Chicago Press.
Singer, Linda. 1998. "Nietzschean Mythologies: The Inversion of Value and War Against Women." In *Feminist Interpretations of Friedrich Nietzsche*, 173–86.
Tirrell, Lynne. 1998. "Sexual Dualism and Women's Self-Creation: On the Advantages and Disadvantages of Reading Nietzsche for Feminists." In *Feminist Interpretations of Friedrich Nietzsche*, 199–224.
Wininger, Kathleen J. 1998. "Nietzsche's Women and Women's Nietzsche." In *Feminist Interpretations of Friedrich Nietzsche*, 236–51.

## 10

# Sexism Is Exhausting

Nietzsche and the Emotional Dynamics of Sexist Oppression

KAITLYN CREASY

Introduction

It might seem odd to look to Nietzsche, a philosopher infamous for his explicitly sexist remarks, for theoretical tools to illuminate the emotional dynamics of oppression.[1] Yet in his descriptions of the social shaping of emotion and the exhausting, obstructive impacts of internalizing harmful social norms, Nietzsche offers us tools for doing just that. My analysis here is situated in the context of gender oppression and sexism.[2] Specifically, I focus on the emotional dynamics of gender oppression in the context of a cis-hetero patriarchy: a socio-cultural milieu characterized by the historical domination of cisgender, heterosexual men and subordination of women via the unequal distribution of power. A patriarchal society will be one that features a predominance of men rather than women in positions of social, political, and economic power, as well as more subtle features (such as the fixing of allegedly gender-typical traits, behaviors, and roles).[3]

The emotional dynamics of oppression—and the oppressive effects of particular socially produced emotions—have been analyzed by numerous scholars in feminist philosophy, critical race theory, and beyond.[4] My claim, then, is not that one *must* read Nietzsche in order to analyze these phenomena or make them intelligible; I cannot even promise that his account will be more illuminating for the reader than these others. Rather, I aim here to add one more account to those on offer, to provide one more way in which the emotional dynamics of oppression, especially gender oppression, might be articulated. In turn, I emphasize how comprehending and articulating these phenomena with the help of a Nietzschean lens might make clearer certain of oppression's characteristic harms.

In this chapter, then, I examine a set of theoretical tools Nietzsche offers for making sense of the emotional dynamics and psychophysiological impacts of sexist oppression. Specifically, I indicate how Nietzsche's account of the social and cultural production of emotional experience (i.e., his account of the transpersonal nature of emotional experience) can serve as a conceptual resource for understanding the detrimental emotional impacts of social norms, beliefs, and practices that systematically devalue certain of one's ends and interests.[5]

To begin, I offer a Nietzschean account of emotional experience that focuses on its transpersonal nature. As I argue below, one's emotional experiences do not occur in isolation from one's social or cultural context; rather, emotional experience—and the transformative force it carries with it—is often a result of the way one's instincts, interests, and ends interface with the interpretation or assessment of them at the levels of society and culture. Then, I demonstrate how certain features of Nietzsche's account help us make sense of one mechanism by which the emotional productions of a patriarchal culture—one with a "patriarchal ideology" that has sexism as its natural "outgrowth"[6]—subject women to certain cultural or social norms and potentially result in exhaustion, detachment from their own values or ends, personal stagnation, and self-loathing.[7]

## Nietzsche on Affectivity

Since emotions are a subset of Nietzschean affects, understanding the emotional dynamics of internalization and the transpersonal nature of emotional experience requires one to understand Nietzsche's account of affectivity.[8] In what follows, I do not intend to offer a comprehensive account of affect. Instead, I aim to provide a characterization of affect that emphasizes the transpersonal nature of emotional experience—that is, the way in which the emotions one experiences first-personally are shaped by socio-cultural milieux that transcend the individual. A key part of the story Nietzsche tells about the transpersonal nature of emotional experience is the tendency of individuals to unwittingly adopt socio-cultural norms and evaluations, even those norms and evaluations that ultimately prove harmful to the individual.

Most basically, Nietzsche understands affects as evaluative feelings.[9] These evaluative feelings—these "reactions of the will" (*KSA* 13:11[71]) often associated with somatic states of arousal (*BGE* 19, 259; *KSA* 13:15[111], [118])—incline or disincline individuals in particular directions (*D* 34), toward or against certain objects (behaviors, beliefs, desires, and even other affects).[10] As inclinations and disinclinations, affects have motivational force: the affects I experience motivate my decisions and behaviors and dispose me to particular beliefs. The "motivational oomph"[11] a particular affect carries with it—the way in which that affect inclines or disinclines me toward a particular object, decision, or behavior—results from the (positive or negative) valence of the affect. Additionally, Nietzsche believes affects originate in drives, which function to "induce" specific affects and affective orientations.[12] Finally, affective states typically have a phenomenal character: there is something it is like to be under the influence of a particular affect.[13]

Recognizing that affects originate in drives allows us to understand why affects are fundamentally *evaluative* feelings. As John Richardson points out, a drive's end-directed nature is such that it always already "'polarizes' the world towards it":[14] a drive is positively disposed toward those features of the world that aid or make possible its expression and negatively disposed toward those features of the world that hinder or make its expression impossible.

## The Sociality of Emotional Experience

Crucially, however, the emotions one experiences (and thus, the beliefs, behaviors, and objects toward which one is inclined or disinclined in virtue of these emotions) are not merely a function of culturally independent individual drives. Indeed, according to Nietzsche, one's emotional experience often results from the ways in which one's drives, qualities, and behaviors are conceptualized and assessed at the level of one's culture or society and how that is implicitly or explicitly communicated to the individual. Such assessments have the power to shape one's emotional experience whether or not the individual is consciously aware of them or able to articulate their value-laden content. Broadly put, emotional experience is transpersonal, or socially shaped: though I understand the emotions I experience as my own, this experience is produced in part by the interaction between myself and the world to which I belong. Thus, the causal story of the vast majority of emotional experiences will exceed or transcend the individual. In Nietzsche's analysis of cowardice and humility from *Daybreak*, we find a clear example of this.

> The same drive evolves into the painful feeling of cowardice under the impress of the reproach custom has imposed upon this drive: or into the pleasant feeling of humility if it happens that a custom such as the Christian has taken it to its heart and called it good. That is to say, it is attended by either a good or a bad conscience! In itself it has, like every drive, neither this moral character nor any moral character at all, nor even a definite attendant sensation of pleasure or displeasure: it acquires all this, as its second nature, only when it enters into relations with drives already baptized good or evil. (*D* 38)

In this example, whether one experiences the emotion of cowardice or that of humility depends on the customary beliefs and norms one assimilates. So it is that "custom" (in the form of customary beliefs or values) taken "to . . . heart" has the power to shape emotional experience (*D* 35). Specifically, those customary beliefs, values, and norms endemic to my socio-cultural context often impact how an emotion shows up for me, shaping the form emotional experience takes, the motivational force that experience (as inclination or disinclination) carries with it, and its intensity.[15]

Understanding the socio-cultural formation of emotional experience requires one to understand that, for Nietzsche, the beliefs, values, and norms assimilated by an individual shape their emotional experience, in turn influencing how the object provoking the emotion shows up in experience.[16] For almost any given emotion, there is an object (or set of objects) that typically provokes that emotion (the "stimulus object"), an object (or set of objects) at which the emotion is directed (the intentional object), and a typical behavioral outcome.[17] In addition, there is an "emotional coloring" to every emotional experience—a felt dimension of emotional experience comprised of its quality (which includes felt intensity) and valence—that both impacts how the intentional object shows up and shapes the particular behavioral response one has.[18] To say that the emotional coloring of a particular emotional experience impacts how the intentional object shows up is to say that it both determines (1) how one assesses the intentional object at hand and (2) which features of the intentional object become salient, standing out to the individual in the throes of a particular emotion, and which go unnoticed. To say that an emotion's coloring shapes the particular behavioral response one has is to say that the specific form that the tended behaviors of a given emotional experience take—the "pattern and the manner of the agent's default response"[19]—is determined by the quality and valence of the emotion at hand. As an example of this mechanism, we can look to Nietzsche's characterization of *ressentiment*.[20] The experience of *ressentiment* as "the most spiritual and poisonous kind of hatred" (*GM* I:7) is such that it typically results in a pursuit of revenge that is especially insidious and all-consuming. Fleeting, comparatively benign forms of *ressentiment*, on the other hand, tend to "[consume] and [exhaust themselves] in an immediate reaction" (*GM* I).

Understanding this structure of emotions is critical for understanding one way in which Nietzsche believes emotional experience to be transpersonal. Indeed, as Nietzsche argues, what functions as the "appropriate" intentional object of a given emotion (in the language of contemporary philosophy of emotion, a "fitting" intentional object)—is shaped by the society to which one belongs. Nietzsche's analysis of the feeling of sin from *Human, All Too Human* (133) illustrates this. In this passage, Nietzsche claims that the phenomenal character of "sin" crucially involves a representation of a deity, God, and that this representation colors the emotional experience itself, adding an extra "sting" or "pang of conscience" to the feeling. Yet importantly, this representation—that of the Christian God or maybe a world created by and for God—is a cultural transmission, communicated to one through a variety of social and cultural institutions. A comprehensive causal story of how emotions feel and the impact they have on the individual thus cannot be reduced merely to the workings of an individual's psychophysiological constitution. Any such story must also include an account of the socio-cultural context in which one finds oneself, given that emotional experiences are frequently a byproduct of this context. Although drives induce affects, a description of the particular drives (and the corresponding activities at which those drives aim) that an individual has will not be enough to explain the origin or character of her emotional experiences. Rather, any explanation of a particular emotional experience for Nietzsche will involve a description of certain socio-cultural facts and features.

My account here neatly dovetails with Peter Poellner's claim that affects are "co-constituted in their phenomenal, experienced character by representations of the world or aspects of it."[21] As we see above, beliefs, values, and norms often play a critical part in constituting my emotional experience (i.e., its emotional coloring, or the quality and valence of the experience). Such content, in turn, impacts how the intentional object shows up, since the intentional object is always already filtered through this emotional coloring.[22] In other words, beliefs, values, and norms that originate from outside of me (from my socio-cultural milieu) frequently play a role in constituting the quality of my emotional experience, which in turn shapes my encounter with a given intentional object. Attending to this helps us understand a critical part of emotional experience's transpersonal nature: that is, my experience of such intentional objects is influenced not only by my drives but by socio-cultural factors (e.g., beliefs, norms, value-laden representations of individuals and behaviors). Otherwise put, my emotional experience is always already informed by the society and culture in which I find myself.

Think back to Nietzsche's remarks on sin and the pangs of conscience from *Human, All Too Human*, where he notes that "if the idea of God falls away, so does the feeling of 'sin' as a transgression against divine precepts, as a blemish on a creature consecrated to god" (133). He continues:

> Then there probably still remains over that feeling of depression which is very much entwined with and related to fear of punishment by secular justice or the disapprobation of other men; the depression caused by the pang of conscience, the sharpest sting in the feeling of guilt, is nonetheless abolished when one sees that, although one's actions may have offended against human tradition, human laws and ordinances, one has not therewith endangered the "eternal salvation of the soul" and its relationship to divinity. (*HH* 133)

In this aphorism, Nietzsche describes how the emotion of guilt, experienced as sin, has a different emotional coloring—a different quality, involving a much more intense "sting"—because I experience the emotion as one who believes in a deity to which I am consecrated (or, at least, as one who has unwittingly, perhaps unconsciously, assimilated it into their mental and moral economy).²³ The intentional object encountered—whether it be certain of one's actions, one's nature, or one's desires—is filtered through the emotional coloring of one's emotional experience, for example the feeling of sinfulness as involving the disapprobation of an entity to which one owes one's existence and the eternal damnation of a sinner's soul. To say that the "sharpest sting" in the feeling of guilt goes away when the idea of god disappears is to acknowledge that the quality of one's emotional experience—the intensity of the feeling, the depth of one's guilt—can be shaped by beliefs, values, or norms that one either consciously adopts or unwittingly assimilates, and that a change in one's beliefs, values, or norm-exposure potentially changes the emotional coloring of an emotional experience, thus changing how one encounters an intentional object. Specifically, when one's emotional experience is no longer influenced by notions of a deity and eternal damnation, the experience of the emotion of guilt (qua sinfulness in the face of god) formerly experienced in relation to one's nature transforms into a different kind of emotional experience (perhaps guilt qua lawlessness), and this changes the way the intentional object shows up: what was formerly encountered as a sinful action is now encountered as a merely antisocial or illegal action. Both the phenomenal character of the new guilty emotion (guilt qua lawlessness) and the intentional object (one's action, newly encountered as merely antisocial or illegal rather than sinful) transform along with one's beliefs. Given the connection between the emotional coloring of an emotion (especially its valence) and its motivational force, the motivational force of the emotion seems likely to transform as well. For example, one might imagine that the "sharpest sting" or pang of conscience unique to guilt qua sinfulness is also uniquely motivational; that is, it disinclines one more intensely against certain actions or desires.

For Nietzsche, then, it is critical to recognize that our emotional experiences are mediated by ideas, values, and norms—beliefs and norms of which one unconsciously or consciously avails oneself that plays an integral role in shaping an emotional experience. And these ideas, values, and norms derive from one's society and/or culture. In other words, one's affects—those feeling-based states most often understood as individual psychological states or processes—are often socially and culturally produced.²⁴ This is the case even though we typically experience those emotions of which we are consciously aware as our own personal feelings in relation to an intentional object: although we experience them as such, our feelings are rarely our own.

## The Sociocultural Construction of Appropriate Emotions

For Nietzsche, our discovery of the surreptitious features of affectivity mentioned above—the malleability of our emotional lives and the incredibly subtle way in which it occurs via ideas, beliefs, values, and norms we (often unwittingly) assimilate in virtue of our social or cultural milieux—is meant to be surprising and perhaps unpleasant. Yet this discovery becomes all the more unpleasant—and the social shaping of emotion all the more pernicious—when one attends to the way in which, for Nietzsche, my emotional responses are "experienced as . . . appropriate response[s] to some feature of the object, as a picking up on some value-aspect pertaining to the object."[25] Otherwise put, I generally experience my emotional responses as fitting responses to the intentional object in question, whether or not they are, in fact, merited by that object.[26] In my emotional encounter with a given intentional object, I typically experience myself as "picking up on" or discovering certain value-laden properties of the object itself; that is, prior to any reflection on my emotional encounters, I experience them as disclosive, rather than deceptive. For example, when someone experiences an emotion of guilt qua sinfulness in response to one of their actions or desires, they experience said action or desire (i.e., whatever intentional object provoked that emotion) as meriting this negative, disapprobatory emotion; that is, they encounter their action or desire as something bad or undesirable *in itself*. This emotional experience disinclines one toward the action or desire in question. The tended behavioral result, then, would be the avoidance of said action or desire.

As another example, imagine the emotional response of love, inspired by the presence of one's partner. When I experience this emotion in the presence of my partner, I *experience* it as merited by features of my significant other that are inherently *worthy* of love (perhaps his compassionate nature or his sense of humor). This experience then tends to result in certain positive behaviors; for example, I might praise him for his compassion or feel inspired to become more compassionate myself. Importantly for Nietzsche, however, this does not indicate that these features—my partner's compassionate nature and sense of humor—are *in fact* worthy of love; rather, this is just the way his compassion appears to me in the throes of that particular loving emotion.

To make this clearer, we can imagine instances in which I might become irritated by my partner's compassionate nature. For example, if my partner decided to donate half of our savings to charity, his compassionate nature might inspire a good deal of anger in me.[27] In the throes of this quite different emotion, I experience his compassionate nature as something negative, something that "calls for" an angry response. This angry emotional response would tend to manifest itself in particular behaviors; for example, I might say unkind things to my partner or sell one of his prized possessions to recoup our lost savings. In the grip of this emotion, however, such assessments and behaviors would seem appropriate, that is, merited by my partner's nature, which I experience as compassionate to a fault.[28] In sum, love might seem a fitting response to his compassionate nature in one case, but in quite another case, anger will seem just as fitting. In either case, we see that the default experience of a given emotional response is to experience the emotion as a fitting response and to experience the intentional object—my partner's compassionate nature, in these examples—as meriting just that response that I do, in fact, have. Part of experiencing an emotion in response to a particular intentional object, then, is an implicit assessment of that intentional object: I "view" the intentional object as worthy of whatever emotional response I experience, such that if my emotional experience is positive, I experience the value of the intentional object as positive, and if my emotional experience is negative, I experience the value of the intentional object as negative.

Though Nietzsche believes I pre-reflectively experience my emotional responses as merited by their intentional objects, he is also keen to indicate that my sense of their appropriateness does not occur in a vacuum. On the contrary, my emotional experiences unfold in a social context permeated by powerfully dominant beliefs, norms, and values, and my sense of their appropriateness can also be shaped by what my society understands as appropriate or inappropriate emotions, given a particular intentional object. Although Nietzsche believes my psychophysiological constitution plays a role in how I experience and come to assess the intentional objects I encounter, this is not the whole picture. Indeed, objects often come to me imbued with a nature and value my society, culture, or ideological community establishes for them. See, for example, *GS* 355:

> Your judgment, "that is right" has a prehistory in your drives, inclinations, aversions, experiences, and what you have failed to experience; you have to ask, "*how* did it emerge there?" and then also, "*what* is really impelling me to listen to it?" . . . But that you hear this or that judgement as the words of conscience, i.e., that you feel something to be right may have its cause in

> your never having thought much about yourself and in your blindly having accepted what has been labelled right since your childhood; or in the fact that fulfilling your duties has so far brought you bread and honors—

It is thus the case *both* that I experience my initial emotional responses as accurately picking up on value-laden aspects of the intentional object *and* that value-laden aspects tend to be "preloaded" into the object of emotional experience as a function of dominant norms and beliefs within a given socio-cultural milieu or ideological community. For example, in a culture dominated by the "morality of compassion [*Mitleid*]" (*TI* "Skirmishes" 37)—a culture in which a belief in the positive value of compassionate action is the norm—selfish actions will be understood as meriting disapprobatory emotions (perhaps disdain). From the perspective of such a culture, the fitting emotional response to selfishness (or a particular selfish action) will be negatively valenced, one that discourages selfish thoughts and behaviors (whether these are actions of one's own or of another).

Let us continue with this typically Nietzschean example—that of compassion—to illustrate this point.[29] According to Nietzsche, his particular Christian socio-cultural milieu is one dominated by the "morality of compassion [*Mitleid*]" (TI "Skirmishes" 37): compassion is a praiseworthy character trait, compassionate acts are worthy of admiration and respect, and a drive to compassion is understood to be a virtuous instinct.[30] In such an environment, compassion is viewed as an objectively positive trait (*BGE* 201–2; *GM* P:5–6), and as such, compassionate actions seem to call for positive emotional responses; that is, such actions appear to warrant respect and admiration in every case. If in such a socio-cultural context I view compassionate actions negatively—experience a negative emotion, such as anger, in response to someone's compassionate deed—my reaction appears to me as errant, one that indicts me and my emotional life rather than the intentional object. In other words, since a compassionate deed in Nietzsche's Christian-moral Europe does not warrant anger, irritation, or frustration, to be frustrated in the face of compassion is to react *inappropriately*. In this way, I encounter compassionate actions qua intentional objects as preloaded with positive value, bestowed by my socio-cultural context. When I experience an approbatory emotion in response to a compassionate action, my emotional life gels with the emotional patterns and values typical of my socio-cultural milieu, insofar as I pick up on positive aspects of the intentional object. My reaction appears, to myself and others, as "normal" and appropriate.

When I experience a disapprobatory emotion in response to a compassionate action, on the other hand, my emotional life seems at odds with dominant beliefs, values, and even emotional patterns. When a compassionate action appears to me, in the throes of a disapprobatory emotion, as undesirable or meriting blame, the social norm that construes compassionate action as objectively positive comes into conflict with my subjective, first-personal emotional experience. My emotional experience here is at odds with what is thought morally appropriate or "normal." In such a case, Nietzsche thinks, I am all too likely to feel I am perceiving wrongly and to develop emotions that discourage the kinds of valuations and behaviors that diverge from the emotional patterns and norms of my socio-cultural milieu (*TI* "Skirmishes" 45). Furthermore, the more one assimilates this dominant norm, the more likely one is to develop positive, approbatory emotional responses to compassion (that I experience as fitting) and the less likely one is to have negative, disapprobatory emotional responses (those that experience compassion as something shameful or blameworthy). After some time, I will not only be in an emotional habit of experiencing positive emotional responses to compassionate actions (which just is, for Nietzsche, to experience them as fitting); I will also eventually judge the former to be morally appropriate responses and the latter morally inappropriate responses.

Before I continue, let me flag something critically important. When talking about the fittingness or appropriateness of emotions, as D'Arms and Jacobson[31] argue, one ought to avoid committing the "moralistic fallacy": conflating the conditions of an emotion's fittingness (i.e., the extent to which it accurately represents its object, or "gets it right") with whether that emotion is morally acceptable to feel (or "morally permissible").[32] Too often, they argue, philosophers commit this fallacy; most often, it involves descriptively designating an emotion as an unfitting (qua unwarranted) response to a given intentional object on the grounds that the emotional response is morally impermissible. In the language of D'Arms and Jacobson, philosophers frequently interpret an emotional response as not "getting it right" simply because it is not "the [morally] right way to feel."[33]

I want to be clear: I grant this conceptual distinction. D'Arms and Jacobson are right that there seems to be two different senses of appropriateness operating in philosophical debates about emotions and their fittingness. My Nietzschean account here, however, is about how one *experiences* one's emotional responses as fitting or appropriate to the intentional objects one encounters (which are encountered through a particularly valenced emotional lens) and how that experience of fittingness is influenced both by what is widely accepted as a fitting emotional response (i.e., an accurate reflection of the object one encounters) and by what is widely accepted as a morally appropriate response. Nietzsche's point, it seems to me, is that insofar as our emotions are mediated by our norm-laden socio-cultural context or ideological community, we are vulnerable to a kind of emotional gaslighting in which we doubt the warrant of our emotional responses because of the internalization of certain norms and values, including norms of moral appropriateness. And indeed, this is one special danger of internalizing or assimilating certain norms or values from my socio-cultural milieu or ideological community. When such internalization or assimilation occurs, I become both alienated from those goals, interests, and values I have that are discordant with the norms and values of my society and alienated from (and discouraged from inhabiting) my own evaluative perspective on the world. Not only do I doubt certain desires or practices of mine, but I doubt the warrant or rationality of my own phenomenological experience.

My socio-cultural context has the power to shape my emotional life, then, by increasing the likelihood that I will experience emotions that are widely deemed appropriate (or warranted) in that context. This happens as I unreflectively assimilate ideas, values, and norms in virtue of my socio-cultural milieu. In such cases, the evaluation of the intentional object manifest in my emotional experience accords with that of my society: I have what my society understands to be an appropriate response to the intentional object of my emotional experience. This happens, for example, when I experience guilt qua sinfulness in response to a cruel action of mine *because* I have assimilated a particular conception of God (in virtue of my belonging to a society dominated by Christian beliefs and norms). At other times, however, my initial emotional experience—and its implicit evaluation of the intentional object—will be incongruous with those emotional experiences deemed appropriate within my broader socio-cultural context. Imagine, for example, that I experience an emotion of pride in response to the same action. Given my assimilation of those beliefs and norms characteristic of my Christian society, I am likely to understand such an emotion as deeply inappropriate and to develop, perhaps, a second-order affect of shame in response. This second-order affect functions to disincline me against my initial prideful response (in relation to the intentional object of my own cruel action). Otherwise put, when one assimilates socially dominant beliefs, values, and norms, one becomes likely to experience second-order affects that discourage emotional responses discordant with those deemed "appropriate"[34] by one's socio-cultural milieu. In short, those second-order affects produced in me by virtue of my assimilating dominant socio-cultural norms and values—feelings of disinclination or inclination toward my first-order affects—nudge me away from "inappropriate" emotions and toward "appropriate" emotions given a particular intentional object. When my emotional responses evaluate the intentional object in a way that conflicts with the dominant social evaluation, these competing emotions will tend to be stifled. At the very least, I come to second-guess those responses.

And indeed, my assimilation of norms that direct me away from "inappropriate" emotional experiences and toward more "appropriate" socially dominant emotional patterns is made all the more likely just in virtue of my continued habitation of a particular social or cultural milieu in which such norms prevail. As Nietzsche makes clear, one's tendency to assimilate such norms is often simply a function of one's exposure to a given norm; the more dominant a norm is in one's society, the more likely one is to absorb it (*GM* II:24). We see this, for example, in Nietzsche's account of the way in which ascetic ideals, as they become more widespread, cause strong-willed individuals to become suspicious of their instincts and drives. When those who embrace ascetic ideals "*shov[e]* their own misery . . . *on to the conscience* of the happy . . . the latter eventually start to be ashamed of their happiness" (*GM* III:14). Through the mere exposure to life-denying beliefs and ideals, strong-willed individuals "begin to doubt their *right to happiness*"—hence, the importance of the *pathos of distance*.[35]

## Internalization, Self-Suspicion, and the Development of a Self-Negating Conscience

If emotions are socio-culturally mediated, regulated, and produced in the ways I describe above—and Nietzsche believes they are—then those emotional evaluations of intentional objects that I experience as merited by the object itself are surreptitiously shaped by the socio-cultural context I inhabit. In particular, I am typically nudged toward those emotional responses deemed appropriate by my socio-cultural milieu and away from those deemed inappropriate. This, in itself, is interesting. But in cases where the intentional objects of emotional experiences are my own actions, desires, traits, or instincts, attending to this structure becomes critically important from a Nietzschean perspective. After all, the more I experience affective aversions to certain of my actions, desires, traits, and instincts as *merited* by these intentional objects—the more I "[view my] natural inclinations with an 'evil eye'" (*GM* II:24)—the more likely I am to develop a second-order evaluative sensibility that turns me against my own instincts, desires, and aims. This aversive sensibility, which I will henceforth refer to as self-suspicion, develops when I habitually experience affective aversions to features of myself, as a function of my assimilating beliefs, values, and social norms (in virtue of their inhabiting a particular socio-cultural milieu) that are at odds with (or in conflict with) my instincts, desires, and aims.[36] Though Nietzsche himself does not employ this specific term, self-suspicion is a psychological sensibility and feature of our inner lives in which he is profoundly interested.[37]

That the socio-cultural production of aversive affects may lead to the development of self-suspicion (given dominant beliefs and norms of a given society that are in tension with one's own instincts, desires, and values) is suggested by the following, taken together:

1. My emotional experiences are fundamentally evaluative; that is, they involve evaluative orientations or assessments of their intentional objects. Nietzsche understands emotional experiences broadly as assessing their intentional objects positively or negatively (depending on whether their valence is broadly positive or negative).

2. The motivational force of an affect (qua inclination or disinclination) is determined by its evaluative orientation. If an emotional experience involves a positive evaluation of its intentional object (via its positive valence), I will feel inclined toward that intentional object. If an emotional experience involves a negative evaluation of its intentional object (via its negative valence), I will feel disinclined toward that intentional object.

3. The motivational force of an emotion determines its *tended* behavioral outcome. If I am positively inclined toward particular actions, desires, or instincts, I become more likely to manifest those actions, desires, and instincts. If I am disinclined toward particular actions, desires, or instincts, I become less likely to manifest those actions, desires, and instincts.

4. Sometimes, the intentional objects provoking my emotional experiences are my own actions, desires, or instincts. That

is, I sometimes experience emotions in response to certain of my actions and/or features of myself.

5. Pre-reflectively—that is, prior to any conscious reflection on my emotional experience—I tend to experience my emotional responses as *appropriate*, or *merited by* the intentional object/s I encounter. Otherwise put, I experience my emotional responses as *fitting*.

6. Thus, when I experience broadly positive/approbatory or negative/disapprobatory emotions in response to my own actions, desires, or instincts, I pre-reflectively experience those emotions as *merited* by these things; that is, I encounter my actions, desires, or instincts as worthy of the emotional experiences they provoke.

7. Yet my emotional experiences are often surreptitiously mediated by ideas, values, and norms typical of the socio-cultural milieu I inhabit (i.e., to say, "customary" beliefs and values). In particular, the intensity and valence of my emotional experience—its emotional coloring—is, in part, a function of ideas, beliefs, and norms I assimilate in virtue of my socio-cultural milieu.

According to Nietzsche, self-suspicion develops when mistrust of my own instincts, desires, and aims takes hold of my psychic life (*GM* II:16). In turn, the development of self-suspicion tends to stifle the outward expression of those instincts (and turn me away from those aims). By connecting the elements outlined above, we can see how this occurs via my emotional experiences and their implicit (allegedly merited) evaluations.

First, the emotional responses I experience in relation to certain of my actions, desires, or instincts have broadly positive or negative valences. As mentioned above, the broadly positive emotions I experience will incline me toward those actions or excite the development or expression of certain desires or instincts, while the broadly negative emotions I experience will disincline me toward those actions or inhibit the development or expression of certain desires or instincts. Additionally, my emotions have the motivational force and tended behavioral outcomes they do in relation to their intentional objects because they are experienced as merited responses to those objects. If I experience a disapprobatory emotion in response to one of my desires, that is, I experience that emotion as appropriate—which is to say I encounter that desire as bad or undesirable *in itself*.

Since I generally experience my emotions as appropriate or fitting (i.e., merited by their intentional objects), when I experience broadly negative or disapprobatory emotions toward certain of my extant instincts, desires, aims, or values (as a function of the socio-cultural milieu to which I belong), I will experience them as justified negative evaluations of these features of myself. The self-suspicion that develops from habitually experiencing such affective aversions commonly functions to suppress these instincts, desires, aims, and values. (At the very least, as mentioned above, it leads me to second-guess them.)

For Nietzsche, the sensibility of self-suspicion is not problematic in itself; it is simply a feature of social existence, a typical result of one's habitual experience of negative, socially produced emotions in response to certain features of oneself. Much like Aaron Ridley's "bad conscience in its 'raw state,'" it is simply part of being a willing, feeling being who belongs to a society and occasionally experiences emotions that conflict with that society's norms.[38] Nor is the mistrust of oneself (or features of oneself) that constitutes self-suspicion necessarily worthy of lament. After all, in the *Genealogy* Nietzsche emphasizes the importance of "mistrust, especially towards our 'first impulses'" for projects of self-cultivation (*GM* III:20). Indeed, in cases where the socially produced, habitual mistrust of certain of my extant instincts, desires, aims, and values pushes me to change in a favorable way, such that my unique form of power is expanded (*GS* 349), for example, or the "social structure of [my] drives and affects" (*BGE* 12) newly unified behind a strengthened drive (*KSA* 13:14 [157; 219]), self-suspicion can even be advantageous, a positive transformative force.

As a transformative force, however, Nietzsche thinks self-suspicion has serious risks. First, if left unchecked by critical reflection, this sensibility of self-suspicion—as an involuntary emotional manifestation of the "herd instinct"—will leave me in a position of unwitting, servile obedience to the herd rather than self-command (*BGE* 199). Otherwise put, self-suspicion can undermine my "will to self-determination, to evaluating on [my] own account, [my] will to *free* will" (*HH* P:3). After all, because I do not typically notice the role that my society plays in producing the emotions I experience (via my assimilation of those customary ideas and values available to me in virtue of my socio-cultural context), when I assess my instincts, desires, aims or values negatively at the emotional level, I experience this as a justified *self*-evaluation. It is easy for me to miss that this emotional evaluation is produced in part by forces from without (and seems merited just in virtue of the phenomenology of emotional warrant).[39] Unfortunately, without honest, critical reflection on these automatic affective self-assessments (involving a recognition of their origin) and subsequent deliberate endorsement of them, I am prevented from truly "evaluating on [my] own account" (*HH* P:3), prevented from attaining this necessary condition of my own self-determination.

Additionally, Nietzsche believes that an individual only counts as a genuine agent (with actions properly their own rather than mere behaviors)—and her affective assessments only count as values proper—if learning more about the origins of her behaviors and affective assessments would not undermine her approval of them (or lead to disapproval).[40] Importantly, however, he also thinks that becoming aware of self-suspicion as the source of my stifled instincts and the motive behind certain of my behaviors will often undermine this approval. Otherwise put, Nietzsche believes I will typically find it troubling that certain of my aims, instincts, and desires are stifled or called into question just in virtue of a socially produced evaluative sensibility that makes me suspicious of nonconforming features of myself. That is, my unknowing, unreflective acceptance of the particular negative self-assessments I experience (and the behaviors motivated by them) is likely to be undermined by a more thorough account of their contingent, socio-cultural origins. The danger of self-suspicion here is that under its influence I become likely to form desires, adopt values, and pursue actions that I would disavow if their origins (in habitual, socially produced emotional self-aversions) were revealed to me.

Finally, Nietzsche believes that there is a particularly insidious result to which self-suspicion can lead. Self-suspicion becomes dangerous when that mistrust of certain features of oneself engendered by self-suspicion turns one against (1) instincts and drives the expression of which are central to one's empowerment, (2) desires and aims the pursuit of which offer opportunities for the expression of one's "most lively" instincts and drives, (3) emotions that facilitate the expression of those drives and instincts central to one's empowerment, and (4) values the adoption of which promotes and increases one's expression of power—in short, when a sensibility of self-suspicion turns into a self-*negating* conscience.[41] We find an example of this in Nietzsche's criminal type from *Twilight of the Idols*. Nietzsche describes him thusly:

> The criminal type is the type of the strong human being under unfavorable conditions, a strong human being who has been made sick. He lacks the wilderness, a certain freer and more dangerous nature and form of existence, in which everything that is a weapon and a defense in the instincts of the strong has a right to be. *His virtues are banned by society; the most lively drives he was born with have been entangled right away with depressing emotions, with suspicion, fear, dishonor. But this is virtually the recipe for physiological degeneration.* Anyone who has to do in secret what he can do best, what he would most like to do—with drawn-out suspense, caution, slyness—becomes anemic. *And since he always reaps only danger, persecution, and disaster from his instincts, even his feelings turn against these instincts—he feels they are fatal. It is society, our tame, mediocre, castrated society, in which a natural human being, who comes from the mountains or from seafaring adventures, necessarily degenerates into a criminal.* Or almost necessarily: for there are cases where such a person proves to be stronger than the society—the Corsican Napoleon is the most famous case. . . . Let us generalize the case of the criminal: let us think of natures who, for some reason, are deprived of public approval, who know that they are not perceived as beneficial, as useful—that chandala feeling of not counting as an equal, but of being excluded, unworthy, a source of impurity. All such natures have a subterranean tint to their thoughts and deeds; with them, everything turns paler than with those on whose existence daylight shines. . . . I draw your attention to the fact that even today, under the mildest ethical regime that has ever held sway on earth, or at least in Europe, every deviation, every long, all too long stay underneath, every unusual, untransparent form of existence approaches that type which is perfected in the criminal. All renewers of the spirit bear the sallow and fatalistic sign of the chandala on their forehead sometime: not because they are thus perceived, but because they themselves feel the terrible gap that separates them from everything that is conventional and honored. (*TI* "Skirmishes" 45, emphasis mine)

Here, we see that the criminal's "most lively drives . . . [are] entangled right away with depressing emotions" as a result of the social stigmatization of her desires, interests, and values. Such an individual—that "criminal type"—is a "strong human being under unfavorable conditions, a strong human being who has been made sick" from being "deprived of public approval," who senses that "[she is] not perceived of as beneficial, as useful" by the socio-cultural milieu to which she belongs. As Nietzsche puts it, such an individual "feel[s] the terrible gap that separates [her] from everything that is conventional and honored"; this leads her to experience emotions of "suspicion, fear, [and] dishonor." Such aversive affects are experienced by the criminal herself as merited by her nature (her "most lively" drives) and values (her "virtues"); given their negative valence, they are experienced as indictments of her nature and values. This indictment leads to disempowerment, weakness, and illness.

In this example, then, we see how the emotional coloring of the criminal's emotional experience (and thus her encounter with her nature and values as intentional objects) results from a complex interaction between her psychophysiological constitution—that individual as the complex of drives she is—and the socio-cultural context she inhabits. In this selection from *Twilight of the Idols*, we find a clear picture of how Nietzsche believes one's society might function to mediate, manipulate, and regulate one's emotional experience, nudging the individual toward certain (allegedly appropriate) emotional responses and away from other (allegedly inappropriate) emotional responses, with the result that desires, instincts, and behaviors incongruous with socio-cultural norms but central to one's own unique form of power are stifled. Otherwise put, the more one is nudged toward socio-culturally "appropriate" responses and evaluations that are at odds with one's own "most lively" desires and instincts—in Nietzschean terms, those desires and instincts that constitute one's own unique form of power—the more likely one becomes to develop a self-negating conscience and to experience a psychophysiological degeneration that makes one's existence paler.

Nietzsche's example of the criminal type—a type in Nietzsche whose aggressive, outlaw instincts and desires typically involve the domination and subordination of others (*Z* I "On the Pale Criminal"; *GM* II:12; *BGE* 201)—might seem an odd example to help illuminate the emotional dynamics of sexist oppression. Yet the basic structure of this example, as involving the pathologizing of an individual's most lively desires, instincts, and goals by her society, parallels the impacts of sexist oppression on a woman whose desires, instincts, and goals conflict with norms of femininity in a patriarchal context. Otherwise put, women whose most empowering desires, interests, and aims are incongruous with the cis-hetero norms of the patriarchal socio-cultural context they inhabit find themselves made into "criminal types," who often cannot help but "feel the terrible gap that separate[s] [them] from everything that is conventional and honored" (*TI* "Skirmishes" 45). In short, in a cis-hetero patriarchy, being a certain kind of woman is criminalized.

## A Nietzschean Account of the Internalization of Sexist Oppression

In this section, I argue that in virtue of being a woman who does not conform to sexist norms (understood as widely shared, socially shaped ideals that communicate what women ought to be, especially as present in widespread sexist stereotyping) in a cis-hetero patriarchal society, one becomes more likely to develop a self-negating conscience, to be nudged away (via socially produced, aversive emotional responses to those desires, traits, and behaviors most central to one's empowerment) from those aspects of oneself incongruous with typical ideals (from one's socio-cultural milieu or ideological community) of womanhood and femininity. Additionally, I argue that the Nietzschean account of affectivity I sketch above offers a set of conceptual tools for analyzing how this occurs. Below, I discuss how this happens as a function of sexist stereotyping (as a form of norm enforcement).

Although all individuals in a patriarchal society are exposed to certain widespread norms of womanhood—those "controlling images" analyzed by Patricia Hill Collins[42]—these norms and images uniquely impact the emotional lives and self-assessments of certain "types" of women in such a way that the development of a self-negating conscience is made more likely.[43] Specifically, women whose desires and behaviors seem to deviate from norms of femininity are uniquely at risk for the development of a self-negating evaluative sensibility, given the aversive emotional responses they are likely to experience as a result of an incongruity between their society's gendered expectations of them and those desires and behaviors central to their well-being and empowerment. In cases where these desires, instincts, and behaviors do not conform to social expectations, one tends to experience a host of emotions, such as "suspicion, fear, and dishonor" (*TI* "Skirmishes" 45) (as a function of one's assimilating beliefs and norms from her socio-cultural milieu) that harm the individual who experiences them by disinclining her against her own desires, instincts, and behaviors.

In a patriarchy in which the historical domination of men and subordination of woman occurs in part via gendered norm enforcement as the involuntary exposure to a variety of sexist beliefs and norms, women are regularly exposed to beliefs and norms about what it means to be a woman that might impel them to second-guess or stifle certain of their instincts, behaviors, and goals, if those instincts, behaviors, and goals are incongruous with norms of femininity. More specifically, a woman who does not conform to gendered social norms will become more likely to experience emotions—produced as one (typically unwittingly) assimilates sexist ideas or values from one's socio-cultural milieu or ideological community—that lead her to assess her desires, instincts, and behaviors incongruous with socio-cultural gender norms negatively. The development of a self-negating conscience—the denial, devaluation, and suppression of those instincts requisite for one's empowerment—is a tended result of this emotional dynamic. In this kind of case, a woman typically develops an aversion to herself or her instincts via the mere assimilation of sexist ideas or values, much in the way Nietzsche's criminal does. Simply put, one's exposure to beliefs about how women *are* (such as gender essentialist beliefs) and norms that fix standards for how women *ought to be* has the power to shape one's emotional life. As Nietzsche indicates, however, this has transformative effects: these emotional impacts potentially shape what I am motivated to do (or to avoid doing) and can ultimately shape who I become. In cases where I develop a self-negating conscience as a result of sexist beliefs and norms, what I do and who I become prevents my empowerment and flourishing.

An example should prove illuminating here. In those patriarchal societies with sexist stereotyping such as the United States, the United Kingdom, and Australia, women are often expected (both by men and other women) to be nurturing caregivers. This expectation is, by and large, a result of stereotypical and sexist representations that depict men and women as having "natural differences."[44] Specifically, women are depicted as "naturally" more submissive and passive, with talents in domestic work including caregiving. Now take the example of a woman who manifests certain desires, character traits, and behaviors and inhabits a social role (expressive of her drives) that do not accord with stereotypical gender norms. Imagine, for example, an ambitious college professor and scholar whose "most lively" drive, a drive central to her empowerment, is the drive to knowledge. She has a personality that is commanding, blunt, and straightforward, and she is protective of her time, so she does not stay on campus beyond her set office hours, even when students ask her to do so. In a patriarchal society with sexist stereotypes, a woman who manifests the abovementioned features—a drive to knowledge; an ambitious, blunt, and commanding personality; a powerful and authoritative social role; and self-preserving behaviors—is liable to be suspect or worse: that is, these features, as intentional objects, may seem to warrant suspicion, disapprobation, and disdain.

According to the account I offer above, through (her own and others') exposure to sexist stereotyping, her patriarchal socio-cultural milieu will encourage her to experience emotions that incline her against (or at least have her "second-guess") these features of herself. Remember from above Nietzsche's description of the way in which a cruel person in a society dominated by the morality of compassion (*Mitleids-Moral*) becomes likely to experience certain of her emotional responses—perhaps joy in cruelty—as inappropriate, not fitting to the intentional object.[45] Nietzsche claims that this happens over time, as a function of being exposed to beliefs and norms that positively value compassion. In this same way, a woman in a patriarchal society dominated by sexist stereotyping might come to experience certain of her initial emotional responses as inappropriate or unfitting. Perhaps, for example, the woman above is proud of her ability to protect her time even when her students ask her to stay past her office hours. In virtue of her being exposed to stereotypical beliefs about women's capacity for nurturing and norms of femininity that lead to expectations of availability,[46] however, this woman might be nudged to adopt a more fitting, appropriate emotional response (by society's lights): these features of herself might slowly begin to provoke wariness or unease. It is not inconceivable that she will be motivated to change these empowering yet nonconforming features of herself or begin slowly (and not necessarily consciously) to adopt values, form desires, and pursue actions that she would disavow if their origin was revealed to her.

The woman in the above example will tend to experience emotions first-personally that either make her averse to a variety of instincts and aims central to her flourishing or transform her in ways she would renounce (if made aware of the origins of that transformation), but she will also experience the potentially transformative emotional evaluations of others. Specifically, she will be likely to encounter patterns of aversive emotional responses (perhaps suspicion, disapprobation, and disdain) from others who believe that such emotions are merited; that is, that they are fitting aversive responses to features that, when manifest by a woman, are negative.[47] Perhaps colleagues dislike her straightforward, assertive personality and find her "untrustworthy."[48] Perhaps they expect her to stay later for the sake of her students or to do other forms of service work; perhaps they bristle and blame her when she does not, experiencing her failure to stay or serve as a deficit of care.[49] Perhaps students write in evaluative comments that she is "cold," "mean," "nasty," and "unfair,"[50] though her behaviors in the classroom are no different than her male colleagues. Perhaps because they expect her "to be available outside of class and care about students' personal lives,"[51] her students react poorly when she protects her time: they consider her "insufficiently available"[52] and understand their negative emotions about her lack of availability as warranted. Perhaps, finally, she notices that she is cited significantly less than her male peers in the field.[53]

The more this woman experiences certain aversive affects in relation to aspects of herself and encounters the aversive emotional responses of others, the more likely she is, Nietzsche thinks, to internalize these emotional responses. This not only leads her to experience disapprobatory emotions in response to aspects of herself; it leads her to experience these emotions as appropriate or fitting reactions to those aspects. Though Nietzsche believes "there are cases where such a person proves to be stronger than the society" (*TI* "Skirmishes" 45), he understands these cases as exceedingly rare. The more she experiences suspicion, disapprobation, and disdain toward herself, then, the more this woman turns away from empowering features of herself that she previously valued. Perhaps her straightforward, commanding nature becomes less appealing to her and she tries to become warmer, more acquiescing in ways that please her students and colleagues, ultimately making her life more frictionless.[54] Perhaps she is motivated to act in more nurturing ways, more selflessly, at her own expense; we can imagine that she might stay just a bit past her office hours and just when students *really* seem to need the help. Perhaps as a function of the lack of citation, she experiences "imposter syndrome," becoming suspicious about her own expertise, her competence, and her ability to contribute substantively to her field.[55] In such a case, the initial empowering impulses and drives she manifested, though still present, become dimmed, inhibited, less actively expressed. Ultimately, she turns against her own desires and instincts at the very level of her affectivity. Those formerly most vigorous desires and instincts become repressed and she no longer is the strong-willed, powerful person that she was.

Suppose this woman unthinkingly accepts her personal transformation and goes about her life. According to Nietzsche, if she should come at a later time to trace the origins of this personal transformation back to a socially produced, self-negating conscience, she would likely be troubled. If that were so, any unreflective acceptance of who she has become (and the process that facilitated her personal transformation) would be undermined; her lack of agency in her own transformation would then be starkly revealed. In a case like this, her emotional revolt against herself—a byproduct of her assimilating beliefs and norms hostile to her mode of existence—will have resulted both in the development of a self-negating conscience and in a fragmentation that results in a loss of agency.[56]

## A Few Final Thoughts

At this point, I wish to add a few remarks and caveats to my account. In the above section, I both analyze the emotional dynamics of sexist oppression and describe the tended results of these dynamics. Importantly, however, cases with end-results like the one I describe just above should be understood as "worst-case scenarios." In such worst-case scenarios, women's emotional lives are manipulated and regulated to such an extent by their sexist, patriarchal societies that they come to devalue their own most empowering instincts and desires, developing a self-negating conscience and losing agency. These cases are the most extreme examples of the ways in which the emotional dynamics of sexist oppression can harm certain women. But there are other, subtler cases to consider that indicate just how insidious the emotional damages of sexist oppression can be.

For example, imagine a woman who becomes aware of a felt pressure to conform her desires, instincts, and behaviors to norms of femininity present in her patriarchal society. Imagine she recognizes that this pressure is the result of certain socially produced emotional responses she experiences and decides that she wants to actively resist that pressure, affirming herself and her instincts in the process. This drive to resist will involve not only striving to overthrow dominant beliefs and norms and subvert their emotional influence; it will also require her to reflect constantly on her own emotional responses, rooting out those emotional responses constituted in part by sexist ideas and values and attempting to abide by those emotional responses that affirm those instincts and values that lead to her empowerment. We can imagine that her constant effort and vigilance will be exhausting. For women in a patriarchal society who do not find their most empowering instincts, desires, and behaviors valued, yet still wish to affirm their modes of existence, such exhaustion is simply an existential hazard—and it is a hazard that others with different modes of existence can avoid, even within a patriarchal socio-cultural milieu. Even if the emotional dynamics of sexist oppression in individual cases do not result in self-negation, then, such dynamics are still likely to harm women whose most empowering desires, instincts, and actions are incongruous to those accepted by her socio-cultural milieu. At the very least, they have the potential to sap energy from such women's attempts to both affirm themselves and to create new and liberating worlds.

I am not arguing, then, that all women in a patriarchal society (with nonconforming empowering desires, instincts, and behaviors) will develop a self-negating conscience, become disassociated from their values and goals, and ultimately lose the urgent need to create a socio-cultural milieu more amenable to their existence. After all, Nietzsche argues that "there are cases where [the criminal type] proves to be stronger than the society" (*TI* "Skirmishes" 45). My claim is much more modest, though still troubling: I argue here that being a certain type of woman in a patriarchy is an existential hazard of sorts, a hazard one encounters simply in virtue of being oneself in a context that is hostile (be it implicitly or explicitly) to who one is. Though this is not a new insight for anyone even mildly familiar with feminist thought, my Nietzschean account of the specifically *emotional* obstacles to one's self-actualization—the way in which a patriarchal socio-cultural milieu might infiltrate one's psychological life by generating emotional responses that turn *oneself* against one's own most lively desires, interests, and goals—does something important. Namely, it fleshes out a critical emotional mechanism of "psychological oppression," the internalization of oppression as described by Sandra Bartky:[57] "To be psychologically oppressed is to be weighed down in your mind; it is to have a harsh dominion exercised over your self-esteem. The psychologically oppressed become their own oppressors; they come to exercise harsh dominion over their own self-esteem. Differently put, psychological oppression can be regarded as the 'internalization of intimations of inferiority.'"[58]

In short, one way in which one might exercise "harsh dominion over [one's] own self-esteem" is via the unwitting assimilation of ideas, beliefs, values, and norms, an assimilation that potentially generates self-harming, aversive emotional responses.

Bartky argues that psychological oppression both fragments (or splits) the self and results in "mystification, [or] the systematic obscuring of both the reality and agencies of psychological oppression so that its intended effect, the depreciated self, is lived out as destiny, guilt, or neurosis."[59] My account supplements that of Bartky by fleshing out the emotional dimension of these two features. First, what Bartky describes as the fragmentation of the self results in part from the fragmentation of one's emotional life, into those emotional responses that seem to affirm one's "true" self (or those instincts and desires central to one's empowerment) and those that seem to devalue it. As one becomes fragmented in this way, it gets more and more difficult to discern which self is the "true" self to affirm. Additionally, the emotional dynamics of sexist oppression described above are a key element of mystification as a process that makes the source of one's psychological oppression, as well as its reality, difficult to discern. After all, a key feature of Nietzsche's account of affectivity as transpersonal is that, though the emotional coloring of my emotional responses (their quality and valence) are informed by the socio-cultural milieux or ideological communities to which I belong, I experience them as my own. When I experience disapprobatory emotional responses in relation to features of myself (perhaps those desires, instincts, or actions that are incongruous to norms of femininity) I tend to understand these disapprobatory emotions and the negative evaluations they carry with them as my own. According to Nietzsche, however, they do not *merely* originate from my psychophysiological constitution; in believing them to do so, the role my socio-cultural milieu or ideological community played in producing them is obscured and my agency is threatened.

Finally, one might ask: Why the focus on women here? Don't we see similar emotional dynamics at work in cases where men possess desires and manifest behaviors outside of the cis-hetero norm of masculinity, for example, in cases of "toxic masculinity?"[60] In response, I say: yes, we do. Indeed, according to the Nietzschean account I sketch here, men within a patriarchal society dominated by sexist beliefs and norms about femininity whose desires, instincts, and actions appear congruous with stereotypically feminine ones would become more likely to internalize sexist beliefs and norm and thus more likely to experience harmful emotions generated in part by their socio-cultural context. But it is especially important to notice that toxic masculinity and its emotional impacts are a result of the *same* sexist, patriarchal context that functions (and has historically functioned) first and foremost to subordinate women and restrict their power, in part by limiting the desires, instincts, behaviors, and roles it deems appropriate for a woman to manifest. Patriarchal socio-cultural milieux involve the systemic subordination and devaluation of women; historically, these milieux have disproportionately harmed women, and they continue to disproportionately harm women today. Thus, though men might also suffer negative emotional impacts, the brunt of the emotional burden of sexism is borne by women—especially women who aspire to positions of power, straightforwardly communicate their desires and ambitions, and refuse to regulate their desires and behaviors.

In his work, Nietzsche asks his reader to imagine a world in which those values we customarily adopt are called into question, a world in which customary norms and understandings of moral appropriateness are disrupted. Such a "revaluation of values" is sorely needed, Nietzsche argues, because the values we have so far are profoundly life-denying: they diminish those who adopt them; though they benefit a particular kind of society, they tend to harm and disempower the individual. Systems of traditional morality idealize selflessness (*GM* II:18); it should be unsurprising that the assimilation of such systems of morality via social norms and values ultimately leads to the loss of oneself. Though Nietzsche was far from interested in subverting patriarchal norms and values, I suggest that there are structural similarities between Nietzsche's critique of certain moral systems (and notions of emotional appropriateness as fittingness that accompany those worldviews) and the critique of patriarchy implied by my account above. The more these structural similarities come into view, the easier it becomes to imagine a world "beyond good and evil" as a world beyond patriarchal norms and values.[61]

## Notes

1. My sincere thanks to Rebecca Bamford, Ian Dunkle, Allison Merrick, and Justin Messmore for their feedback on early versions of this chapter.

2. In discussing gender oppression and sexism, it is important not to ignore the fact that these phenomena are experienced and lived differently depending on other aspects of one's identity and circumstance, such as race (Crenshaw 1989; Hill Collins 1991; Lorde 1984), gender identity or sexuality (Bettcher 2007, 2017; Serano 2007; Whittle 2006), and other factors.

3. A cis-hetero patriarchy will also be characterized by (1) the domination of cisgender men and the subordination of individuals who are not cisgender and (2) the domination of heterosexual men and the subordination of individuals who are not heterosexual. Explaining the complex, interwoven dynamics of domination and subordination that occur as a function of these is not something I have space to do in this chapter.

4. Lorde 1981; Pierce 1974; Berlant 2011; Pratt-Clarke 2014; Smith, Allen, and Danley 2007; Sullivan 2017; Whitney 2018.

5. On this point see Merrick (in this volume) "How We Became Who We Are: Concerning Nietzsche's Genealogy of Politicized Identity."

6. Manne 2019, 33.

7. When I speak of the (typically unconscious) assimilation of certain attitudes, norms, and beliefs, I am describing what is colloquially referred to as internalization. Importantly, however, "internalization (*Verinnerlichung*)" is a term with a specific meaning and significance in Nietzsche's work: it results when instincts that cannot

be discharged, or expressed outwardly, are then expressed inwardly (*GM* II:16). It is important to attend to this difference, especially because Nietzschean internalization, as the turning of one's instincts against oneself, seems to result when certain socio-cultural norms and beliefs are (colloquially) internalized.

8. The topic of affect in Nietzsche has been treated by a variety of scholars in recent literature (Poellner 2007; Janaway 2009a; Anderson 2012; Clark and Dudrick 2012; Bamford 2014; Katsafanas 2016; Mitchell 2017; Creasy 2018, 2020, 2022; Kail 2018; Bamford 2019; Leiter 2019; Fowles 2020). Not only does Nietzsche catalog a variety of specific emotions and their characteristic impacts, he also describes certain general functions that affects play (e.g., in shaping perceptual and moral experience, epistemic perspectives, and evaluative orientations).

9. His reflections on value-feelings (*Werthgefühlen*), both in his published work (*D* 148; *BGE* 4, 186) and in the *Nachlass* (*KSA* 12:6[25], 6:[26], 9:[1], [62], 10:[2], [23], [49], [168]; and *KSA* 13:14[185], 15[17]) are illuminating here, especially as he sometimes uses "Werthgefühlen" and "Affekte" interchangeably (*KSA* 12:6[26], 10[168]; and *KSA* 13:14[185]).

10. Though Nietzsche very frequently associates affects with somatic states (and even sometimes seems to identify them as such), it is unclear whether Nietzsche intends to establish a strict identity between affects and somatic states.

11. Leiter 2019, 70.

12. Katsafanas 2016, 94.

13. Mitchell 2017, 41; Kail 2018, 238; Leiter 2019, 70. I say "typically" here because Nietzsche seems to think that affective states are not always consciously experienced or articulable by the individual who is subject to them.

14. Richardson 1996, 36.

15. Creasy 2020.

16. My account here expands upon that of R. Lanier Anderson (2012) and utilizes the helpful terminology he employs. In his work distinguishing between Nietzschean drives and affects, R. Lanier Anderson suggests that unlike drives, which have a characteristic "aim/object structure," affects involve (1) a "stimulus object," (2) "a *default* behavioral response," and (3) a specific "emotional 'coloring'" that shapes the way the intentional object is encountered in experience (2012 218–19).

17. I say "almost" here because a select number of affects lack a clear intentional object.

18. Again, this language of emotional coloring comes from Anderson (2012, 219). Although this term is helpfully broad when speaking generally about the felt dimension of emotional experience, the emotional coloring of an emotional experience can be separated into (at least) two critical constituent parts: its quality (which includes the intensity of the experience) and its valence. Doing justice to Nietzsche's various descriptions of emotional experiences and their functions requires one to specify these.

19. Anderson 2012, 219.

20. Anderson 2012 does the same.

21. Poellner 2009, 161.

22. The behavioral outcomes that follow are also determined, in part, by these features.

23. For an example of how one might profess disbelief in a god but still assimilate the idea of a god into their mental economy (in a way that impacts emotional experience), see Lindeman et al. (2014). In this study, an explicitly stated disbelief in god did not prevent emotional states that seemed to result from assimilating the idea of a deity or god. Cases such as those outlined by this study show that the quality of one's emotional experience can still be shaped by an idea that is not an explicitly avowed belief. Such an idea can then play a role in shaping one's encounter with the intentional object at hand: in the case of the study, a requested curse on one's family.

24. Of course, Nietzsche wants to leave room for individuals who work to lessen the influence of dominant socio-cultural beliefs and norms on their emotional lives through practices of genealogy, self-knowledge, and self-genealogy. See Creasy 2020 for more on this.

25. Poellner 2009, 162.

26. Note here, by the way, that I use "appropriate" and "fitting" interchangeably, to refer to emotional responses that are warranted by the object that provokes them. Importantly, however, my claim here is not about the *actual* fittingness of one's emotional responses but the perceived fittingness of one's emotional responses. Additionally, whenever I intend to refer to the apparent *moral* appropriateness or moral permissibility of emotions, I will indicate that. If there is no such indication, "appropriate" should be read as non-moral fittingness.

27. Susan Wolf's description of allegedly fitting responses to moral sainthood comes to mind here.

28. This example is perhaps a bit tricky, since apart from this angry emotional response seeming fitting or appropriate to me in the throes of that emotional experience, such a response might seem to be *actually* appropriate. Here, it might seem my partner's compassionate nature is *actually* worthy of an angry response. Thus, the assessments and behaviors I describe above are in fact fitting. Otherwise put, while my emotional response might shape my experience of the intentional object (my partner's compassionate nature) in this example, I have good reason to judge his nature negatively here. (Thanks to Ian Dunkle for suggesting I address this worry.) I include the above example just to illustrate how affectivity shapes one's experience and evaluation of a given intentional object, in such a way that one immediately takes one's evaluation to be fitting (i.e., one understands it to be picking up on value-laden properties of the object itself). But it might be helpful to include another example in which it is perhaps less likely that the intentional object is *actually* worthy of my particular emotional response. Imagine that early in the week I promise my partner that I would do the dishes as soon as I get

some free time. Noticing that I am extraordinarily busy revising a book chapter and that the dishes are continuing to pile up, he decides late in the week to do the dishes himself, hoping it will relieve me of a burden and prove helpful. When I see the empty sink and he explains that he wanted to help out, I feel insulted, patronized, and annoyed. Here too my emotional response leads me to experience his compassionate nature as something negative, something that calls for a feeling of insulted frustration. Seized by insult and annoyance, I put the dishes from the dishwasher back into the sink so that I can do them myself. As long as I am still "in the grip" of this experience, I experience my evaluations and actions as fitting responses to my partner's compassionate nature, which I feel patronized by. In this case, although it is perhaps less obvious that my emotional response is *actually* fitting (and that his compassionate nature is *actually* worthy of insulted frustration), I still experience it as such. This leads me to negatively assess his compassionate nature.

29. Note here that I am translating *Mitleid* as compassion rather than pity. I do this to keep this portion of the chapter consistent with the example above of my partner's compassionate nature.

30. On the other hand, "strong ages, *noble* cultures see in compassion [*Mitleid*], in 'loving one's neighbor,' in a lack of self and of self-esteem, something contemptible" (*TI* "Skirmishes" 37).

31. D'Arms and Jacobson 2000.

32. D'Arms and Jacobson 2000, 66.

33. D'Arms and Jacobson 2000, 66.

34. I put "appropriate" in scare quotes here to indicate that sense of an emotion's alleged fittingness that is widespread within a given socio-cultural context/ideological community.

35. The contagion of emotion—made possible by a fundamental affective vulnerability that characterizes all individuals—is another, less subtle way in which emotion is transpersonal. See Bamford 2019, 78, on emotional contagion.

36. Insofar as self-suspicion is a sensibility that turns me against *features* of myself that may be more or less central to who I *genuinely* am, the sense of "self" employed here is extremely thin.

37. Though Nietzsche does not use the term self-suspicion to describe the evaluative sensibility I explore above, he refers to such a sensibility with some frequency throughout his body of work. In *Daybreak*, he explains how customary morality inspires one to become "more distrustful [*misstrauischer*] of all excessive well-being" (*D* 18), including one's own (given that this suspicion results in "self-chosen torture." In *BGE*, his treatment of self-suspicion (or self-mistrust) as a socio-culturally produced evaluative sensibility is pronounced. In one aphorism, he describes how, due to conventional morality, "everything that elevates the individual above the herd . . . is henceforth called *evil*; and the fair, modest, submissive, conforming mentality, the *mediocrity* of desires attains moral designations and honors. Eventually . . . every severity, even in justice, begins to disturb the conscience; any

high and hard nobility and self-reliance is almost felt to be an insult and arouses mistrust [*erweckt Misstrauen*]" (201). Later, he refers to "the internal *mistrust* [*das innerliche Misstrauen*] which is the sediment in the hearts of all dependent men and herd animals" (206) and claims that those who assimilate conventional, "slavish" morality are "skeptical and suspicious, *subtly* suspicious, of all the 'good' that is honored [in the virtues of the powerful]" (260). Throughout the *Genealogy*, he describes how shame, as an emotional response to features of oneself inspired by one's belonging to a society or ideological community, results in a mistrust of oneself and one's instincts (*GM* II:7; *GM* III:9; GM III:14). (Note that he refers to *D* 18 and *BGE* 260 in *GM* III:9.) In *TI*, he describes how the criminal's society inculcates in him a "Chandala feeling" involving suspicion [*Verdacht*] of himself ("Skirmishes" 45); in *The Antichrist*, he describes how assimilating beliefs endemic to a Christian socio-cultural context "arouses mistrust [*Misstrauen*]" in "everything natural in the instincts,—everything beneficial and life-enhancing in the instincts" (43). Finally, in his late unpublished notes, he argues that "man, imprisoned in an iron cage of errors became a caricature of man, sick, wretched, ill-disposed toward himself, full of hatred for the impulses of life, full of mistrust [*voller Misstrauen*] of all that is beautiful and happy in life" (*KSA* 13:15[73]).

38. Ridley 1996, 134.

39. We see this in the case of the sick nobles who, after becoming "ashamed of their happiness," exclaim, " 'It's a disgrace to be happy!' " (*GM* III:14). Rather than reflecting and recognizing that the negative valuation of "their happiness" has its origin in the values of miserable others "shov[ed]" on to [their] conscience," they understand the negative evaluation present in their emotional experience as merited by that experience's intentional object: happiness itself.

40. Katsafanas 2016, 132, 192. Katsafanas describes learning more about the origins of one's behaviors as gaining "knowledge of the drives and affects that figure [into their] etiology" (193).

41. The sense of "self" used in "self-negating conscience" is more robust than that used in "self-suspicion." The self-negating conscience does not merely involve turning against more or less central features of oneself; it involves turning against those features of oneself that are most central to one's flourishing, those instincts, desires, aims, and values most central to one's empowerment. Note also here that I am understanding power as growth in one's abilities over time (Dunkle 2020).

42. Hill Collins 1991, 266.

43. Note that these widespread beliefs and norms vary not only along the axis of gender but along the axes of race, class, and more. For example, those emotions, desires, and behaviors deemed "feminine" by one's socio-cultural milieu will also frequently vary along lines of race, class, and more.

44. Manne 2019, 88.

45. Again, my claim here is not that such an individual experiences the emotion as morally inappropriate but as unfitting, as inaccurately representing the

evaluative features of the object in question (here, it might be a cruel action or a cruel emotion). Nietzsche's use of *Mitleids-Moral* (*GM* P:5, 6; *TI* "Skirmishes" 37) follows Schopenhauer's use of the same term but is used by him more broadly: to refer to the modern Christian system of value dominating Europe in the late nineteenth century. This system of value, of course, positively assesses compassion.

46. Bennett 1982, 177.

47. See El-Alayli et al. (2018), who note that "descriptive stereotypes also align with people's prescriptive stereotypes regarding how women and men should behave (Barreto et al. 2009), resulting in negative impressions being formed of those who violate gender expectations (Connell 1995; Sibley and Wilson 2004)."

48. See Ridgeway (2001), who notes that "when women in mixed-sex groups present their ideas in an assertive or self-directed style, they are disliked or perceived as untrustworthy and achieve less influence over men compared to similarly acting men or less assertive women" (648–49).

49. Misra et al. 2011.

50. Manne 2019, 275.

51. El-Alayli 2018, describing research from Burns-Glover and Veith 1995.

52. Bennett 1982, 177.

53. As per Mitchell et al. (2013), who notes that "articles published by women are significantly less likely to be cited than articles written by men."

54. As El-Alayli et al. (2018) indicate: "In order to please students, female professors must walk a line between warmth and agency, a fine balance not as strictly required of male professors (Basow 1998; Cuddy et al. 2004)."

55. Interestingly for my case here, Clance and Ames (1978) find that "later introjection of societal sex-role stereotyping appear[s] to contribute significantly to the development of the impostor phenomenon" (241).

56. Nietzsche would likely insist that such a transformation happens without one's being aware of it.

57. Bartky's account is inspired by Franz Fanon's account from *Black Skin, White Masks* (1967) and a 1970 paper by Joyce Mitchell Cook.

58. Bartky 1990, 22; citation to Cook, 1970.

59. Bartky 1990, 23.

60. See, for example, the 2018 "APA Guidelines for Psychological Practice with Boys and Men." American Psychological Association. https://www.apa.org/about/policy/boys-men-practice-guidelines.pdf.

61. Not to mention a world beyond nationalisms and white supremacy.

# References

"APA Guidelines for Psychological Practice with Boys and Men." American Psychological Association. 2018. https://www.apa.org/about/policy/boys-men-practice-guidelines.pdf.

Bamford, Rebecca. 2014. "Mood and Aphorism in Nietzsche's Campaign Against Morality." *Pli: The Warwick Journal of Philosophy* 25: 55–76.
———. 2019. "The Relationship Between Science and Philosophy as a Key Feature of Nietzsche's Metaphilosophy." In *Nietzsche's Metaphilosophy: The Nature, Method, and Aims of Philosophy*, edited by Matthew Meyer and Paul S. Loeb, 65–82. Cambridge: Cambridge University Press.
Bartky, Sandra L. 1990. *Femininity and Domination: Studies in the Phenomenology of Oppression*. New York: Routledge.
Bennett, Sheila Kishler. 1982. "Student Perceptions of and Expectations for Male and Female Instructors: Evidence Relating to the Question of Gender Bias in Teaching Evaluation." *Journal of Educational Psychology* 74, no. 2: 170–79.
Berlant, Lauren. 2011. *Cruel Optimism*. Durham, NC: Duke University Press.
Bettcher, Talia Mae. 2007. "Evil Deceivers and Make-Believers: On Transphobic Violence and the Politics of Illusion." *Hypatia* 22, no. 3: 43–66.
———. 2017. "Trans Feminism: Recent Philosophical Developments." *Philosophy Compass* 12, no. 11: e12438.
Burns-Glover, A., and D. Veith. 1995. "Revising Gender and Teaching Evaluations: Sex Still Makes a Difference." *Journal of Social Behavior and Personality* 10: 69–80.
Clance, Pauline Rose, and Suzanne Ament Imes. 1978. "The Imposter Phenomenon in High Achieving Women: Dynamics and Therapeutic Intervention." *Psychotherapy: Theory, Research, and Practice* 15, no. 3: 241–47.
Cook, Joyce Mitchell. 1970. Paper delivered at Philosophy and the Black Liberation Struggle Conference, University of Illinois, Chicago Circle, Nov. 19–20. As cited in Bartky 1990.
Creasy, Kaitlyn. 2018. "On the Problem of Affective Nihilism." *Journal of Nietzsche Studies* 49, no. 1: 31–51.
———. 2020. *The Problem of Affective Nihilism in Nietzsche: Thinking Differently, Feeling Differently*. London: Palgrave Macmillan.
———. 2022. "Nietzsche on the Sociality of Emotional Experience." *European Journal of Philosophy*. https://onlinelibrary.wiley.com/doi/10.1111/ejop.12818.
Crenshaw, Kimberlé. 1989. "Demarginalizing the Intersection of Race and Sex: A Black Feminist Critique of Antidiscrimination Doctrine, Feminist Theory and Antiracist Politics." *University of Chicago Legal Forum* 140: 139–67.
D'Arms, Justin, and Daniel Jacobson, 2000, "The Moralistic Fallacy: On the 'Appropriateness' of Emotions," *Philosophy and Phenomenological Research* 61, no. 1: 65–90.
Dunkle, Ian. 2020. "On the Normativity of Nietzsche's Will to *Power*." *Journal of Nietzsche Studies* 51, no. 2: 188–211.
Eckes, Thomas. 2002. "Paternalistic and Envious Gender Stereotypes: Testing Predictions from the Stereotype Content Model." *Sex Roles* 7, no. 3: 99–114.
El-Alayli, A., A. A. Hansen-Brown, and M. Ceynar. 2018. "Dancing Backwards in High Heels: Female Professors Experience More Work Demands and Special

Favor Requests, Particularly from Academically Entitled Students." *Sex Roles* 79: 136–50.
Fanon, Franz. 1967. *Black Skin, White Masks*. New York: Grove Press.
Fasching-Varner, Kenneth, Katrice Albert, Roland Mitchell, and Chaunda Allen. 2015. *Racial Battle Fatigue in Higher Education*. New York: Rowman & Littlefield.
Fowles, Christopher. 2020. "The Heart of Flesh: Nietzsche on Affects and the Interpretation of the Body." *Journal of the History of Philosophy* 58, no. 1: 113–39.
Heyes, Cressida. 2003. "Feminist Solidarity after Queer Theory: The Case of Transgender." *Signs: Journal of Women in Culture and Society.* 28, no. 4: 1093–1120.
Hill Collins, Patricia. 1991. *Black Feminist Thought*. New York: Hyman Press.
Kail, Peter. 2018. "Value and Nature in Nietzsche." In *The Nietzschean Mind*, edited by Paul Katsafanas. New York: Routledge.
Leiter, Brian. 2019. *Moral Psychology with Nietzsche*. Oxford: Oxford University Press.
Lindeman, Marjaana, Bethany Heywood, Tapani Riekki, and Tommi Makkonen. 2014. "Atheists Become Emotionally Aroused When Daring God to Do Terrible Things." *International Journal for the Psychology of Religion* 24, no. 2: 124–32.
Lorde, Audre. 1981. "The Uses of Anger." *Women's Studies Quarterly* 9, no. 3: 7–10.
———. 1984. *Sister Outsider: Essays and Speeches*. Trumansburg, NY: Crossing Press.
Manne, Kate. 2019. *Down Girl*. Oxford: Oxford University Press.
Mitchell, Jonathan. 2017. "Nietzsche on Taste: Epistemic Privilege and Anti-Realism." *Inquiry* 60, no. 1–2: 31–65.
Mitchell, Sara McLaughlin, Samantha Lange, and Holly Brus. 2013. "Gendered Citation Patterns in International Relations Journals." *International Studies Perspectives* 14: 485–92.
Misra, Joya, Jennifer Hickes Lundquist, Elissa Holmes, and Stephanie Agiomavritis. 2011. "The Ivory Ceiling of Service Work." American Association of University Professors. Jan.–Feb. https://www.aaup.org/article/ivory-ceiling-service-work#.XiZyMBdKjBK.
Nietzsche, Friedrich. 1982. *Daybreak*. Translated by R. J. Hollingdale. Cambridge, MA: Cambridge University Press.
———. 1974. *The Gay Science*. Translated by Walter Kaufmann. New York: Vintage Books.
———. 1967–77. *Sämtliche Werke: Kritische Studienausgabe in 15 Bänden*. Edited by G. Colli and M. Montinari. Berlin: De Gruyter.
———. 1996. *Human, All Too Human*. Translated by R. J. Hollingdale. Cambridge, MA: Cambridge University Press.
———. 1997. *Untimely Meditations*. Translated by R. J. Hollingdale. Cambridge, MA: Cambridge University Press.
———. 2002. *Beyond Good and Evil*. Translated by Judith Norman. Cambridge: Cambridge University Press.
———. 2005. *Nietzsche: The Anti-Christ, Ecce Homo, Twilight of the Idols, and Other Writings*. Translated by Judith Norman. Cambridge: Cambridge University Press.

———. 2006. *Thus Spoke Zarathustra*. Translated by Adrian Del Caro. Cambridge: Cambridge University Press.
———. 2007. *On the Genealogy of Morality*. Translated by Carol Diethe. Cambridge, MA: Cambridge University Press.
Pierce, C. M. 1974. "Psychiatric Problems of the Black Minority." In *American Handbook of Psychiatry*, edited by G. Caplan. New York: Basic Books.
Pratt-Clarke, Menah. 2014. "Racial (and Gender) Battle Fatigue: The Transdisciplinary Applied Social Justice Approach." In *But You Can't Take Our Souls: Racial Battle Fatigue in Higher Education*, edited by Kenneth Fasching-Varner, Katrice Albert, Roland Mitchell, and Chaunda Allen. New York: Rowman & Littlefield.
Ridgeway, Cecilia L. 2001. "Gender, Status, and Leadership." *Journal of Social Issues* 57, no. 4: 637–55.
Ridley, Aaron. 1996. "Nietzsche's Conscience." *Journal of Nietzsche Studies* 11: 1–12.
Serano, Julia. 2007. *Whipping Girl: A Transsexual Woman on Sexism and the Scapegoating of Femininity*. Emeryville, CA: Seal Press.
Smith, William, Walter R. Allen, and Lynette L. Danley. 2007. "'Assume the Position . . . You Fit the Description': Psychosocial Experiences and Racial Battle Fatigue Among African American Male College Students." *American Behavioral Scientist* 51, no. 4: 551–78.
Sullivan, Shannon. 2017. *The Physiology of Sexist and Racist Oppression*. New York: Oxford.
Whitney, Shiloh. 2018. "Byproductive Labor: A Feminist Theory of Affective Labor Beyond the Productive–Reproductive Distinction." *Philosophy & Social Criticism* 44, no. 6: 637–60.
Whittle, Stephen. 2006. "Where Did We Go Wrong? Feminism and Trans Theory—Two Teams on the Same Side." In *The Transgender Studies Reader*, edited by Susan Stryker and Stephen Whittle, 194–202. New York: Routledge.
Wolf, Susan. 1982. "Moral Saints." *Journal of Philosophy* 79, no. 8: 419–39.

## 11

# "The Great Seriousness Begins"

## Nietzsche's Tragic Philosophy and Philosophy's Role in Creating Healthier Racialized Identities

JACQUELINE SCOTT

> Another ideal runs ahead of us, a strange, tempting [*Versucherisches*], dangerous ideal to which we should not wish to persuade anybody because we do not really concede *the right to it* to anyone: the ideal of a spirit who plays naively—that is, not deliberately but from overflowing power and abundance—with all that was hitherto called holy, good, untouchable, divine; for whom those supreme things that the people naturally accept as their value standards, signify danger, decay, debasement, or at least recreation, blindness, and temporary self-oblivion; the ideal of a human, superhuman well-being and benevolence that will appear *inhuman*—for example, when it confronts all earthly seriousness so far, . . . and in spite of all of this, it is perhaps only with him that *great seriousness* really begins, that the real question mark is posed for the first time, that the destiny of the soul changes, the hand moves forward, the *tragedy* begins.
>
> —Friedrich Nietzsche, *GS* 382

In the epigraph for this chapter, Friedrich Nietzsche foretold of a potential philosophical ideal that would counter the reigning "holy, good" ideals of traditional philosophy and would signal a "great health" (the title of the section). This new ideal, its accompanying health, and the people who will embody it portend the beginning of "the tragedy." What is this tragedy? How is it related to Nietzsche's criticisms of traditional philosophy, his philosophy of the future, and health in the late works? In this chapter, I will argue that "tragic philosophy" is a key component of Nietzsche's metaphilosophical project in the late works—though he left the term underdeveloped in his published works. In particular, my focus will be less on the content of Nietzsche's tragic philosophy and more on the role he assigned to it in helping us understand and move away from the "diseased" philosophical approach of the traditional philosophy that wills truth.[1] In this sense, I will argue that Nietzsche's tragic philosophy was meant to act as a counterpoint to the bad conscience and the ascetic ideal. As a result, it is meant to guide those who embrace it out of the *ressentiment* and world-weariness resulting from the "truths" of traditional philosophy to a more creative way of affirming life.

In making this argument, I will argue that one of Nietzsche's goals in the late works was to experiment with ways in which those of his time might rethink the aims and methods of philosophy so that the healthiest among them might affirm meaningful lives in the face of a tragic view of life. Nietzsche characterized this approach as a "pessimism of strength" in which the problematic nature of existence served as a stimulus for life affirmation (*BT* "Attempt" 1; *TI* "Skirmishes" 24). This metaphilosophical project, then, is not primarily focused on the traditional disinterested pursuit of knowledge, but instead on the subjective creation of values that are derived from an affirmation of the only "truth" we have about our lives (that they are, at root, meaningless). Nietzsche referred to this as "tragic wisdom" and he proclaimed himself as the "first tragic philosopher" because of a profound self-knowledge he had acquired as a sufferer of the diseased traditional philosophy (*EH* "Books," BT 3, 4).

In the final section of the chapter, I will conclude by pointing toward the importance of this understanding of Nietzsche's tragic approach for contemporary philosophy. In particular, I will argue that this tragic metaphilosophical approach is potentially quite fruitful for those of us looking for healthier ways of enacting race in our society. I will argue that we need to adopt a tragic view of our racialized lives: an acceptance of the endemic and chronic nature of racism in our society without falling victim to the bad conscience-induced resignation and resentment that plague so many people today. In doing so, I will contend that we should draw from aspects of Nietzsche's tragic philosophy to aid us in affirming our lives as racialized subjects and as a racialized society. This is not solely an American cultural problem. It is also one that plagues our own discipline. I will argue that the discipline of philosophy itself needs to undergo this process of attaining tragic wisdom.

## Background Information—Nihilism and the Problem of Decadence

In his reassessment of his first book, *The Birth of Tragedy*, Nietzsche emphasized the philosophical import of this book in its analysis of ancient Greek tragic pessimism as a sign of health and vitality. Nietzsche lauded the ancient tragic Greek method for contending with the pessimism that plagues human existence. He characterized this pessimism in *The Birth of Tragedy* in terms of the Wisdom of Silenus: "What is best of all is utterly beyond your reach: not to be born, not to *be*, to be *nothing*. But the second best for you is—to die soon" (*BT* 3). Given this deeply gloomy view of our existence (avoid existing altogether or exit it as soon as possible), Nietzsche marveled at how these Greeks understood this view of life, embraced it (by portraying it in their religion and tragic plays), and still managed to affirm their lives.

Space limitations do not permit me to fully flesh out the relationship between nihilism, pessimism, and decadence in his late works. While it is well established in the scholarship that nihilism and pessimism are important technical terms in his arguments and that these terms played important roles throughout his writings, "decadence" is less universally acknowledged as a technical term. That being said, I, along with scholars such as Daniel Conway, Randall Havas, and Daniel Ahern, have argued that in the late works, the terms "decadence" and "decadent" took on a technical status and were important for Nietzsche in terms of how he characterized his post-*Zarathustra* critical and positive projects as well as his own role in carrying them out.[2] As Bernard Reginster has argued, Nietzsche often used the terms nihilism and pessimism interchangeably, and therefore it is difficult to settle on a rigid characterization of their relationship.[3] The same goes for decadence. For the purposes of this chapter, I suggest that we understand the relationship between these three terms in the following way. Nihilism is both the fact that the history of human existence is characterized by ceaseless and meaningless suffering and also our response to this suffering (*GM* III:28).[4] The fact of this meaningless suffering causes "disorientation" and eventually suicidal despair in us when we realize that our highest values that would render this existence ultimately meaningful are not realizable (*BGE* 10).[5] The assumption here is that in response to this meaningless suffering and to avoid the despair, we create a meaning in life as well as the values that are attendant to this meaning. For example, Christianity offers its followers a meaningful life by requiring that they accept Jesus Christ as their savior and devote their lives to following his teachings. The meaning in a Christian's life then is formed by organizing one's life according to the established Christian values.

Nietzsche also held that though philosophy is generally regarded as a theoretical and rational activity, it is actually guided by instinctual drives that reflect an autocratic desire to impose our preferences on the world around us (*BGE* 13, 22, 211, 230).[6] In imposing these values ("I prefer this and do not prefer that") to fashion a meaningful life, humans—particularly philosophers—utilize subconscious instincts and drives. As Reginster, Conway, Paul Katsafanas, and I have claimed, Nietzsche's argument is that this value creation emerges out of a particular physiological attunement. This attunement is Nietzsche's will to power (*BGE* 9; *GM* III:7).[7] As humans, we attempt to contend with this nihilistic disorientation by putting our stamp on the world, saying that certain things are more important than others (valuation), and thus rendering our lives meaningful.[8] An unhealthy organization of the drives and impulses engenders an unhealthy creation of values.[9]

While in the short term this philosophy has held off nihilism, Nietzsche argued that in the long term it had introduced an additional set of problems for its adherents: any values that we create will eventually "decay." In this sense, these values are organic. By this I mean that due to changes in the individuals or external circumstances, values lose their efficacy in helping to make life meaningful for their believers. This is the problem of decadence: we must create values to hold off suicidal despair, but any values we create will decay. There is thus no permanent escape from the threat of suicide-inducing nihilism because there is no cure for the disease of decadence (*TI* "Socrates" 11).[10]

Traditionally, philosophers have attempted to create a cure for decadence so as to end it as a problem altogether. I have argued that these philosophers can be divided into two groups and both exhibit a weakly decadent approach: optimists and weak pessimists. Optimists attempt to treat decadence using universal and unconditional values (like "good" and "evil").[11] Their claim is that there is an inherent meaning to life, they have discovered it, and these values will render life meaningful for all who adhere to them. In the late works, Nietzsche charged Socrates and Plato with being such optimists. The weak decadent counterpart to the optimists is the group of weak pessimists. This group accepts that there can be no permanent cure for decadence in terms of our lives on earth—that suffering in life is inevitable. Their goal instead is to help their followers escape from our problematic existence on earth. In terms of value creation, then, these types teach a hatred of the animalistic instincts behind our expressions of the will to power and claim that it is these instincts that make life problematic (*EH* "Destiny" 8; *TI* "Skirmishes" 35). Christian values are an example of this type of treatment for decadence, in that Christianity claims that the suffering in our lives is caused by sinning. But if people are "good" and avoid the "evil" of acting on our instincts (expressing our individual will to power) while we are alive, then we will be rewarded with a life free of suffering in the afterlife (*GM* III:8–23). Based on this view, our lives are made meaningful by dutifully following the dictates of the ascetic priest. Nietzsche likened this approach to that of a physician who offers a treatment that lessens the symptoms of the disease but leaves the underlying disease untreated (*GM* III:5–17).

In this sense, decadence is the physiological underpinning (I refer to it as health) of the philosophical issue of nihilism.[12] Pessimism is the emotional response to the fact of nihilism and the problem of decadence.[13] This emotional response, for most of human history, has been a weak pessimistic evaluation on the whole of life. Nietzsche argued that the Greeks of the tragic age stood out because while they acknowledged this nihilistic fact of human existence (marked by ceaseless and meaningless suffering), they still affirmed their lives. Nietzsche then characterized this as a pessimism of strength (*BT* "Attempt" 1).

Both types of weak decadence are characterized by a twofold denial of the necessity of creating values as well as of the ability of these values to help us affirm our lives on earth (*GS* 370). As a result, they do not prepare their followers for either the inevitable decline of these values or for the necessary creation of new values needed to hold off nihilism. Nietzsche's project, as described for example in *The Gay Science* (382), was to propose a healthier, more effective alternative to these two forms of decadence. I have characterized this approach as "strong decadence." It is decadent in that it accepts the fact that there is no inherent meaning to life and so life is characterized by inexplicable suffering. But it is strong in that it proposes an antidote to this disease of decadence that emphasizes the abilities of individuals to create values that aid them in affirming their own lives (*BGE* 59). In this sense, this strong decadence acts as an antidote to the disease of decadence by strengthening the body to withstand the most pervasive symptoms of decadence.[14]

This strong decadence is characterized by what I call a "strong pessimist" view of life: life is meaningless, unpredictable, and rife with inexplicable suffering and this void in meaning offers individuals the opportunity to express their wills to power and affirm their lives (*BT* "Attempt" 1). In this sense, the suffering brought about by the meaninglessness of life can act as a stimulus for growth and not merely serve as a burden to be endured in our earthly existence (*GM* III:2; *BGE* 225). As I will argue, Nietzsche's personal role was to act as a philosophical physician for his time and to foster a philosophical and cultural transition from weak pessimism to strong pessimism by cultivating future strong types who might be able to enact this transition. Returning to *The Gay Science* 382, this transition requires "great health" both on the part of Nietzsche (the physician) and his future physician colleagues: "Another ideal runs ahead of us, a strange, tempting [*versucherisches*], dangerous ideal to which we should not wish to persuade anybody because we do not reality concede *the right to it* to anyone: the ideal of a spirit who plays naively—that is, not deliberately but from overflowing power and abundance—with all that was hitherto called holy, good, untouchable, divine." Here Nietzsche wrote of a future alternative to the ideals of weak decadence, and this ideal will be "strange" in that it will be different from the dominant traditional approaches. Nietzsche used the term *versucherishes* to describe it, and the German verb *versuchen* can mean to attempt, to experiment, or to tempt (*BGE* 42). This future ideal is *versucherisches* in that it attempts to push Nietzsche's contemporaries to experiment with value creation, and it thereby tempts its followers to overcome the traditional approaches that those of his time considered to be "holy, good, untouchable, divine."

Note also that these future types are engaged in what Daniel Conway has called "the dangerous game" of the philosophers. Conway has argued that Nietzschean philosophers must attempt, and experiment with, the task of creating values that make life meaningful and acknowledge that any values they create will eventually decay. They then are always tempting the specter of nihilism, and it was because of this temptation that Nietzsche called this ideal dangerous.[15] Nietzsche's future healthy types who will create strong decadent values are a select bunch because they will have the ability to create instinctively by using their will to power ("the ideal of a spirit who plays naively—that is, not deliberately but from overflowing power and abundance"). In other words, contrary to the ideals of weak decadence, it is the unconscious desires and instincts that will be most valued as opposed to an emphasis on conscious rational creation. Also note that these future types will see the weak decadent "value standards" that are "naturally accept[ed]" by most people as symptoms of "danger, decay, debasement, or at least recreation, blindness, and self-oblivion" (*GS* 382). In other words, these future Nietzschean strong decadents will understand that the values of traditional philosophy "signal" a decay of values and thus the slide toward nihilism.

Most importantly for my purposes in this chapter, these future types will signal the transition to a different approach for contending with the problem of decadence and the threat of nihilism. In this sense, these types will pose "the real question mark . . . for the first time" about the health of these traditional values and thus "[confront] all earthly seriousness so far." For Nietzsche, this would signal the beginning of a "tragedy," which would necessitate a new type of physiological health ("the ideal of a human, superhuman well-being and benevolence") and would change the "destiny of the soul."

*The Gay Science* 382 thus epitomizes Nietzsche's concept of tragic philosophy in the late works because in that section Nietzsche connected three aspects of tragic philosophy: first, as a response to weak decadence; second, as involving physiological and philosophical health; and third, as the cultivation of a new type of philosopher. In other words, I am arguing that this section describes a future new type, a new goal, and also a new means for attaining that goal. In the rest of this chapter, I will argue that if one engages in a close analysis of *The Gay Science* 382 and connects it to other references in the late works to "tragedy" and "tragic," then one will emerge with a fairly detailed sketch of this tragic philosophy and its role in Nietzsche's positive philosophy of the late works as well as of Nietzsche's own role in cultivating this "new ideal." Now that I have provided some background information on my view of Nietzsche's general positive philosophy in the late works, I will focus on this analysis of "tragic philosophy."[16]

## Tragedy and the Tragic

In this analysis, I will delineate three characteristics of this tragic philosophy:

1. Harbinger for a healthier philosophy of the future
2. Artistic acceptance of the meaningless nature of human existence
3. Metaphor for Nietzsche's own critical work in assessing weak decadent philosophy[17]

Returning to Nietzsche's "Attempt at a Self-Criticism," in his preface to *The Birth of Tragedy*, he argued that his call in the previous edition of the text for a rebirth of tragedy out of the spirit of Wagner's music was wrongheaded. Instead, his emphasis should have been on understanding and replicating the tragic Greek "pessimism of strength [*Stärke*]" as a sign of their "intellectual predilection for the hard, gruesome, evil, problematic aspect of existence" as it derives from an overflowing health (*BT* "Attempt" 1). In other words, fourteen years after publishing *The Birth of Tragedy*, Nietzsche wanted his readers to focus on his understanding of an aspect of the ancient Greek strong decadent approach to value creation. He considered it to be healthy because the Greeks did not deny the nihilistic foundational state of human existence ("the hard, gruesome, evil, problematic aspect of existence"), as did Nietzsche's contemporaries, but instead cultivated an "intellectual predilection for it." Nietzsche, then, was using his own value system of weak and strong decadence to engage in a retrospective diagnosis of the Greeks of the tragic period.[18]

In terms of the second characteristic of tragic philosophy, throughout the published late works Nietzsche characterized this pessimism of strength as involving the ability to both accept the frightful and evil nature of existence and to use the pain involved in this acceptance as a stimulus to create values that allow one to affirm one's present-day life. For Nietzsche, this way of contending with the "problematic aspect of existence" was something in which the artists of the tragic period excelled:

> The psychology of the orgy as an overflowing feeling of life and energy within which even pain acts as a stimulus provided me with the key to the concept of the *tragic* feeling, which was misunderstood as much by Aristotle as it especially was by

our pessimists. Tragedy is so far from providing evidence for pessimism among the Hellenes in Schopenhauer's sense that it has to be considered the decisive repudiation of that idea and the *counter-verdict* to it. Affirmation of life even in its strangest and sternest problems, the will to life rejoicing in its own inexhaustibility through the *sacrifice* of its highest types—that is what I called Dionysian, *that* is what I recognized as the bridge to the psychology of the tragic poet. *Not* so as to get rid of the pity and terror, not in order to purify oneself of a dangerous emotion through its vehement discharge—it was thus Aristotle understood it—: but, beyond terror and pity, *to realize in oneself* the eternal joy of becoming—that joy which also encompasses joy in destruction. (*TI* "Ancients" 5)

Here Nietzsche contrasted the weak modern Schopenhauerian pessimism of his time that was characterized by resignation and weariness about the meaninglessness of human existence with the strong pessimism of the tragic poet. This latter pessimism was an expression of an "overflowing feeling of life and energy" that allowed suffering to be a stimulus to life affirmation as opposed to a reason for negating life. In the tragic plays, the Greeks affirmed life "even in its strangest and most sternest problems" and because of the "the *sacrifice* of its highest types." These heroes played the "dangerous game," and while they usually perished because of the view of life they attempted to embody, this attempt or experiment with life affirmation should be viewed as a celebration of the creation of something out of the possibilities offered by life and of the "joy" they experienced while engaging in this project.

Nietzsche was giving his readers the historic roots of his strong decadent approach and an interpretation of the ancient "tragic feeling" (as distinct from that offered by Aristotle) that could, if his future readers played their cards right, serve as "the bridge to the psychology of the tragic poet." It could serve as the bridge to a future instantiation of this philosophical and psychological approach to life (*BGE* 23). In a different section of *Twilight of the Idols*, Nietzsche developed this psychological assessment of tragic artists.

> A psychologist asks on the other hand: what does all art do? does it not praise? does it not glorify? does it not select? does it not highlight? By doing all this it *strengthens* or *weakens* certain valuations. . . . Is [the artist's] basic instinct aimed toward art, or is it not rather directed towards the meaning of art, which is

life? towards a *desideratum of life?*—Art is the great stimulus to life: how could it be thought purposeless, aimless, as *l'art pour l'art*? One question remains: art also brings to light much which is ugly, hard, and questionable in life—does it not thereby seem to suffer from life? . . . *What does the tragic artist communicate of himself?* Does he not display the condition of fearlessness in the face of the fearsome and questionable?—This condition itself is a high desideratum: he knows it bestows on it the highest honours. He communicates it—he *has* to communicate it if he is an artist, a genius of communication. Bravery and composure in the face of a powerful enemy, great hardship, a problem that arouses aversion—it is this *victorious* condition which the tragic artist singles out, which he glorifies. In the face of tragedy the warlike in our soul celebrates its Saturnalias; whoever is accustomed to suffering, whoever seeks out suffering, the *heroic* man extols his existence by means of tragedy—for him alone does the tragic poet pour this draught of sweetest cruelty.—(*TI* "Skirmishes" 24)

Nietzsche described the tragic artist as one who displays "fearlessness in the face of the fearsome and questionable." It is this artistic approach that involves knowledge of this "truth" of existence without being engulfed by the enormity of it. Also note that here Nietzsche's emphasis is on the artistic aspect of this tragic approach. Art "strengthens or weakens certain valuations" in terms of the subject matters it attempts to portray.[19] In terms of the psychology of this artistic type and its propensity to affirm life, in this sense, art is "the great stimulus to life." Tragic artists in particular portray the nihilistic state of human existence and affirm their ability to do so without fear. Like Nietzsche's philosophers of the future, he described these tragic artists as having the "courage" to affirm life not only *despite* but also *because* of its problematic nature.[20] Beyond this artistic propensity to portray their fearlessness in face of the "fearful and questionable," another characteristic of tragic artists that Nietzsche hoped his future philosophical colleagues would cultivate is the cheerfulness of artists who know how to be "superficial out of profundity" (*GS* P:4). This cheerfulness is meant to distinguish them from weak decadents who favor the will to truth but who then blanch when they confront the basic naturalistic truth of the nature of existence and either deny this truth in favor of their own "truth" that is meant to serve as a cure for decadence (optimists) or whose truth is despair about the terrible and questionable aspects of life (weak pessimists) (*BGE* 59).

Instead, Nietzsche says that if convalescents still need art, then it is an art that portrays the artistic cheerfulness and are convalescents (Nietzsche calls them "we convalescents" and thus he includes himself in this group) in the sense that they had suffered from weak decadence, as well as from the "profound" knowledge that life is inherently meaningless and rife with senseless suffering, and have recovered from it. Now they approach the "truth" of life in a different way. They embrace the truth of "art for artists, for artists only." This artistic truth requires a cheerful approach that involves forgetting and being "good at *not* knowing" (*GS* P:4). I think what Nietzsche means by this is that it involves contending with the profound nihilistic truth of life but not drowning in the despair it inspires. Instead, they consciously "paint" on this life their affirmative value systems and as such they are "superficial out of profundity."[21]

The final characteristic is Nietzsche's use of tragedy as a metaphor for the work in his own time period of putting an end to traditional, dogmatic philosophy—as evinced by my analysis of *The Gay Science* 382. In his *Ecce Homo* discussion of *BT*, Nietzsche referred to himself as the "first tragic philosopher," which means that he alone was able to transpose "the Dionysian into a philosophical pathos" because he had the requisite "tragic wisdom" (*EH* "Books" BT:3). I understand this as Nietzsche's boast that he had adopted the artistic approach to knowledge of the truth of life (tragic wisdom) and from that Dionysian rebirth of himself from a weak decadent follower of Schopenhauer and Wagner into a philosopher who could be the harbinger to a healthier philosopher.

In the next section of his discussion of *The Birth of Tragedy* in *Ecce Homo*, Nietzsche then promised "a tragic age: the highest art in saying Yes to life, tragedy, will be reborn when humanity has weathered the consciousness of the hardest but most necessary wars *without suffering from it*" (*EH* "Books" BT:4).[22] In terms of tragedy as a metaphor, this age represents both a future period in time (a rebirth of the tragic age of the Greeks) and the rebirth of the physio-philosophical health of that time period (*BGE* 23). In the penultimate section of *Genealogy of Morals*, Nietzsche described this same historical event:

> Here I touch on my problem, on our problem, my *unknown* friends (for as yet I *know* no friend): what meaning would *our*

whole being possess if it were not this, that in us the will to truth has become conscious of itself *as a problem*? As the will to truth thus gains self-consciousness—there can be no doubt of that—morality will gradually *perish* now: this is the great spectacle [*Schauspiele*] in a hundred acts reserved for the next two centuries in Europe—the most terrible, most questionable, and perhaps also the most hopeful of spectacles. (*GM* III:27)

Note that Nietzsche here likens the historical event of the overcoming of the weak, decadent "will to truth" to a "spectacle" of great length that will play out over the next two hundred years. So not only did Nietzsche seem to be likening this epistemic event to a play, but the adjectives he used to describe this play ("the most terrible, most questionable") are similar to the language that he used to describe the ancient Greek tragic view of life. In at least a metaphorical sense then, Nietzsche here used tragedy as a metaphor to describe his own as well as future time periods (*GS* 343, 371, 372, 377).

## The Historical and Epistemic Meanings of Tragic Wisdom

Now that I have highlighted many of the ways that Nietzsche used the terms "tragic" and "tragedy" in describing aspects of his positive philosophy, I want to focus on the historic and epistemological meanings of this "tragic wisdom." Notice that, in the quotes from both the second edition of *The Gay Science* and *Ecce Homo*, the issue is about the psychological (and resulting philosophical) response to the "findings" of the will to truth (*GS* P:4; *EH* "Books" BT:3). In this sense, this historic tragedy and the resulting tragic wisdom are, at least in part, epistemic issues. Nietzsche thus intended tragic wisdom to be part of his healthier alternative to the weak decadent will to truth. It is, in part, these historic and epistemic understandings of tragic wisdom that I will argue our society and philosophy as a discipline should adopt in contending with the American disease of racism.

In order to carry out this analysis, I will focus on Nietzsche's argument in *Beyond Good and Evil* 32.[23] For the purposes of this chapter, one might read this section as a microcosm for the overarching historical and epistemic argument in the three essays of the *Genealogy of Morals*. In other words, just as *Genealogy*'s three essays trace the lineage of the contemporary will to truth, *BGE* 32 does the same (*GM* P:2, 3, 6). There, Nietzsche also explicitly described his healthier alternative to that offered by *Genealogy*'s bad conscience and the acetic ideal. On a close reading of *Genealogy*, one can see in each of these essays gestures to this Nietzschean healthier alternative, but they are more implicit than in the statement in *BGE* 32 (*GM* I:6, 17; II:16–19; III:20–27).[24]

In *BGE* 32, Nietzsche divided human history into three periods. The first is the "pre-moral" period, in which the value of an action was determined by looking at its consequences. The second period he called the "moral period," and he argued that he and his contemporaries were still in it. This second period was a result of "the first attempt at self-knowledge [*der Erste Versuch zur Selbst-Erkenntnis*]" and the value of an action was determined by the intention driving it. Nietzsche then called for another "reversal and fundamental shift in values" that would be brought about by "another self-examination of man, another growth in profundity [*Vertiefung*]." He called this third period the "extra-moral" [*aussermoralische*] period. In this time period in the future, the value of an action would be determined by what is unintentional in it.

I recommend that we understand this move from one period to the next in terms of Nietzsche's genealogy of morals. The pre-moral period seems to correspond to the time period of the nobles of the first essay. The *Erste Versuch zur Selbst-Erkenntnis* seems to have come about as a result of the slave morality described in the first essay, during which "man first became an interesting animal, that only here did the human soul in a higher sense acquire depth [*Tiefe*] and become evil" (*GM* I:6). As Nietzsche argued in the second essay of *Genealogy*, this new depth [*Tiefe*] in humans was brought about by the bad conscience in which expression of the instincts was turned inward and repressed. In this sense, the sufferers of bad conscience were expected to focus on their intentions and repress them. There was a resultant inward turn of the instincts—especially those instincts for hostility, cruelty, destruction, and joy in attacking (*GM* II:16). With this depth, humans acquired a soul and also began to suffer from the "gravest and uncanniest illness" that also rendered humans "pregnant with a future" (*GM* II:7). I contend that one should understand this pregnancy as the ability for those of us in the moral period to give a Dionysian birth to a different (healthier) type of human being via another self-examination and growth in profundity [*Vertiefung*].[25] This growth in profundity was meant to come about through this "artists' cruelty, this delight in imposing a form upon oneself as a hard, recalcitrant, suffering material" (*GM* II:18).

Here, then, I want to argue that this next historical growth in profundity of the third moral period is connected to Nietzsche's tragic wisdom. This profundity is meant to come about by deepening our self-knowledge ("self-examination") of our instincts and desires (the unintentional) with the aim of utilizing them. It is this aspect of our human selves that Nietzsche argues traditional philosophy had either denied or devalued out of shame at discovering our "animal," beastly selves (*GM* III:2) while at the same time prioritizing the rational "angel" side of ourselves. It is this hierarchy that has led to the cultivation of the Nietzsche's weak contemporaries, and this value system emerged out of a weak pessimistic approach to the knowledge of our human existence—that is, the animalistic part of our natures. On this reading, those suffering from bad conscience gained knowledge of this non-rational animalistic aspect of themselves and were ashamed of it. As a result, they were nauseated and frozen in inaction. The ascetic ideal of the ascetic priest rescued us from this potentially nihilistic sickness in the short term, but of course Nietzsche argued that in the long term it was leading straight to suicidal nihilism (*GM* III:28).[26]

I am thus arguing that Nietzsche's tragic philosophy, because of his own tragic wisdom, was meant to be a third alternative for dealing with the problem of our existence (beyond those offered by optimistic Socratism and the weak pessimism of the bad conscience and the ascetic ideal). Nietzsche's particular tragic approach was meant to push us to accept this animalistic self and to use its powers to creatively shape our wills and to create healthier values. Note that in *GM* II:18 Nietzsche called this "active bad conscience" an expression of an artist's "cruelty, this delight in imposing a form upon oneself as a hard, recalcitrant, suffering material." I see this description of a preferable alternative to the regular passive bad conscience of Nietzsche's formulation as an expression of the strong pessimism of the tragic artist. These artists delight, as did the Greeks of the tragic age, in creating a system of values and imposing it on themselves.[27]

In short, in order to emerge out of the bad conscience of *GM* II, Nietzsche argued that we need to adopt a more artistic approach to value creation, self-formation, and self-procreation. But Nietzsche did not mean that one who engaged in this approach would simply be an artist or that the product of this engagement would be a work of art itself. Instead, Nietzsche emphasized that this approach is still philosophical. My claim, then, is that this aspect of Nietzsche's positive philosophy involves revaluations of both art and philosophy and of their roles in engendering vibrant individuals and cultures (*GM* III:3–5, 16, 18).[28]

## Nietzsche's Tragic Philosophy and the Philosophy of Race

Given my arguments for understanding Nietzsche's tragic metaphilosophical approach in the late works, I will briefly highlight ways in which it could (and should) be put into practice today.[29] In this concluding section, I will suggest ways in which a tragic philosophic approach could address and ameliorate the "disease" of American racism. We in the twenty-first century are still grappling with problematic racialized identities that can often leave us suffering from a Nietzschean *ressentiment* and world-weariness. In response, I will contend that we should draw from aspects of Nietzsche's tragic philosophy in order for us to affirm our lives as racialized subjects and as a racialized society. We first need to learn to think and feel our racialized identities and racialized instincts and desires. This is akin to the self-knowledge that results from the bad conscience. We then need to engage in creative life-affirming racialized *Versuche* of the sort Nietzsche argued could result from the second *Versuch* in self-knowledge (*BGE* 32). I recommend that this might be a way to get ourselves out of the despair and resignation that plague our racist society and into experimentations with racialized identities that are more mutually beneficial. Also, as Nietzsche, foretold, any such engagements are dangerous because we need to come to terms with the potential fact that racism might be like decadence in the sense that there is no permanent escape from it. If this might be the case (as Derrick Bell and others have claimed), then I argue the Nietzsche's tragic philosophy might be instructive.[30]

Neither philosophy as a discipline nor our culture wants to actually deal with the "hard, gruesome, problematic aspect of" our racially imbued past and present. As a result, some reject the pessimistic view that racism was baked into the American foundation from the start, continues to exude its toxic gas, and infects all who breathe in this country, or they optimistically claim that racism was all in the past and that we have since cured ourselves of it (optimism). Some other folks take a Nietzschean weak pessimistic approach and accept a pessimistic view of systemic racism (that it is incurable and infects us all), drown in this self-knowledge of themselves and/or the culture, and fall into world-weariness (bad conscience) or engage in ritualistic self-flagellation and hope that admissions of guilt will bring redemption in some far future time (ascetic ideal). I propose that we in philosophy try to be like Nietzsche's future strong types and endeavor to adopt Nietzsche's strong decadent approach: to engage in another "reversal and fundamental shift in values" that would be brought about by "another self-examination of man, another growth in profundity." By this I mean that we should adopt a version of Nietzsche's tragic approach by having the courage to understand our racialized selves (particularly our unconscious racialized instincts and habits) and not be sickened by them and thus frozen in inaction; by recognizing the role that we might play in supporting a racialized system of advantages and disadvantages; by having the courage to engage in open and honest attempts and experiments [*Versuche*] to revalue and redefine the racialized identities that characterize the racism of our time; and by adopting an artistic approach to crafting racialized identities at both the individual and group levels that express self-mastery of our racialized selves and help to affirm our lives.

This is not solely an American cultural problem. It is also one that plagues the profession of philosophy. There are some who call for a revaluation of the type of discourse and content of philosophy to potentially open it up to groups who are underrepresented in the communities of philosophy majors, graduate students, and professors.[31] Others have forcefully responded that such a change might signal the end of philosophy as we know it (philosophy will become too much like English, with its focus on gender and race, and more "touchy-feely, good-natured, friendly, mutually supportive").[32]

What is at stake here in revaluing philosophy? Of what are we afraid if we were merely to become open to changing the style of the practice of philosophy, its content as well as its practitioners? What would happen if we were to experiment (*versuchen*) with a philosophy that is more focused on gender and race and more "mutually supportive"? We might lose a philosophy that has been combatively argumentative as well as hostile to groups of people, and we might also lose something that has historically been distinctive about philosophy and perhaps even has made it more successful in the past.[33]

In this sense, philosophy as a discipline is a microcosm for our larger society where protests against a rash of deadly shootings of African American men by police officers result in long discussions about the patriotism of the protesters, their method of protest, or the ramifications of the ability of all police officers to do their job and little about the subject of the protest itself. We in the United States, and in the American philosophical community in particular, are running away from the "fearsome and questionable" roles that a traditional understanding of race (as well as gender, class, sexual orientation, etc.) has played in weakening our culture. As Nietzsche instructed us through his tragic philosophy, I then want to charge those of us in philosophy who have the courage and the strength to play "naively—that is, not deliberately but from overflowing power and abundance—with all that was hitherto called holy, good, untouchable, divine; for whom those supreme things that the people naturally accept as their value standards" (like those values of white supremacy) to engage in *Versuche* with our racialized identities that are often understood as "untouchable," god-given, and attached to unchanging or unchangeable value standards and focus on cultivating a great racialized health (*GS* 382).

Elsewhere, I presented a contemporary example of this sort of healthy racialized experiments.[34] For example, Lani Guinier and Gerald Torres describe the case of white prisoners on work-release and Black and Latino workers who could have formed a coalition to improve their work conditions in a meat processing plant in North Carolina. The white prisoners were unwilling to work in solidarity with the others because they did not see themselves as being part of the category of people who were being systematically disadvantaged in that work place. Using the Guinier and Torres's technical language, they needed to see themselves being treated as "politically Black" (as a target of systemic power), and not solely according to traditional racial categories. In this example, a white prisoner who was assigned to work in the same area of the plant as Latinx workers "complained that the work stinks 'but at least I ain't a nigger. I'll find work soon. I'm a white man.' To which a black worker responded, 'You might be white, but you came in wearing prison greens and that makes you as good as a nigger.'"[35] Because he was a prisoner, he was not working the same sort of jobs as unincarcerated white workers. He needs to experiment with his racial identity within the context of this workplace and see himself regarded as politically Black not just in the plant but also once he is released from prison and is categorized as an "ex-offender." Once he thinks and feels himself as being part of this category (as being a target of power), he can then also draw from group solidarity and use this group identity to try to affect change (to see this identity as a vehicle for change).[36]

Another example of healthy racialized *Versuche* is the work I do with a nonprofit credit building organization called Working Credit, NFP, where I am board president. I have argued that there is a particular type of weak racial pessimism that negatively affects people of color. I have coined the term "meta-oppression" describing an existential state brought on by the longevity, depth, and intransigence of racialized oppression—particularly systemic racism. In short, it is the oppression of being oppressed.[37] In other words, "Just as prolonged anxiety can trigger a clinical oppression, prolonged racialized oppression seems to be triggering a profound sense of resignation, weariness, and despair at the looming realization that American racism will not change significantly—ever" (Scott 2022). I argue that we can see this meta-oppression particularly in post–civil rights Black communities in America.

Working Credit's mission is to partner with individuals and communities to interrupt structural racism by providing credit-building education, one-on-one counseling, and access to the products people need to thrive financially.[38] American credit systems have been used to oppress people of color (e.g., the exclusion of people of color from mortgages guaranteed by the GI Bill just after WWII, "redlining," and contemporarily "in unregulated, high-interest, and often predatory financial services providers") (Scott 2022). This credit-based oppression has contributed to the racial wealth gap in the US, and the resulting meta-oppression has led many Black folks to believe that the type of credit that is a tool for wealth building (credit cards and bank loans) for many white middle-class people is "not for us," as a Working Credit client reported. One of the symptoms of meta-oppression is resignation to the current racial stasis, which is analogous to the nihilistic resignation of weak pessimistic decadence. Working Credit partners with participants of color to understand the systemic racism in credit systems, the resulting meta-oppression, and how to interrupt them. This interruption is not meant to be a cure for systemic racism, but it is meant to interrupt the ways it normally functions and to open up possible alternate ways of responding to it. This is similar to the way that Nietzschean tragic wisdom is meant to be an alternative response to the weakly pessimistic value system of the second period of *BGE* 32. Working Credit does this by educating participants about how to access credit products in order for them to flourish financially.

With this interruption, credit is revalued from an instrument of racism to a tool for resisting it. This educational interruption allows participants to adopt a strong pessimist approach to contending with racism. It enables them to experiment (*versuchen*) with their inner strengths (the ability to accrue a prime FICO score) and utilize the helpful credit that comes from it to realize their dreams and affirm their lives. In other words, they utilize the resulting "great [financial] health" to overcome traditional racist assumptions and affirm their lives despite the racism that still exists in society. Interviews with Working Credit participants reveal that they feel "empowered to combat systems of oppression, have expanded views of their life possibilities, and experience a renewed sense of self-worth" (Scott 2022).

In my view, these participants are engaging in Nietzschean joyful affirmation of the tragic heroes, who affirm their lives despite "hard, gruesome, evil, problematic aspects" of racism.

Working Credit has used my Nietzschean-influenced conceptions of racialized meta-oppression and racialized strong pessimism (Scott 2014) to understand why so many people of color are suspicious of credit, why they have resigned themselves to the fact that revolving credit (credit cards, mortgages, and lower-interest bank loans) is not for them, and how effective knowledge has been in these communities about how to access these credit products. Working Credit is currently partnering with the Urban Institute "to better understand how past experiences with—and feelings about—the credit system affect credit gains among Black, Latinx and White participants" (Scott 2022). They will then use this research to inform their program design and expand research in the field at large.

It is only with this sort of courageous racial experimentation will a "great seriousness" begin, will "the destiny of our [racialized collective] soul" change, and will the tragedy begin (*GS* 382). As I have argued in this chapter, philosophy as a discipline can do this if we can cultivate the great health and tragic wisdom to undertake such a task.

## Notes

1. See also the chapter in this volume that engages with the themes of race, tragedy, and identity: Jeremy Fortier "'To Affirm while Resisting': Ralph Ellison and Friedrich Nietzsche on Overcoming History." The chapters by Paul Kirkland, "Nietzsche and Tragic Identity," and Rebecca Bamford, "Disability, Power, and Life," also engage with the themes of tragedy and identity.

2. I develop my arguments about these connections in Scott 1998 and 2014. In terms of the secondary literature, Conway 1997; Havas 1995; and Reginster 2006 are book-length analyses of Nietzsche's positive philosophy that place an importance on nihilism, pessimism, and decadence.

3. Reginster 2006, 28–31.

4. As Paul Loeb 2008 has argued, the *Übermensch* is meant to signal a break in this fact of human existence in that this type will give meaning to past and present existence.

5. Reginster 2006, 8–11.

6. In the preface to *The Gay Science*, Nietzsche describes philosophy in this way: "A philosopher who has traversed many kinds of health, and keeps traversing them, has passed through an equal number of philosophies; he simply cannot keep

from transposing his states every time into the spiritual form and distance: this art of transfiguration *is* philosophy" (*GS* P:3).

7. See Paul Katsafanas 2016, chaps. 4 and 5, for this relationship between the drives, instincts, and values.

8. Loeb 2008, 167.

9. Katsafanas 2016 has presented a careful and incisive analysis of this aspect of Nietzsche's moral psychology. See also Havas 1995; Ahern 1995, chap. 2.

10. See also Conway 1997; Scott 1998.

11. Scott 2014.

12. Scott 2014, 303–8.

13. Loeb 2008, 172.

14. See Scott 2014 for a clarification of my use "cure" versus "antidote."

15. Conway 1995, 2–3.

16. While I am focusing on *GS* 382, I also want to contend that of the forty sections that comprise Book V of *The Gay Science*, nineteen sections discuss the role of art, the artist, and particular artistic media (acting, music, literature) in philosophical approaches to creating values and affirming life (both weak and strong decadent approaches). In particular, several of these sections are focused on describing Nietzsche's future strong types (he consistently refers to these types using the pronoun "we") as well as his relationship to them. It is beyond the scope of this chapter to make the argument for this claim, but it would seem that *GS* 382 is not unique in its description of what I am calling this tragic approach to philosophy. Instead, *GS* 382 can be read as an exemplar of Nietzsche's attempt in the second edition of *GS* (the new preface and Book V) to clarify the role of the tragic and tragedy (in terms of both its artistic and philosophical commitments) in Nietzsche's positive philosophy.

17. Ahern 1995, 46.

18. See Hatab 2008, 50–62, for a similar assessment of Nietzsche's reading of the Greeks of the tragic era.

19. In *GM* III:5, Nietzsche remarks that artists do not create values on their own, and as such they are "mere valets" to philosophers. It is because of statements like this that I contend that Nietzsche's tragic philosophy is not meant to be an art form itself and instead is meant to take on healthy characteristics exhibited by artists.

20. Several scholars have presented important discussions of Nietzsche's artist as a type and the role for this type in his positive philosophy as well as the role of the tragic artist. See Havas 1995, 45–68; Gillespie 1988; Ridley 1998, chap. 4; Register 2006, 191–92; Nehamas 1985.

21. The subtitle of *The Gay Science* is "La gaya scienza," and the title of section 343 is "The Meaning of Our Cheerfulness." In this section Nietzsche explained why those who engage in this new science he is introducing are happy, gay, and "cheerful." These new philosophers are responding to the developing realization of the death of God that Nietzsche likened to the setting of the "sun" of this traditional ideal. While this event is still remote for the majority in the culture, for these "firstlings

and premature births of the coming century" this event is a pressing and inevitable one and in them it inspires a "kind of light, happiness, relief, exhilaration, encouragement, dawn." This cheerfulness is occasioned by the hope that this coming event of the demise of these dominant weak decadent values signals the opportunity for new value creation: "At long last the horizon appears free to us again, even if it should not be bright; at long last our ships may venture out again, venture out to face any danger; all the daring of the lover of knowledge is permitted again; the sea, *our* sea, lies open again; perhaps there has never yet been such an 'open sea'—." See also Havas 1995, chap. 2.

22. See Reginster 2006, 242, 248–50.

23. See Janaway 2007, 253–54, for a comprehensive list of traits of Nietzsche's positive philosophy (or more specifically, a list of negative traits of this positive philosophy).

24. See Janaway 2007; Ridley 1998; Owen 2007; Hatab 2008; Conway 2008; Acampora 2006; and May 2011.

25. Note here the Dionysian reference to rebirthing oneself.

26. Reginster 2006, 29; Janaway 2007, 118–19, 122–23; Owen 2007, 98–102; Hatab 2008, 75–81; May 1999, 65–70, 116–18; Loeb 2010, 219; Acampora 2008, 40–42.

27. For more on this artistic procreative cruelty to the self, see, for example, Ahern 2012, 40–45; Richardson 2013, 770–71.

28. It is beyond the scope of this chapter to delve fully into the relationship between art/artists and Nietzsche's positive philosophy in the late works. See the following for informative discussions of this topic: Ridley 1998; Owen 2007, 132–34; Hatab 2008, 101–3, 180–82; Ahern 2012, 55, 63; Young 1992, 117–18, 126, 148; Ridley 1992, 419–23; Gardner 2013, 600.

29. I have developed this argument more fully in Scott 2014; Scott 2017; and Scott 2022.

30. Derrick Bell 1992; Tommie Curry 2014; and Scott 2017.

31. See, for example, Alcoff 2005; Davidson 2010; Medina 2012; and Zack 2017.

32. Wilson 2014.

33. The American Philosophical Association (2018) reports that of its members in 2017, 25 percent are women, 2.6 percent are African American, 1 percent are Native American/Alaska Natives, 6.8 percent are Asian, and 2.3 percent are Latinx.

34. Scott 2014.

35. Guinier and Torres 2009, 6.

36. Guinier and Torres 2009, 9–10, 52–53.

37. I have written an article introducing this concept: " 'This land of thorns is not habitable': Diagnosing the Despair of Racialized Meta-Oppression," *Critical Philosophy of Race*, forthcoming.

38. For more information about Working Credit's approach and methods, please see: https://www.workingcredit.org/.

# References

Acampora, Christa Davis, ed. 2006. *Nietzsche's "On the Genealogy of Morality": Critical Essays*. Lanham, MD: Rowman & Littlefield.

———. 2008. "Forgetting the Subject." In *Reading Nietzsche at the Margins*, eds. Steven Hicks and Alan Rosenberg, 34–56. West Lafayette, IN: Purdue University Press.

Ahern, Daniel. 1995. *Nietzsche as Cultural Physician*. University Park: Pennsylvania State University Press.

———. 2012. *The Smile of Tragedy: Nietzsche and the Art of Virtue*. University Park: Pennsylvania State University Press.

Alcoff, Linda. 2005. *Visible Identities: Race, Gender, and the Self*. Oxford: Oxford University Press.

American Philosophical Association. 2018. "Demographic Statistics on the APA Membership, FY2015 to FY2017." http://c.ymcdn.com/sites/www.apaonline.org/resource/resmgr/data_on_profession/FY2017-Demographic_Statistic.pdf.

Bell, Derrick. 1992. *Faces at the Bottom of the Well*. New York: Basic Books.

Curry, Tommy. 2014. "Chapter One: We Who Must Fight in the Shade: Derrick Bell's Philosophy of Racial Realism as the Basis for a Black Politics of Disempowerment." Unpublished manuscript, 1. https://www.academia.edu/2922493/Illuminated_in_Black_Chapter_1_We_Who_Must_Fight_in_the_Shade.

Conway, Daniel. 1997. *Nietzsche's Dangerous Game*. Cambridge: Cambridge University Press.

———. 2008. *Nietzsche's "On the Genealogy of Morality."* London: Continuum Books.

Davidson, Maria del Guadalupe, Kathryn Gines, and Donna-Dale Marcano, eds. 2010. *Convergences: Black Feminism and Continental Philosophy*. Albany: State University of New York Press.

Gardner, Sebastian. 2013. "Nietzsche's Philosophical Aestheticism." In *The Oxford Handbook of Nietzsche*, edited by Ken Gemes and John Richardson, 599–628. Oxford: Oxford University Press.

Gillespie, Michael Allen. 1998. "Nietzsche's Musical Politics." In *Nietzsche's New Seas*, eds. Michael Gillespie and Tracy Strong. Chicago: University of Chicago Press.

Guinier, Lani, and Gerald Torres. 2009. *Miner's Canary*. Cambridge, MA: Harvard University Press.

Hatab, Lawrence J. 2008. *Nietzsche's "On the Genealogy of Morality": An Introduction*. Cambridge: Cambridge University Press.

Havas, Randall. 1995. *Nietzsche's "Genealogy": Nihilism and the Will to Knowledge*. Cornell, NY: Cornell University Press.

Janaway, Christopher. 2007. *Beyond Selflessness: Reading Nietzsche's "Genealogy."* Oxford: Oxford University Press.

Katsafanas, Paul. 2016. *The Nietzschean Self: Moral Psychology, Agency, and the Unconscious*. Oxford: Oxford University Press.

Loeb, Paul S. 2008. "Suicide, Meaning, and Redemption." In *Nietzsche on Time and History*, ed. Manuel Dries, 163–90. Berlin: De Gruyter.
———. 2010. *The Death of Nietzsche's Zarathustra*. Cambridge: Cambridge University Press.
May, Simon. 1999. *Nietzsche's Ethics and his War on Morality*. Oxford: Oxford University Press.
———. 2011. *Nietzsche's "On the Genealogy of Morals."* Cambridge: Cambridge University Press.
Medina, José. 2012. *The Epistemology of Resistance: Gender and Racial Oppression, Epistemic Injustice, and Resistant Imaginations*. Oxford: Oxford University Press.
Nehamas, Alexander. 1985. *Nietzsche: Life as Literature*. Cambridge, MA: Harvard University Press.
Nietzsche, Friedrich. 1966. *Beyond Good and Evil*. Translated by Walter Kaufmann. New York: Vintage Books.
———. 1967. "Attempt at a Self-Criticism." In *The Birth of Tragedy*, translated by Walter Kaufmann. New York: Vintage Books.
———. 1967. *On the Genealogy of Morals*. Translated by Walter Kaufmann. New York: Random House.
———. 1968. *Twilight of the Idols*. Translated by R. J. Hollingdale. London: Penguin Books.
———. 1974. *The Gay Science*. Translated by Walter Kaufmann. New York: Vintage Books.
Owen, David. 2007. *Nietzsche's "On the Genealogy of Morality."* Montreal: McGill-Queen's University Press.
Richardson, John. 2016. "Nietzsche on Life's Ends." In *The Oxford Handbook of Nietzsche*, edited by Ken Gemes and John Richardson, 756–83. Oxford: Oxford University Press.
Ridley, Aaron. 1998. *Nietzsche's Conscience: Six Character Studies From the Genealogy*. Ithaca, NY: Cornell University Press.
Reginster, Bernard. 2006. *The Affirmation of Life: Nietzsche on Overcoming Nihilism*. Cambridge, MA: Harvard University Press.
Scott, Jacqueline. 1998. "Nietzsche and Decadence: The Revaluation of Morality." *Continental Philosophy Review* 31, no. 1 (Jan.): 59–78.
———. 2014. "Racial Nihilism as Racial Courage." *Graduate Faculty Philosophy Journal* 35, no. 1–2: 297–329.
———. 2017. "Effortful Agon: How to Think and Feel Differently about Race." In *Oxford Handbook on Race*, edited by Naomi Zack, 411–19. Oxford: Oxford University Press.
Scott, Jacqueline. 2022. "The Dual Credit Market Dilemma: How Working Credit Interrupts Structural Racism." *Working Credit NFP* (blog), Feb. 28. https://www.workingcredit.org/blog/financial-wellness/the-dual-credit-market.

Wilson, Robin. 2013. "Women Challenge Male Philosophers to Make Room in Unfriendly Field." *Chronicle of Higher Education*, Jan. 13, 2013. https://www.chronicle.com/article/Female-Philosophers-Shake-Up/136629.dilemma-how-working-credit-interrupts-structural-racism/.

Young, Julian. 1992. *Nietzsche's Philosophy of Art*. Cambridge: Cambridge University Press.

Zack, Naomi, ed. 2017. *The Oxford Handbook of Philosophy and Race*. Oxford: Oxford University Press.

## 12

# "To Affirm while Resisting"

## Ralph Ellison and Friedrich Nietzsche on Overcoming History

JEREMY FORTIER

Three decades after publishing one of the greatest American novels, *Invisible Man*, Ralph Ellison remarked to a correspondent, "My problem is to affirm while resisting."[1] With this remark, Ellison captured in a concise phrase something essential about his thought, along with the thought of an author he was quite familiar with—Friedrich Nietzsche.[2] But the thought is (for both authors, not to mention for their readers) just as Ellison suggests: a *problem*. For why should we *want* to be affirmative (rather than adopting a stance of principled, thorough-going criticism)? And how is it possible to affirm *while* resisting? Both Nietzsche and Ellison wrestled with these questions, and both concluded that finding something to affirm in one's history is a precondition for effectively resisting it.

Affirmation is arguably Nietzsche's highest ideal, but readers continue to question whether Nietzsche lived up to it, and whether the ideal is even coherent enough to be worth aspiring to.[3] Ellison shows how the ideal might be made useful for Americans, as part of his answer to an essential question for the country: how to understand its present and future in relation to its past. Ellison explicitly placed the problem of affirmation within that context. Thus, his statement that "[m]y problem is to affirm while resisting" appears in an exchange of letters about whether it would be fair to attribute to his thought a kind of "patriotism." This question had long troubled Ellison. His view of the United States had been by shaped the perspective he gained from living abroad, in Rome. Yet Ellison resisted attempts to frame his point of view as that of an "exile" (a category white journalists often applied him, as well to his contemporaries James Baldwin and Richard Wright). Ellison preferred to characterize his point of view as "vindictively American": "While I sympathize with those Negro Americans whose disgust with the racial absurdities of American life leads them to live elsewhere, my own needs—both as citizen and artist, make the gesture of exile seem mere petulance . . . I am too vindictively American, too full of hate for the hateful things in this country, and too possessed by the things I love here to be long away."[4] Returning to this line of thought toward the end of his career, Ellison commented: "I have never been able to dismiss democratic ideals so easily as have some of my colleagues whose racial background makes the rewards of democracy more easily available. Therefore I would affirm the principles while insisting that they be extended to all and on the basis of equality. It ain't the theory which bothers me, it's the practice. My problem is to affirm while resisting."[5] The problem would not have weighed so heavily on Ellison if principle and practice could be cleanly separated. But for Ellison, affirmation required understanding the United States, and *himself*, as a product of its history[6]—and so affirming himself as, in deeply meaningful ways, a product of the same forces that he was obligated to resist.[7] Was that really possible? Was it even desirable?

In this chapter, I will contend that Ellison's entire body of work constitutes a reflection on this question of how (or whether) his predicament as a product of American history was in fact something that could be affirmed. Ellison's thought has generally not been read in terms of the problem of affirmation, but readers of Nietzsche should be well-placed to correct that oversight. After all, Nietzsche set himself apart by claiming to speak on behalf of those "who seek our honor in being *affirmative*" (*TI* "Morality" 6; emphasis in original). And Ellison's notion of affirming *while resisting* should resonate with readers of an author who declared, "All in all and on the whole: some day I wish to be only a Yes-sayer," (*GS* 276) despite admitting that "[m]y taste, which is very much the opposite of a tolerant taste, is far from saying yes indiscriminately: it is very loath to say yes, and prefers to say no" (*TI* "Ancients" 2). Nietzsche is an author who can "say yes" and "say no" in the same breath ("denying and destroying are the conditions for yes-saying": *EH* "Destiny" 4). Ellison's *Invisible Man* does the same ("I condemn and affirm, say no and say yes, say yes and say no"[8]). And for Nietzsche no less than for Ellison, the challenge to be wrestled with—the object to be both affirmed and resisted, to which one says yes and says no—is the awareness of one's world and one's self as the product of a deeply troubling, unwanted historical inheritance. To that end, both Ellison and Nietzsche offer readers first-person narratives (fictional or autobiographical) which illuminate the thought that there is always a personal history to an individual's becoming affirmative, and that process of personal development is bound up with a process of coming to terms with one's embeddedness in a larger world history (as the inheritor of traditions, values, and obstacles that one would not choose for oneself but which shape one's position and possibilities in the world). To complete this task successfully is to square the circle of affirming while resisting: that is to say, to adequately come to terms with oneself as a product of history without allowing oneself to be defined by it.

There remain large differences between Ellison and Nietzsche, starting with the fact that equality was not a principle Nietzsche wanted to affirm. I will conclude this chapter by commenting on the inadequacy of Nietzsche's project, from Ellison's point of view. But those differences do not preclude the possibility of a productive dialogue. To the contrary: the fact that authors with significantly different histories and moral-political outlooks nevertheless reached some strikingly similar conclusions about how one should face and overcome one's history ought to be a cause for reflection.[9] And since Ellison himself reflected on Nietzsche, let me begin with an overview of the relationship between them.

## Ellison and Nietzsche: Elective Affinities

Ralph Ellison was no "Nietzschean," but Nietzsche was part of the intellectual atmosphere in which his ideas incubated. Ellison was not influenced by other authors in a conventional scholarly sense. He was an eager and ecumenical reader from childhood on, but he did not look for intellectual authorities so much as for thought-provoking echoes of, and variations on, his own experiences.[10] And, in that spirit, he circled around a constellation of concerns he shared with Nietzsche.

Throughout his formative years Ellison encountered Nietzsche regularly, although as ancillary to other interests. He first read Nietzsche around the age of ten, connecting the German philosopher's ideas to questions of ritual and folklore that he had already been considering in the plays of George Bernard Shaw (one of Nietzsche's earliest advocates in the English-speaking world).[11] Later, Ellison studied authors for whom Nietzsche was a crucial influence, notably the literary critic Kenneth Burke[12] and the French existentialist André Malraux.[13] His interest in Malraux was shared by his close friend and interlocutor Richard Wright, who was an avid reader of Nietzsche.[14]

Ellison was also closely engaged with two authors who had made a powerful impression on Nietzsche. The first was Ralph Waldo Emerson, one of Nietzsche's very favorite authors[15]—and Ellison's namesake—whose writings are commended to the skeptical protagonist of *Invisible Man* by a somewhat clueless older white character (thereby introducing into the novel the theme of "Fate," which is a key concern for all three members of the Nietzsche/Emerson/Ellison axis).[16] Another point of contact is Dostoevsky: in the prologue to *Invisible Man*, the protagonist calls to mind Dostoevsky's Underground Man,[17] whom Ellison acknowledged as a distant ancestor of his creation,[18] and *Notes from Underground* is the novel that (in a bowdlerized French edition) sparked Nietzsche's great admiration for Dostoevsky.[19] The relationships between Nietzsche and Dostoevsky, on the one hand, and Dostoevsky and Ellison, on the other, have been the subject of several studies; the relationship between Nietzsche and Ellison has only received a few scattered comments.[20] Yet in important respects Ellison's concerns overlapped with Nietzsche's more than either's did with Dostoevsky.

To see why, consider an intriguing-but-misleading comparison between the Underground Man and the Invisible Man suggested by Dostoevsky's leading English-language biographer, Joseph Frank. According to Frank, the Russian and American protagonists face the same problem: "The impossibility . . . of being able to live humanely within categories that, although he has learned to accept them about himself, have been imposed on him by others."[21] In other words, the Underground Man accepts as factually accurate the intellectual frameworks of a Western European culture he despises, and that frustrate all of his natural instincts, while "the invisible man stands in relation to white American culture and *its* ideas and values as Dostoevsky's underground man stands in relation to West European culture."[22] It is true enough that both characters struggle to define themselves in the shadow of a dominant culture that has deeply distorted a more natural sort of self-understanding, and they both alternate between resolute assertions of that more natural understanding and ambivalent concessions to the dominant culture.[23] But the Invisible Man does not actually reject the *ideas* of that culture out of hand because Ellison's own position was virtually the opposite of the one suggested by Frank: "It ain't the theory which bothers me, it's the practice." More precisely, Ellison thought that white Americans were deeply confused about the ideals that they claimed for themselves and projected much of their internal confusions and conflicts onto their images of Black Americans.[24] Since Ellison's objection was not so much to the ideals as to the distorted and distorting ways they had played out on the stage of American history, he saw his task as that of bringing to light how patterns of the past continued to shape the present, without presenting individuals as so locked in to those patterns as to be incapable of shaping a more productive future for themselves.[25] In short: Dostoevsky's question was how one could act in light of ideas whose force one was compelled to accept on one (intellectual) level and reject on another (instinctual) level; Ellison's question was how one could act in light of a historical inheritance whose power one could not avoid both acknowledging and resisting.[26] This latter question was also Nietzsche's, as we shall see in detail shortly.[27]

Before turning to Nietzsche, however, we should note that not only do Ellison and Dostoevsky sketch different predicaments, but they also point readers in different directions. For whereas Dostoevsky's depiction of the Underground Man's dilemma was part of a broader effort to lay the groundwork for a turn to Russian nationalism buttressed by Orthodox Christianity,[28] the Invisible Man is not impressed by representatives of traditional religious authority,[29] and he stays at a distance from advocates of racial separatism.[30] More generally, where Dostoevsky's portrait of the Underground Man amounts to an "attack on Western secular individualism,"[31] Ellison has been plausibly read as part of individualist traditions of American social thought,[32] and when he remarked that his protagonist "represents the Negro individualist," he meant it as a point of praise.[33] So although Ellison and Nietzsche did not share the same politics, they might have agreed about the insufficiency of Dostoevsky's more bluntly rejectionist response to the modern predicament.[34]

How, then, should modern human beings understand the relationship between their past and their future? For both Ellison and Nietzsche, the answer is not to reject the past but to affirm—*while* resisting. Moreover, both Ellison and Nietzsche argue that affirming the history one has unwillingly inherited is a precondition for successfully *overcoming* it (on this line of argument, sheer resistance, without affirmation, is inevitably ineffectual and self-frustrating). Since this conclusion is not an obvious one, I want to trace out how each author arrived at it, as follows.

## Nietzsche on Affirmation

In the words of one recent study, "Nietzsche regards the affirmation of life as his defining philosophical achievement."[35] The last word in that formulation deserves the most emphasis: for Nietzsche, affirmation is very much an *achievement*—an ideal whose desirability one has to discover gradually and then struggle to put into practice. In his own experience, affirmation had been not just an abstract ideal or the result of a logical argument but a deeply felt disposition that was characteristic of particular moments of his life and particular stages of his work as an author. To understand affirmation as a feature of Nietzsche's thought, then, we need to understand how he *became* affirmative.[36]

Nietzsche went out of his way to help readers do exactly that. One of his very last compositions was the autobiographical *Ecce Homo* (*Behold the Man*), which included a survey of all his earlier books, designed to help readers grasp the development of his thought.[37] To that end, Nietzsche classifies three of his books as "affirmative," "yes-saying" works: twice referring to *Dawn* as "a *Yes-saying* book," then adding, "This is true once again and in the highest degree of the *gaya scienza*" before introducing *Thus Spoke Zarathustra* by stating that "the basic conception of the work" is "the *thought of eternal return*, this highest possible formula of affirmation" (*EH* "Daybreak" 1; "Gay Science," "Zarathustra" 1). These books were written in succession between 1881 and 1885, so they belong to a particular period of Nietzsche's life.

But it was more than just Nietzsche's books that were affirmative during the early 1880s. *Ecce Homo* makes clear that the affirmativeness of the books was an extension of developments in his life. He makes this point by commenting that his highest possible formula of affirmation (the thought of eternal return) required a gestation period of eighteen months, during which

1. He experienced "a sudden and profoundly decisive alteration in my taste, in music above all."

2. He worked on both *The Gay Science* and *Thus Spoke Zarathustra* (the latter of which "may perhaps be counted as music";[38] as

for the former work, Nietzsche had emphasized its musical features just a few lines earlier[39]).

3. "The *affirmative* pathos par excellence, which I call the tragic pathos, dwelt within me to the highest degree."

4. And as a "symptom" of that "*affirmative* pathos," he was moved to set to music a *Hymn to Life* (Nietzsche stresses the importance of this little-known work by expressing the hope that one day it will be sung in his memory, though he notes that the text for the piece was actually "the astonishing inspiration" of his acquaintance Lou Salomé) (*EH* "Zarathustra" 1).[40]

These points are all connected: Nietzsche's affirmative pathos inspired him to create a new piece of music (the *Hymn to Life*), along with a piece of quasi-music (*Thus Spoke Zarathustra*), plus a book that included several songs (*The Gay Science*), and the music of each work reflects a distinctive disposition toward life. Anyone familiar with the works in question will spot the similarity: they all speak of Life as a kind of romantic partner to be passionately embraced and whole-heartedly loved.[41] This was the apex affirmation that Nietzsche encountered in himself, and expressed in his work, around the time he was working on *Thus Spoke Zarathustra*.

To affirm life in Nietzsche's fullest sense is, then, to love it with the passion of one's heart, to the point of being moved to express one's passion through music. Nietzsche had been concerned with the proper disposition toward life from the very outset of his career, initially stressing the obstacles to embracing it. What he eventually discovered was not that the obstacles to loving life could be entirely dispensed with so much as that they could be approached from a different perspective, which would make them more manageable. This complex dynamic—which integrates "No" into "Yes" rather than bypassing the former in favor of the latter—points to a kind of affirmation that is less inspired and ecstatic than what is suggested by passages such as the one from *Ecce Homo* I have just summarized. Yet the more nuanced picture is arguably truer to the whole of Nietzsche's experience and more feasible for others to emulate.

Nietzsche's wrestling with the problem of affirmation is evident from his first book, *The Birth of Tragedy Out of the Spirit of Music*, which proposes that the ancient Greek world was imbued with the deeply disturbing awareness that human beings exist in a chaotic, uncaring universe, resulting in the wisdom of Silenus (according to which it would be best to have never been born, and, failing that, best to die soon; see *BT* 3). According to the early Nietzsche, the Greeks were able to manage their disturbing awareness of the harsh reality of human existence through invigorating festivals of music, dance, and drama. In his words: "Art alone can re-direct those repulsive thoughts about the terrible or absurd nature of existence into representations with which man can live" (*BT* 7). Nietzsche hoped that a similar trick could be pulled off in his own time through the artwork of Richard Wagner (*BT* 15, 24). However, in the modern world artists would have to help audiences overcome a difficulty that the Greek world had not faced: consciousness of one's history. Nietzsche reflected on this problem in a series of essays written after *The Birth of Tragedy*. At this point Nietzsche was still part of the academic profession, but he was worried that the scholarly study of history would harm the broader culture, by showing people truths about themselves that would impair their future development: "When the historical sense reigns *without restraint*, and all its consequences are realized, it uproots the future because it destroys illusions and robs the things that exist of the atmosphere in which alone they can live" (*HL* 7).[42] Nietzsche notes that it can seem like a matter of justice to recognize the forces that have made us into what we are, but he stresses that the results will be stultifying: "The reason is that historical verification always brings to light so much that is false, crude, inhuman, absurd, violent, that the mood of pious illusion in which alone anything that wants to live can live necessarily crumbles away: for it is only in love, only when shaded by the illusion produced by love, that man is creative" (*HL* 7).[43] Nietzsche knew that the sources of a culture's problems sometimes had to be exposed.[44] But he was also convinced that anyone concerned with the future of a culture would ultimately have to choose between either: Life, including love and art, supported by the power of illusions (especially in the form of religion, and myth more generally) *or* Knowledge, especially historical knowledge, along with science, and the pursuit of truth more generally. In Nietzsche's estimate, the modern world was pushing people ever more in the direction of knowledge, without consideration of the consequences. What was needed in response were artists capable of redirecting people back toward life—and away from the scholar's deadening depictions of "empirical truth," in favor of inspiring illusions (*HL* 6; see further *HL* 9).[45]

    This was the mission Nietzsche assigned to Richard Wagner. Nietzsche believed that Wagner's operas could mold Germans' understanding of their history into a mythical form that would inspire them to create a new future

(*RWB* 3). As a result, both Wagner's artwork and Nietzsche's commentary on that work play with the possibility of creating a culture on the basis of semi–self-conscious illusions.[46] Ultimately, however, Nietzsche realized that Wagner offered only illusions—not illusions that could generate new forms of life.[47] Wagner was a symptom of modern problems, not a solution to them (*NCW*, "We Antipodes"; *CW* "Preface; *EH* "Human" 3).

At first Nietzsche admitted Wagner's failings only privately, but he acknowledged them publicly beginning with *Human, All Too Human*. In the process, he came close to inverting his earlier trade-off between life and knowledge: that is to say, *Human, All Too Human* often seems to be committed to the study of history and pursuing the truth at the expense of art or love.[48] At one point Nietzsche raises the question: Is his newfound commitment to truth at odds with life or not? His answer is suggestive, but not conclusive: the effect of knowledge on our attitude toward life is, he initially says, determined by our "temperament," but perhaps, in certain cases, a positive attitude toward life could be cultivated. Yet Nietzsche pointedly refrains from saying exactly how that would work, or the degree to which it has in fact worked for him (*HH* 34)[49]. Accordingly, the work looks at life through a lens that is more conflicted or melancholic than simply affirmative.[50]

But in Nietzsche's next work, *Dawn*, his disposition begins to change. This is, after all, the first of his writings that he retrospectively classified as "affirmative" (*EH* "Dawn" 1). Within the work itself, a key statement on affirmation is found in an aphorism that presents a character who claims to have emerged from a debilitating skepticism "healthier than ever, again in possession of my instincts," thereby having "learned to *affirm*!" (D 477). As this suggests, to become affirmative is to find a new relationship to one's instincts: to learn how those instincts can be engaged and acted upon, rather than held at bay.[51] Bound up with this new confidence in his instincts is Nietzsche's new emphasis on the "passion for knowledge"—that is to say, an aspect of existence that demands to be whole-heartedly embraced (*D* 429; see further *D* 450).[52] This, in turn, changes his relationship to things he might otherwise disapprove of: for instance, the undeniable pain entailed in suffering from a protracted illness, or learning that one is the product of a historical process in which one finds much that is objectionable—these fates have something to recommend them, insofar as they give us new ways of exercising the passion for knowledge (new challenges spur us on to new discoveries, broadening and deepening our understanding of ourself and of the world) (*D* 114 and 197).[53] In an extension of this line of thought,

Nietzsche contends that the world as it is offers a kind of beauty that is sufficient to bring happiness, not because all things immediately win one's approval but because, as objects whose investigation serves to enhance our knowledge, they contribute to our genuine enjoyment of existence (*D* 550).

With *Dawn*, then, the reader no longer faces such a stark a choice between life and love *or* knowledge and commitment to truth. We can have both, but with a caveat. "Love at first sight" is an illusion; we must learn to love, especially in cases where we are initially inclined to see nothing loveable (*GS* 334).[54] Thus, in *The Gay Science* affirmation moves to center stage, particularly in the opening aphorism of the fourth book, where Nietzsche declares "what I wish from myself" for the new year, namely, the *amor fati* (love of fate) that would allow him to be "only a Yes-sayer!" (*GS* 276; see further *GS* 341 and the quotation from Emerson used as the epigraph to the first edition). As inspiring as this wish of Nietzsche's is, less prominent passages provide a more nuanced picture of what affirmation entails—a picture that is less about being *only* a Yes-sayer than about becoming *primarily* a Yes-sayer.

For Nietzsche, the relationship between "yes-saying" and "no-saying" is complex because the desire to affirm is a natural instinct that it is easily misdirected (what we say yes to may be what we see least clearly because we long so deeply for something—*anything*—to say yes to; see further *GM* III.I and III.28). As a result, in order to learn how to affirm properly we need to focus less on where we are initially inclined to say yes and more on where we say no. This point emerges in the first book of *The Gay Science*. Here Nietzsche discusses the *renouncer*—someone who "wants to fly higher and further than all affirmers." But at the end of the aphorism, Nietzsche pivots: he now refers to the renouncer as "this affirmer!" The renouncer and the affirmer, it turns out, are driven by the same desire—the difference is that the first type of person "strives for a higher world," and, to that end, renounces the all-too-human world. In other words, what makes people renounce the world is not a lack of desire to affirm but a feeling that our world cannot satisfy the desire (*GS* 27).[55] This implies that the renouncer might be made into an affirmer in the sense Nietzsche admires if the renouncer can be persuaded to revalue the all-too-human world (finding something within that world capable of satisfying their desire). Consequently, there is—as Nietzsche explains in the fourth book (i.e., after having declared his wish to be "only a Yes-sayer")—something to be said "*in favor of criticism*": "When we criticize, we are not doing something arbitrary and impersonal; it is, at least very often, proof that there are living, active forces within us shedding skin. We negate and have to negate because something in us wants to live and affirm itself, something we might not yet know or see!—This in favor of criticism" (*GS* 307). So notwithstanding Nietzsche's commitment to "yes-saying," he identifies a partial or qualified point in favor of criticism insofar as that criticism reflects a desire for something *worth* affirming. It follows that the inclination to renounce or criticize is not as much of a problem as it first seems to be, because that inclination amounts to a frustrated and submerged desire for something to affirm. And so although Nietzsche aspires to some day be "only a Yes-sayer," that "Yes" is one that will have to grow out of, and reflect back on, an initial "No!"[56] What distinguishes a properly affirmative human being is therefore not that they find nothing in the world worth opposing. To the contrary: an affirmative individual will be distinguished by knowing how to select the most rewarding enemies because they understand that a "No" worth having is one that can be made instrumental to a larger "Yes!"[57]

It is for this reason that, beginning with *Dawn*, Nietzsche's approach to history changes; it becomes part of a "revaluation of values," which means that Nietzsche does not shy away from scrutinizing what is at first sight ugliest in the historical legacy which he is an heir to, because he looks to it confident that he can find something worth loving (affirming) in it.[58] But while Nietzsche no longer wants to conceal the facts of history, he does want to change how they are interpreted.[59]

This task has to be carried out not just at the cultural level but at the personal level. This point—and Nietzsche's understanding of affirmation more generally—may be most revealingly articulated in the epilogue to a work from the end of his career, where Nietzsche looked back on a figure who had dominated his beginning: *The Case of Wagner*.[60] Here Nietzsche discusses affirmation in relation to both his personal history (via his relationship to Wagner) and world history (via Wagner's relationship to the question "What is modern?"). He also cites what is now probably the most famous result of his historical inquiries: his contrast between "master morality" and "slave morality" (a footnote directs the reader to his longer statement about the contrast in the first essay of *On the Genealogy of Morality*; in the present text, Nietzsche will refer to "slave morality" as "Christian morality"). He distinguishes the two positions specifically with respect to their capacity for affirmation: "Master morality *affirms* just as instinctively as Christian morality *negates*." But he also makes clear that this dichotomy is only provisional. Nietzsche is not claiming to be simply on the side of "master morality" over and against "Christian morality." In fact, he says,

"These opposite forms in the optics of value are *both* necessary,"[61] and in any case you can't simply negate "Christian" negation—it is a fact of life to be confronted, not something that can be accepted or dispensed with at will (that is to say, for modern human beings, Christianity's perspective is part of our shared inheritance, shaping how we see and are disposed toward the world, whether we like it or not). However, what one can do is what Wagner did not do: face what one has inherited and admit the internal conflict that it generates (which requires, first of all, recognizing that there *is* an opposition between "master morality" and "Christian morality," rather than hoping for a seamless synthesis). Nietzsche therefore claims to differ from Wagner not in the fact of being "modern" (which is also to say, Christian), but in being willing to face squarely the conflict that this entails.[62] I take it, then, that Nietzsche has to say both "Yes" and "No" because he wants to affirm Christianity's contribution to what he is, without affirming its evaluation of what he is.

Accordingly, in the final paragraph of the epilogue to *The Case of Wagner*, Nietzsche says both "No" and "Yes" in the following way: on the one hand, he associates himself with Goethe's instinctive aversion to what the symbol of the Christian cross represents in world history;[63] on the other hand, he emphasizes that insofar as a "case" of "Christian morality" such as the case of Wagner proves to be "*instructive*," it is also something for which he can be grateful (grateful, that is, for what it contributes to his understanding[64]). The fact that Nietzsche presents these thoughts side by side suggests that he does not expect to transcend the tension between them in any straightforward way; rather, for Nietzsche, the ability to affirm becomes all the more impressive insofar as it has to confront things that provoke one's serious resistance.[65]

Because Nietzsche wants readers to *become* affirmative in this self-reflective and self-critical way, one of his aims as an author is to jolt readers into recognizing and wrestling with tensions embedded in human existence, and because he thought that it was typical of modern individuals (such as Wagner) to try to evade those tensions rather than engage with them, he often employs very extreme forms of anti-modern rhetoric (as if he is trying to convince readers that there is still much in the world that is worth fighting over).[66] By making his "No" so prominent—and so intemperate—Nietzsche made it too easy for his thought to be appropriated for reactionary purposes.[67] This is a serious failing of his work, but it is a failing which makes it all the more important to emphasize what he was ultimately aiming for, which was to integrate every "No" into a greater "Yes" (which requires that one find a way to affirm what one would at first prefer to reject outright). Merely resisting (saying "No") came easily to Nietzsche; the challenge that he set for himself, and for readers, was to affirm *while* resisting. One of the readers to take up that challenge was Ralph Ellison.

## Ellison on Affirmation

Ralph Ellison and Fredrich Nietzsche were both writers who would have liked to be musicians. In fact, they both played with the notion that they really were musicians: we have already seen Nietzsche's suggestion that *Thus Spoke Zarathustra* "may perhaps be counted as music"; Ellison, while working on *Invisible Man*, commented to a correspondent, "I told Langston Hughes in fact, that it's the blues, but nobody seems to understand what I mean."[68] Twelve years after the novel was published, Ellison returned to this line of thought in the introduction to his first volume of essays, *Shadow and Act*, disclosing in the opening sentence that at one point in his writing career he regarded himself "in my most secret heart at least—as a musician."[69]

For Ellison as for Nietzsche, the aspiration to be a musician was bound up with an aspiration to be affirmative. For both, music was significant insofar as it embodied and engendered an overall attitude toward life. In the introduction to *Shadow and Act* Ellison draws this connection by explaining how he and his childhood friends absorbed and transformed the different forms of popular culture they encountered:

> Behind each artist there stands a traditional sense of style, a sense of the felt tension indicative of expressive completeness, a mode of humanizing reality and of evoking a feeling of being at home in the world. It is something which the artist shares with the group, and part of our boyish activity expressed a yearning to make any-and-everything of quality *Negro American*—to appropriate it, possess it, re-create it in our own group and individual images. And we recognized and were proud of our own group's style wherever we discerned it. . . . We did not fully understand the cost of that style but we recognized within it an <u>affirmation of life</u> beyond all question of our difficulties as Negroes.[70]

It was this approach to making art, Ellison says, that he eventually brought with him to his career as a writer.[71] But Ellison found that approach to art above all in music, and he comments on it most extensively with respect to the blues and flamenco. In these different artforms, Ellison detected a similar source of appeal: "Perhaps what attracts us most to flamenco, as it does to the blues, is the note of unillusioned affirmation of humanity which it embodies."[72] To draw out the parallels a bit further: in both, Ellison saw "a communal art," or "ritual,"[73] representing both "a total way of life" and "an attitude toward life,"[74] which confronts "a world viewed as basically impersonal and violent" by celebrating "man's ability to deal with chaos,"[75] thereby challenging familiar dualities of pessimism and optimism by "speak[ing] to us *simultaneously* of the tragic and comic aspects of the human condition . . . precisely because [the participants'] lives have combined these modes."[76] In other words, for Ellison, the blues and flamenco were "affirmative" artforms precisely because they were *tragicomic*. As he observed, "[The] flamenco voice resembles the blues voice, which mocks the despair stated explicitly in the lyric, and it expresses the great human joke directed against the universe, that joke which is the secret of all folklore and myth: that though we be dismembered daily we shall always rise up again."[77] What Ellison admires, then, are forms of art that can give a world-affirming meaning to a world that would otherwise be meaningless.[78]

This was, to repeat, an accomplishment that Ellison associated above all with music, but it was not exclusive to music (e.g., he admired the way Romare Bearden's paintings captured "abiding rituals and ceremonies of affirmation"[79]). And in one of his most important essays Ellison contended that at a particular point of world history it also became a task for novelists:

> Perhaps the novel evolved in order to deal with man's growing awareness that behind the façade of social organization, manners, customs, myths, rituals and religions of the post-Christian era lies chaos. Man knows, despite the certainties which it is the psychological function of his social institutions to give him, that he did not create the universe, and that the universe is not at all concerned with human values. . . . We cannot live, as someone has said, in the contemplation of chaos, but neither can we live without an awareness of chaos, and the means through which we achieve that awareness, and through which we assert our humanity most significantly, is in great art. In our time the most articulate art form for defining ourselves and for asserting our humanity is the novel.[80]

Ellison concluded this essay by asserting that although the novelist was needed at a particular point in time, the task to which novelists are called is to identify features of human life that are timeless in order to show readers how to "affirm that which *is* stable in human life."[81] For some readers, Ellison is torn somewhat incoherently between this appreciation of stability and awareness of chaotic flux.[82] But from Ellison's perspective, this is an unavoidable tension which underscores the importance of giving readers a better sense for the "tragicomic"[83]—that is to say, a perspective from which human life *can* be affirmed.

To frame the issue of affirmation at the level of communal ritual is, however, to miss an important dimension of the issue. Ellison may have aspired to play the role of Wagner (i.e., giving a new life and meaning to a larger culture),[84] but he also played the role of Nietzsche in the sense that I outlined above (i.e., giving meaning to an individual life, apart from or prior to any communal project). Affirmation is therefore a theme that Ellison raises not just in the context of the rituals of blues or flamenco but also in the context of how an individual can make sense of themselves as a product of, but not defined by, a larger history.

Ellison highlighted this more individual perspective on affirmation in his response to a criticism of *Invisible Man* by the influential literary critic Irving Howe. In his response to Howe, Ellison commented, "Being a Negro American involves a *willed* (who wills to a Negro? *I* do!) affirmation of self as against outside pressures—an identification with the group as extended through the individual self which rejects all possibilities that do not involve a basic resuscitation of the original American ideals of social and political justice."[85] Ellison sharpens this line of thought in an interview that touches upon the relationship of artists to their history. After the interviewer questions whether African American authors ought to leave the United States in order to gain a perspective from which to understand themselves more clearly, Ellison responds that he would rather change the conventional understanding of the situation that he has inherited: "Despite the historical past and the injustices of the present, from *my* perspective there is something further to say. I have to *affirm* my forefathers and *must* affirm my parents or be reduced in my own mind to a white man's inadequate—even if unprejudiced—conception of human complexity."[86] In this way, Ellison binds himself to his history in order to better determine his place within it.[87]

And so I would say of Ellison, much as I said of Nietzsche: he is looking for a way affirm the contribution of a historical inheritance to what he is, without affirming its evaluation of what he is. Yet here we should recall that Ellison also spoke of affirmation as a problem, and he treated it as a problem most extensively in *Invisible Man*.

### Ellison's *Invisible Man* as a Fable About Affirmation

Affirmation becomes a prominent, explicit theme of *Invisible Man* only toward its end, but when it emerges, it does so as the culmination of the (unnamed) narrator's long process of self-development, and particularly as the result of the narrator's recurring reflections on the dying words of his grandfather.

The novel's main narrative traces the narrator's development from his time as a fairly timid and conventional high school graduate in a Southern town through his life as a resident of Harlem, where he becomes politically active and, as a consequence, much more confident and independent-minded but also embroiled in controversies that eventually drive him into a self-described "state of hibernation."[88] Throughout the main narrative, the narrator is vexed by the advice of his grandfather, who had been born into slavery and on his deathbed declared,

> Son, after I'm gone I want you to keep up the good fight. I never told you, but our life is a war and I have been a traitor all my born days, a spy in the enemy's country ever since I give up my gun back in Reconstruction. Live with your head in the lion's mouth. I want you to overcome 'em with yeses, undermine 'em with grins, agree 'em to death and destruction, let 'em swoller you till they vomit or bust wide open.[89]

For the narrator, these words had "a tremendous effect": it became "a constant puzzle which lay unanswered in the back of my mind," how this ostensibly "quiet old man who never caused any trouble" could have understood his way of living to be a contribution to a *war effort*.[90] The narrator is especially puzzled by—and uncomfortable about adopting—the duplicity ("treachery") that his grandfather's advice seems to recommend.[91] In the early stages of his odyssey the narrator will be equally uneasy when older Black men instruct him about the importance of lying, above all for dealing with (and manipulating) whites.[92] The narrator accepts this as a practical necessity,[93] but he cannot reconcile himself to that fact as comfortably as the older characters (and he is angry when he learns that *they* have been lying to *him*[94]). The narrator's preference for truth over lies also drives the action near the end of the novel. Here, after becoming disillusioned with his erstwhile political allies, the narrator tries to put his grandfather's advice into practice and "overcome them with yeses," but when he finds that this means saying "yes" always only to the false and repellant beliefs of others ("saying 'yes' against the nay-saying of my stomach—not to mention my brain"), he becomes "ill of affirmation" and consequently driven into hibernation.[95] So the narrator's first attempts at following his grandfather's advice teach him that he cannot affirm what he does not believe.

Although the narrator is unable to follow his grandfather's advice about being affirmative, he does not lose his sense of fight. To the contrary: when we first meet the narrator, in the prologue to the novel (which is discontinuous with the main narrative), he speaks to us from out of his state of hibernation, and it quickly becomes evident that although he is living in isolation, his "hibernation" is part of a stealthy but persistent struggle against the society that he has retreated from. In particular, the narrator is proud of having learned that it is possible to "carry on a fight" against others "without their realizing it"—for instance, by his living, undetected, "rent-free in a building rented strictly to whites," in a basement where he siphons off power from the city's electrical grid at no expense.[96] This scheme reflects the narrator's confidence and ingenuity, rather than his capacity for deceit (the very first anecdote that the narrator tells us about himself involves him fighting a man who insults him in the street[97]). Accordingly, the narrator is prepared to enter into direct conflict as circumstances require: "A hibernation is a preparation for a more overt action."[98]

This promise is picked up in the epilogue, where we see the narrator in his hibernation again, only now strongly hinting that he is preparing to leave it.[99] He does so, however, on the basis of a renewed reflection over his grandfather's dying words. For notwithstanding the failure of his initial attempt to follow his grandfather's advice about yes-saying, the narrator still wants to make sense of the old man's words. To that end, the narrator ponders: "Could he have meant—hell, he *must* have meant the principle, that we were to affirm the principle on which the country was built and not the men, or at least not the men who did the violence? Did he mean say 'yes' because he knew the principle was greater than the men, greater than the numbers and the vicious power and all the methods used to corrupt its name?"[100] This passage has attracted a lot of attention because of its apparent political salience: it has seemed (to both friendly and critical readers) to be an assertion of the basic goodness of the foundational institutions and ideals of the United States (as embodied by the Constitution and the Declaration of Independence), notwithstanding their flawed applications over the course of American history.[101] Ellison sometimes spoke along those lines.[102] But Ellison's narrator is not making an argument from authority or presenting a patriotic dogma.[103] The context makes clear that the situation is more complex, for at least three key reasons.[104]

Most obviously, the narrator's suggestion that his grandfather may have wanted him to "affirm the principle on which the country is built" is not really presented as the solution to his problems; it is, rather, the first *question* that he asks in a long string of questions (none of which is given a straightforward answer). Moreover, in one of his next questions the narrator makes clear that if the "principle" is superior to "the men," it is not so much because the principle *as established* was superior but because *his understanding* of it is.[105] Most importantly, the narrator in the epilogue is the same character, in the same scene, that we encountered in the prologue: that is to say, someone who is "carrying on a fight" with the society around him.[106] Accordingly, in the epilogue the narrator questions his grandfather with respect to affirmation but not with respect to whether "our life is a war," and the narrator's problem is therefore to determine whether his grandfather's instruction to affirm can be integrated into the resistance that he is already engaged in.[107] By the end of *Invisible Man*, then, readers are not left with a solution so much as a problem: to affirm while resisting.

## Concluding Remarks

To recapitulate: Ellison and Nietzsche both recognize themselves as the products of a historical inheritance whose evaluations they contest, and in response, they both search for something to affirm from within that history, not in order to passively acquiesce to it, but to show that it can have a meaning that is superior to the one that has been commonly attributed to it. So understood, affirmation is not at odds with resistance; affirmation is the precondition of effective resistance.[108]

For both Nietzsche and Ellison, then, self-knowledge and historical knowledge are intertwined, because when one devotes careful attention to oneself, one discovers that one is in many ways quite different from how one is "supposed" to be (whether by one's self or by others), and that insight can help one to recognize that the history of which one is a part may also be different from what it has generally been supposed to be.[109] This way of proceeding can render one troublingly uncertain about the truth of any particular set of political or moral principles, as Ellison recognized.[110] But he also recognized that it promised to make the principles which one eventually arrived at more truly one's own.

That said, Ellison also challenges Nietzsche by suggesting that self-knowledge ultimately serves purpose beyond self-affirmation. From Ellison's perspective, Nietzsche's career would have seemed myopic or stunted, insofar as Nietzsche remained preoccupied with autobiographical inquiry to the end of his life (continually reexamining and reinterpreting his life in order to find something worth affirming from within it).[111] Ellison's Invisible Man also turns inward and tells the story of his life, but, as we have seen from the novel's epilogue, the Invisible Man's self-reflection leads him gradually away from studying himself and toward searching for political principles that he could affirm along with others—"on the basis of equality," as Ellison would emphasize at the end of his career. By this Ellison meant not so much that equality is a state to be brought about, as it is a buried truth about the United States to be brought to light—that the nation has always been no less Black than white.[112] And this is why, for Ellison, his protagonist's development is a movement "from invisibility to visibility" (or, in the narrator's words, a search for "recognition").[113] In short: for Ellison, seeking self-knowledge was a way to find a more just place in the social order, rather than a more secure place beyond it. Viewed in that light, Nietzsche's kind of affirmation (self-affirmation) can only be a beginning, not an ending.

This is not to say that Nietzsche's notion of affirmation has no relevance for contemporary criticisms of racial domination. For instance, Christopher Lebron's pioneering account of the Black Lives Matter movement finds one of its major sources of inspiration in Zora Neale Hurston's "spirit of Emersonian self-affirmation"—a spirit that resonates with elements of Nietzsche as well as Emerson.[114] But both Hurston and Emerson avoided concrete political commitments and social movements to protect their sense of individual independence and self-sufficiency. Nietzsche might have sympathized with their disposition; Ellison would not have.[115]

Yet if Ellison gives us reason to question the sufficiency of Nietzsche's ideal of self-affirmation, both authors can help us to see why coming to terms with oneself as a product of one's history demands neither passively accepting that history nor attempting to escape from it, but instead, finding a way to affirm *while* resisting.

## Notes

1. Ellison 2019, 797.
2. Ellison mentioned his youthful reading of Nietzsche in conversation (see Ellison 1991a, 247). Textual parallels between *Invisible Man* and works of Nietzsche are noted by Germana (2018, 57–68). I give a more detailed overview of the relationship between the two authors in the next section of this chapter—since, as we will see, the relationship has generally been given less attention than it deserves by the scholarly literature. Ellison's interests in Nietzsche may have been overlooked in part because he has been both praised (see Morel 2004, 16n33) and criticized (see Foley 2010, 1, 340) as a relatively straightforward sort of Cold War liberal. Ellison's interest in Nietzsche doesn't fit easily into that picture.
3. On affirmation as Nietzsche's highest ideal, see Reginster 2007 and Richardson 2020. For some of the difficulties, consider Loeb 2021 and Stern 2021.
4. Ellison 2019, 545. Throughout his career, Ellison generally preferred the term "Negro American" (see Ellison 1995b, 69, 131–32).
5. Ellison 2019, 797.
6. See Brand 2022, 192; Warren 2003, 59.
7. Ellison 1995a, 740–41.
8. Ellison 1995c, 579.
9. See also the following essay in this volume that engages with the themes of race, tragedy, and identity: Jacqueline Scott, "'The Great Seriousness Begins': Nietzsche's Tragic Philosophy and Philosophy's Role in Creating Healthier Racialized Identities."
10. Ellison 1995a, 141, 185–86.
11. Ellison 1995b, 247.
12. See Ellison 1995a, 60; as well as Hawhee 1999; and Eddy 2003, 52–53, 84–85.
13. See Ellison 1995a, 205; as well as Jackson 2002, 169–70; and Anderson 2005, 84–85.
14. Wright 2006, 25, 127. On Richard Wright and Nietzsche, see Ward and Butler 2008, 283–84.
15. See Zavatta 2019.
16. Ellison 1995c, 41–44. On Ellison's name, see Jackson 2002, 2–3, explaining that Ellison's father chose the name as a signal of his intention to raise his son as a poet. But Ellison's father died when he was three, and he grew up "puzzle[d]" by the name, and "uncomfortable" with it (see Ellison 1995a, 194–96). In connection with this detail, it is worth noting Marc Conner's characterization of Ellison's ambiguous relationship to his namesake (and, thereby, to the inheritance of both his family and his country): "*Invisible Man* offers not merely a satire of Emerson, as many have argued, and not merely an apology for Emerson; rather, Ellison (characteristically) both *affirms and denies* the Emersonian heritage" (2004, 181; emphasis added). Although the relationship between Emerson and Ellison will not

be my topic, the question of how to respond to an unwelcome inheritance will be. On Ellison's critical revision of Emerson's notions of fate, see Eddy 2003, 16–18.

17. See Cash 2003 and Cope 1976.

18. Ellison 1995c, xix; Ellison 1995a, 541; Ellison 2019, 680.

19. See Clowes 2016. Nietzsche's most emphatic commendation of Dostoevsky is in *TI* "Skirmishes" 45.

20. On Nietzsche and Dostoevsky, see the essays collected in Love and Metzger 2016. On Ellison and Dostoevsky, see the sources cited in n17, above.

21. Frank 1990, 35.

22. Frank 1990, 35 (emphasis in original).

23. This problem that Ellison was dealing with has also been read in terms of W. E. B. Du Bois's notion of "double consciousness" (see Lyne 1992).

24. "Since the beginning of the nation, white Americans have suffered from a deep inner uncertainty as to who they really are. One of the ways that has been used to simplify the answer has been to seize upon the presence of black Americans and use them as a marker, a symbol of limits, a metaphor for the 'outsider' " (Ellison 1995a, 586); "It was our Negro 'misfortune' to be caught up associatively in the negative side of this basic dualism of the white folk mind, and to be shackled to almost everything it would repress from conscience and consciousness" (Ellison 1995a, 102); "Race became a major cause, form, and symbol of the American hierarchical psychosis. As the unwilling and unjust personification of that psychosis and its major victim, the Afro-American took on the complex symbolism of social health and social sickness" (Ellison 1995a, 783).

25. See Ellison 1995a, 581–88, 855–60.

26. In the words of Ealy (2013): "Where Underground Man's puzzle is theoretical or philosophical, the Invisible Man's is historical. Invisible Man's puzzle begins with his family history, but can only be resolved by placing this personal history within the context of the larger American history" (188).

27. The parallel between Ellison and Nietzsche on this point is noted by Germana 2018, 64–68.

28. For a penetrating analysis, see Orwin 2007, 6–7. On Dostoevsky's nationalism in particular, see Scanlan 2002.

29. Ellison 1995c, 133. Here, the Reverend Homer A. Barbee gives a fantastic account of the history of the college that the narrator is attending—an account which justifies the authority of the college in very much the terms which Nietzsche says are typically used to ground the authority of law, namely, "God *gave* it, the forefathers *lived* it" (see *A* 57). But after Barbee's sermon, the narrator observers, "Barbee was blind." The novel's account of the college is modelled after Ellison's disenchanting experience at Tuskegee University. Ellison himself has been described as "thoroughly secular" (Harriss 2017, 17).

30. Ellison 1995c, 375–76. Ellison criticized what he called "the illusion of secessionism" (Ellison 1995a, 583)—although he was not altogether dismissive of its appeal (see Seaton 2004, 29–30; as well as Warren 2003, 17–19).

31. Orwin 2007, 25.

32. See Albrecht 2012.

33. Ellison 1995a, 344 (see further Ashe 2002, 53).

34. "A word in the Conservatives' Ear.—What we did not know before, what we know today, could know today—a *regression*, any about-turn of any kind or to any extent, is just not possible" (*TI* "Skirmishes" 43); "We 'conserve' nothing, neither do we want to return to any past" (*GS* 377). On the contrast between Nietzsche and Dostoevsky in this regard, see further Gillespie 2017, 157–60.

35. Reginster 2006, 2–3, 50, 228. See further Richardson 2020, 39–80, 353–93.

36. On the approach to philosophy that this implies, consider a comment by Pierre Hadot: "We ought not to forget that many a philosophical demonstration derives its evidential force not so much from abstract reasoning as from an experience which is at the same time a spiritual exercise" (1995, 107; see also 272). On reading Nietzsche in the spirit suggested by Hadot, see further Fortier 2020, 1–3; Meyer 2019, 87–88; and Ure 2019, 1–2.

37. The importance of this autobiography has recently been highlighted from a variety of perspectives by the essays collected in Martin and Large 2021.

38. On the self-consciously musical qualities of the work, see further Parkes 2005, xxviii–xxxi.

39. See *EH* "Gay Science," where Nietzsche singles out for discussion two sections of the work: "The Songs of Prince Vogelfrei" (which he says are reminiscent of "that unity of *singer*, *knight*, and *free spirit* which distinguishes the marvelous early culture of the Provençal people") and "To the Mistral" ("a boisterous dancing song," and "a perfect Provençalism"). Although these songs are probably the least well-known part of the work, Higgins (2000, 16–21) shows that they illuminate its animating spirit.

40. For the text, score, and history of the "Hymn to Life," see Schaberg 1995, 140–49. The development of the work is much more complex than Nietzsche's remark in *Ecce Homo* suggests, but he evidently wanted to associate it with this period of his life in particular.

41. From the "Hymn to Life": "Surely—thus a friend loves a friend / As I love you, inscrutable Life!"; "With all my strength, I embrace you / Let your flame ignite my soul!" See also *GS* 339 and *TSZ* III.10.

42. This discussion is an extension and completion of themes from the first *Untimely Meditation* (see Brooks 2018, 29, 70).

43. See further Lemm 2009, 98–99.

44. As Brooks (2018, 103–11) points out, Nietzsche is engaging in such an exercise himself, but that fact only intensifies his emphasis on the dangers of "critical history."

45. To be sure, in the optimal case people will strike an appropriate balance between historical and unhistorical awareness (see *HL* 1 [Nietzsche 1997, 63]), but in the current context that demands rebalancing our awareness very much toward the latter (cf. Franco 2011, 4–5; Lampert 2017, 61–62).

46. See Fortier 2020, 106–9; Gemes and Sykes 2014, 97–100.

47. See Franco 2011, 9–10; as well as Lampert 2017, 106, 115–16.

48. On studying history, see *HH* 1 and 2 (and, on the contrast between this approach to history and the approach proposed in *HL*, see Richardson 2020: 331–32). On committing oneself to the pursuit of truth (which Nietzsche, at this point, distinguishes from possessing truth in some definitive way), see the quotation from Descartes used "In Place of a Preface" and aphorism 633. On the limitations that this new posture places on art, see Franco 2011, 40–41; for the limitations on the capacity for love, see Fortier 2020, 186n4.

49. Lampert (2017, 171–72) attributes the ideal temperament to Nietzsche, but to my mind it is more striking that at this point Nietzsche does not quite claim this for himself (particularly when this aphorism is compared to the emphatic affirmations of later works).

50. This point is made in different ways by Clark 2015, 229; Fortier 2020, 65–66; Franco 2011, 47–48; Meyer 2019, 95–98; Ure 2019, 56–57.

51. Nietzsche's point here is not that skepticism is to be abandoned but that it needs to be refined into a more life-affirming form that supports action and experimentation. On this point, see Ansell-Pearson and Bamford 2020, 31–32; Miner 2017, 28–29; Ure 2019, 56–57.

52. *D* 429; cf. 450.

53. As this suggests, Nietzsche is not straightforwardly affirming the predicaments he describes, but, rather, affirming and resisting in different respects. For a discussion of the nuances at play, see Ansell-Pearson and Bamford 2020, 38–41, 118–20.

54. See further the discussion by Anderson and Cristy 2017, 1521–1522.

55. For related remarks, see *GS* 111 (on the desire to affirm as a natural instinct); *D* 298 (on the tendency of the desire to get misdirected); *D* 32 (on denying the world, not for the sake of denying, but for the feeling of affirming something greater than the world). Also significant are the sequence of songs in the middle of Book Two of *Thus Spoke Zarathustra*: in the first ("Night Song") Zarathustra laments that "a need for love is within me"; in the second ("Dance Song"), he sings of his frustrated love for Life; in the third ("Grave Song") he identifies all-too-human frustrations that have made it difficult for him to love Life, but then admits that he perseveres regardless, due to "*my will*"—in other words, Zarathustra's need for love drives him onward, almost in spite of himself. The difficulty, then, is not to make oneself *capable* of loving, but to find a non-self-frustrating way of doing so. I would therefore amend Robert Pippin's characterization of the modern predicament as being, on Nietzsche's analysis a "failure of desire" (see Pippin 2010, 54–56, 64). This is a helpful formulation, but it's important to see that the problem is not so much that the desire has mysteriously disappeared as that doubts about whether our desires can be satisfied have transformed those desires into less healthy, self-denying forms.

56. In *BGE* 56 Nietzsche makes this point more directly: someone who has really "looked down into the most world-denying of all possible ways of think-

ing," he writes there, "may just thereby—without really meaning to do so—have opened his eyes to the opposite ideal: the ideal of the most high-spirited, alive, and world-affirming human being."

57. For the importance of having good enemies, see *TSZ* I.10; *EH* "Wise" 7. More generally, see Acampora 2013.

58. See *EH* "Dawn" 1, which explains that the project of revaluation involves "saying 'yes' to and placing trust in everything that has hitherto been forbidden, despised, condemned. This *yes-saying* book [*Dawn*] pours out its light, its love, it delicacy over nothing but bad things, it gives them back their 'soul,' their good conscience, the lofty right and *prerogative* of existence." On this point, see further Meier 2019, 120.

59. Consider *GS* 58 ("*what things are called* is unspeakably more important than what they are") and Meredith, forthcoming ("Revaluation is . . . repetition with a difference").

60. I offer a more detailed exegesis of this often-overlooked text (placing the epilogue within the context of the larger essay) in Fortier 2020, 99–101.

61. On this remark, see further Satkunanandan 2015, 48–49 (also see Miner 2017, 76–77). As Nietzsche's remark indicates, despite the fact that he often associates the ability to affirm life with a "noble" (aristocratic, anti-modern, anti-Christian) character-type (e.g., *GM* I.10), he is less of a straightforward partisan of "nobility" than he sometimes appears, because he recognizes that, in the contemporary context, being affirmative has to include an affirmation of "Christian/slave morality."

62. "What alone should be resisted is that falseness, that deceitfulness of instinct, which *refuses* to experience these opposites ["master morality" and "Christian morality"] as opposites—as Wagner, for example, refused" (*CW* "Epilogue"; Nietzsche's emphasis). In a comment on this passage, LaMothe (2006, 242n4) observes that Nietzsche can "overcome the life-denying effects of Christianity" only by first "acknowledging his debt to Christianity." More broadly, LaMothe—along with Benson 2008, 11–12; and Hutter 2006, 179–81—makes the point that although Nietzsche recognizes that having to say both "Yes" *and* "No is the result of an internal tension, he also sees that there are admirable ways of learning to live with that tension (for instance, practices of dancing, in which internal tensions are consciously embodied, controlled, and made creative). On Nietzschean affirmation as a kind of learned, second-order affirmation see Andersson and Cristy (2017).

63. Nietzsche alludes—both here and in *TI* "Skirmishes" 51—to the blasphemous remark in Goethe's *Venetian Epigrams* 66.

64. In the first postscript to *The Case of Wagner*, Nietzsche comments on *Parsifal* (which he deemed Wagner's most Christian, and therefore most corrupted and corrupting, work): "I admire this work; I wish I had written it myself; failing that, *I understand it*."

65. There is a connection between the thought suggested here and Nietzsche's notion of "great health" (after all, "Wagner is merely one of my illnesses" [*CW*

"Prologue"] and Christianity is akin to "an illness of the eye" [*CW* "Epilogue"]). For Nietzsche, "great health" is not the absence of illness but the ability to emerge ever stronger from ever greater illnesses; so "illnesses" like Wagner or Christianity can be appreciated for their capacity to spur one on to greater health. On "great health" see *GS* 382 (and on health more generally, *GS* 120), as well as the commentaries by Faustino 2011, 214–15; Fortier 2020, 159–60; and Richardson 2020, 519–20. I think that the dynamic of the "great health," along with the epilogue to *CW*, supports the judgment of Acampora (2013, 3) to the effect that, for Nietzsche, "agents want both to win and be perpetually overcoming, not simply *to have overcome*" (see, similarly, Satkunanandan 2015, 48: "The kind of greatness now available to humans could be the attainment of a civil war within the soul").

66. Acampora (2013, 204–5) elaborates on Nietzsche's aim of generating an appreciation for tension and enmity, not because he wants to resolve conflicts so much as because he wants to set them back in motion. I would add that because Nietzsche's rhetoric is so extreme, it can be an obstacle to arriving at well-reasoned judgments about the subjects he is discussing (even when he has something of value to say beyond the rhetoric). One example is his tendency to characterize his opponents (such as Wagner or Christianity) in pathological terms, making them out to be symptoms of disease. Gemes (2021) shows that this kind of rhetoric is more nuanced than it first appears because Nietzsche is suggesting how "sickness" can become productive of health, but Gemes also comments on the "deep irresponsibility" of this kind of rhetoric, notwithstanding the nuances that Nietzsche had in mind.

67. See the forceful but fair criticism by Beiner 2018, esp. 148n63, which draws on remarks by Karl Löwith to suggest that Nietzsche never got beyond "No-saying" (the same criticism is suggested by Benson 2008, 206).

68. Ellison 2019, 301.
69. Ellison 1995a, 49.
70. Ellison 1995a, 54 (second emphasis added).
71. Ellison 1995a, 55.
72. Ellison 1995a, 24.
73. Ellison 1995a, 23, 286.
74. Ellison 1995a, 287.
75. Ellison 1995a, 22 287.
76. Ellison 1995a, 22, 286 (emphasis added).
77. Ellison 1995a, 24–25.

78. For a comment on "the existential affirmation of life" in Ellison's "blues ontology," see Headley 2009, 250–51. Headley points to related remarks by Ellison's close friend Albert Murray, who draws a link back to the outlook of "ancient tragedy" (see Murray 1973, 36). Gordon (2014, 110–11) connects Ellison's analysis to Nietzsche's *Birth of Tragedy*. I would add that in Ellison's admiration for Flamenco one finds echoes of Nietzsche's enthusiasm for the life-affirming art of the Provence (see n40, above) and Bizet's "Mediterranean" alternative to Wagner (see Fortier, 2020,

78–80). On the importance of southern Europe for Nietzsche more generally, see d'Iorio 2016 and Prange 2013.

79. Ellison 1995a, 696. On Ellison's interest in Bearden, and the visual arts more generally, see Hill 2014, 185.

80. Ellison 1995a, 703–4.

81. Ellison 1995a, 728. In an introduction for the thirtieth anniversary edition of *Invisible Man*, Ellison commented that "my task [in the novel] was one of revealing human universals within the plight of one who was both black and American" (Ellison 1995c, xxii). Foley

82. Alison (2017) treats Ellison's remark as evidence of conflicted feelings about social progress. Foley (2010, 282) also criticizes Ellison for shying away from chaos.

83. Ellison 1995a, 177. Consider also Allen 2004a (on Ellison's "tragi-comedy of citizenship"); and Albrecht 2012, 297–306 (on Ellison's "tragicomic ethics").

84. Danoff (2020, 35) argues that "Ellison aspired to be a leader even if he did not label himself as such."

85. Ellison 1995a, 178.

86. Ellison 1995a, 740–41.

87. The following words that Ellison wrote as part of a tribute to Alain Locke seem like they could apply equally to Ellison himself: he was one of those "people who in their own way defined what the American experience was, who defined that which was affirmative beyond all contradictions of social hierarchy and racism. . . . This is all one can really ask of any individual: that he not deny where he comes from, and that he plumb this background with all of the conscious thought that he possibly can" (Ellison 1995a, 448).

88. Ellison 1995c, 6.

89. Ellison 1995c, 16.

90. Ellison 1995c, 16; cf. 147, 170, 354, 380, 462, 508.

91. Ellison 1995c, 17.

92. Ellison 1995c, 138–44, 154.

93. Ellison 1995c, 38.

94. Ellison 1995c, 194; cf. 402–3. Nietzsche famously asks, "*What* in us really wants 'truth'?" and "*why not rather* untruth?" (*BGE* 1), so he might not seem to share the narrator's scruples (cf. *TI* "Errors" 5). But Nietzsche also observes that, in the modern world, certain "rare, noble, and select" cases—whom he also refers to as "free, very free spirits"—will be strongly attached to truth (*GM* III:23–24; cf. Fortier 2020, 33–34). So, from Nietzsche's point of view, although one's attachment to truth needs to be interrogated, it is not a sign of bad character—and he therefore might be able to sympathize with the predicament of Ellison's earnest young narrator.

95. Ellison 1995c, 573; cf. 508–9. Albrecht (2012, 304) comments on the many "models of 'yessing' duplicity" whom the narrator encounters, and his determination to find a more honest alternative.

96. Ellison 1995c, 5–6

97. Ellison 1995c, 4–6.
98. Ellison 1995c, 13.
99. Ellison 1995c, 581.
100. Ellison 1995c, 574.
101. For a friendly reading in this vein, see Danoff 2020, 48–49. Danoff argues that in passages such as this, Ellison follows Abraham Lincoln in holding that "it is a key task of leadership—whether that leader is an artist, activist, or elected official—to reaffirm, reapply, and rearticulate the nation's founding principles, in order to help the nation move further toward their realization." For a critical view, see Foley 2010, 282, who claims that in the epilogue the narrator "rediscover[s] the sagacity of the Founding Fathers and offer[s] himself as a spokesperson for universal humanity."
102. Ellison 1995a, 197, 457–58. See further Seaton 2004, "Affirming the Principle," 25–27.
103. Contrary to the suggestion of Foley 2010, 282 (as quoted in n102, above). Foley's judgment is part of a broader effort to criticize Ellison for falling away from his early-career identification with Marxism, thereby "avoid[ing] the dull certainties of political commitment" in favor of a wishy-washy Cold War liberalism (see Foley 2010, 344). Lena Hill counters that this criticism does not do justice to Ellison's principled judgment that the problems for Americans were more psychological than material (cf. n24, above), so by directing his protagonist (and readers) to focus on acquiring greater self-knowledge, Ellison is in fact making a political statement (see Hill 2014, 182, 203).
104. Larkin (2015, 93, 121–23) gives an overview of assessments to the effect that in its final pages "the novel asserts a universal humanist vision that, grounded on transracial and individual identifications . . . exceeds the novel's particular critique of racial exclusion," but argues that this assessment reads the epilogue without the same kind of literary subtlety that is generally granted to the rest of the text.
105. "Was it that we of all, we, most of all, had to affirm the principle, the plan in whose name we had been brutalized and sacrificed—and not because we would always be weak nor because we were afraid or opportunistic, but because we were older than they in the sense of what it took to live in the world with others and because they had exhausted in us, some—not much, but some—of the human greed and smallness, yes, and the fear and superstition that that kept them running?" (Ellison 1995c, 574). In his own voice, Ellison once remarked: "We continue to assert the old received values, *modifying them as seems necessary*, but seeking to affirm them nevertheless." Ellison 1995b, 601, emphasis added.
106. Whitaker (2021, 437) comments: "The protagonist has amassed power unto himself, and he plans to take even more of it."
107. Allen 2004a, 115. Allen argues that the narrator comes to understand his grandfather's advice as a lesson about "the subversive power of apparent agreement"—in other words, as a strategy of resistance (cf. Beltrán 2010, 144). Warren

(2003, 33) proposes that the grandfather's advice alludes to several different strategies of (more and less overt) resistance that he adopted in response to different circumstances during and after the Civil War, so part of the puzzle for future generations is to determine which strategy to adopt at any given time.

108. For a related line of thought in James Baldwin, consider Shulman 2018, 158–59 ("In a Nietzschean sense, accepting the past diminishes the power it accrues from denial").

109. On the interrelatedness of historical knowledge and self-knowledge in Nietzsche, see Parkes 1994, 214–15; for this issue in Ellison, see Booth 2008, 689–90, 694, 699.

110. The narrator of *Invisible Man* remarks of his grandfather: "He never had any doubts about his humanity—that was left to his 'free' offspring" (Ellison 1995c, 580).

111. Autobiography was a preoccupation of Nietzsche's from a young age (see Blue 2016), although it is in *Ecce Homo* and the 1886 prefaces that he focuses on interpreting his life to make it worth affirming (on this strategy for becoming affirmative, consider Creasy 2020, 157–63; Fortier 2020, 150–52; Hough 1997, 116). My view is that autobiography is decisive for Nietzsche because he thinks that one can affirm life only if—and only insofar as—one can affirm oneself. See Fortier 2020, 100, 198–99 n91; see also Lampert 2017, 267–68, on how "self-affirmation leads to world affirmation."

112. Ellison 1995a; 1995c, 577; Bland 2022, 166; Pippenger, forthcoming.

113. Ellison 1995a, 215; 1995c, 14. This dimension of the novel is emphasized by Krause 2015, 61–62.

114. Lebron 2017, 57. Lebron quotes Hurston's remark, "Sometimes I feel discriminated against, but it does not make me angry. It merely astonishes me. How *can* any deny themselves the pleasure of my company! It's beyond me." Referring to the same remark, Lawler (2019, 196) suggests, "a better example of Nietzsche's aristocratic pathos of distance would be difficult to find." Yet, as we have seen, Nietzsche's self-affirmation is not straightforwardly aristocratic because it has to overcome the psychological burden of its own history—as does Hurston's. See further Stewart 2021 and Lebron 2017 (139–40).

115. On Hurston, see Plant 1995, 55–56, who finds Hurston explaining her political agnosticism with apparently Nietzschean tropes, e.g., "I do not have much of a herd instinct." On Ellison's friendly-yet-firm criticism of Emerson's brand of individualism, see Albrecht 2012, 305; and Bland 2022, 28.

# References

Acampora, Christa Davis. 2013. *Contesting Nietzsche*. Chicago: University of Chicago Press.

Albrecht, James. 2012. *Reconstructing Individualism: A Pragmatist Tradition from Emerson to Ellison*. New York: Fordham University Press.
Allen, Danielle. 2004a. "Ralph Ellison on the Tragi-Comedy of Citizenship." In *Ralph Ellison and the Raft of Hope: A Political Companion to Invisible Man*. Edited by Lucas Morel. Lexington: University Press of Kentucky.
———. 2004b. *Talking to Strangers: Anxieties of Citizenship Since Brown v Board of Education*. Chicago: University of Chicago Press.
Alison, Cheryl. 2017. "Writing Underground: Ralph Ellison and the Novel." *Twentieth Century Literature* 63, no. 3: 329–58.
Anderson, R. Lainer, and Rachel Cristy. 2017. "What Is 'the Meaning of Our Cheerfulness'? Philosophy as a Way of Life in Nietzsche and Montaigne." *European Journal of Philosophy* 25, no. 4: 1514–1549.
Anderson, Paul Allen. 2005. "Ellison's Music Lessons." In *The Cambridge Companion to Ralph Ellison*. Edited by Ross Posnock. New York: Cambridge University Press.
Ansell-Pearson, Keith, and Rebecca Bamford. 2015. *Nietzsche's Dawn: Philosophy, Ethics, and the Passion of Knowledge*. Hoboken, NJ: Wiley-Blackwell.
Ashe, Bertram D. 2002. *From within the Frame: Storytelling in African American Fiction*. New York: Routledge.
Beiner, Ronald. 2018. *Dangerous Minds: Nietzsche, Heidegger, and the Return of the Far Right*. Philadelphia: University of Pennsylvania Press.
Beltrán, Cristina. 2010. *The Trouble with Unity: Latino Politics and the Creation of Identity*. New York: Oxford University Press.
Benson, Bruce Ellis. 2008. *Pious Nietzsche: Decadence and Dionysian Faith*. Bloomington: Indiana University Press.
Bland, Sterling Lecater Jr. 2022. *In the Shadow of Invisibility: Ralph Ellison and the Promise of American Democracy*. Baton Rouge: Louisiana State University Press.
Blue, Daniel. 2016. *The Making of Friedrich Nietzsche: The Quest for Identity, 1844–1869*. Cambridge: Cambridge University Press.
Booth, W. James. 2008. "The Color of Memory: Reading Race with Ralph Ellison." *Political Theory* 36, no. 5: 683–707.
Brooks, Shilo. 2018. *Nietzsche's Culture War*. Cham, CH: Palgrave Macmillan.
Cash, Earl A. 1973. "The Narrators in *Invisible Man* and *Notes from Underground*: Brothers in Spirit." *CLA Journal* 16, no. 4: 505–7.
Clark, Maudemarie. 2015. *Nietzsche on Ethics and Politics*. New York: Oxford University Press.
Clowes, Edith. 2016. "Mapping the Unconscious in *Notes from Underground* and *On the Genealogy of Morals*." In *Nietzsche and Dostoevsky: Philosophy, Morality, Tragedy*. Edited by Jeff Love and Jeffrey Metzger. Evanston, IL: Northwestern University Press.
Conner, Marc C. 2004. "The Litany of Things: Sacrament and History in Invisible Man." In *Ralph Ellison and the Raft of Hope: A Political Companion to Invisible Man*. Edited by Lucas Morel. Lexington: University Press of Kentucky.

Cope, Jonas. 2006. " 'Shaking Off the Old Skin': The Redemptive Motif in Ellison's *Invisible Man* and Dostoevsky's *Notes from Underground*." *Dostoevsky Journal* 7, no. 1: 75–91.
Creasy, Kaitlyn. 2020. *The Problem of Affective Nihilism in Nietzsche: Thinking Differently, Feeling Differently*. Cham, CH: Palgrave Macmillan.
Danoff, Brian. 2020. *Why Moralize upon It? Democratic Education through American Literature and Film*. Lanham, MD: Lexington Books.
d'Iorio, Paolo. 2016. *Nietzsche's Journey to Sorrento: Genesis of the Philosophy of the Free Spirit*. Translated by Sylvia Mae Gorelick. Chicago: University of Chicago Press.
Ealy, Steven D. 2013. "Speaking on the Lower Frequencies: *Notes from Underground* in Ralph Ellison's America." In *Dostoevsky's Political Thought*, edited by Richard Avramenko and Lee Trepanier. Lanham, MD: Lexington Books.
Eddy, Beth. 2003. *The Rites of Identity: The Religious Naturalism and Cultural Criticism of Kenneth Burke and Ralph Ellison*. Princeton, NJ: Princeton University Press.
Ellison, Ralph. 1995a. *The Collected Essays of Ralph Ellison*. Edited by John F. Callahan. New York: Modern Library.
———. 1995b. *Conversations with Ralph Ellison*. Edited by Maryemma Graham and Amritjit Singh. Jackson: University Press of Mississippi.
———. 1995c. *Invisible Man*. 2nd edition. New York: Vintage International.
———. 2019. *The Selected Letters of Ralph Ellison*. Edited by John F. Callahan and Marc C. Conner. New York: Random House.
Faustino, Marta. 2011. "Philosophy as a 'Misunderstanding of the Body' and the 'Great Health.' " In *Nietzsche on Instinct and Language*, edited by João Constâncio and Maria João Mayer Branco. Berlin: De Gruyter.
Foley, Barbara. 2010. *Wrestling with the Left: The Making of Ralph Ellison's Invisible Man*. Durham, NC: Duke University Press.
Fortier, Jeremy. 2020. *The Challenge of Nietzsche: How to Approach His Thought*. Chicago: University of Chicago Press.
Franco, Paul. 2011. *Nietzsche's Enlightenment: The Free Spirit Trilogy of the Middle Period*. Chicago: University of Chicago Press.
Frank, Joseph. 1990. *Through the Russian Prism: Essays on Literature*. Princeton:, NJ Princeton University Press.
Gemes, Ken. 2021. "The Biology of Evil: Nietzsche on Degeneration (*Entartung*) and Jewification (*Verjüdung*)." *Journal of Nietzsche Studies* 52, no. 1: 1–25.
Gemes, Ken, and Chris Sykes. 2014. "Nietzsche's Illusion." In *Nietzsche on Art and Life*, edited by Daniel Came. New York: Oxford University Press.
Germana, Michael. 2018. *Ralph Ellison: Temporal Technologist*. New York: Oxford University Press.
Gillespie, Michael Allen. 2017. *Nietzsche's Final Teaching*. Chicago: University of Chicago Press.
Gordon, Lewis R. 2014. "Fanon's Decolonial Aesthetic." In *The Aesthetic Turn in Political Thought*, edited by Nikolas Kompridis. New York: Bloomsbury Academic.

Hadot, Pierre. 1995. *Philosophy as a Way of Life: Spiritual Exercises from Socrates to Foucault*. Translated by Michael Chase. Oxford: Blackwell.
Headley, Clevis R. 2009. "A Study in Comparative Ontologies: Root Metaphors of Existence." In *Conversations in Philosophy: Crossing the Boundaries*, edited by F. Ochieng' Odhiambo, Roxanne Burton, and Ed Brandon. Newcastle, UK: Cambridge Scholars.
Harriss, M. Cooper. 2017. *Ralph Ellison's Invisible Theology*. New York: New York University Press.
Hawhee, Debra. 1999. "Burke and Nietzsche." *Quarterly Journal of Speech*. 85, no. 2: 129–45.
Higgins, Kathleen Marie. 2000. *Comic Relief: Nietzsche's Gay Science*. New York: Oxford University Press.
Hill, Lena. 2014. *Visualizing Blackness and the Creation of the African American Literary Tradition*. Cambridge: Cambridge University Press.
Hough, Sheridan. 1997. *Nietzsche's Noontide Friend*. University Park: Pennsylvania State University Press.
Hutter, Horst. 2006. *Shaping the Future: Nietzsche's New Regime of the Soul and Its Ascetic Practices*. Lanham, MD: Rowman & Littlefield.
Jackson, Lawrence Patrick. 2002. *Ralph Ellison: Emergence of Genius*. New York: Wiley.
Krause, Sharon. 2015. *Freedom Beyond Sovereignty: Reconstructing Liberal Individualism*. Chicago: University of Chicago Press.
LaMothe, Kimerer L. 2006. *Nietzsche's Dancers: Isadora Duncan, Martha Graham, and the Revaluation of Christian Values*. New York: Palgrave Macmillan.
Lampert, Laurence. 2017. *What a Philosopher Is: Becoming Nietzsche*. Chicago: University of Chicago Press.
Larkin, Lesley. 2015. *Race and the Literary Encounter: Black Literature from James Weldon Johnson to Percival Everett*. Bloomington: Indiana University Press.
Lawler, Kristin. 2019. "Labor's Will to Power: Nietzsche, American Syndicalism, and the Politics of Liberation." In *Nietzsche and Critical Social Theory*, edited by Christine A. Payne and Michael James Roberts. Leiden, NL: Brill.
Lebron, Christopher. 2017. *The Making of Black Lives Matter: A Brief History of an Idea*. New York: Oxford University Press.
Lemm, Vanessa. 2009. *Nietzsche's Animal Philosophy: Culture, Politics, and the Animality of the Human Being*. New York: Fordham University Press.
Loeb, Paul S. 2021. "Ecce Superhomo: How Zarathustra Became What Nietzsche Was Not." In *Nietzsche's Ecce Homo*, edited by Nicholas Martin and Duncan Large. Berlin: De Gruyter.
Love, Jeff, and Jeffrey Metzger, eds. 2016. *Nietzsche and Dostoevsky: Philosophy, Morality, Tragedy*. Evanston, IL: Northwestern University Press.
Lyne, William. 1992. "The Signifying Modernist: Ralph Ellison and the Limits of Double Consciousness." *PMLA* 107, no. 2: 318–30.

Martin, Nicholas, and Duncan Large, eds. 2021. *Nietzsche's Ecce Homo*. Berlin: De Gruyter.

Meredith, Thomas. Forthcoming. "Nietzsche's Critique of Power: Mimicry and the Advantage of the Weak." *American Political Science Review*.

Meyer, Matthew. 2019. *Nietzsche's Free Spirit Works: A Dialectical Reading*. Cambridge: Cambridge University Press.

Miner, Robert. 2017. *Nietzsche and Montaigne*. Cham, CH: Palgrave Macmillan.

Morel, Lucas. 2004. "Recovering the Political Artistry of Invisible Man." In *Ralph Ellison and the Raft of Hope: A Political Companion to Invisible Man*, edited by Lucas Morel. Lexington: University Press of Kentucky.

Murray, Albert. 1973. *The Hero and the Blues*. Columbia: University of Missouri Press.

Nietzsche, Fredrich. 1996. *Human, All Too Human*. Translated by R. J. Hollingdale. Cambridge: Cambridge University Press.

———. 1997. *Untimely Meditations*. Translated by R. J. Hollingdale. Cambridge: Cambridge University Press.

———. 1999. *The Birth of Tragedy and Other Writings*. Translated by Ronald Speirs. Cambridge: Cambridge University Press.

———. 2000. *The Basic Writings of Nietzsche*. Edited by Walter Kaufmann. New York: Modern Library.

———. 2001. *The Gay Science*. Translated by Josefine Nauckhoff. Cambridge: Cambridge University Press.

———. 2005. *Thus Spoke Zarathustra*. Translated by Graham Parkes. New York: Oxford University Press.

———. 2007. *Ecce Homo*. Translated by Duncan Large. New York: Oxford University Press.

———. 2011. *Dawn*. Translated by Brittain Smith. Stanford: Stanford University Press.

Orwin, Donna. 2007. *Consequences of Consciousness: Turgenev, Dostoevsky, and Tolstoy*. Stanford: Stanford University Press.

Parkes, Graham. 1994. *Composing the Soul: Reaches of Nietzsche's Psychology*. Chicago: University of Chicago Press.

———. 2005. Introduction to *Thus Spoke Zarathustra*, by Friedrich Nietzsche. New York: Oxford University Press.

Prange, Martine. 2013. *Nietzsche, Wagner, Europe*. Berlin: De Gruyter.

Pippenger, Nathan. 2023. "Reading Ellison Through Herder: Language, Integration, and Democracy." *Journal of Politics* 85, no. 2: 749–59.

Pippin, Robert B. 2010. *Nietzsche, Psychology, and First Philosophy*. Chicago: University of Chicago Press.

Plant, Deborah G. 1995. *Every Tub Must Sit on Its Own Bottom: The Philosophy and Politics of Zora Neale Hurston*. Urbana: University of Illinois Press.

Reginster, Bernard. 2006. *The Affirmation of Life: Overcoming Nihilism*. Cambridge, MA: Harvard University Press.

Richardson, John. 2020. *Nietzsche's Values*. New York: Oxford University Press.
Satkunanandan, Shalini. 2015. *Extraordinary Responsibility: Politics Beyond the Moral Calculus*. New York: Cambridge University Press.
Scanlan, James P. 2002. *Dostoevsky the Thinker*. Ithaca, NY: Cornell University Press.
Schaberg, William H. 1995. *The Nietzsche Canon: A Publication History and Bibliography*. Chicago: University of Chicago Press.
Seaton, James. 2004. "Affirming the Principle." In *Ralph Ellison and the Raft of Hope: A Political Companion to Invisible Man*, edited by Lucas Morel. Lexington: University Press of Kentucky.
Shulman, George. 2017. "Baldwin, Prophecy, and Politics." In *A Political Companion to James Baldwin*, edited by Susan J. McWilliams. Lexington: University Press of Kentucky.
Stern, Tom. 2021. "Against Nietzsche's Theory of Affirmation." In *Nietzsche on Morality and the Affirmation of Life*, edited by Daniel Came. New York: Oxford University Press.
Stewart, Lindsay. 2021. *The Politics of Black Joy: Zora Neale Hurston and Neo-Abolitionism*. Evanston, IL: Northwestern University Press.
Ure, Michael. 2019. *Nietzsche's "The Gay Science": An Introduction*. New York: Cambridge University Press.
Ward, Jerry W. Jr., and Robert J. Butler. 2008. *The Richard Wright Encyclopedia*. Westport, CT: Greenwood Press.
Warren, Kenneth W. 2003. *So Black and Blue: Ralph Ellison and the Occasion of Criticism*. Chicago: University of Chicago Press.
Whitaker, Cord J. 2021. " 'We Were outside History': The Middle Ages in *Invisible Man* and the Struggle for Black Lives in 2020." *PMLA* 136, no. 3: 432–40.
Wright, John S. 2006. *Shadowing Ralph Ellison*. Jackson: University Press of Mississippi.
Zavatta, Benedetta. 2019. *Individuality and Beyond: Nietzsche Reads Emerson*. Translated by Alexander Reynolds. New York: Oxford University Press.

13

# Disability, Power, and Life

REBECCA BAMFORD

Nietzsche's philosophy has been deployed to support accounts of disability as a positive political identity.[1] There is broad agreement amongst the available accounts that Nietzsche's philosophy has held significance for disability justice in the past and that it continues to be relevant today. However, a difference in emphasis on the relevance of various aspects of Nietzsche's philosophy means that we lack a unified account of reasons why Nietzsche's philosophy can count as a liberatory resource: some accounts emphasize Nietzsche's critique of *Mitleid* as a means to sustaining disability as a positive political identity, while others focus more on tragedy or health and pay little attention to *Mitleid*.[2] The available scholarship is further complicated by ongoing debate concerning the scope and justice implications of the social model of disability. As David Peña-Guzmán and Joel Michael Reynolds have discussed, the medical model of disability has tended to treat disability as a personal tragedy, hardship, or health problem resulting from factors such as disease, congenital abnormality, environmental accident, or old age; in contrast, the social model of disability holds that a person is *impaired* insofar as their body is different in ways that impact their ability to function in the world as compared to most people, whereas a person is *disabled* insofar as they are negatively impacted by the treatment of others on account of their impairment, including through such negative impacts as arise through wider societal norms and social institutions.[3]

What is needed, therefore, is a clearer understanding of how Nietzsche's critical engagement with *Mitleid* might make a meaningful contribution to structural disability justice projects that use the social model of disability to address problems created by the medical model, why Nietzsche's critique has been taken to be helpful toward such ends in the past, and whether it can continue to play this role going forward. I propose to shift the trajectory of the available scholarship by connecting the individual and structural dimensions of liberatory resources of Nietzsche's critique of *Mitleid* more clearly, including through assessment of its implications for philosophy itself. I argue that Nietzsche's critique of *Mitleid* is a useful tool that can support treating disability as a positive political identity on group and individual levels owing to its implications for social power relationships.[4] I also suggest that Nietzsche's critique opens up a point of support for Shelley Tremain's work on "de-naturalizing disability" within philosophy itself, which further supports the case for treating disability as a positive political identity.[5]

In the first part of my account, I review two important previous accounts that have made use of Nietzsche's critical engagement with *Mitleid* in accounting for disability as a positive political identity. I raise some concerns with the previous scholarship focusing on the available textual evidence and the significance of power relationships to structural accounts using the social model of disability, following work by Joe Stramondo. In response, I show how Nietzsche's thinking on *Mitleid* can be squared with analyses of structural power that attend to power relationships, and thus how it can still count as having meaningful liberatory potential.[6] In the final part of this chapter, I build on this approach by turning to the issue of power relationships within philosophy. I consider a problem that has been identified by Shelley Tremain—ableism in philosophy itself.[7]

## Nietzsche's Philosophy in Disability Justice

I begin by examining two accounts that discuss Nietzsche's influence on disability activism as part of examining his relevance to disability justice projects.[8] As I show, these accounts have paid close attention to Nietzsche's critique of *Mitleid* and leave room for more sustained explanation of the structural relevance of Nietzsche's critique.

Steven R. Smith has defended an account of the disability rights movement in which he identifies Nietzsche as a "surprising" yet helpful ally to this movement.⁹ Smith points out that there are four particularly promising areas of overlap between Nietzsche and the disability rights movement that may prove useful to ongoing research: (1) Nietzsche's anti-essentialism, (2) Nietzsche's critique of pity and compassion, (3) Nietzsche's critique of ideals and dualism, and (4) Nietzsche's eternal recurrence thesis, especially as linked to notions of individual empowerment and identity-assertion.¹⁰ Smith acknowledges that claims for equal rights, such as those advanced by the disability rights movement, do not sit well with appeals to Nietzsche's wider philosophy—not least since equal rights demands may be grounded in customary morality [*Sittlichkeit der Sitte*] (e.g., D 9), against which, as I have discussed in previous work, Nietzsche develops a sustained campaign, especially in *Dawn* and other free spirit writings.¹¹ Even so, Smith maintains that Nietzsche is a useful resource for scholars and activists seeking to advance disability justice. Smith argues that Nietzsche's philosophy aligns with the social model of disability on the basis that (1) the medical model assumes an essentialism foreign to Nietzsche's wider philosophy and (2) as he claims, " 'being disabled' (understood as a personal loss or tragedy) is not an inevitable characteristic of impairment possession, but rather relates to cultural and social conditions and prejudices which are not fixed or 'essential' but which are highly variable and contingent."¹²

For Smith, this variability and contingency means that there is no single, complete definition of disability available on a Nietzschean account; instead, Smith proposes that Nietzsche's philosophy allows for a series of perspectives on disability, which affect disabled people's lives "variously (and often detrimentally) as they relate to social conditions."¹³

As part of his account, Smith provides some detailed discussion of why Nietzsche's critique of *Mitleid* has proven helpful within disability rights activism. He points out that according to Nietzsche, the moral emotion of *Mitleid* (his translation of this term is "pity") is problematic on several fronts: it diminishes individuals' capacities for self-creativity and assertiveness; it obscures individuality generally, as well as individual differences in how people respond to suffering; and it compounds human suffering.¹⁴ Smith turns to *Antichrist* 7 for textual evidence to support his explanation of Nietzsche's critique of pity. There, as Smith discusses, Nietzsche remarks, "Pity stands in antithesis to the tonic emotions which enhance the energy of the feeling of life: it has depressive effects," and Nietzsche also notes the loss of force "when one pities" and that pity increases the "loss of force which life has already sustained through suffering," giving "life itself a gloomy and questionable aspect."[15] As Smith explains, this is why Nietzsche's critical account of *Mitleid* is a sustaining critical tool for disability rights activism, for example in demonstrations that have formed a crucial part of the disability rights movement such as those held to protest the BBC's *Telethon* charity fundraising event.[16] Such events have warranted protest from disability justice advocates, according to Smith, because they present a picture of disabled people as "passive and tragic victims of impairment" rather than as self-determining, self-creative, individuals whose lived experiences of impairment may involve the impairment contributing "positively to their lives" in a range of possible ways.[17] As Smith notes, even if an impairment does cause physiological or psychological suffering, disabled people nonetheless have the capacity to use their experiences "to their advantage in respect to personal development and fulfilment."[18] That Nietzsche's philosophy affords us this critical perspective on *Mitleid* and its consequences and political implications is, for Smith, why Nietzsche's philosophy still counts as an important liberatory resource for disabled people and for disability justice as a form of structural as well as individual justice.

Susan Stocker has drawn on Nietzsche's critique of *Mitleid* alongside resources from Aristotle in order to analyze the relationship of the self to injury, rehabilitation, and disability. Stocker contrasts Nietzsche's thinking on pity and will to power with Aristotle's thinking on empathy in order to illuminate how the ethical itself begins in "the throes of lived human experience."[19] Attending to the value of lived experience of disability in accounting for disability, Stocker also discusses how she experienced "serious mobility challenges for two and a half years," first using "crutches and then a wheelchair full-time for another eight months."[20] Stocker explains how she encountered two distinct but related philosophical concepts as part of experiencing disability. First, she describes an experience of "empowering empathy," a concept drawn from Aristotle that she characterizes as "an interest in, attunement to, and responsiveness to the subjective inner experience of the other at a cognitive and affective level."[21] Second, she describes experiencing what, according to her, Nietzsche, along with rehabilitation professionals, already understood as "a pity that is demeaning for both the pitier and the one pitied."[22]

To illustrate what she means by pity or *Mitleid* as being demeaning to the person who is pitied, Stocker takes an example from disability pride activism that is also noted by Smith, namely the well-known disability rights slogan "Piss on Pity."[23] Stocker thinks that both Aristotle's empowering empathy and Nietzsche's view of *Mitleid* as demeaning to the pitied person are helpful to her wider project of "facing" disability.²⁴ For Stocker, Nietzsche's critique of *Mitleid* (which she translates as pity) is especially useful to her project. She defines Nietzsche's critique of *Mitleid* as a response to vulnerability, in which our independence from others is highlighted.²⁵ In light of this, Stocker argues that Nietzsche's critique of *Mitleid* shows us that we can preserve our individual self-determination as an emotional and moral option "free of either a malingering self-pity or a hankering for pity from others."²⁶

In other words, Stocker holds that Nietzsche's critique of *Mitleid* is useful to the aims of disability justice because Nietzsche's work shows us how disabled people can sustain a positive self-relation with disability, without disability constituting an objection to life. According to Stocker, Nietzsche recommends our "saying an affirming 'yes' to our lives, suffering and all" and that "only the rancorous emotions are put down as symptoms of a pathetic life-denying 'will to power.' "²⁷ Stocker claims in light of this that what we owe to others as well as to ourselves is "own vitality, a life-affirming 'will to power.' "²⁸ Stocker thus draws a direct connection between Nietzsche's critique of *Mitleid* and his concept of will to power. This point by Stocker is helpful for theorizing disability as a positive political identity since it identifies a potential way to ground understanding of disabled identity as itself powerful and empowering, in addition to providing a basis for the affirmation of disabled life.

However, it is not clear that Stocker is right to imply that merely experiencing the feeling of *ressentiment* on a single occasion is what is problematic for Nietzsche, nor is it clear that rancorous emotions are life-denying in themselves: rather, what is problematic for Nietzsche is whether *ressentiment* festers over time and in which social system and affective economy the rancorous emotion is expressed. For Nietzsche, noble psychological types can express their painful or rancorous feelings—it is the slave type who cannot do so, for structural and social reasons, and who may therefore be consumed by those feelings. It is also problematic that Stocker relies on only three aphorisms from Nietzsche to develop her assessment of his relevance to disability justice—*GS* 290; *BGE* 43; and *BGE* 44—and she gives none of these aphorisms significant detailed analysis. I shall examine these aphorisms in turn, in order to determine how far we may support Stocker's position in light of this textual evidence.

*GS* 290 receives Stocker's most detailed attention, and she quotes the following excerpt from the aphorism: "One thing is needful: that a human being should attain satisfaction with himself, whether it be by means of this or that poetry or art; only then is a human being at all tolerable to behold. Whoever is dissatisfied with himself is ready for revenge; and we others will be his victims, if only by having to endure his ugly sight." Stocker presents this claim from *GS* 290 as a remark by Nietzsche on the importance of learning to experience "loss or thwartedness without resenting it."[29] However, there is more to say of the aphorism than this. Nietzsche's point on self-satisfaction is preceded in this aphorism by his point that that "to 'give style' to one's character" is "a great and rare art" (*GS* 290). As Paul Franco has emphasized, the type of artistry that Nietzsche discusses in this aphorism "puts the emphasis on working with and arranging the natural aspects of ourselves," in the same way that artists work with what they are given even if it is ugly with the purpose of focusing on transformation rather than on denial.[30] According to Franco, Nietzsche's point here is that the great and rare art is practiced "by those who survey all the strengths and weaknesses of their nature and then fit them into an artistic plan until every one of them appears as art and reason and even weaknesses delight the eye" (*GS* 290).[31] And as Nietzsche makes clear a little later in the aphorism, his sense of weakness here refers to weak characters, who are, he claims, "without power over themselves" and who "*hate* the constraint of style" (*GS* 290). There is much more of affirmation in the aphorism than Stocker's discussion of it allows, and Franco's emphasis on transformation in this aphorism is crucial to properly understanding the liberatory potential of Nietzsche's critique.[32]

Stocker also discusses *BGE* 43 and *BGE* 44 as part of examining Nietzsche's critique of *Mitleid* (which she translates consistently as pity). She claims that, for Nietzsche, pity is mistaken because (1) it wrongly affirms external goods as important, (2) it misaligns fault as lying elsewhere instead of with oneself—"Anyone with the Nietzschean virtues evaluates accordingly and without self-pity," and (3) identifying with the supposed good of others is "putrid," since there are no common goods.[33] Stocker's source of textual evidence for her third claim here is *BGE* 43, and she quotes the following portion of the aphorism to support her point: "'Good' is no longer good when one's neighbor mouths it. And how should there be a 'common good'! The term contradicts itself: whatever can be common always has little value" (*BGE* 43). Stocker further contends that Nietzsche disparages pity because it's "a pretense that life should be easy and that hardships are a misfortune" (141). She also claims, paraphrasing *BGE* 44, that Nietzsche "chastises those pathetic moralists who insist on security and comfort 'and an easier life for everyone' because 'suffering itself they take for something that must be abolished' " (141). In addition, Stocker claims—referring to *Genealogy* and paraphrasing *Twilight* "Maxims" 8—that "the "herd" would rid us of conditions that actually enhance our species: whatever doesn't kill us makes us stronger."[34] We should note that *TI* "Maxims" 8 in fact reads, "*From the Military School of Life*: Whatever does not kill me makes me stronger."

There are some issues with Stocker's account. First, Stocker's criticism of Nietzsche's stoicism with regard to experiences of disabled embodiment assumes a dualism of mind and body and also seems to assume that therefore, according to Nietzsche, we must disengage from all external goods in order to affirm experiences of disability. Second, the phrasing of Stocker's objection to Nietzsche as delegitimizing rancorous emotion as life-denying is problematic, since the form of this objection conflates a positive conception of the ethical with customary morality, between which Nietzsche himself distinguishes.[35] A third problem with Stocker's argument has been raised by Joe Stramondo, to the examination of which I now turn.

## Power and the Ideology of Pity

In his account of the ideology of pity, Stramondo calls attention to the problem that the harms of disability have been naturalized, which further entrenches these harms and requires a structural response to address them properly. This poses a problem for using Nietzsche's critique of *Mitleid* to pursue disability justice, since as Stramondo suggests, Nietzsche's approach may be unable to address the social and structural dimension of disability injustice. In this section, I explain Stramondo's concern with naturalizing disability harms in more detail and then show how, in my view, Nietzsche's account can count as aligned with Stramondo's structural approach to disability justice.

Drawing on resources from Sartre, Stramondo shows that Stocker analyzed Nietzsche's account of *Mitleid* in the context of disability in terms of individual emotion rather than in terms of power differentials in social contexts.[36] As he points out, Stocker's analysis falls short since she seems not to acknowledge that "the folks with disabilities who would wear a 'Piss On Pity' t-shirt do not see their disability as a misfortune or hardship at all and so her reading of Nietzsche falls far short of an explanation."[37] Stramondo directs our attention to this social context, arguing via Sartre that "for pity to exist, one group must have more power than another"; moreover, as he claims, a "power differential is a necessary condition" for pity, and that the power differential is "what creates harm" in the case of pity.[38] According to Stramondo, what is of prime importance in understanding how pity harms disabled people as a group is how "some members of the non-disabled class of people derive benefits from the system of domination of people with disabilities."[39] As Stramondo shows, pity leads to social oppression of disability by means of naturalizing the harms of disability; according to him, the process of naturalization involves framing disability as a biological rather than a social phenomenon, which results in social and political institutions promoting a biotechnological cure for disability as the primary response to disability, rather than acknowledging that "it is social oppression that does the harming by creating a system of domination."[40] Stramondo provides helpful examples of naturalization at work, including (1) autonomy-limiting public policy that directs government funds supporting disabled people toward nursing homes rather than toward disabled people, thus making it harder for many disabled people to sustain their freedom and autonomy by utilizing in-home or community care; (2) financial gain, for instance from biotechnological disability cures, through remuneration via fundraising, and through earmarking public funds for biotechnological research aimed at disability cures.[41] The root of the process by which the harms of disability become naturalized is, Stramondo claims, the distinction between the medical and social models of disability, according to which the medical model is grounded in the liberal view that "there is a universal human nature," even while that view simultaneously includes and constructs "a separate category of people who somehow fail to meet the criteria for inclusion" in universal human nature.[42]

Stramondo proposes that this exclusionary move is made possible by "the ideology of pity."[43] It is pity that, he suggests, enables "denial of the social nature of the harms of disability" and the accompanying claim that a disabled person is "just wrong" to describe these harms as social rather than biological or, to put it slightly differently, intrinsic to the disability itself.[44] What makes pity in the context of disability especially problematic is that certain forms or displays of pity or compassion constitute a social harm to disabled people. To illustrate Stramondo's point, imagine a person who has sustained a permanent impairment to their body's capacity to perform certain movements under particular environmental conditions and who needs to wear an orthotic device under conditions, such as ice and snow or on a beach or a path covered in gravel, that raise a slipping and further injury hazard to ensure their safe movement (different environmental conditions, such as warm dry weather or stable paths make the device unnecessary). Expressions of pity or *Mitleid* for this person when they wear their orthotic device (which people might do by saying, for example, "I'm so sorry you're still having to wear that device—aren't you getting better?" or "It would be good not to see you wearing that thing any more") may be well-intentioned but do nothing useful to support or include this person. Moreover, such expressions fail to recognize the feeling and the expression of strength of device users. It is not that such a device always replaces an absent strength but that it supports a joint in safe movement and thus a body in expressing its strength and power, no matter that the feeling and expressed degree of strength and power may differ from body to body. Moreover, pity expressions undercut the feeling and expression of strength and power of the device wearer, for instance in the workplace, when a pity expression is spoken by, say, a senior line manager who wields economic and institutional power over the continued employment of the individual. And because the utterance is one of pity, which is assumed to be morally appropriate owing to customary morality, it is especially difficult to call out or challenge as unjust.

Such expressions of *Mitleid* may also be collectively harmful, making the workplace less welcoming and accessible to disabled people as a group, and potentially making them less likely to seek accommodations to which they are entitled, or more likely to practice device use in ways that help them to avoid expressions of pity or compassion that disempower them even when doing so is less safe, or assistive, or sustaining of their feeling and expression of strength and power. As Stramondo puts this point, pity understood as a power relation "veils and reinforces power relations of subjugation."[45] Through the practice of *Mitleid*, the disabled person is forced to occupy a disempowered position in relation to the pitier: this may be unintentionally done or it may be deliberate, but the structural injustice of ableism is perpetuated regardless.

According to Stramondo, Sartre provides the conceptual tools to "move away from an understanding of pity as a mere moral emotion and toward an understanding of how pity rests on and obscures a certain type of power relation"; given this, he thinks, we would do better to attend to social power relations in order to properly understand the harm of pity and how the ideology of pity plays a key role in disability oppression.[46] While Stramondo is right to direct our attention to social power relations, I have two suggestions in reply to his account. First, while I think he is right to say that for Nietzsche pity rests on a type of power relation, I do not think Stramondo is right to also hold that pity obscures that power relation—rather, for Nietzsche, pity overtly signifies the power relation in question. Second, Nietzsche's analysis of *Mitleid* does incorporate an analysis of social and structural power relationships that can help us understand and identify *Mitleid* as harmfully ableist, as well as expanding on the rationale supporting disability justice activists' past use of Nietzsche as a resource for challenging disability oppression.[47]

Several sources of support are available to support my view, including some key aspects of Nietzsche's engagement with *Mitleid*, which are helpful to identifying how *Mitleid* signifies a power relation and constitutes a harm. The first aspect concerns Nietzsche's distinction between expressing *Mitleid* for an unfortunate person and having *Mitleid* for such a person. As I have discussed in previous work, Nietzsche points out in *Human, All Too Human* that "[o]ne should, to be sure, *manifest* [Mitleid], but take care not to possess it" (*HH* 50).[48] His reasoning is that while pity is often taken to be a great good, it can still be used by the unfortunate person to strengthen their power against a seemingly strong person pushed by the unfortunate person to express pity: the unfortunate possess the power to hurt the strong, to a point where the strong feel it essential to make an expression of pity (*HH* 50). This manifestation of the unfortunate's power prompts a gain in pleasure for them, according to Nietzsche (*HH* 50). Thirsting for pity is, Nietzsche suggests, "a thirst for enjoyment . . . at the expense of one's fellow men" (*HH* 50). Nietzsche extends this point to social life more generally, suggesting that in three-quarters of social discourse, questions and answers are given to cause pain to the other party and to thereby gain a sense of one's own strength (*HH* 50). Nietzsche further suggests that most people are insufficiently honest to admit this (*HH* 50). As I have shown in earlier discussion of this aphorism, there is no truly passive or powerless subject position in the type of power relationship expressed through *Mitleid*, even for the person appearing, from a customary moral position, to occupy the least powerful position.[49]

Examining Nietzsche's campaign against customary morality as the grounding framework of his critique of *Mitleid* also helps to support my view. There has been significant attention drawn to ways in which Nietzsche addresses social embeddedness and social power relations as part of his moral psychological inquiries, for example by Christopher Janaway and by Mark Alfano.[50] Textual evidence also supports this view: consider that in *Dawn* 467 Nietzsche explores why *Mitleid* might contribute to an agent's need for forbearance or patience, which he characterizes as "*forbearance twice.*" The aphorism asks us to consider how someone may warn us about taking a particular action by saying, "You will cause a lot of people pain that way" (*D* 467). The aphorism suggests the following reply to such a warning: "I know it; and know as well that I will suffer doubly for it, once from compassion [*Mitleid*] with their suffering and then from the revenge they will take on me. Nevertheless, it is no less necessary to act as I am acting" (*D* 467). Through this exchange, as Ansell-Pearson and I have demonstrated, Nietzsche is making clear that according to him, agents are embedded in a web of social connections and that this social aspect of customary morality, of which *Mitleid* is part, helps shape ethical agency in group context.[51] Customary moral agents, especially those who express or solicit *Mitleid*, are always already part of a group and understand morality in social and power relationship context.[52]

Work by Henry Staten also provides support for my view. Staten has shown how *Dawn* 113 provides an example of how power relationships amongst empathic agents are understood by Nietzsche in his free spirit writings.[53] In this aphorism, Nietzsche emphasizes the importance of power in ethical and social action. He argues that the empathy and "being-in-the-know" that the drive for distinction requires is not "harmless or compassionate or benevolent" and is better understood as the "striving for domination" (*D* 113).[54] Any joy experienced through the striving for domination is brought about by someone having placed their "*imprint*" on the soul of another person (*D* 113). As Katsafanas discusses, Nietzsche connects this analysis of *Mitleid* with an account of the function of psychophysical drives.[55] As one brief example, Nietzsche discusses drives in *Dawn* 119, which he clearly prefaces in *Dawn* 113 when he identifies the striving for distinction as a "drive [*Trieb*]." Nietzsche finds the notion that social groups are united by *Mitleid* (as did Schopenhauer, for example) to be ultimately implausible.[56] This is not least because he sees *Mitleid* as a form of power relation; therefore, he thinks that our risking censure along with our own and others' suffering by challenging customary morality would be giving up on a harmful illusion about morality (and one that creates the conditions for perpetuating ableism), not giving up on the possibility of the ethical itself.[57] Similarly, in *Dawn* 146, Nietzsche suggests that while we may be under the impression that *Mitleid* is always humanizing, this impression is false since *Mitleid* can also be dehumanizing as well as hypocritical (*D* 146). Under the auspices of customary morality, everyone remains superstitiously afraid of contravening custom, incurring divine wrath and garnering negative consequences for their community; as Nietzsche proposes, this is a "narrow and petty bourgeois morality"; in contrast to this form of morality, a "higher and freer" way of thinking would look beyond immediate consequences and work toward more distant aims, such as furthering knowledge and including ethical understanding, even if doing so comes at the cost of our own or others' suffering (*D* 146).[58] Nietzsche again connects his account to feelings of power, claiming that through sacrifice of obedience to moral custom, we "strengthen and elevate the feeling of human *power*, even though we might achieve nothing further" and that therefore, "even this would be a positive increase in *happiness*" (*D* 146). The "we" of whom Nietzsche speaks in the aphorism are alternative, possible, ethical agents who are focused on self-fashioning and who, as an emergent possible community of the future, are engaged in throwing off old values and experimenting with new values.[59]

A recent paper by Ian Dunkle, which discusses Nietzsche's relevance to contemporary disability studies, also offers some support for my view.[60] Dunkle's account focuses primarily on developing an account of the concept of health that Nietzsche held by the late 1880s, rather than on disability.[61] Dunkle addresses Nietzsche's thinking on *Mitleid* within a wider discussion of how Nietzsche requires strength for health and how he claims that weakness entails illness; as Dunkle points out, *Antichrist* 7 provides a good example of Nietzsche developing this claim: "Through pity, that loss of strength [Kraft] which suffering in itself already brings to life increases and is reproduced. Suffering itself becomes contagious through pity. [ . . . ] Nothing is less healthy within our unhealthy modernity than Christian pity" (*A* 7).[62] As Nietzsche also points out earlier in this aphorism, "—Pity is nihilism put into practice. [—Mitleiden ist die Praxis des Nihilismus]" (*A* 7). Moreover, as Dunkle claims, pity is unhealthy according to Nietzsche since pity causes weakness, and weakness entails illness. Nietzsche requires health for strength, since as he claims, "In the struggle with the beast, making sick can be the sole means of making it weak" (*TI* "Improvers" 2)—though Nietzsche does not directly equate health and strength or weakness and illness, as Dunkle shows using evidence from *A* 14.[63] The reason why, as Dunkle claims, Nietzsche identifies pity as inhibitory of strength and health is since the latter two concepts are tied together by Nietzsche given the importance he places on "enabling one's basic instincts to express themselves."[64] Dunkle further points out that for Nietzsche, while functional impairments can detract from health, they may also not detract from it and may sometimes contribute to health. Dunkle here follows Elizabeth Barnes's value-neutral account of disability in suggesting that Nietzsche's concept of health allows us to oppose any categorical definition of disability as health- and welfare-detracting, in line with the contemporary social model of disability.[65]

Nietzsche's critique of *Mitleid* explains the structure of power relations in and through which *Mitleid* empowers and disempowers groups as well as individuals. Following Nietzsche, and in line with Stramondo's wider analysis, it makes sense to treat *Mitleid* as a value to be challenged, as well as to note that when understood in terms of power relationships, moral psychological concepts can be important in addressing structural as well as individual injustice.

## Disability and Power

Even if, as I have suggested, Nietzsche's critique of *Mitleid* is brought into alignment with Stramondo's structural account, a further problem remains: the naturalization of disability. As mentioned earlier, Stramondo suggests that the process of naturalization frames disability as a biological, not a social, phenomenon, which is what grounds disability injustice as a structural problem.[66] Shelley Tremain has pointed out that the naturalization of disability also occurs within philosophy understood as itself a social institution. Critical engagement with moral philosophy's dependence on this feature of moral psychology is therefore needed in order to fully explain the continuing relevance of Nietzsche's thought, and in particular his critique of *Mitleid*, to disability justice. In this section, I discuss Tremain's analysis of disability within philosophy and then explain how Nietzsche's critique, set within the context of his free spirit writings, can support the ongoing work of denaturalizing disability within philosophy as a part of pursuing disability justice.

Shelley Tremain's feminist philosophy of disability gives significant emphasis to disability oppression as a structural social problem. What is especially important about Tremain's feminist account is that she shows how disability is problematically naturalized within philosophy itself, understood as a social structure, as well as how disability is naturalized in other social structures.[67] Tremain points out that the discipline of philosophy has been assessed as an ableist social institution that requires transformation, and she contends that disability has, problematically, been naturalized in philosophy, which she explains as a process whereby disability becomes treated as a "non-accidental and disadvantageous biological human characteristic, attribute, difference, or property that ought to be corrected or eliminated."⁶⁸ According to Tremain, disability continues to be naturalized in philosophy by means of "epistemologies and ontologies of domination," and she also points out that even while it may seem as if addressing the structural problem of the naturalization of disability may only appear relevant to philosophers of disability and other applied and social philosophers, "the ways in which disability is naturalized in philosophy and what can be done to de-naturalize disability in philosophy and elsewhere ought to be of interest and concern to every philosopher."⁶⁹

As part of her analysis, Tremain notes how Nietzsche's genealogical method influenced Foucault's work on "limit-attitude," and specifically Foucault's account of how genealogy as a method can reveal the ways in which limits are imposed upon us within the context of the philosophical life.⁷⁰ What Tremain finds helpful about Foucault's work is how "genealogies denaturalize us," and how genealogy shows us to be "artifactual," which she uses to provide an account of disability.⁷¹ The context of the critique of *Mitleid*—Nietzsche's campaign against morality in his free spirit works, particularly *Dawn*—is of particular importance to my view, since it is as a part of this campaign that Nietzsche shows how moral philosophical assumptions or prejudices hinder collective social and ethical innovation as well as stifling individual moral reflection and understanding. Let me provide some support for this point from recent scholarship.

In our 2020 book on Nietzsche's *Dawn*, Keith Ansell-Pearson and I discuss how the primary ethical project embedded within *Dawn* is the development of a substantial challenge to what Nietzsche terms customary morality [*Sittlichkeit der Sitte*] and to its grounding ethic of compassion, which is set alongside Nietzsche's development of a set of experimental, playful, aphorisms that encourage exploration of new ethical alternatives to customary morality. Nietzsche shows that customary morality inhibits us from having or exploring new experiences, correcting old customs even when they are doing harm to individuals or groups, and developing new, better, customs to inform our actions (*D* 19).⁷²

As discussed by Ansell-Pearson and I, Nietzsche's survey of customary morality as a problem in the first book of *Dawn* discusses how social context is significant to Nietzsche's critique of pity. Nietzsche identifies that a way must be found to counter three specific issues: (1) overcoming reluctance to develop criticism owing to fear of moral censure by a community; (2) limited moral vocabulary—only having words for "superlative" aspects of psycho-physical processes and drives such as "compassion" and not for milder or lower processes and drives, which form our characters even though we are unaware of them; and (3) the specifically social mood of fear created by customary morality, which helps to inhibit challenges to its authority.[73] As Nietzsche points out in *Dawn*, human social feeling for custom (including customs that are concerned with expressions of *Mitleid*) is based on the age-induced sanctity of each custom rather than on the practical utility or the ethical value of the custom (*D* 19). Nietzsche also suggests that our obedience to traditions and moral customs is increased through our susceptibility to superstitious fear that arises out of our concern for the consequences of transgressing against an "inexplicable, indeterminate power" (*D* 9).[74] This superstitious fear is best understood as a mood, because our fear of transgression against an unseen and unknowable power is not directed toward any single action or event, but rather surrounds us and frames our experiences, moral reflections, and moral discourse.[75] Nietzsche is a useful resource for—and sees himself as offering ways of—challenging harmful habits of thought that are perpetuated in and through philosophical discourse.[76]

This commitment to challenging harmful habits of thinking, including of philosophical thinking, includes Nietzsche's critique of *Mitleid* along with wider moral discourse, as Ansell-Pearson and I have shown.[77] In *Dawn*, for example, Nietzsche points out that the teachers of morality have been too ambitious in identifying "precepts" by which everyone ought to live; according to Nietzsche, the "animals" who have been advised by these teachers of morality to turn into "humans" through following these precepts find their moral education tedious (*D* 194).[78] Nietzsche praises the ancient Greek virtue of personal distinction and criticizes Germans, including Kant, for treating morality as a means to secure obedience (*D* 207). He contrasts this with scholars who, he envisages, would be "the embryonic state of something higher": as he claims, we may yet expect great things of them (*D* 207). These embryonic new philosophers are revisited by Nietzsche in *Beyond Good and Evil*. There, he points out, "The stiff yet demure tartuffery used by the old Kant to lure us along the clandestine, dialectical path that leads the way (or rather: astray) to his 'categorical imperative'—this spectacle provides no small amusement for discriminating spectators like us, who keep a close eye on the cunning tricks of the old moralists and preachers of morals" (*BGE* 5). In a later aphorism, Nietzsche distinguishes between current philosophers and philosophers of the future as "very free spirits" since, as he claims, these philosophers "will not be free spirits merely, but something more, higher, greater, and fundamentally different" (*BGE* 44).

As he suggests, these philosophers may be described as *"those who attempt."* (*BGE* 44). Rather than seeking a moral law to obey, the new philosophers will seek to make their own judgments. As Nietzsche claims, they will be "philosophers of the dangerous," whose "taste and inclination are somehow the reverse of those we have seen so far" (*BGE* 2). And as Nietzsche says, the new type of thinker that he envisages will have to test themselves to see if they are ready, and specifically whether they are "destined for independence and command" rather than stuck to old places, people, and values, including old virtues (*BGE* 41).

Obedience to the customary moral emotion and virtue of *Mitleid*, then, is a feature of the kind of moral philosophy that Nietzsche's critique of this concept challenges—along with his revealing of *Mitleid* as a power relation—as a core part of the campaign against morality that forms the core component of his free spirit works. This, I propose, is another key facet of the liberatory value of Nietzsche's critique to disability justice. Examining Nietzsche through Tremain's feminist philosophy of disability and in particular her discussion of the problem of how disability is naturalized, including within philosophy, shows us that the structural problem of ableism is reinforced by the lack of challenge to the forms of moral philosophy that incorporate *Mitleid* and cognate moral emotions as essential and as being beyond question. As well as pissing on pity itself, disability justice activists and scholars adopting the social model of disability may also need to relieve themselves from forms of moral, social, and political philosophy that uncritically depend on *Mitleid* in order to free themselves from the oppressive effects of *Mitleid's* negative consequences for the material-social conditions of disabled people's lives.[79] As Allison Merrick has pointed out, Nietzsche's view is not purely that moral concepts (e.g., good, justice) shift and are variable and contingent but that such concept shifts track power relations that, post-shift, appear "natural" or "given" or beyond question to us—"*that* a will to power," as he writes, "has become master of something less powerful and imposed upon it the character of function" (*GM* II:13).[80] This is why Nietzsche's position can offer further support to Tremain's argument that disability is too often naturalized within philosophy, to the point where ableism may secure professional advantage and that disability needs to be denaturalized within the discipline as well as in wider society in order to make disability justice possible.

Available scholarship offers support for the critical approach to *Mitleid* and to this critical engagement with philosophy itself as developed by Nietzsche. As Allegra Reinalda has recently pointed out, Hannah Arendt raised serious and compelling concerns about the political limitations of pity and compassion in her essay "The Social Question," in which Arendt discusses how pity can reduce people to victims and add to the power of those who speak on behalf of (or in place of) victims, and how compassion can turn from natural fellow-feeling to performative virtue signaling.[81] More recently, Jacqueline Scott has developed an account of how Nietzsche's thinking on experimentation can facilitate the vital importance of revitalizing our unhealthy racialized identities through value experiments in order to make possible new identities and thus possible projects of solidarity and justice.[82] As part of her account, Scott suggests that the same revitalizing move is necessary for philosophy itself.[83] In this respect, Scott's analysis is similar to that of Tremain: both identify philosophy as naturalizing what are fundamentally social groups and identities and naturalizing harms experienced by relevant groups owing to structural injustices. Notably, Scott makes use of Nietzsche's tragic philosophy from his later writings, understood as a counterpoint to the ascetic ideal, in order to develop this account.[84]

Like Scott, Thomas Abrams and Brent Adkins focus on Nietzsche's thinking on tragedy, but they use Nietzsche's early account of tragedy to argue that tragedy is real and part of life, including disabled life, so as to fully include disabled lives within life itself.[85] To do so, they assess a case study focusing on boys with Duchenne muscular dystrophy (DMD) using theory from Nietzsche, Spinoza, and Sharp to propose an account of tragedy as supportive of the liberatory goals of disability studies.[86] They claim that Nietzsche's affirmation of tragedy in opposition to pessimism in *EH* "Books" BT shows us that tragedy is both real and part of life.[87] It cannot be wished or pretended away, or ignored. As they contend, the experiences of boys with DMD, such as Simon, attest to the Nietzschean account of tragedy that they present: as they describe, Simon expresses curiosity about future effects of DMD on his body, and, upon learning that he will need a tracheotomy and wheelchair use in the future, responds by asking whether he can be a doctor in a wheelchair.[88] Abrams and Adkins point out that Simon's focus is on "exploring his life" as his life in fact is, rather than on mourning the loss of a hypothetical possible life that he could have lived in the absence of DMD.[89] Abrams and Adkins support their analysis with evidence from *GS* 120 on health, noting that for Nietzsche in this aphorism, life is treated as a series of expressive and creative forces in which both healthy and unhealthy states are found, and in which an objective account of "health as such" does not exist.[90] As Nietzsche claims, instead of "health as such," there is health for one's horizon, powers, goal, mistakes, and "ideals and phantasms of your soul" (*GS* 120). For Abrams and Adkins, similarly to Stramondo's analysis of pity on this point, the widespread assumption that "health as such" exists is a prime factor in generating the conditions in which whole lives are deemed tragic or not by virtue of one fact about that life, perpetuating a situation in which disability is treated as a totalizing tragedy and disabled identities are wrongly treated as essential, tragic, powerless negatives.[91]

## Conclusion

As I have discussed, in the past, support for disability justice has been found in Nietzsche's thought, including in his critique of *Mitleid*. I have shown that *Mitleid* still counts as a key prop for the problem of structural ableism and how Nietzsche's critique of *Mitleid* incorporates attention to power relationships that make his critique structural as well as individual.[92] In developing this account, I do not claim that Nietzsche's critique of *Mitleid* is the only liberatory tool that is available to disability justice activists and scholars of disability. All I have claimed is that Nietzsche's critique of *Mitleid* and the free spirit works in which it is to be found still count as a helpful resource for disability justice projects and that it makes sense for scholars and activists to continue to appeal to them in pursuit of their projects. Moreover, as I have suggested, critical engagement with forms of moral philosophy that depend on *Mitleid* is an important avenue for further scholarly engagement in order to remove *Mitleid* as a source of support for ableism as experienced at the individual and group levels. Nietzsche's critique of *Mitleid* can help to unpick the structural conditions that perpetuate ableism and can promote disabled people's agency and independence, enabling freedom from institutions, groups, and social structures that use *Mitleid* to disempower and dominate either advertently or inadvertently. We can, therefore, use Nietzsche to understand how moral, social, and political philosophical assumptions and prejudices, particularly when these are predicated on the universal moral and social correctness of *Mitleid*, hinder the elimination of ableism from philosophy as well as from wider society.[93]

## Notes

1. I use identity-first language throughout, and so I shall refer, for example, to "disabled people." When using the term "disability" in a general sense, I include intellectual, cognitive, and physical disability.

2. *Mitleid* may be translated into English as pity or as compassion. To limit the difficulties presented by translation in this case, I leave the term untranslated wherever possible and quote the translations of the term that are provided in the scholarship that I discuss.

3. Peña-Guzmán and Reynolds 2019, 205–42, 215. See also Reynolds 2022.

4. Kaitlyn Creasy discusses the transpersonal and transmissible nature of affect in Nietzsche (2020, 79). See also my work on emotion as socially contagious (Bamford 2019, 65–82).

5. Tremain 2020.

6. I am grateful to Ofelia Schutte for pointing this out and for pushing me to think more carefully about it.

7. Tremain 2020. Before proceeding, let me address two likely points of immediate resistance to my approach here. First, given that my view involves putting Nietzsche to liberatory ends within broadly democratic contexts, note that in what follows I do not argue that Nietzsche is a democrat. Making such a claim is unnecessary to support my view; moreover, as Lawrence J. Hatab (1995) and Alan Schrift (2000) have both shown, Nietzsche's philosophy can be used to support democratic political philosophy and specific democratic political projects without holding that Nietzsche maintains any specific democratic commitments. Second, I do not develop a complete account of Nietzsche's concept of health or a full account of disability; doing so is unnecessary for my view in this chapter to hold.

8. Smith 2005; Stocker 2002.

9. Smith 2005, 554–76.

10. Smith 2005, 560.

11. Smith 2005. See also Ansell-Pearson and Bamford 2020.

12. Smith 2005, 561.

13. Smith 2005, 561.

14. Smith 2005, 562.

15. Smith 2005, 562.

16. Smith 2005, 562.

17. Smith 2005, 562.

18. Smith 2005, 562.

19. Stocker 2002, 138.

20. Stocker 2002, 139.

21. Stocker 2002, 138.

22. Stocker 2002, 138. In rehabilitation contexts, care is generally and typically taken to avoid incorporating negative value judgments into clinical discussions and interactions. When discussing an injured body part, for instance, US physical therapists do not refer to an "injured" or "bad" or "problem" body part but to "involved" or "uninvolved" body parts, and they encourage patients to use this same terminology when referring to their own bodies and bodily experiences.

23. Stocker 2002, 139. Smith 2005, 562, also refers to this slogan.

24. Stocker 2002.

25. Stocker 2002, 141.
26. Stocker 2002, 143.
27. Stocker 2002, 141.
28. Stocker 2002, 142. She also points out that when Aristotelian empathic enlargement is available to us, we can respond joyfully, but when it is not available, "we can respond with the vitality of what is our own, with strength and without seeking pity." Stocker 2002, 144.
29. Stocker 2002, 139.
30. Franco 2018, 69.
31. Franco 2018, 69.
32. Franco 2018, 69.
33. Stocker 2002, 142.
34. Stocker 2002, 142.
35. I have discussed this in Bamford 2014; see also Ansell-Pearson and Bamford 2020. Bernard Williams (1986) also draws a distinction between ethics and morality in Nietzsche's works.
36. Stramondo 2010. Stramondo uses Sartre's *Anti-Semite and Jew*, and in particular Sartre's discussion of the relationship between pity and the creation of categories of racial oppression as well as remarks on disability, to develop his own account of pity as a problem for understanding disability.
37. Stramondo 2010, 124.
38. Stramondo 2010, 125.
39. Stramondo 2010, 128.
40. Stramondo 2010, 128–29, 124.
41. Stramondo 2010, 128–29. This is not to claim that all biotechnological research is intrinsically ableist.
42. Stramondo 2010, 130. See also Peña-Guzmán and Reynolds 2019.
43. Stramondo 2010, 130.
44. Stramondo 2010, 131.
45. Stramondo 2010, 129.
46. Stramondo 2010, 125, 132.
47. Of course, Nietzsche is one amongst many resources to this end, not the only possible resource.
48. Bamford 2007, 242.
49. Bamford 2007, 243–45.
50. Janaway 2007. Alfano 2019, 192–215.
51. Ansell-Pearson and Bamford 2020, 100–1.
52. By virtue of their experiences, the disabled moral agent may have access to an important ethical perspective that the nondisabled customary moral agent lacks.
53. Staten 1990. See also Ansell-Pearson and Bamford 2020; Bamford 2014; and Bamford 2007.
54. Staten 1990.

55. See Katsafanas 2016.
56. Ansell-Pearson and Bamford 2020, 98.
57. Katsafanas 2016.
58. Katsafanas 2016; Ansell-Pearson and Bamford 2020.
59. I shall have more to say about these alternative possible agents later in this chapter.
60. Dunkle 2022.
61. Dunkle 2022.
62. Dunkle 2022, 298.
63. Dunkle 2022, 298–99.
64. Dunkle 2022, 298.
65. See Barnes 2016, 78; and Dunkle 2022, 308–9. Dunkle does also claim that his account of Nietzsche's concept of health allows us to acknowledge that disabilities do not "always come with health-/welfare-benefits outweighing their harms," though since his account is not focused on disability, it is hard to determine whether this claim involves a naturalization of disability harms. I will discuss the problem of naturalization in the next section. See Dunkle 2022, 309.
66. Stramondo 2010, 128–89.
67. Tremain 2020.
68. Tremain 2020.
69. Tremain 2020.
70. Tremain 2020.
71. Tremain 2020.
72. Ansell-Pearson and Bamford 2020. On Nietzsche's critique of customary morality, see also Robertson 2012.
73. Ansell-Pearson and Bamford 2020; Bamford 2014.
74. See also Bamford 2014.
75. Ansell-Pearson and Bamford 2020.
76. Bamford 2014; Ansell-Pearson and Bamford 2020.
77. Ansell-Pearson and Bamford 2020.
78. Ansell-Pearson and Bamford 2020, 65.
79. See also Stramondo 2010.
80. For a detailed working out of this claim, see Merrick 2021.
81. See Reinalda 2022. See also Arendt 1963. Arendt distinguishes between pity and compassion but treats both as problematic in a political context. Nietzsche receives only a passing mention from Arendt (1963, 69).
82. Scott, this volume; and Scott 2019.
83. Scott 2019.
84. Scott 2019. See also Scott's revised chapter in this volume.
85. Abrams and Adkins 2022, 120–21.
86. Abrams and Adkins 2022.
87. Abrams and Adkins 2022, 121.

88. Abrams and Adkins 2022, 122.
89. Abrams and Adkins 2022, 122.
90. Abrams and Adkins 2022, 122–23.
91. Abrams and Adkins 2022, 123. On *GS* 120 and health, see also Dunkle (forthcoming).
92. Creasy 2020; Bamford 2019.
93. My thanks to audiences at Royal Holloway, SPEP, members of Justin Remhof's online Nietzsche research group, and especially to Allison Merrick, Ofelia Schutte, Joel Michael Reynolds, and Keith Breen, for their many helpful comments and suggestions.

## References

Abrams, Thomas, and Brent Adkins. 2022. "Tragic Affirmation: Disability Beyond Optimism and Pessimism." *Journal of Medical Humanities* 43: 117–28.

Alfano, Mark. 2019. *Nietzsche's Moral Psychology*. Cambridge: Cambridge University Press.

Arendt, Hannah. 1963. "The Social Question." In *On Revolution*, 59–114. Harmondsworth, UK: Penguin.

Ansell-Pearson, Keith, and Rebecca Bamford. 2020. *Nietzsche's Dawn: Philosophy, Ethics, and the Passion of Knowledge*. Oxford: Wiley-Blackwell.

Bamford, Rebecca. 2007. "The Virtue of Shame." In *Nietzsche and Ethics*, edited by Gudrun von Tevenar, 241–61. Berne: Peter Lang Verlag.

———. 2014. "Mood and aphorism in Nietzsche's campaign against morality." *Pli: The Warwick Journal of Philosophy* 25: 55–76.

———. 2019. "The Relationship between Science and Philosophy as a Key Feature of Nietzsche's Metaphilosophy." In *Nietzsche's Metaphilosophy: The Nature, Method, and Aims of Philosophy*, edited by Paul S. Loeb and Matthew Meyer, 65–82. Cambridge: Cambridge University Press.

Barnes, Elizabeth. 2016. *The Minority Body: A Theory of Disability*. Oxford: Oxford University Press.

Creasy, Kaitlyn. 2020. *The Problem of Affective Nihilism in Nietzsche: Thinking Differently, Feeling Differently*. London: Palgrave Macmillan.

Dunkle, Ian. 2022. "Nietzsche's Concept of Health." *Ergo: An Open Access Journal of Philosophy* 8 (34): 288–311. https://doi.org/10.3998/ergo.2235.

Franco, Paul. 2018. "Becoming Who You Are: Nietzsche on Self-Creation." *Journal of Nietzsche Studies* 49.1: 52–77.

Hatab, Lawrence J. 1995. *A Nietzschean Defense of Democracy: An Experiment in Postmodern Politics*. Chicago: Open Court.

Janaway, Christopher. 2007. *Beyond Selflessness: Reading Nietzsche's Genealogy*. Oxford: Oxford University Press.

Katsafanas, Paul. 2016. *The Nietzschean Self: Moral Psychology, Agency, and the Unconscious*. Oxford: Oxford University Press.
Merrick, Allison. 2021. "Knowing Ourselves: Nietzsche, the Practice of Genealogy, and the Overcoming of Self-Estrangement. *Genealogy* 5.2: 41.
Nietzsche, Friedrich. 1974. *The Gay Science*. Translated by Walter Kaufmann. New York: Vintage.
———. 1998. *Beyond Good and Evil*. Translated by Marion Faber. Oxford: Oxford University Press.
———. 2003. *Twilight of the Idols and The Antichrist*. Translated by Reginald J. Hollingdale. London: Penguin.
———. 2006. *On the Genealogy of Morality*. Edited by Keith Ansell-Pearson. Translated by Carol Diethe. Cambridge: Cambridge University Press, 2006.
———. 2011. *Dawn: Thoughts on the Presumptions of Morality*. Translated by Brittain Smith. Stanford: Stanford University Press.
Peña-Guzmán, David, and Joel Michael Reynolds. 2019. "The Harm of Ableism: Medical Error and Epistemic Injustice." *Kennedy Institute of Ethics Journal* 29.3: 205–42.
Reinalda, Allegra. 2022. "The Cruel and Benevolent Knife: Hannah Arendt's Critique of Compassion in Politics." *Critical Horizons* 23.2: 188–202.
Reynolds, Joel Michael. 2022. *The Life Worth Living: Disability, Pain, and Morality*. Minneapolis: University of Minnesota Press.
Robertson, Simon. 2012. "The Scope Problem: Nietzsche, the Moral, Ethical, and Quasi-Aesthetic." In *Nietzsche, Naturalism, and Normativity*, edited by Christopher Janaway and Simon Robertson, 81–100. Oxford: Oxford University Press.
Schrift, Alan D. 2000. "Nietzsche For Democracy?" *Nietzsche-Studien* 29: 220–33.
Scott, Jacqueline. 2019. "'The Great Seriousness Begins': Nietzsche's Tragic Philosophy and Philosophy's Role in Creating Healthier Racialized Identities." In *Nietzsche's Metaphilosophy: The Nature, Method, and Aims of Philosophy*, edited by Paul S. Loeb and Matthew Meyer, 247–64. Cambridge: Cambridge University Press.
Smith, Steven R. 2005. "Equality, Identity and the Disability Rights Movement: From Policy to Practice and from Kant to Nietzsche in More than One Uneasy Move." *Critical Social Policy* 25.4: 554–76.
Staten, Henry. 1990. *Nietzsche's Voice*. New York: Cornell University Press.
Stramondo, Joseph A. 2010. "How an Ideology of Pity Is a Social Harm to People with Disabilities." *Social Philosophy Today* 26: 121–34.
Stocker, Susan. 2002. "Facing Disability with Resources from Aristotle and Nietzsche." *Medicine, Health Care and Philosophy* 5: 137–46.
Tremain, Shelley. 2020. "Field Notes on the Naturalization and Denaturalization of Disability in (Feminist) Philosophy: What They Do and How They Do It." *Feminist Philosophy Quarterly* 6.3: Article 1.
Williams, Bernard. 1986. *Ethics and the Limits of Philosophy*. Cambridge, MA: Harvard University Press.

# Contributors

**Rebecca Bamford** is Reader in Philosophy at Queen's University Belfast. She is the coauthor (with Keith Ansell-Pearson) of *Nietzsche's Dawn: Philosophy, Ethics, and the Passion of Knowledge* (2020) and the editor of *Nietzsche's Free Spirit Philosophy* (2015). She has also published numerous articles on post-Kantian European philosophy and on bioethics. She developed many of the ideas informing her chapter in this volume during physical therapy and through experiences of disability.

**Daniel Conway** is professor of philosophy and humanities, affiliate professor of film studies and religious studies, and courtesy professor of law at Texas A&M University, where he also serves as a core faculty member in the Philosophy for Children program and the Space Governance Research Group. Conway lectures and publishes widely on topics in post-Kantian European philosophy, political theory, aesthetics (especially film and literature), and genocide studies. His most recent publications include essays on Nietzsche, Kierkegaard, Camus, Arendt, law and humanities, philosophy for children, and treatments of genocide in the cinematic genre of science fiction.

**Kaitlyn Creasy** is associate professor of philosophy at California State University, San Bernardino. She is the author of *The Problem of Affective Nihilism in Nietzsche* (2020) as well as several articles and papers on Nietzsche. She also works in moral psychology, the philosophy of emotion, and environmental philosophy. She wrote this piece as an attempt to make sense of the subtle ways in which sexist oppression disempowers women at the level of their emotional lives, endangering their agency and flourishing. She also aims to show in this piece how an individual's perception of her world and herself is surreptitiously shaped by sociocultural sources, some of which have the potential to harm.

**Robert Guay** is professor of philosophy at Binghamton University, SUNY. He is the author of *"On the Genealogy of Morality": A Critical Guide Introduction and Guide* (2022) and the editor of *Dostoevsky's "Crime and Punishment": Philosophical Perspectives* (2021). He is currently working on a project about the philosophical foundations of reparations for historical injustice and a project on Nietzsche's relational ethics.

**Lawrence J. Hatab** is Louis I. Jaffe professor of philosophy emeritus at Old Dominion University. He has published seven books and over sixty articles, mainly on Nietzsche, Heidegger, and ancient Greek thought. His latest work is a two-volume study on language, *Dwelling in Speech* (2017, 2019). He is also the author of *A Nietzschean Defense of Democracy* (1995), *Nietzsche's Life Sentence* (2004), and *Nietzsche's "On the Genealogy of Morality"* (2008). His chapter in this volume was inspired by Nietzsche's unique relevance for contemporary culture, especially with urgent questions about identity, immigration, and nationalism.

**Paul Kirkland** is associate professor of political science at Carthage College. He is the author of *Nietzsche's Noble Aims* (2009), author of several articles on Nietzsche and political thought, and coeditor of *Joy and Laughter in Nietzsche's Philosophy* (2022). His current book project is on Nietzsche, tragedy, and political philosophy.

**Rebecca Longtin** is an associate professor of philosophy at SUNY New Paltz. Her research brings together critical phenomenology, decolonial feminist philosophy, aesthetics, and the history of ideas to examine experiences that transform how we see the world and ourselves. She is interested in how Nietzsche's understanding of perspectivism can contribute to a more complex concept of political identity.

**Allison Merrick** is associate professor of philosophy at California State University, San Marcos. With a keen interest in how moral values shape self-understanding Merrick has written numerous articles on the philosophical methods and moral philosophy of Nietzsche that have been published in the *European Journal of Philosophy*, the *Journal of Nietzsche Studies*, *History of Philosophy Quarterly*, and edited volumes. Merrick, also having trained as a psychoanalyst at the Institute of Contemporary Psychoanalysis, Los Angeles, is interested in using Nietzsche's work to show how an individual's sense of self is shaped and formed by socio-cultural norms.

Contributors | 349

**Rebecca Aili Ploof** is assistant professor of political science at Leiden University. Her research interests include the history of political thought, rhetoric, and the environment. Her work has appeared in *Contemporary Political Theory*, *History of Political Thought*, *Political Theory*, and the *Review of Politics*. Ploof's current book project examines how Nietzsche, among other political philosophers, understood humanity's relationship to nature and how this can inform environmental politics today.

**Jeremy Fortier** is visiting assistant professor in the Department of Political Science at Colgate University. He is the author of *The Challenge of Nietzsche*, and he has published articles on a variety of topics in *American Political Thought*, the *Journal of Politics*, *Polity*, and the *Review of Politics*. He was inspired to work on the chapter for this volume partly by walking past Elizabeth Catlett's memorial for Ralph Ellison in Riverside Park, on his way to teach at the City College of New York.

**Jacqueline Scott** is associate professor of philosophy at Loyola University, Chicago. Her research interests include Nietzsche, nineteenth-century philosophy, critical philosophy of race, and African American philosophy. She is the coeditor (with Todd Franklin) of *Critical Affinities: Nietzsche and African American Thought* (2006), and she has published numerous articles on Nietzsche, critical philosophy of race, and the intersections of those two areas. Scott is currently completing a book manuscript entitled *Nietzsche's Worthy Opponents: Socrates, Wagner, the Ascetic Priest, and Women*. She is also at work on a book project entitled *Ending the Racial Nightmare: Re-Thinking Racial Identities and Alternate Paths to Racialized Health*. In terms of her research, teaching, and nonprofit work, she is interested in formulating healthier and more effective ways of engaging in anti-racism work. This interest and arguments regarding these formulations are informed by reading Nietzsche, his conception of individual and cultural health, and his strong pessimistic approach to contenting with nihilism. As she argues in her contribution in this volume, adopting a "strong pessimist" view of racism (racism is incurable, a focus on curing it has led to other problems, and attempting to affirm life despite/because of this racism) is potentially a quite generative approach to anti-racism work.

**C. Heike Schotten** (she/her) is professor of political science and affiliated faculty in women's, gender, and sexuality studies at the University of Massachusetts Boston, where she teaches political theory, feminist theory, and queer theory. Her research interests lie at the various and unlikely intersections of queer theory and Nietzsche studies, which ground a wide array of publications focusing, most recently, on the theoretical presuppositions animating right-wing ideologies, including but not limited to settler colonialism, anti-queerness, neoconservatism, "terrorism" policy and the "War on Terror," anti-Muslim racism, Zionism, and trans-exclusionary feminism.

**Elif Yavnık** is a visiting instructor at Sabancı University. She works on ethics, feminist thought, Nietzsche, and how Nietzsche's work may provide resources for thinking about certain contemporary debates. She wrote the piece in this volume after going through the peculiar experience of reading Nietzsche as a woman. Since early on in that encounter, she was tempted to explore what Nietzsche was saying to/about his non-masculine audience. The question became more interesting for her as she came to realize the possibilities it offers for non-masculine subjectivities and the ethical and political consequences that that entails.

# Index

Ableism, 10, 11n.6, 91, 324, 331, 333, 338, 340
Abolitionism, 92
Abrams, Thomas, 339–340
Adkins, Brent, 339–340
Affectivity, 230, 236, 248, 254, 257n.28
Affects, 5, 39, 66, 91, 102–103, 109, 115n.16, 230–231, 233–235, 240–242, 244, 247, 251, 256n.8, 10, 16, 17, 259n.40
African American, 4, 280, 285n.33, 303
Africans, 32, 115n.24
Agency, 5, 10, 64–65, 85, 213, 224n.22, 252, 254, 333, 340, 347
Agon, 145
Agonism, 5, 18, 20–25, 28, 31, 40, 155
Ahern, Daniel, 267
Alcoff, Linda Martín, 114n.13
Al-Qaeda, 187
Alienation, 70, 75, 112
Americans, 20–21, 176, 182, 289, 293, 315n.103
Ancient Athens, 42
Ansell-Pearson, Keith, 333, 336–337
Anti-Black, 4, 104

Antichrist, the, 12n.21
Anti-Semitism, 4, 104, 150n.27
Anzaldúa, Gloria, 7, 101, 105–108, 108, 110–113, 114n.1, 8, 116n.38
Appiah, Kwame, Anthony, 38, 52, 54n.4
Arabic, 30–31
Arabs, the, 192
Arendt, Hannah, 197n.47, 338–339, 343n.81
Argentina, 215
Armstrong, Louis, 131
Ascetic ideal, the 3, 7–8, 124, 140–141, 143–147, 150n.35, 153–155, 159, 163–165, 241, 266, 278–279, 339
Asceticism, 73, 135, 141, 145–146, 159–164
Ascetic priest, the, 7, 123–124, 132–135, 140–147, 149n.21, 150n.35, 150n.37, 159–162, 164, 269, 278
Asian American, 30
Australia, 249
Authoritarianism, 215
  neo, 190
Autonomy, 29, 37, 54n.4 106, 225n.50 330

## 352 | Index

Babich, Babette, 167n.18, 210, 224n.23
Bad conscience (*see also* good conscience), 156, 158–162, 232, 244, 266, 277–279
Bad faith, 66
Baldwin, James, 290
Bamford, Rebecca, 115n.24, 256n.8, 258n.35, 283n.1, 311n.50, n.53
Barnes, Elizabeth, 334
Bartsky, Sandra, 9, 253
Baubô, 210
Bayoumi, Moustafa, 182–183
Beauvoir, Simone de, 210
Bell, Derrick, 279
Bergoffen, Debra B. 212, 214–217
Bernasconi, Robert, 3–4, 115n.24
Bettcher, Talia Mae, 255n.2
Blond beast, the, 157, 159, 167n.12, 13
Bray, Mark, 190, 199n.53
Brogan, Walter, 109
Brooks, Roy L., 75
Brown, Kristen, 212, 214–216
Brown, Wendy, 3, 11n.7, 61, 71–74, 172–175, 193n.6
Burke, Kenneth, 292
Bush, George W., 187, 198
Butler, Judith, 67–69, 113, 196n.38

Caesar, Julius, 85
Call, Lewis, 212–213
Capitalism, 114n.2, 124, 175, 183
Chazelle, Damian, 7, 126–128, 134, 139, 141–142, 145–146, 148–150
Christ, Jesus, 268
Christianity, 12n.21, 22, 159, 172, 268–269, 293, 300, 312n.62, 313 nn.65–66

Citizenship, 21–22
Clark, Maudemarie, 4, 55n.19, 93n.9, 114n.14, 155, 210, 223n.4, 8, 225n.48, 311n.50
Class, 1, 3, 7, 37, 88, 114n.2, 125, 156, 173, 177, 190, 251, 259n.43, 280, 282, 330
Collins, Patricia Hill, 248
Colonialism, 12n.21, 29, 92, 106, 114n.2, 115n.24, 186, 191
Comedy (*see also* tragedy and tragicomedy), 168n.20
Communism, 186–187, 197n.47
Compassion (*see also* pity and *mitleid*), 10, 212, 236, 239, 250, 258, 260n.45, 325, 330–331, 336, 339, 341n.2, 343n.81
Conscience, 61–64, 66, 182, 233–235, 237, 241, 245, 247–249, 251, 251n.37, 309n.24, 312n.58
Conservatism (*see also* neoconservatism), 28, 173–174, 192, 194n.11, 198n.49
Constâncio, João, 109–110
Contempt (*see also* hatred), 56, 93, 103, 147–148, 179
Conway, Daniel, 7, 198n.49, 267, 270
Cook, Joyce Mitchell, 260n.57, n.58
Cosmopolitanism, 28, 34n.15, 38, 54n.4
Cox, Christoph, 109
Creasy, Kaitlyn, 9, 95n.32, 115n.16, 223n.3, 316n.111, 341n.4, 344n.4
Crenshaw, Kimberlé, 11, 38, 52, 53n.3
Crouch, Stanley, 148n.9–10, 149n.19
Cuba, 186

D'Arms, Justin, 239

Davis, Angela Y., 92
Decadence, 44–48, 50, 267–272, 275, 279, 282, 283n.2
Democracy, 1, 4, 8, 21–23, 40, 53n.2, 155, 159, 165, 167n.18, 172, 176, 186, 188–191, 290
Dent, Gina, 92
Derrida, Jacques, 34n.18, 209–211, 213, 224n.23, 225n.48
Descartes, René, 109, 311n.48
Dionysian, the, 48, 50, 150n.39, 273, 275, 277
Dionysius, 48, 50, 109, 150n.39, 273, 275, 277, 285n.25
Discrimination, 20–21
Disability, 1, 323–332, 334–340, 341n.7, 342n.36, 343n.65
justice, 10, 323, 327, 329, 331–332, 335, 338–340
Dohm, Hedwig, 209
Dostoevsky, Fyodor, 292–292, 309nn.19–20, 28, 310n.34
Drives, 5–6, 17–20, 30, 37, 39, 46–47, 51, 56nn.25–26, 71, 84, 94n.22, 99, 103, 109–110, 231–234, 237, 241, 244–247, 249, 251, 256n.16, 259n.40, 268, 284n.7, 333, 336–337
Drochon, Hugo, 40, 198n.49
Du Bois, W. E. B., 54n.4, 309n.23

Egalitarianism, 8, 25, 28, 172
Ego, the, 18, 82, 112
Eliminativism, 22
Elitism, 4, 8, 166n.2, 174–177, 181, 189, 198n.49
Ellison, Ralph, 10, 149n.19, 289–293, 301–304, 306–309, 314–316
Emden, Christian, 94n.11

Emerson, Ralph Waldo, 292, 298, 307, 308n.16
Emotions, 102, 229–233, 235–241, 243–251, 254, 265n.8, 257n.26, 259n.43, 325, 327, 338
Empowerment, 11, 245, 248–249, 252, 254, 259n.41, 325
Enlightenment, the 25, 28, 32
Enmity, 37, 41–43, 126, 313n.66
Epistemology, 102, 114n.15
Erdem, Esma, 188
*eros*, 132, 141
Eternal recurrence, the, 23, 325
Eternal return, the, 216, 298
Ethnicity, 1, 5, 20, 28, 114n.6, 116n.38
Equality, 8, 21, 42–43, 51, 154–155, 161, 165, 172, 290–291, 307
Europe, 17, 24–29, 32, 34n.12, 40, 43, 70, 100, 107, 114n.2, 126, 145, 187–188, 199n.53, 238, 246, 260n.45, 276, 292

Fanon, Frantz, 73, 260n.57
Fascism, 187, 190, 198n.49
Feminine, the, 4, 9, 208, 211–222, 225n.49
Femininity, 212, 220–221, 225n.49, 247–250, 252, 254
Feminism, 4, 104, 114n.2, 172, 174, 193n.5, 194n.12, 211, 225n.49
Feminist border thinking, 100–101, 105, 114n.8
Feminine subjectivity, 9, 207–222, 224n.22, n.23
Fortier, Jeremy, 10, 55n.23, 283n.1
Foucault, 3–4, 38, 40, 54n.8, 55n.18, 56n.25, 72, 336

Franco, Paul, 166n.9, 311nn.47–48, n.50, 328
Frank, Joseph, 292
Franklin, Todd, 4
French, the, 61, 64
Frye, Marilyn, 105–106
Futurity, 41–42

Gender, 1, 20, 29, 32, 53n.3, 67, 69, 72, 114n.2, 194n.12, 229–230, 249, 259n.43, 260n.47, 280, 349
Genealogy, 1–4, 40, 79–80, 92–93, 336
Germany, 26, 186
GI Bill, the, 282
Gillespie, Michael, 40, 54n.13
Globalism, 24
God, 73, 157, 233–234, 240, 284n.21
Goethe, Johann Wolfgang von, 49, 56n.28, 300, 312n.63
Good conscience (*see also* bad conscience), 163, 232, 312n.58
Good European, the, 17, 25–27, 126
Gordon, Lewis, 4, 313n.78
Graybeal, Jean, 223n.8
Greatness, 42–43, 127–128, 136, 148n.6, 149n.21, 163–164, 166, 174, 191
Greeks, the, 23, 267, 269, 272–273, 275, 278, 284n.18, 296
Guay, Robert, 6, 168n.22
Guinier, Lani, 9, 281

Habermas, Jürgen, 53n.2
Hadot, Pierre, 310n.36
Hanisch, Carol, 1
Haritaworn, Jin, 188
Hatab, Lawrence J., 5, 155, 341n.7

Hatred (*see also* contempt), 23, 56n.25, 157, 179, 188, 233, 259n.37, 269
of the self, 92, 145, 180
Havas, Randall, 267
Hawaii, 30
Hedonism, 83
Hegel, 29, 41, 53n.2, 54n.4, 135, 145, 150n.39
Hegelianism, 54n.4, 145, 150n.39
Heraclitus, 56n.29
Hermit, the, 48
hooks, bell, 92, 95n.27
Hollywood, 145
Holocaust, the, 188, 198, 199n.49
Homogeneity, 6, 24–25, 32, 72, 155
Hume, David, 29
Hurston, Zora Neale, 307, 316nn.114–115

Idealism, 64
Identity
 cultural, 17, 116n.44
 ethnic, 30, 32, 126n.8
 national, 24–25
 personal, 17, 21, 25, 28
 political, 3, 8–9, 11 17, 27, 37–38, 72, 74, 124 323–324, 327
 self, 106
Identity politics, 3, 12n.1, 17, 20–22, 172, 174
Ideology, 28, 65, 68, 183, 185–187, 190–192, 198n.49, 199n.53, 230, 237–238, 240, 248–249, 254, 259n.37, 329–331 ("of pity, the")
Immigration, 17, 21, 27–28, 32–33
Individualism, 19
Invisible Man, the, 292–293, 307
Iran, 186

Irigaray, Luce, 4, 207, 211–213, 216, 220, 223n.4, 224n.23
Islam, 182–183, 186–188, 192
Islamic fundamentalism, 186
Islamophobia, 176, 182–183, 197n.47
Israel, 176, 187–190, 197n.47
Israelis, the, 176, 184, 187–188

Jacobson, Daniel, 239
Janaway, Christopher, 114n.14, 150n.38, 168n.21, 332
Jerusalem, 184
Jews, the, 174, 176, 187, 191
Jones, Jo, 129–131, 135, 137, 144, 148n.9

Kant, Immanuel, 28–29, 41, 54n.4, 109, 337
Kirkland, Paul, 5–6, 283n.1
Kofman, Sarah, 209–210, 223n.2, 8

Latin America, 107, 183
Latin American, 7, 100, 114n.6, 116n.44
Latinx, 114, 281, 283, 285n.33
  decolonial feminist philosophy, 99, 101, 105, 108, 112
Lebron, Christopher, 307, 316n.114
Left, the, 187, 197n.47
Left Nietzscheanism, 3, 172
Liberalism, 3, 29, 38, 74, 172, 191, 315n.103, 330
Liberty, 29, 38, 155
Libya, 186
Longtin, Rebecca, 6–7, 12n.21
Lorraine, Tamsin, 212, 214, 216–217
Lugones, María, 7, 101, 105–106, 108, 110, 113, 114n.1, 2

Malraux, André, 292
Marginalization, 6, 20, 38, 40, 55n.18, 72, 80, 100, 105, 107, 112, 173, 207
Marxism, 186, 315n.103
Masculine, the, 211–215, 222
Masculinity
Mastery, 18, 177, 179, 181, 189, 192, 280 (self)
May, Simon, 94n.22
Meysenbug, Malwida von, 223n.5
Meiners, Erica R., 92
Merrick, Allison, 6, 12n.21, 171, 338
*mestiza*, 107–108, 116n.38
  consciousness, 105
  new, 111–113
Mexican, 107
Middle East, the, 183, 186, 188
Mill, John Stuart, 29, 38, 155, 166n.9
Miller, Stephen, 68
Mirabeau, Comte de, 90
Misogyny, 137, 210, 223n.4
*Mitleid* (*see also* compassion and pity), 10, 238, 258n.29, 30, 323–329, 331–338, 340–341
*Mitleids-moral*, 250, 260n.45
Modernity, 8, 42, 64, 161, 172–173, 334
Modern mobility, 24–25, 28
Moralism, 175–176, 181, 183–184, 187, 190, 192
Morality, 6, 27–28, 46, 73, 79, 81–82, 85–87, 89–90, 93n.8, n.10, 102, 124, 153, 156–159, 162, 178, 185, 187, 192–193, 255, 258n.37, 333, 336–338
  Christian, 299–300
  of compassion, 238, 250

Morality *(continued)*
  customary, 81–82, 258n.37, 325, 329
  master, 19, 299–300, 312n.62
  slave, 8, 19, 158–159, 162, 171–181, 189–190, 192, 194n.11, 198n.49, 277, 299, 312n.62
Morphology, 80–83, 85, 94n.11
Moynihan, Daniel Patrick, 186, 197n.47
Multiplicity, 5, 37–39, 41–42, 44, 48, 52, 55n.18, 56n.28, 109–113
Muslims, the, 182, 191

Naber, Nadine, 183
Nationalism, 17, 21, 24–25, 28, 186, 260n.61, 293
Native American, 30, 32, 34
Nazism, 186–188, 198n.49
Nazis, the, 184–188, 199n.49
Nehamas, Alexander, 49, 58n.26, n.28, 110
Neoconservatism (*see also* conservatism), 194n.47
*nepantla, la*, 111–113
Netanyahu, Benjamin, 184–187, 198n.49
Nihilism, 34n.18, 70, 104, 171, 187–188, 190, 192, 212–213, 267–269, 271, 278, 283n.2, 334
Nobility, 42–47, 51, 87–88, 91, 135, 157, 189, 259n.37, 312n.61
North Korea, 186
Nussbaum, Martha, 85–86

Obama, Barack, 182
Oliver, Kelly, 207, 211–216
Ontological freedom, 7, 154–156, 159, 162–165, 167n.11, n.13

Oppel, Frances Nesbitt, 221
Optimism, 279, 302
Ortega, Mariana, 7, 111–113
Otherness, 21, 23, 31–32, 115n.37, 225n.50

Pacifism, 19
Palestine, 199n.55
Palestinians, the, 199n.55
Pamerleau, William, 127, 147n.6, 149n.16
Parker, Charlie (The Bird), 127, 129–131, 135, 137–139, 142–144, 148nn.9–10, 149n.19
Parochialism, 28
Patriarchy, the, 9, 104–105, 175, 212, 215, 229–230, 247–250, 252–255
Patriotism, 280, 290
Peña-Guzmán, David, 323
Perspectivalism, 155
Perspectivism, 6–7, 20, 22, 25, 99–110, 113, 114n.14
Performativity, 67–70
Pessimism, 266–267, 269–270, 272–273, 278, 281, 283, 302, 339
  Schopenhauerian, 273
  of strength, 266, 269, 272
  of the tragic poet, 273
Pickens, Slim, 147
Pity, 10, 181, 258n.29, 273m 325–332, 334, 336, 338–340, 341n.2, 342n.28, 36, 343n.81
Plato, 40–41, 46–47, 54n.13, 269
Platonism, 55n.19
Ploof, Rebecca Aili, 7–8
Plumb, Ali, 149n.26, 150n.30
Poellner, Peter, 234
Post-human, 144

Index | 357

Prejudice, 2, 8, 10, 20, 27, 30–32, 81–83, 86, 88, 94n.10, 218, 303, 325, 336, 340

Race 1, 4, 9, 25, 30, 34n.5, 37, 53n.3, 54nn.5–7, 67, 72n.2, 107, 114n.10, 114n.15, 115n.24, 116n.7, 190n.22, 229, 255n.2, 259n.43, 266, 279–280, 283n.1, 308n.20, 309n.24
Racism, 4, 9, 11n.6, 91, 176, 195n.24, 199n.49, 266, 276, 279–283, 314n.87
Rana, Junaid, 183
Reconciliation, 24, 37–39, 48, 52, 53n.2, 75
Reginster, Bernard, 84, 87–88, 93n.4, 114n.14, 267–268
Reinalda, Allegra, 338
Resentment/*ressentiment*, 3, 8, 23, 73, 77n.23, 79, 90–91, 102, 125, 133, 146, 157, 163, 174, 177–178, 180–181, 192, 195n.17, 233, 266, 279, 327
Revenge (*see also* vengeance), 23, 73, 125, 132–133, 135, 157, 179–181, 233, 328, 333
Reynolds, Joel Michael, 323
Richardson, John, 231
Richie, Beth, 92
Ridley, Scott, 147, 166n.10, 244
Rivera, Omar, 100
Robin, Corey, 173, 192
Romanticism, 86
Rousseau, Jean-Jacques, 155
Ruíz, Elena, 100, 114n.8

Sartre, Jean-Paul, 65–66, 329, 331, 342n.36

*Schauspieler*, 62, 75n.2, 137
Schutte, Ofelia, 3, 100–101, 103–104, 114n.13, 115n.23, 116n.44, 209–211
Schopenhauer, 69, 273
Schotten, C. Heike, 3, 8, 104
Scientism, 8, 161, 165
Schrift, Alan D., 155, 341n.7
Scott, Jacqueline, 4, 9–10, 308n.9, 339
Selfhood, 5, 17018, 20, 32, 99–100, 189, 221
Self-knowledge, 10, 19, 103, 217, 257n.24, 266, 277–279, 306–307, 315n.103
Sexism, 11, 91, 229–230, 254–255
Sexuality, 1, 67, 194n.12, 213, 255n.2
Shame, 7, 124–130, 132–134, 141, 144, 147n.2, 158–159, 185, 240, 259n.37, 278
Shari'a law, 182
Sharp, 339
Shaw, George Bernard, 292
Silenus, 267, 296
Simmons, J. K., 7, 126
Singer, Linda, 209, 211, 223n.8
Slavery, 30, 75, 115n.24, 175, 177, 181, 304
Smith, Steven R., 324–326
Socrates, 40–42, 44–46, 56n.30, 268–269
Socratism, 41, 50–51, 56n.30, 278
Solidarity, 10, 21, 38, 52, 193, 281, 339
Soul atomism, 39, 109
Sovereign individual, the, 28–29, 34, 52n.1
Soviet Union, the, 183, 186
Spinoza, Baruch, 56, 339

Stampnitzky, Lisa, 185
Staten, Henry, 333
Stegmaier, Werner, 103
Stocker, Susan, 326–329
Stoicism, 28, 329
Stramondo, Joseph A., 324, 329–331, 335, 340
Symptomatology, 81
Syria, 186

Taquir, Tamsila, 188
Taylor, 38, 53n.24
Teller, Miles, 7, 126
Terrorism, 8, 24, 175–176, 182–192, 194n.35, 197n.47, 199n.57
Tirrell, Lynne, 210, 225n.37
Tocqueville, Alexis de, 155
Torres, Gerald, 9, 281
Totalitarianism, 183–184, 186–187, 195n.25
Toxic masculinity, 254
Tragedy (*see also* comedy and tragi-comedy), 39, 44, 48–49, 52, 266, 271–276, 283, 283n.1, 284n.16, 308n.9, 323, 325, 339–340
Tragi-comedy, (*see also* tragedy and comedy), 163, 314n.83
Tragic philosopher, the, 49–51, 56n.28, n.29, 206, 275
Tremain, Shelley, 324, 335–336, 338–339
Tribalism, 21, 25, 28, 32
Trump, Donald, 174, 191
Tyranny, 22, 40–41, 46, 85, 184

*Übermensch*, the, 25, 40, 112, 283n.4

Underground Man, the, 292–293, 309n.26
United Kingdom, the, 249
United Nations, the, 183
United States, the, 8, 30 175–176, 182–184, 186–192, 249, 280, 290, 303, 306–307
Universalism, 28, 104, 107

Vengeance, 24, 133
Victimization, 71, 189, 191–192
Virtue signaling, 68, 339

Wagner, Richard, 272, 275, 296–297, 299–300, 303, 312n.62, 313n.65, n.66
WASP, 32
West, the, 144, 187–188, 190
White supremacist, 92, 174
Will to power, the, 19–24, 26–28, 31, 79–81, 83–85, 89, 94n.12, 104, 167n.13, 187, 268–271, 326–327, 338
Williams, Bernard, 11n.6, 89
Williams, Patricia, 3
Wininger, Kathleen J., 223n.5
Womanhood, 248
WWII, 282
Wright, Richard, 290, 292

Yavnik, Elif, 9

Zarathustra, 25, 86, 144, 214, 219–220, 222, 223n.5, 267, 311n.55
Zionism, 195n.19, 198n.49

www.ingramcontent.com/pod-product-compliance
Lightning Source LLC
Chambersburg PA
CBHW031703230426
43668CB00006B/96

www.ingramcontent.com/pod-product-compliance
Lightning Source LLC
Chambersburg PA
CBHW031703230426
43668CB00006B/96